RANDELL MILLS
and the
SEARCH
for
HYDRINO ENERGY

Brett Holverstott
illustrated by Matt Schmidt

Randall Mills and the Search for Hydrino Energy
Brett Holverstott
Copyright © 2016 Brett Holverstott
All rights reserved
Published by KRP History

ISBN: 978-0-692-76005-5

Illustrations copyright © 2016 Brett Holverstott

Cover art and design copyright © 2016 Brett Holverstott

Interior design copyright © 2016 KRP History

All rights reserved. Except for brief quotations in critical articles or reviews, the purchaser or reader may not modify, copy, distribute, transmit, display perform, reproduce, publish, license, create derivative works from, transfer or sell any information contained in this book without the express written permission of Brett Holverstott. Requests to use or quote this material for any purpose should be addressed to Brett Holverstott.
http://www.brettholverstott.com/

Disclaimer

This book is provided for general educational purposes. While the author has used his best efforts in preparing this book, KRP History makes no representation with respect to the accuracy or completeness of the contents, or about the suitability of the information contained herein for any purpose. All content is provided "as is" without warranty of any kind.

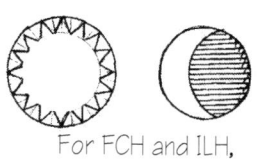

For FCH and ILH,
my sun and my moon

FOREWARD

We all need a little dose of hope in these times of trouble.
I did when I met the pioneers at Brilliant Light Power (then BlackLight Power) in the early 2000s. I worked at Greenpeace at a time when we were fighting to get the United States back into the game at the United Nations negotiations on climate change after the Bush Administration threw a stick in the spokes. The impacts of climate change were becoming more and more obvious. The scientific community's clarion call was ringing with more urgency.

The vision of a green and peaceful future, both then and now, hinged on a transition away from dirty and dangerous energy sources and toward green, renewable energy along with efficiency and conservation. We envisioned a world where the world's most needy would have access to distributed solar power. Where "quality of life" the world over would be improved, along with the obvious benefits of reduced fossil fuel consumption, such as cleaner air, cleaner water, and less risk of oil spills.

And the bottom line: protecting the ecological security of the planet that supports all life on earth.

As Research Director for Greenpeace, I was allowed to think big, to search for solutions and find companies we could partner with who were working toward innovative solutions. We worked with odd bedfellows including CocaCola, PepsiCo and Unilever, on innovations in refrigeration. Blacklight Power fit into my solutions file. BLP became a big source of hope.

The first time I met Randell Mills and his team, Randy gave a presentation that blew my mind. The lab demos were even more impressive.

Anyone's first thought at the presentation would be, this can't be real. But there it was. Unless this was some elaborate ruse, with fake energy monitors hooked up to fake plasma generators, with some hidden fuel source invisible to the naked eye, these scientists were doing something really quite extraordinary.

The idea at the time was to develop a basketball-sized metal sphere with photovoltaic cells lining the interior, tuned to capture the exact light emissions of the BLP plasma and convert this energy to electricity.

All powered by just adding water.

Magical thinking. Science fiction. This generator would power your home, and emit only hydrinos.

I put a poster of Mills's orbitsphere on my office wall. I would glance at it and think, 'there's hope.' Or more often, 'hurry up!'

Through the years I introduced BLP to various environmental community contacts and tried to get science reporters from the New York Times and other outlets to take interest. Later on, I introduced BLP to some scientists we worked with and they were soon as jazzed as I was. This validation helped to counter the predictable skepticism even within Greenpeace.

And now, many years later, the company has come back to a similar design—solar power from plasma.

Brett Holverstott has undertaken a monumental effort to tell the elusive and unknown details of the BLP story. This is at once a science history treatise and a business mystery story. The evolution of this technology and its emergence into the real world has been slow and difficult journey, filled with quick right turns and dead ends. This book captures it all, and doesn't short change the intense complexity of the scientific material for the background drama of how such a revolution in thought upset a lot of apple carts.

In chapter 19, Brett plays out the global energy challenge and climate change drama in a compelling compact treatment. This is truly the challenge of our era.

In the early 2000s, Mills and team didn't seem to grasp how incredibly important their breakthrough work could be to the planet and its people. Instead, and with good reason, they were focused on proving their business model and viability within the electricity market. They were making a business case that they would make money.

Profit is an easy motivation to understand, but I frankly didn't care about BLP's profitability, I just wanted them to produce clean power.

I have a higher goal: to protect the planet from runaway climate change. To stop the Arctic sea ice, the Greenland ice sheet and Antarctica from melting and swamping hundreds of coastal cities over the next century.

The atmospheric concentration of carbon dioxide now tops 400 ppm for the first time in at least 800,000 years. To keep the world below a net 1.5 °C rise in average global temperature (a level indicated by the scientific and policy arena as a glaring red "Stop" sign), halting and reversing the climb in atmospheric CO_2 levels is crucial.

We cannot burn even a fraction of the known oil, coal and natural gas supplies, even that which is already on the books of major fossil fuel companies as "reserves".

Not only do we have to keep fossil fuels in the ground, but we have to somehow clean up the carbon that is already in the atmosphere. Where do you get the energy to do that without creating more pollution?

We literally need a miracle.

As detailed in the pages of this book, BLP has needed to pass a hundred laugh tests in order to show they are a real and viable alternative energy source. BLP will probably be passing laugh tests forever.

Let's all hope they get the last laugh. Because the world needs a clean energy breakthrough now more than ever.

Kert Davies
Executive Director
Climate Investigations Center
July, 2016

ACKNOWLEDGEMENTS

Special thanks to T. Stolper and E. Baard whose prior writings were invaluable to the project. Special thanks to those who allowed themselves to be interviewed for this book, including: E. Baard, R. Booker, S. Bowyer, A. Bykanov, N. Cohen, K. Davies, N. Glumac, G. Gagnon, G. Goedecke, W. Good, D. Goodman, J. Farrell, P. Jansson, A. Marchese, R. Mills, P. van Noorden, S. Patz, J. Phillips, W. Reiff, L. Setzer, T. Stolper, E. Wishnow, F. Witteborn, and others. Special thanks to those who helped fund the Kickstarter to support the illustrations, and to Matt Schmidt for his beautiful work. Thanks to B. Kelly for the translations from Dutch, and to S. Mention, Jeff and John Driscoll. Special thanks to those who read early manuscripts and encouraged the project, including N. and H. Hogle, S. and R. Wallick, as well as the members of the Drunken Philosophers, the Capital Hill Writing Meetup, and the Society for Classical Physics. Thanks to M. Hinchliff for advising my thesis project which originated much of the philosophical material. Thanks to R. Engelmann for early discussions. Thanks to J. Laik and L. Cutter for publishing advice, and to S. Read and V. Murr for editing. Thanks to A. Holverstott for everything.

Note:
No part of this work was financially supported by BLP.

Note on the Figures:
All data plots have been redrawn by the author for stylistic consistency.

*Nature
is always simple
and ever consonant
with itself*

NEWTON

CONTENTS

Foreward by Kert Davis	i
Acknowledgements	v
Chapter 1: The Fire of the Gods	1
Chapter 2: A Farmer's Son	17
Chapter 3: Unobservable Magnitude	27
Chapter 4: The Hydrino	49
Chapter 5: The Cold Shoulder	71
Chapter 6: The Electron, Olympian	95
Chapter 7: Greater Than Fire	111
Chapter 8: Spheres, Ellipsoids, and the Void	137
Chapter 9: South of the South Pole	167
Chapter 10: The Semmelweis Effect	187
Chapter 11: The Blacklight Rocket Engine	207
Chapter 12: The Fulcrum of Physics	217
Chapter 13: Theory and Practice	237
Chapter 14: The Hydrino Universe	253
Chapter 15: The Eternal Tide	273
Chapter 16: The Arbiter of Truth	295
Chapter 17: The Cosmic Conspiracy	311
Chapter 18: The Quantum Quagmire	323
Chapter 19: The Power of the Sun	343
Chapter 20: Truth and Delight	371
Chapter 21: The Path to the Stars	387
Bibliography	401

CHAPTER 1

THE FIRE OF THE GODS

In which a highly irregular event occurs at the United States Patent Office; and in which the author first discovers the controversy of the hydrino atom.

In 1846, the general hospital of Vienna was in the midst of an epidemic. Childbed fever, a disease which affected delivering mothers and their infants, was widespread at the time but especially potent at the hospital, where it killed 459 women that year. The disease had been known since antiquity, and there were many theories as to its cause, yet still it raged on.

The next year, a new assistant of obstetrics, Ignaz Semmelweis, arrived and took an interest in the disease. He apprenticed himself to practitioners who were beginning to understand medicine from a modern scientific perspective. Ignaz was open to these ideas, dedicated to a cause, and, as it turns out, fearless in his ability to reject bad ideas of prior thinkers while looking for fresh insight. He sifted through hospital records. He spent week after week in the morgue.

When a friend and mentor was accidentally pierced in the finger with a knife during an autopsy, and later died from symptoms similar to childbed fever, Semmelweis conjectured that perhaps invisible "cadaverous" particles had been transmitted into his body from that of the fever victim on the table. Perhaps the disease was *transmissible*, but not contagious by conventional means.

It was routine for university students to perform autopsies on cadavers at the hospital and, often in the same day, meet with patients at the laying-in ward. Semmelweis quickly put an end to this and instituted new procedures for washing hands and bedding in a chloride of lime, a solution hitherto used for removing odors.

Within a year, incidence of fever had sharply declined in reaction to the new method. Semmelweis's progress was celebrated by his colleagues at the hospital. The disease lingered, but the parishioner's bell was seldom heard in the ward; new mothers and their infants were returning to their homes flush with the joy of new life. Vienna, already an attraction for students and practitioners, was poised to become the epicenter of a new way of doing medicine.

At the conclusion of Semmelweis's two year assistantship, the director of the laying-in hospital fired him.

In the course of history, there are moments when one individual rises above his or her peers with a fresh understanding of nature, overturning years of thought, to usher in a new era of technological advance. We would like to believe that, as a society, we are able to quickly absorb new discoveries, but in fact the barrier is high. First, we must recognize when a discovery has been made, and second, we must be willing to accept it.

Serendipitous events are often ignored until there is a good theory to explain them. They may be absorbed *ad hoc* by the dominant theory, revealing that just as the human body defends itself from disease, established ideas defend themselves from disconfirming evidence. When a new theory does emerge, it must compete with its predecessors, sometimes with extraordinary effort by those few who are willing to undertake unpopular research. Major discoveries are by nature disruptive; the more disruptive, the more reluctantly we accept them.

Semmelweis struggled against the inertia of ideas held by older practitioners. He was in a mix of social and political tensions in Vienna. And he carried a message that no one wanted to believe: that doctors carried death on their hands. Somehow, his ideas were communicated poorly, misunderstood, and in the eyes of his peers, quickly debunked. Like a stone skipping off the surface of a pond, his ideas were rejected, even while he perfected his technique and virtually eliminated the fever from his wards.

As decades went by, Semmelweis was consumed by frustration and lashed out in anguish and spite at his fellow practitioners. It was not until after his death, *thirty years* after his initial discovery that the medical community came around.

Thirty years of broken families, thirty years of heartbreak.

We might call this the '*Semmelweis Effect*,' when an idea meets fierce and seemingly irrational resistance and is forgotten for a generation.

It is painful to realize that this happens time and again in modern science; each case due to a unique combination of circumstance and bias. It is more painful to accept that it may be happening now, *today*, in our scientifically enlightened age. Perhaps, we are still learning how to do science.

Our scientific community has grown, and so has the volume of scientific publications. In the daily barrage of new ideas, we have learned to make fast judgments on incomplete information using a variety of context-sensitive clues. These heuristics may work for the slow advancement of science along predictable lines, but not unusual cases.

If a major discovery presents in the wrong context, it may be ignored, the discoverer deemed a fool.

It is perhaps for some of these reasons that Randell Mills has had such trouble.

On March 1, 2000, Jeff Melcher stood outside the courtroom of the United States Federal Circuit Court. He set down his briefcase and loosened his tie. He was exhausted. His client, Randell Mills, had filed one of the longest patents in US history, containing 499 claims, each claim adding to the breadth and scope of an invention that would rank either among the most important, or most infamous, in the history of the US Patent Office.

The patent had been issued, but the fallout had just begun.

Melcher had been the only patent attorney at his firm willing to take on Mills's project. Mills spoke of a new fundamental source of energy and a new theory of the physics of the atom. He even spoke of a new kind of atom, a sort of shrunken hydrogen atom that he called a *hydrino*, an atom that the prevalent theory of atomic physics–quantum mechanics–said should not exist.

The history of the patent office is rife with cases of applications for inventions based on flawed, discredited, or mystical theories, ones that violate physical laws, authored by individuals who are deluding themselves or defrauding others.

Energy technologies top this list: from gas-mileage enhancing fuel-additive cocktails or super-carburetors to undisguised "perpetual motion" machines, which (conceivably) once started could generate energy forever.

The history of false patents and techno-mythical inventions is long and entertaining: pulsed electromagnetic motors that give 500% efficiency; motors that covert static electricity to DC power; motors that are motionless, or claim to use magnetic fields in mysterious ways; those that use particles (N-rays, G-rays) that don't exist; those that produce power from time itself by way of gyroscopes and pendulums; or from space itself such as Zero-Point Energy or the Aether Electric Accumulator.

And my favorite: a "Cosmic" energy source, which legend tells was dumped into a river. And therefore lost to man.

These technologies have their advocates; after all, if it has been written, it must be true. Though these were allegedly patented or demonstrated to someone, they never had a chance: those that were not stolen, classified by government, bought out by big oil interests, or dumped into rivers, are—at the very least—ignored.

And for good reason. We have a sharp sensitivity to "fringe" physics. If you are making energy in a new way, making new kinds of materials, manufacturing diamonds, or demonstrating anti-gravity; if you are not highly credentialed in your field, or are in business for yourself, or being ignored by your peers for unknown reasons; if you are struggling to publish, struggling to patent, but finding investors and occasional positive press: you are, my friend, a crackpot.

Mills had a history of making claims to the press about a new power source that would make energy cheap, clean, and abundant. He often claimed this would be unveiled in a matter of months, or maybe a year or two, but by the year 2000, ten years had already gone by without a product. He justified his technology with a theory that was often waved off as nonsense by Nobel Laureates.

The scientific community ignored and ridiculed the man, whom one could easily mark as a lonely fool caught up in his own infinite energy fantasy. Many did not glance twice at Mills.

But those who *did* found something unusual.

Mills was flush with tens of millions in venture capital from private sources that included energy utilities, which he funneled into a large laboratory just outside Princeton, New Jersey. Working for him there was a team of PhD scientists, including highly trained specialists in plasma physics, microwave physics, electrochemistry, and chemical engineering, with backgrounds in industry and academia. His company, named BlackLight Power (BLP) after the ultraviolet light produced by his reaction cells, was becoming a factory of experimental research. With his team, Mills was publishing dozens of papers presenting evidence of the formation of hydrogen atoms with electron orbits smaller than was previously believed to be possible.

Mills reported significant heat gains from his small prototype reactor cells. He also reported spectroscopic evidence such as light emissions from the reactors as well as unique signatures of hydrino atoms and molecules.

These results were not something that could be easily explained away, unless they were the result of gross scientific incompetence, or truly fabricated in an act of wholesale fraud. Mills's papers were climbing a slow and agonizing ladder of reputability and were appearing in better known scientific journals. He was an idea-entrepreneur, conducting basic research for the purpose of technological advancement, and making strides where it counted, in the research literature.

But Mills had promised the world a power generator based on his discovery and he was long overdue on his promise. Critics were skeptical that Mills would *ever* deliver; many assumed he was a fool, or a fraud, or both; few bothered to look at the data, and those who did assumed some conventional explanation had to exist.

The patent office had already developed a thick skin for frivolous inventions when the 1989 rise–and fall–of cold fusion elevated the situation to a crisis. While scandal unraveled the saga of cold fusion, a river of applications flowed into the office from researchers claiming power production from alleged nuclear reactions occurring in small, bench-top electrochemical cells. Mills, who began work at the same time using similar experimental equipment, was easily lost in the noise.

Suffice it to say, everyone in Melcher's office knew that it would be a firestorm, an all-consuming battle for scientific legitimacy, even if Mills was right.

Mills's first patent applications took two years to work their way through the requirements of the examiners. His case files included thousands of pages of supplementary material filled with his own experimental studies and outside scientific literature backing up his claims.

The two examiners of record in charge of Mills's case, Stephen Kalafut and Wayne Langel, were initially skeptical, but after reviewing Mills's data, they were both convinced. They allowed Mills's first patent, "Lower Energy Hydrogen Methods and Structures," number 6,024,935, containing 499 claims, to successfully issue on February 15th, 2000.

BLP had several more patent applications in queue, and the next, number 09/009.294, was due to issue days later, on February 28th, as patent number 6,030,601. Mills received a letter that the patent would be issued, and paid the required fee.

However, a few days later, he received a notice that his patent was being withdrawn, with no explanation. Mills was also notified that the review process for his five other pending applications would effectively start over.

It may have been the first time in the history of the patent office that a patent was rejected *after* it had been issued a number and the fee had been paid. The resulting 'ghost' patent would even appear in the monthly periodical of granted patents issued by the office.

When Jeff Melcher began to investigate, he found the patent examiners themselves were furious. While they technically held full authority over the granting of the patents, their supervisors had held some kind of unofficial review, and the decision had come down to reject the patents. They also said they were asked to lie so that it would appear they agreed with the decision. One of the examiners took himself off the case in protest. They didn't know who was now in charge of Mills's applications, the reasons for the rejection, or whom at the patent office the scientists at BLP needed to convince.

Two years of work had been swept clean; Melcher was facing an unnamed opponent. He sighed. The storm was not over yet.

Nick Wheeler is a crumpled man with a large head and a slow swagger, a professor of physics at Reed College, whose shiny scalp is so prominent that his body seems hung from his powerful brain. He walks through the hallway with eyes unfocused as students spill around him; he sees only the infinity of time; he is as old as the universe; he was there when the foundations of the physics building were laid, and they were laid around him.

Standing outside Wheeler's office, I peer in to see him sitting amidst high shelves of books, bathed in the light of a nearby window.

I knock; there is no answer.

I wait, then knock again.

Still nothing as seconds tick away.

I venture in, around a set of open shelves, and come up behind him.

I am within inches of the man's tweed jacket. I reach out my hand to touch his shoulder, and hesitate. Changing my mind, I escape out of the office unseen.

NICK WHEELER

It was September of 2001. I was in my first week at Reed College in Portland, Oregon. I was wooed by the population of intelligent and weirdly obsessed students, and by the school's deep commitment to a "life of the mind" enjoyed on sprawling green lawns.

The school is liberal, but the curriculum is staunchly conservative in the academic sense: all students participate in a traditional core curriculum grounded in works of philosophy, history, and literature, going back to ancient Greece and Rome. Knowledge changed slowly at Reed.

I was excited to be there, and on the first day of orientation, I spent three hours in philosophical debate with a fellow student while walking the sunny streets of downtown Portland, before, as we were about to part, remembering to introduce ourselves.

When I reentered Wheeler's office some minutes later, he spun about in his office chair and leaned back to inspect me. His eyes peered through heavy spectacles, his silver hair was pushed back over a balding scalp stamped with the imprint of time. With a friendly gentleness he invited me to sit.

I pulled out a heavy black book with a gold-embossed logo on the front that consisted of a triangle with a circle inscribed within it and arrows drawn on the points–it resembled the emblem of a space-dwelling civilization more than a company logo. The cover read *The Grand Unified Theory of Classical Quantum Mechanics* by Randell Mills (Mills, 1990)[1]. Wheeler looked at it skeptically and took it. I began to tell him the story.

---

[1] Mills has since renamed his theory "The Grand Unified Theory of Classical Physics" to avoid some confusion. The logo has also since been changed to something more conventional.

The book had sat on my shelf for a year, as I finished high school and set my sights on Reed. It was the theoretical treatise in which Mills 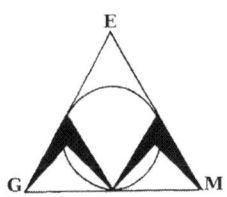 presented his new theory of the atom, one that predicted the existence of hydrinos, but also described the structures of other atoms, molecules, and fundamental particles. It proposed elegant solutions to fundamental, century-old problems in physics. It even offered a revision to Einstein's theory of gravity, and Mills claimed that he had completed Einstein's quest to unify the forces of physics.

It was a theory of nature, and if true, we have not seen the likes of it since Newton or Darwin.

A NASA engineer named Luke Setzer had set up an online message group to discuss Mills's theories, called the Hydrino Study Group. It was a magnet for those who wanted to talk about the topic, whether layman or seasoned physicist, supporter or critic.

For a few years, Mills participated in the discussion. Debates on the forum often concerned some theoretical or experimental detail, and I watched the conversations unfold to get a clue of the forces at play.

My impression was that there were few serious academics on the forums, but many with an electrical engineering degree struggling to work through subtle details.

I was most surprised to find that there were critics (such as Peter Zimmerman, from the US State Department, but several more who were anonymous) who trolled the forum for years, posting almost daily, yet didn't seem to have any real interest in Mills's work. They had not yet bothered to grasp the specifics of Mills's theoretical claims, and were uninterested in scrutinizing published experimental data, except by imagining ways in which it could be forged.

Mills himself was a question mark. He remained aloof but was willing to respond to highly technical questions. His posts would give clarifications or corrections, often with direct quotes and references to his publications, or supporting literature.

Beyond the forum, secondary literature on Mills's work was scarce. The media was varied and often of poor quality. Erik Baard, reporting for New York City's *Village Voice*, wrote a series of articles about BLP from 1999-2002. He surveyed well-known scientists for opinions on Mills. The reactions were brief, emotional, and sweepingly dismissive.

Dr. Phillip Anderson, a Nobel Laureate in physics at Princeton University, said to the press: "If you could fuck around with the hydrogen atom, you could fuck around with the energy process in the Sun. You could fuck around with life itself" (Baard, 1999a).

From theoretical physicist Michio Kaku: "the only law that this business with Mills is proving is that a fool and his money are easily parted." From Steven Chu (later Secretary of Energy in the Obama Administration), "it's extremely unlikely that this is real, and I feel sorry for the funders, the people who are backing this" (Baard, 1999a, 1999b). Howard Georgi, professor of physics at Harvard, called it "just silliness."

One of the most vocal critics, Robert Park, the public spokesman for the American Physical Society in DC, said "There is virtually nothing that science does not know about the hydrogen atom... [The hydrino] has no credibility whatever" (Reuters, 1997).

But Mills was attracting energy utilities who were looking for a competitive edge in a recently deregulated market, and convincing those who were willing to look at his work in depth.

Investors included Conectiv, an energy utility, whose senior vice president David Blake wound up on BLP's board. He told a reporter: "We're past the scientific verification stage. The talk now is about commercial applications" (Baard, 1999a).

Executives at Eastbourne Capital Management put in five million dollars after in-depth due diligence with PacifiCorp, a utility in Oregon (Baard, 2000).

BLP had also met with Morgan Stanley Dean Witter, to discuss the possibility of a billion dollar initial public offering.

Mills was attracting board members that any tech-startup would die for, including Aris Melissaratos, former director of Westinghouse's Science and Technology Center, and Shelby Brewer, a nuclear engineer and physicist who was Assistant Secretary of Energy under the Reagan Administration. Brewer had seen many inviable energy schemes over the years, and lent his support to Mills after cautious due diligence. "I'm convinced that there is something of enormous impact here and it's only a question of time until we can garner the capital and infrastructure to take it into commercialization" he said (Baard, 1999a).

Tom Cassel of Reading Energy was warned by an Ivy League professor that "these types of people are dangerous," but when he investigated the theory and experiments himself, was convinced that Mills's work could be on the magnitude of a scientific revolution (Baard, 1999a).

Was Mills blinding those with dollar signs in their eyes?

Or were physicists blinded by a fear of new realities?

From the discovery of the electron in 1900 to roughly 1925, physicists sought a model for understanding the atom that was based on the physical laws known at the time, now known as the *classical* laws of nature. These laws, familiar on the scale of everyday life, include the laws of electricity and magnetism (Maxwell's equations) and Newton's mechanics. These laws presented a vision of a clear, deterministic universe, and physicists expected that the atom would behave accordingly.

But physicists were unable to explain the behavior of the atom in classical terms. In 1925, a revolution in thought occurred. Physicists invented *quantum mechanics*.

This described particles in terms of probabilities, in a highly mathematical scheme that remained somewhat agnostic about the underlying physics. It didn't speak the same language as classical laws, and it was the beginning of a rift that would divide the foundations of our knowledge. On the one hand, the familiar physics on the macroscale, and on the other, the weird world of the quantum.

Central to quantum mechanics was the problem of the hydrogen atom. With one electron orbiting one proton, it was simple enough to be one of the only real scenarios that a quantum physicist could solve exactly, without any approximations.

By this I mean that the theoretical model used to calculate *observable* properties of the hydrogen atom (such as the frequencies at which it absorbs and emits light) produced numbers that corresponded very well to experimental findings. As a result, the hydrogen atom became an exemplary problem in quantum mechanics, the center of an entire body of knowledge.

And it was the hydrogen atom that came under attack by Mills.

His theory was *classical*.

Against the backdrop of a scientific community obsessed with strings in eleventh-dimensional space and multiple universes, Mills returned to the questions that faced the physicists of 1925: Why is the atom stable? How does the electron move? He approached them afresh, as if classical laws had not withered on the vine.

It is well known that the electron in the atom can jump between orbits (so-called "quantum" jumps), by absorbing and emitting discrete frequencies of light. But there exists an orbit that the electron in any atom cannot fall below (this is known as the "ground state") and why it is stable has never been clearly understood. It is a feature that classical atomic theorists such as Bohr struggled to understand.

Mills's theory used the latest advances in electrodynamics to understand the stability of the ground state. But Mills also predicted that under certain conditions, the electron of a hydrogen atom may occupy a *lower* orbit than the ground state. Instead of jumping to this orbit by releasing light, the hydrogen atom must collide with another atom, called a catalyst, and exchange energy in a process known as resonant coupling. The catalyst must be able to absorb just the right amount of energy in the process of ejecting electrons or breaking chemical bonds.

According to Mills, the electron in the hydrogen atom then releases light as it falls to an orbit that is an integer fraction (1/2, 1/3, 1/4... etc.) of the ground state, forming what Mills named a *hydrino*.

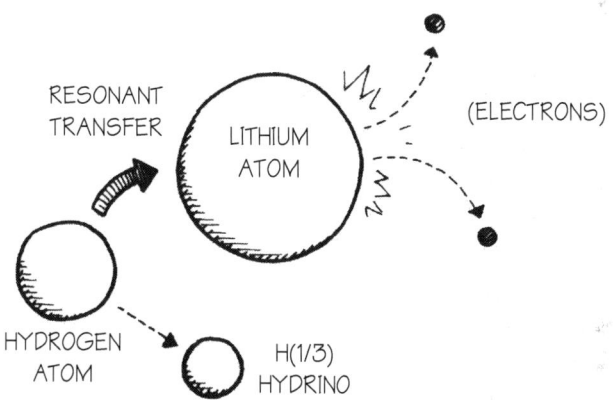

HYDRINO CATALYSIS

Since the electron and proton attract, you must release energy from the electron orbit in order to produce a hydrino state. The release is predicted to be substantial; not as great as nuclear energy, but far greater than that yielded from chemical combustion.

And what of the hydrino itself? Mills began to explore its commercial usefulness in a host of new hydrino hydrides with unusual properties.

Mills's astonishing claims piled up: he had made a historic discovery in physics, discovered a new, potentially limitless energy source, and opened up a new field of hydrogen chemistry.

But the idea struck at the heart of a theory that had been around for eighty years, that had been labored over by thousands of physicists, that had been described repeatedly as the most successful theory of all time. Physicists snarled at the thought of overturning quantum mechanics; its inventors—Heisenberg, Born, Pauli, Schrödinger, Dirac—are gods of physics. To question them is heresy.

Playing offense as well as defense, Mills rallied against the contradictions inherent in quantum theory, and the fuzzy and often confusing picture of the world that has forced scientists to question everything from causality to an objective world outside our skulls. Mills also argued the unbelievable – that quantum was simply a *bad* theory.

After all, the world has changed since 1925. We look out into space and see mysteries everywhere: dark matter, dark energy, the neutrino imbalance of the Sun, the diffuse emissions of galaxies, and the tempo of quasars.

Quantum mechanics was always a struggle to apply to systems more complex than hydrogen, and it has been at an utter loss to explain some simple experiments such as electron bubbles trapped in liquid helium. The theory has waned, its technological potential gone sterile, yet its philosophical controversies linger endlessly on.

I began to perceive Mills's ideas as *conservative*; instead of advocating some weird new physics, he advocated a return to established classical laws of Newton and Maxwell. He portrayed quantum theory as new and suspect, unproven and full of holes.

When Mills started a company to develop his idea, it was a bold move. He did so, as Shelby Brewer put it, "without largess from the US government, and without benediction of the US scientific priesthood" (Brewer).

In 1901, scientists believed that commercial interests tainted the purity of science; they toasted the discovery of the electron by saying "let it prove no commercial value." Though we live in an age of electronics, the vestiges of that attitude remain today in a distrust between business and academia. Mills, perhaps inadvertently, was drawing a line in the sand.

But it allowed him to raise money without the National Science Foundation, to the frustration and perhaps envy of his peers.

Robert Cava, a materials scientist commenting on Mills, told a reporter: "…when someone comes along and makes a big splash without going through the rigor of peer review, it makes us think that the guy has no business doing it" (Baard 2002).

In time, Mills became too busy with his own theoretical and experimental work to worry much about academia, and academia returned the favor.

But the question at the heart of the issue was unresolved: *Does the hydrino exist?*

Is Mills a modern-day Prometheus, bringing fire down from the gods?

I was 17 when I discovered the controversy and decided to proceed with eyes open, to understand the science and the issues, and make up my own mind. At stake was everything: new technological possibilities and new ways of looking at the universe.

When I presented the book to Nick Wheeler, he agreed to take a look. A few days later he called me back to his office. Flipping it open, he briefly pointed out that while it had very thorough citations (often a rule of thumb to gauge whether a scientist has done his research), he could not make any sense of it. He nonchalantly snapped it closed and tossed it back with assurances that as I proceeded with my education, I would learn to understand the topic myself, and would soon reject it.

Perhaps Mills's theories *were* bunk. But there was something about the way Wheeler disposed of the topic that told me he was either unable or unwilling to engage it completely.

I put the book back on the shelf, and over the next several years, I occasionally came back to it. By studying both physics and chemistry, I was arming myself with the tools to understand both the theories and experiments.

Contrary to Wheeler's prediction, as my understanding grew, so did my interest.

I sought out a local professor in electrical engineering, Reinhart Engelmann, who was working at the Oregon Health and Science University and had voiced his support for Mills's work (Engelmann, 1996). Engelmann and I would sit down occasionally and go over his thoughts and criticisms about Mills's theory. His comments were insightful and complex, revealing to me that some physicists took Mills seriously.

After three years of undergraduate work I applied for a summer internship at BLP. I had the opportunity to do experimental work in the lab and work closely with Mills, and I extended my stay to over a year.

After returning to Reed with renewed enthusiasm, I again tried to bring Mills's ideas to professors. But it would always end up the same. I would leave their office with an emptiness that made me realize that not all scientists had the curiosity Newton once described as, "only a child playing on the beach, while vast oceans of truth lie undiscovered before me."

Had they lost their spirit of discovery?

Or was this stuff really junk?

Perhaps I was just a self-deceiving pawn of a perpetual-motion ploy, a follower of a charismatic but irrational leader, my inexperience and *desire* for Mills to be right clouding my perception of the facts.

"I once had a student who claimed she was from Venus," Wheeler said some months later. He let the thought drop with the heaviness of implication, and I bit my lip.

After twenty-five years, Mills's story is, like that of Semmelweis, a complex enigma sewn in layers of history, sociology, and politics.

Here I will explore Mills's theories and discoveries, critics and collaborators, legal battles and technological efforts. I will set his story against questions fundamental to progress in science: How do we identify major discoveries? Good science from bad? Great minds from peddling fools? Why are we bound by the inertia of past beliefs?

We may find that in our pursuit of science, we carry with us the baggage that is human nature, with its hopes and dreams, biases and frailties, and bursts of genius that push us forward to a better future.

CHAPTER 2

A FARMER'S SON

In which a young scientist with a medical degree publishes a stunning article in Nature, *and then moves on to other interests.*

Randell Lee Mills was born in 1957, in Lancaster, Pennsylvania, and grew up on the family farm. When not attending to the requisite chores of farm life, Mills had an early interest in science. He filled his room in his family's old farm house with scientific and mechanical gadgets, including chemistry and microscope sets. He enjoyed farm life, which gave him the opportunity to solve problems in biology and chemistry, and operate powerful machines.

By the time Mills was sixteen, he had his own agribusiness. He formed the Mills Brothers Grain Company with his older brother Robert, and the two continued to expand, growing corn for exporters in Philadelphia and Baltimore. The Soviet Union had become a major buyer, and prices were soaring. In his junior year, Mills was making more money than his teachers.

To make room for this venture, Mills did work-study and was excused from hours of classes at the Octoraro High School in rural Pennsylvania. He would be out for a week at a time, show up for a day, read the class material and ace the exams. Despite this unorthodox arrangement, he rarely had less than perfect scores on his college prep courses. His chemistry professor thought he was a natural genius on the topic.

After graduating, Mills farmed for two more years. By 1978 he and his brother were managing a thousand acres of land and growing cash crops worth $300,000. The two brothers worked the fields themselves, hiring extra hands only at the busiest times. They worked round the clock at harvest time and caught up on sleep when it rained.

In 1978, a freak accident occurred; Mills almost bled to death after putting his hand through the locked glass door of his office. He spent six hours in surgery and five days in the hospital.

As he lay on the hospital bed, he decided that if he survived, he wanted to understand it all before he died, from physics to biology to intelligence.

By now Mills had made enough money from agriculture to finance a college education. He was accepted by Franklin and Marshall College, and on the day he enrolled, he declared his intention to major in Chemistry.

John Farrell, a professor of Chemistry who would become Mills's mentor and friend, remembered fellow professor Jerry Scheiber talking excitedly about the new student; Scheiber thought Mills would be the best student the department had ever had.

Farrell had Mills as a student in two physical chemistry classes, and immediately marked him as unusual. Mills asked complex and interesting questions in class, questions he spent ten to fifteen minutes framing, tying together all his knowledge on the topic. They were questions that Farrell needed another ten to fifteen minutes to answer. Farrell soon asked him not to ask questions in class, but to save them for office hours. Mills also had perfect scores on every exam.

Mills appeared to be blessed with a photographic memory and could recite almost anything he had read. He spent days at a time in the laboratory or in the library, surviving on very little sleep. He did turn out to be a star student, with an almost perfect record, graduated first in his class, with the only *summa cum laude* degree awarded that year.

Both the Johns Hopkins School of Medicine and the Harvard Medical School accepted Mills for graduate studies. He told the admissions committee that he had no intention of becoming a doctor, but rather to start a company inventing medical technologies.

This was not unusual for Harvard, as it was a magnet for those interested in doing research. Although Johns Hopkins offered a generous scholarship, Mills wanted to study at Harvard. Profits from the farm paid most of his tuition.

In 1982, Mills started at Harvard Medical School. He moved rapidly through the required coursework, taking six or seven classes per term.

John Taplin at the Harvard Technology Licensing Office introduced him to a senior professor there, Carl Walter: a medical inventor and entrepreneur, who had invented steam sterilization and plastic blood transfusion equipment. Walter understood Mills, became his mentor, and introduced him to his network of scientists and engineers in the Boston area who were interested in developing new technologies.

By the fall of 1985, after only three years, Mills had completed all the required coursework at Harvard Medical School. This was unheard of, and Harvard asked Mills complete a final year, so Mills spent it at the Graduate School of Electrical Engineering at MIT.

While still at Harvard, Mills began to invent.

In 1984, Mills witnessed the silent hopelessness of doctors treating breast cancer patients with traditional radiation cancer therapy. The purpose of the radiation was to destroy cells that were rapidly growing, of which cancer cells were a large fraction. But this killed *all* cells, both healthy and unhealthy, indiscriminately. Perhaps there was a way for radiation to *target* the cancerous cells.

Mills had heard of a phenomenon called the Mossbauer Effect. According to this, a Cobalt-57 isotope can be made to decay to Iron-57, releasing a high-energy gamma ray in the process. This gamma ray can then be almost perfectly absorbed by another Iron-57 atom; say, one that is bound to a cancerous string of DNA.[2]

Using a very low dosage of radiation, one too low to cause any side effects, the absorbing Iron-57 atom becomes a mini-bomb, releasing its absorbed energy as an explosion of electrons that shatter the DNA strand. The cancer cell would be unable to repair the damage, and die.

Mills called it *Mossbauer Isotropic Resonant Absorption of Gamma Emission*, or MIRAGE.[3]

There was interest in Mills's idea. A Japanese chemical company invited Mills in 1986 to give a presentation, and afterwards they offered him a research laboratory to develop the idea further. Mills declined this offer, a decision he later regretted.

Once back in Boston, Mills's mentor Carl Walter helped set him up at a laboratory in Brigham and Woman's Hospital where Mills could begin tests. His first paper on MIRAGE was published in 1988 in *Nature*, one of the world's most prestigious scientific journals. In Mills's study, the tumors either grew much more slowly than the control, or shrank (Mills 1988).

---

[2] If the emitting isotope is embedded in a crystal and unable to move, there is very little recoil by the atom when it decays. As a result, the gamma ray is very finely tuned to a specific frequency. Amazingly, this frequency can then be Doppler shifted by moving the source at a rate of as little as one centimeter per second during the emission. This is enough to match the absorbing frequency of the Iron-57 atom, resulting in almost perfect absorption. The 1957 discovery of this phenomenon earned Rudolf Mossbauer the Nobel Prize.

[3] In 1985 he filed for a patent, which was later issued as patent number 4815447.

However, Mills had not exposed his control mice to the same radiation, and some questioned whether the effect was due only to the radiation exposure.

An oncologist, Gregory Gagnon at the Department of Radiation Medicine at Georgetown University, remembered reading the article in *Nature* and inviting Mills to give a talk. Gangon thought it was an extremely clever and elegant idea, and asked William Rieff at Northeastern University to bring his Mossbauer source down to run some preliminary in-vitro tests on cell lines. Because Iron-57 and Iron-56 are identical chemically, he ran a clean control, exposing both samples to radiation, and the Iron-57 killed more cancer cells.

The topic would get some serious traction in the literature, with some researchers backing the proposal and some skeptical that Mossbauer resonance could be achieved with molecules in a warm biological environment.

Mills teamed up with Reiff and Farrell to perform further studies (Reiff 1990). Bristol Meyers expressed interest in the concept on two occasions, but never took it into development.[4]

In 1987, Mills got his second major idea. Because blood is paramagnetic, he designed an imaging system based on differences in its magnetic susceptibility. Magnetic Susceptibility Imaging (MSI) may have had advantages over Magnetic Resonance Imaging (MRI). First, MRI could only produce two-dimensional visual slices, whereas MSI had the potential to make three-dimensional images with higher resolution and contrast than MRI, with a speed capable of making real time movies.

Hewlett-Packard expressed interest but the chief mathematician there voiced concerns over the complexity of the math needed to make it work, so Mills was on his own to develop a prototype. He scrounged up old parts junked by Franklin and Marshall and built a proof of concept. Afterward, he used his contacts at Harvard to meet a star in the field of medical imaging, William Moore, who was intrigued and enabled Mills to build a second prototype. Moore was impressed that Mills, with degrees

---

[4] For more information see Brenner 1989; Ortalli 1992a; Ortalli 1992b; Ortalli 1996; Barbieri 1998. Also see the conceptually similar proposal by Chia-Gee Wang for low-dose radiation therapy using monochromatic X-rays (US patent number 7981928).

in chemistry and medicine, was able to solve the many mathematical problems that came up.

Then tragedy struck: Moore died of a heart attack, leaving Mills to fend for himself. Again other researchers expressed interest, such as Dr. Samuel Patz, an assistant professor at Harvard Medical School with an appointment at Brigham and Women's Hospital's Department of Radiology, who told a reporter he was excited by the idea (Baard 2000b).

But Mills was unable to get the idea funded. This may have been in part due to the fact that the only experts available to comment on MSI were themselves experts in MRI, which was rapidly advancing. Mills continued to think about the technology and incorporated some recent advancements of MRI into a refined proposal: Resonant Magnetic Susceptibility Imaging (ReMSI) which he patented in 2002 (Mills 2002b).

While working on his idea for a new cancer therapy, Mills encountered a problem that led to still another seminal idea. Getting his Mossbauer-resonant drug into cancerous cells at doses low enough to be safe for healthy cells was hard to do. Many promising drugs that were developed had been scratched (or substantially modified, weakening their potency) because they were unable to penetrate the cell's defenses against foreign molecules. The drugs could only be administered in doses that were poisonous to other parts of the body in which they indiscriminately made contact.

Instead of modifying his Mossbauer-resonant drug to make it less poisonous, Mills tried to think of a good way to get it into the cell–a "carrier compound." In 1988, he designed a new carrier that could potentially be used with almost *any* drug.

Mills took a chemiluminescent molecule and combined it with a photochromic molecule, then bound a drug to the end. He knew that cells were full of highly reactive free radicals of oxygen; when his molecule encountered one of these oxygens, the free radical would react with the chemiluminescent piece, which would then react with the photochromic piece; what would typically result in the emission of light, would instead produce a bond-breaking dissociation, releasing the drug inside the cell.

It was a molecular chain reaction, analogous to the mechanism that allows fireflies to glow. Mills called his carriers, "luminides."

In 1988, Mills's resources were stretched to the limit; he was living in a cheap apartment furnished with only a mattress on the floor and working out of John Farrell's small office and laboratory at Franklin and

Marshall. Although luminides had potential applications in herbicides and insecticides, Mills focused his efforts on pharmaceuticals.

In particular, he wanted to see if he could administer the drug phosphatoformate, which blocks an enzyme necessary to the replication of HIV, without killing the patient. He improvised a mouse testing facility out of an 800-gallon milk tank from an old barn on his father's farm. The studies were successful, and the luminides eliminated HIV without killing the mice.

A research unit at DuPont wanted Mills to attach some of their compounds to his carriers. But another corporate upheaval intervened, and DuPont sold the unit to Merck, which didn't pursue the research.

Unfazed, Mills started a company in 1992, Luminide Technologies, to develop them, funded in part by Montgomery Medical Ventures, a venture capital fund. Eventually, a starter contract with the National Institutes of Health was approved, and Mills raised a million dollars to capitalize his Luminide Pharmaceuticals Corporation.

This led to ongoing research with a small staff; a paper published in 2003 found the luminide carrier to be five times more potent in suppressing HIV than the drug alone (Mills 2004). He also found his carrier effective at suppressing the Friend Leukemia Virus (FLV). Mills hoped his luminides would allow the industry to revitalize a long list of promising drugs that had been discarded due to poisonous side effects.

Jim Turpin, the manager of a retrovirology lab at Serquest, a Southern Research Institute company, tested Mills's technique and reported " a minimum nine-fold enhancement of antiviral activity in tissue culture," he told a reporter (Baard 2000b).

In other words, it worked.

In the mid 1980s Mills also struggled with a concept for a genomic sequencer. He had the opportunity to present his concept to Millipore, a large medical technology company, and interacted closely with the executive and top scientists there, who were interested.

Again disaster struck: only a week after their first meeting, the executive died in a helicopter accident, and Mills never took the idea further.

Perhaps most revealing of Mills's mathematical creativity was his concept for artificial intelligence that was, simultaneously, a proposal for how the brain computes. In his proposal, information was encoded as Fourier series, and association tasks were carried out through spectral analysis and probability functions. Mills developed the scheme in depth but did not carry the idea beyond the initial design, publishing on the topic twice, and filing patents (Mills 2006c; Mills 1998d). Mills never raised funds for the project, which languishes to this day, but remains close to his heart.

Mills's ideas had many traits in common: they were genuinely innovative, often spanning problems in mathematics, physics, chemistry, and medicine; they looked at the world anew, solving important problems in a fresh way; they had high potential impact for the benefit of mankind; and none of them were brought to market.

Is it possible that Mills's early career was a tragedy of coincidence, a string of bad luck, with the deaths of key individuals or corporate upheavals intervening at the wrong time? There is no doubt that many of his ideas were radical and required a wide range of expertise to implement successfully. But Mills was brilliant and hard-working, and he could have dedicated himself to any one of his medical ideas to build a career and garner financial success, perhaps even obtain a Nobel Prize in Medicine.

Why did Mills not pursue those ideas? By 1989, he had something else on his mind, something he felt was more important than treating cancer or enabling a host of new pharmaceuticals; something so demanding that it was occupying most of his time, delegating his other ideas to the back-burner, until it came to consume his life and career.

CHAPTER 3

UNOBSERVABLE MAGNITUDE

In which physicists abandon a house under construction; and a rift forms in modern physics.

The history of science may well be written as a history of great experimental apparatus. The telescope gave us access to the planets and stars, which in turn gave us the physics of Galileo, Kepler, and Newton. The microscope gave us access to the world of the very small, which gave us the medical knowledge of Pasteur and Salk.

Less celebrated is the vacuum chamber, a glass tube evacuated of air, which allowed us to determine the true weights of elements, and the role of oxygen in respiration. Modify the chamber with electrodes at either end, and you have a *cathode ray tube*, which gave us the discovery of the electron. And of course, the television set.

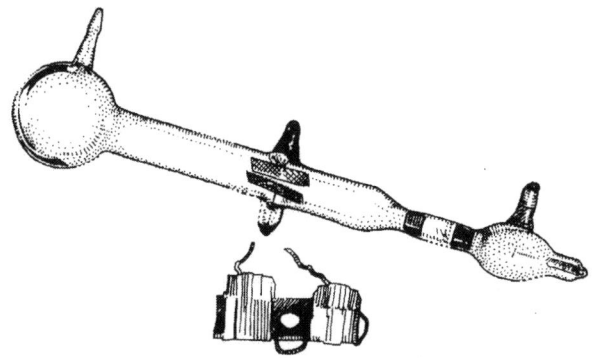

THOMPSON'S CATHODE-RAY TUBE

Prior to the turn of the century, theoreticians and philosophers speculated on the nature of the atom. Vortex theory imagined atoms as vortical modes of motion in an ether fluid that filled space, an idea popular among British physicists. Others imagined pulsating spheres, or fountains of flowing ether (the unfortunately named "ether squirts"). With little experimental evidence to offer, atomic theory was perhaps not conversation for polite company in the world of science.

But in 1887, J.J. Thompson was able to isolate cathode rays: faint trails of illuminated, ionized gas in an imperfect vacuum, which may be bent in a magnetic field, with a fixed ratio between their charge and mass.

Because the mass was thousands of times smaller than that expected for an atom, he rightfully concluded that these were *subatomic* particles. For years scientists had speculated about charged particles in the atom, and now Thompson had found it. He called the particles "corpuscles," though soon they adopted the term long in use by theorists, "electrons."

Thompson's atomic model was the first of the modern era. His first question: since atoms are neutral, what might the positively-charged something in the atom be? He proposed something akin to a spherical ball of positively-charged fluid, in which electrons, small point-particles, stood at rest or rotated in circular paths within a plane.[5]

Suppose we plop one electron in this atom; it could reside at rest in the center of this ball of positive fluid. Doing so creates a very symmetrical state in which the negative charge at the center could perfectly balance the positive charge surrounding it.

Suppose now we plop two electrons in the atom; because they repel, they will push apart from one another.

Now plop three in; they will form an equilateral triangle.

All this is intuitively clear. But what happens as we continue to add more?

A good way to study this is to do as Alfred Mayer did in 1878. He placed a number of corks in a bowl of water under the positive end of a magnet; he then placed an electrolyzed pin in each cork and watched as the corks assumed the optimal positions.

Some number of corks in each ring could be made stable, but beyond about seven, the ring would rearrange itself, ejecting a cork into a new outer ring which could then be populated with more.

A series of stable rings produced a kind of periodic relationship in the structure of the atom resembling the periodicity of the chemical properties of atoms, which chemists had already begun to notice.

Drawing on this idea, Thomson imagined various three-dimensional arrangements of electrons in the atom, static or orbiting the center. He found that if they orbit, they were less likely to be knocked out of position. He imagined various arrangements of them, in flat planes or forming three-dimensional arrangements about the center of the atom.

---

[5] For further reading see (Friedman 1965) and (Kragh 2010). Also see the original sources by (Thomson 1904a, 1904b, 1907).

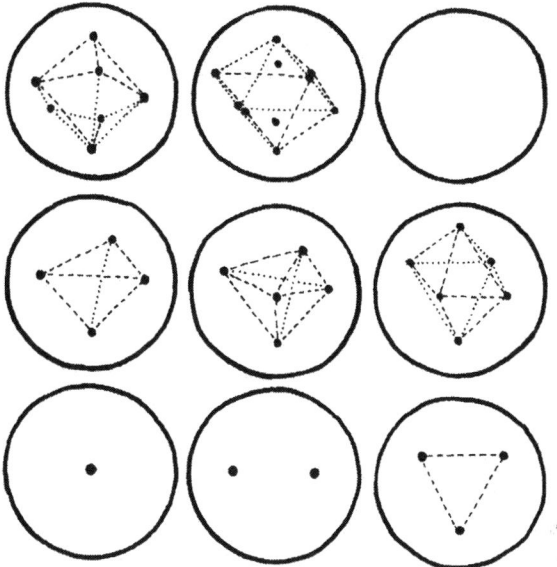

THOMPSON'S THREE-DIMENSIONAL ARRANGEMENTS
OF ELECTRONS IN THE ATOM

When confined to a plane, he also found a series of rings naturally formed, each stable only if inner rings were present, much like Mayer's initial findings.[6]

However, Thompson saw an early problem with his model. Each electron orbiting within the atom must follows a curved path, so it must be in a constant state of acceleration. According to the laws of electricity and magnetism (Maxwell's equations), a negatively-charged particle undergoing acceleration should be shedding energy.

This process is called *radiation*, energy released as light.

---

[6] If the positions of the electrons are disturbed for any reason, they will push and pull on one another like a mass on a spring (coupled oscillators) with distinct frequencies of vibration (normal modes). Thompson hoped that this would explain the light emitted and absorbed by the atom, but unfortunately, there was no clear relationship between the two. Because of how each electron can move when vibrating, the number of normal modes is three times the number of electrons. This was far fewer than the known spectral lines emitted by atoms, although it did suggest that perhaps there were many more electrons even in the lightest atoms—something that ultimately was shown to be false.

So although orbiting electrons in Thomson's model are more stable than static electrons to perturbations, the radiation drain should cause their movement to slow down and, eventually, stop.

ALFRED MAYER'S EXPERIMENT

CONDUCTED IN 1878, CORKS WITH ELECTRIFIED PINS WERE PLACED IN A WATER DISH UNDER AN ELECTROMAGNET. CONCENTRIC RINGS NATRALLY FORMED UNDER THESE CONDITIONS, RESEMBLING THE PERIODICITY OF CHEMICAL PROPERTIES OF ATOMS.

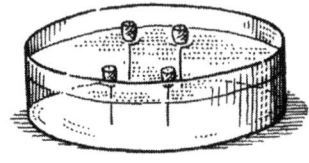

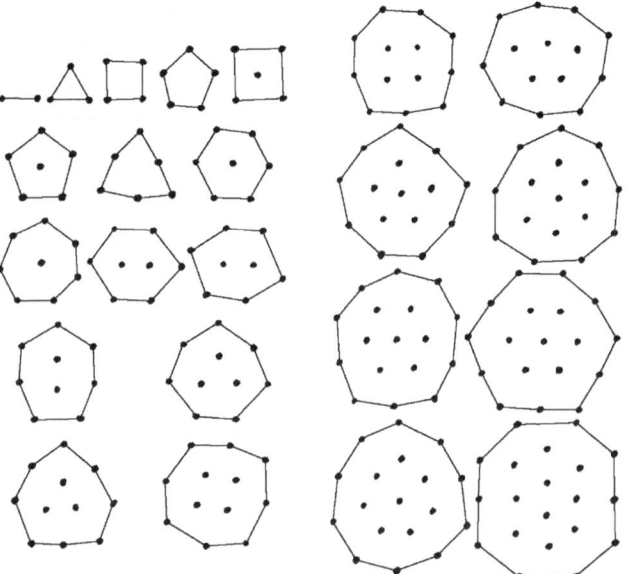

Thomson found, however, that the *more* electrons that were placed in each ring, the *less* radiation was emitted overall. In fact, the radiation from many electrons was deconstructively interfering. Especially if the electrons were orbiting at low velocities, the radiation drain could be reduced by several orders of magnitude for each new electron placed in the same orbit.

RADIATION FROM ELECTRON ORBITS

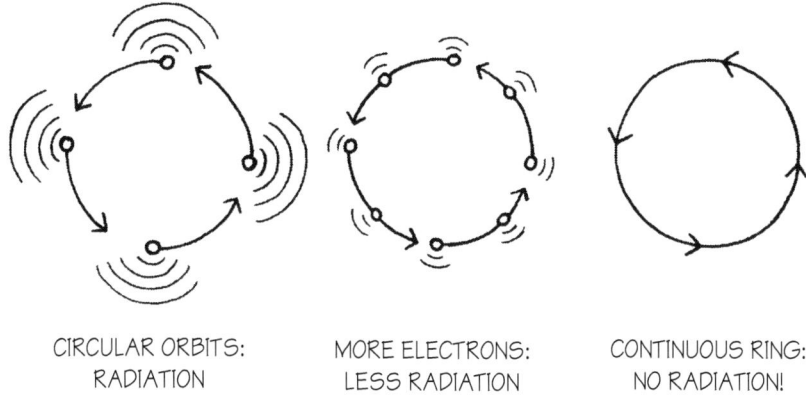

CIRCULAR ORBITS: RADIATION | MORE ELECTRONS: LESS RADIATION | CONTINUOUS RING: NO RADIATION!

THOMSON FOUND THAT THE MORE ELECTRONS WERE PLACED IN AN ORBIT, THE LESS RADIATION IS EMITTED OVERALL.

Perhaps, Thomson speculated, atoms radiated continuously, but at such low levels that it was very difficult to observe.[7] And he discovered that if electrons were packed into an orbit to form a *continuous* ring of charge, the radiation drain would theoretically drop completely to zero.[8]

In the first decade of the century, there were other theoreticians, model-builders, mostly British, who imagined the internal structure of the atom. Kelvin's Aepinus atom; Oliver Lodge's concept of interlocked positive and negative electricity; Philip Leonard's neutral dynamids, doublets of positive and negative electrons; James Jean's concentric shells of alternating charges (Kragh 2010). These models were not always assumed to be a literal picture of the atomic world, but illustrative. Some were mathematically complex. None, including Thomson's, were fully developed.

Perhaps inspired by the idea of radiationless rings of current, Hantaro Nagaoka, a Japanese physicist who studied in Germany, speculated that rings of electrons orbited like the rings of Saturn, about a ball of positive charge (Nagaoka 1904).

---

[7] If electrons do radiate continuously while slowing in their orbit, the atom might eventually become critically unstable, causing it to rearrange or eject electrons from the atom; Thomson thought this might be a good way to explain the radioactivity of some substances.

[8] This has become a classic example in electrodynamics, see Jackson 1999.

RADIATION FROM A POINT-CHARGE

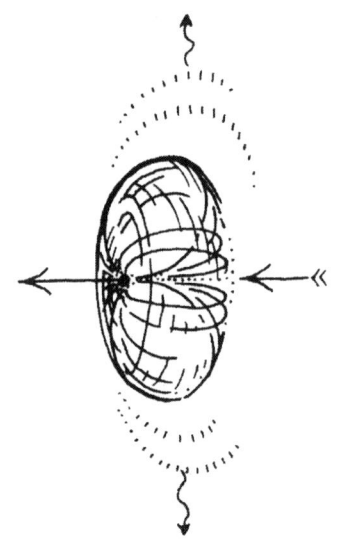

AN ACCELERATING POINT-CHARGE RELEASES A FRONT OF RADIATION IN THE SHAPE OF A TOROID.

He even used similar mathematics that Maxwell had used in calculating the stability of Saturn's rings. A fascinating scheme, it is somewhat obscure today, because it represents a dead end in the exploration of possibilities, like a trickle of water running against a rock in its search for the ocean.

New theories are driven by new experiments, and what physicists needed was an experiment that told them something, *directly*, about the positive half of the atom.

Recall the familiar sight in old westerns: a shady transaction between highwaymen. One of them opens the chest, revealing a hoard of gold coins. The other reaches in, takes one, brings it to his mouth, and takes a bite.

If you have ever wondered why this is, it turns out that gold (unlike fool's gold) is soft. It can be hammered into an almost transparent foil, only 1500 atoms thick. In 1911, Geiger, Rutherford, and Marsden famously fired particles through such a foil, giving each particle a small chance of hitting one of the 1500 atoms as it went through.

They were surprised to find that the particles were deflecting at high angles; not what you would expect from a Thomson-like atom with a spread out positive charge, but as if there was a heavy, concentrated mass in the atom: the *nucleus*.

Following these developments in atomic theory was the young Danish physicist Niels Bohr. After earning his doctorate in Copenhagen in 1911, Bohr traveled to England where he finally met J.J. Thomson, whom he idolized. Once in the presence of the great man, he rather tactlessly pointed out a line in a paper where Thomson had been wrong, disheartening the older by the younger. They never got along.

Bohr, however, continued the work of Thomson and Nagaoka, and proposed a new model for the atom that is now taught in grade school everywhere: the "planetary" model, in which the electrons orbit the nucleus in circular orbits, much like planets orbit the Sun. The orbit of each electron is balanced by two forces: first, the electron's attraction to the positive charge of the nucleus; and second, its outward momentum.[9]

But what about the radiation drain? In fact, it didn't go away. The electron, in constant acceleration on a circular path, should radiate, losing energy and spiraling into the nucleus within a fraction of a second! In a Bohr universe, matter is unstable, and should quickly disintegrate.

Bohr, for some reason, was either not interested in solving this problem, or unable to imagine how it could be solved. Bohr was familiar with Thomson's work and we can imagine him late at night, paging through Thomson's description of the radiation of orbiting charges. Perhaps electrons did have an internal structure that allowed them to remain stable, but they were small enough to approximate as a point. At least, it was a start. In the tradition of the model-builders, a model did not need to be perfect, just illustrative, and one could ignore the defects until someone had a better idea.

For the atom to exist, some electron orbits simply *had* to be stable, so Bohr made a strong, theoretically unjustified declaration that there exists a stable ground state orbit in the atom. When electrons in this state absorbed light, they jumped to a higher orbit, in which (unlike the ground state) the electron was unstable and must radiate energy, falling out of its orbit within a fraction of a second to return to the ground state orbit.

The great advantage of this idea was that it could reproduce the spectroscopic absorption and emission lines found from experiments with hydrogen. The electron will only absorb light of discrete frequencies as it jumps to higher orbits, and similarly as it emits radiation, dropping to lower orbits. These frequencies had been captured in a simple formula, which Bohr used to postulate his electron orbits in the atom.

The Bohr model is taught even today as a useful heuristic, but work along this vein stopped around 1914. A generation of physicists were recruited to the war effort or lost on the battlefield.

---

[9] The planetary model was an idea that had been shuffled around philosophically in the previous century: the analogy between physics on the macroscopic scale and physics on the microscopic scale.

The atom was a house under construction but abandoned (as Philip Pearle put it) by the workmen on receiving news of an approaching plague (Pearle 1982).

The next generation would be that of Heisenberg, of Pauli, of Dirac, of de Broglie, of those who would look at physics in a new way.

The plague, in Pearle's analogy, was quantum theory.

The history of science may also be written as a history of ideas; borrowed from one century, carried into another, sometimes reborn, sometimes hybridized. An idea written down takes on a life of its own, trickling down through centuries, flowing from one thinker to another, evolving, diversifying, and spreading to new minds.

In 1920, Germany was still the premier nation in the world for science. But the younger generation was upset, at politics, at physics, at the heritage of their forerunners. They would rebuild postwar Europe in their own image.

At a gathering in Bad Nauheim for the 86th Assembly, a young prodigy, Wolfgang Pauli, stood to speak. He was still a year away from his doctorate, but already well-regarded in the physics community.

"None of the erstwhile theories," Pauli began "not even the Einstein theory, has up to now succeeded in solving the problem of the elementary electric quanta in a satisfactory manner; thus it is desirable to look for a deeper reason for this failure" (Mehra et al. 1982, p. 279).

Since its inception, physicists did not love the Bohr model. It had a radiation problem. In addition, the frequency of light emitted from electrons in the Bohr atom did not properly correspond to the calculated orbital frequency of the electron. It was unclear if electrons would be stable enough in their orbits to withstand perturbations. And what of the interaction with light, which must be absorbed and released in discrete quanta? What of the wave properties of light? These problems must have seemed overwhelming to physicists of the time; even as they do today.

Pauli and others were dissatisfied with the canonical scientific method. It was applicable in the last century, perhaps, but times had changed. It was a time of relativity, in which common preconceptions could be thrown out; a time in which anything could and would be questioned.

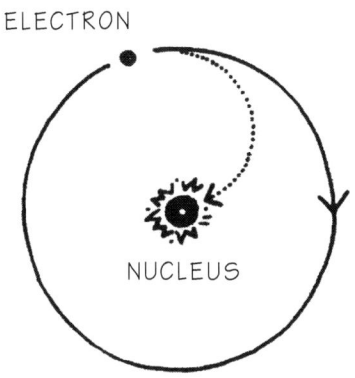

THE BOHR MODEL

ACCORDING TO MAXWELL'S EQUATIONS, AN ELECTRON DESCRIBED AS A POINT, CONSTANTLY ACCELERATING AS IT MOVES IN A CIRCULAR ORBIT, SHOULD SHED ENERGY AND COLLAPSE INTO THE NUCLEUS WITHIN A FRACTION OF A SECOND. BOHR COULD NEVER EXPLAIN WHY AN ELECTRON ORBIT IS STABLE IN HIS MODEL.

Pauli's suggestion was ripe for the time, but the root of the idea first emerged in Germany, in 1781. Immanuel Kant was an aging German philosopher who broke a decade of silence with a massive tome, *The Critique of Pure Reason*. In it he outlined a theory of knowledge, and made a biting argument about the nature of the senses.

Kant asked the question: do our senses help us know the world?

Our sense organs, Kant reasoned, are like messengers; if we really wanted direct knowledge of the world, we would need to bypass our sense organs, which is clearly impossible. Instead, Kant proposed that the world we experience is artificial, conditioned.

In his *Prolegomena To A Future Metaphysics*, Kant wrote that "things as objects of our senses existing outside us are given, but we know nothing of what they may be in themselves, knowing only their appearances, that is, representations which they cause in us by affecting our senses" (Kant 1951, p. 36).

This argument threw a wrench in the Enlightenment machine, built by intellectuals such as Francis Bacon, Isaac Newton, and John Locke, who believed that the scientific method, reason, and freedom of thought enabled man to come to know the world. But Kant's ideas found fertile ground in Germany; and over the next hundred years, they grew in favor.

Even today they are well received.[10]

Reason and science, as advocated by the Enlightenment thinkers, were a way to know the world, an alternative to faith or endless scholasticism. Kant was rejecting this view in a fundamental way; perhaps more fundamentally than he himself realized.

Seventy years later, Kant's *Prolegomena* would fall into the hands of Ernst Mach (1838-1916). Mach found Kant's book in his father's library when he was fifteen years old; it made a "powerful and ineffaceable impression upon me, the like of which I never afterwards experienced in any of my philosophical reading" (Mach 1914).

Mach would write several books, including *The Science of Mechanics* and *The Analysis of Sensations*. Many German philosophers were disciples of Kant at the time; a neo-Kantian philosophy of Helmholtz, Cohen, and Cassirer had become part of German scientific common sense. Mach's neo-Kantianism was less dominant but also widespread, with influence especially in Gottingen, Berlin, and the Kaiser Wilhelm Institutes, where the new physics would emerge.[11]

Like Kant, Mach held that our representations of such things as substance, natural laws, their mathematical relations, and causality were products of human cognition. We arbitrarily focus on those aspects of the world, Mach argued, because we are capable of representing them in our mind, and we do so only in ways that are important or useful to us.

> In speaking of cause and effect we arbitrarily give relief to those elements to whose connection we have to attend in the reproduction of a fact in the respect in which it is important to us. There is no cause nor effect in nature; nature has but an individual existence; nature simply *is*. (Mach 1960)

---

[10] Partly still popular, I think, due to a confusion over what he was trying to do. I still remember late night debates with other students who believed that Kant was defending reason and the Enlightenment program. But a friend, philosopher Stephen Hicks, put it well when he wrote, "Any thinker who concludes that in principle reason cannot know reality is not fundamentally an advocate of reason" (Hicks 2004, p. 40).

[11] Posthumously, Mach would receive the honor of having the speed of sound in air named after him ("Mach 1"), which I agree has a good ring to it.

Soon after reading the *Prolegomena*, Mach began to question Kant, and decided that the role the "thing-in-itself" plays in Kant's philosophy was superfluous (Mach 1914).[12] Kant may have believed that the substance (or substratum) of the world was inaccessible, but he still believed it was there. It was, for him, a kind of universal common denominator of changes in shape, color, and composition (Kant 1951).

Whereas for Mach, substance could only be what was left over after all its sensory qualities were subtracted, and when you did that, you have nothing left. In short, for Mach, we are under the illusion that the things around us are made of stuff, when in fact they are aggregates of sense experiences only (Mach 1914).

Overall, Mach's view on the nature of reality was as follows: that all that exists are appearances (or *phenomena*), and sensations are the fundamental constituents of reality. "Bodies do not produce sensations, but complexes of elements (complexes of sensations) make up bodies" (Mach 1914).[13] According to Mach, our minds are swimming in a sea of sensations, and the more we seek to understand them, the more we discover that there is nothing there but more sensations, nothing solid to grab on to. To reach out into the world was only to reach deeper within.

Mach resisted the idea of the atom altogether, as did some others[14], but instead of questioning the hypothesis on the basis of scientific evidence, he questioned whether something that could not be directly observed could be claimed to exist at all. Atoms were the latest incarnation of Lock's hard substratum of the world, guided by natural laws. Mach interpreted atoms as a "mathematical *model* for facilitating the mental reproduction of facts" and only a segue to constructing what he called *direct descriptions* of phenomena, that are able to omit the unobservables, leaving just the mathematical equations and relations that allow us to make predictions (Mach 1960).

At first glance, this seems like a very efficient way of thinking. If we throw out all the theoretical apparatus of a theory, and retain only the

---

[12] Incidentally, other thinkers obsessed with Kant realized this also, such as Hegel.

[13] The enlightenment idea that very small particles somehow carried information between our senses and the world around us so repelled Mach that he refused to use even the word "sensations," instead using what translates as a more neutral word "elements" to refer to our perceptions of the world.

[14] See Fleck 1963.

ERNST MACH
(1838-1916)

BELIEVED THAT ALL THAT EXISTS ARE APPEARANCES; THAT SENSATIONS ARE THE FUNDAMENTAL CONSTITUENTS OF REALITY. HIS IDEAS INFLUENCED EINSTEIN AND THE FOUNDERS OF QUANTUM THEORY.

things that really matter, perhaps we are left with something cleaner and stronger.[15] This idea fueled the creativity of those who would rewrite atomic theory. But first, it passed by way of a young Austrian physicist.

---

[15] In a later chapter we will discuss how a theory's ability to make inferences to new situations makes it far more useful than such direct descriptions. Also see Hempel 1965, p. 222.

Somewhere, an idea makes a leap into a new mind. As it stretches into a new fertile consciousness, it is reborn with new meaning.

Albert Einstein was a devoted student of Mach. He picked up a copy of *The Science of Mechanics* around 1897, and it made a "deep and lasting impression" upon him (Holton 1968).

In it, Mach had fiercely attacked Newton's concepts of absolute space and time. This influenced Einstein's thoughts, perhaps encouraging him to work through the counterintuitive aspects of travel at near light speed from the point of view of observers taking measurements, instead of a third-person omniscient narrator. This resulted in his theory of Special Relativity, and later, General Relativity, which modified Newton's theories. Einstein was a careful and methodological thinker, a philosophical role model for the younger generation, and a sensation in the scientific community.

Einstein and Mach corresponded and occasionally met; they often found agreement. But Einstein's views would change slowly throughout his career. As he was finishing up his theory of gravity, he would admit that he was fundamentally opposed to Mach's views.[16]

Relativity theory was a huge challenge to physics at the time; and in Germany, it flourished primarily at those schools sympathetic to Mach's point of view, such as Göttingen and Berlin.

In Göttingen, Minkowski gave a series of lectures on relativity, with a strong emphasis on Mach's ideas, and presenting what came to be called "Mach's Principle."[17] Those who attended the talks included Max Born, a professor there, and Werner Heisenberg, an assistant nearing his doctorate.

The idea, as Heisenberg later recalled, was that "real things are those which you can observe, and everything else has no meaning" (Mehra 1982, p. 274).

The goal was to construct a theory in terms of *observables*, things which can be seen and measured. The interior of the atom was not observable; no experiment could give the instantaneous position and velocity of

---

[16] See Chapter 17 for further discussion.

[17] The principle in this form is somewhat more broad than that mentioned by Einstein in his General Theory, in which the large-scale distribution of matter of the universe establishes a reference frame for local inertial motion. This principle is interesting, however, and I will discuss it in a later chapter.

electrons, only the energies of their stationary orbits and the frequencies and intensities of their transitions.

The principle was a synthesis of two elements from Mach's philosophy: first, a general skepticism of what cannot be directly observed. If you could not see it, how did you know it was really there? How did you know it behaved the way you thought it did?

And second: a theoretical definition must be operational to be meaningful. All you needed to know is enough to calculate numbers seen in experiments, anything else was considered inessential theoretical jargon.

As Born expressed it: "the principle states that concepts and representations that do not correspond to physically observable facts are not to be used in theoretical description" (Born 1964).

Pauli, the godson of Ernst Mach, had extensively read his philosophical works. Born, Pauli, Heisenberg, and Pascual Jordan discussed the principle as a group. By 1924, this way of interpreting theoretical models of the atom was catching on more widely. It appeared in a letter to *Nature* by Hendrik Kramers (based in Copenhagen) on dispersion theory (Kramers 1924). It also appeared in a note by Sommerfeld on the theory of periodic systems (Sommerfeld 1925, p. 70).

Even the Bohr model began to be spoken about as a scheme for calculating experimental numbers rather than as physical theory of the atom (Born 1927, p. 114).

Physicists were dropping the physics out of their math, and the idea was embraced even by those who had built classical electron theory; Bohr himself was a quick and lasting convert.

Why was this idea so persuasive?

Physicists had hit a dead end with the theory but were able to continue working even without a clear theoretical foundation. New data such as spectral lines for atoms could usually be understood with simple formulas derived from experiments, not from theory. By 1925, there was a wealth of this data. If a computational scheme could suffice, why postulate a physical mechanism?

After earning his degree from the University of Munich, Heisenberg returned to Göttingen as a lecturer and assistant to Born, and began to work on atomic theory. Armed with a guiding principle "Der Erfolg heiligt die Mittel" ("Success sanctifies the means") he would try out new assumptions, experiment with different mathematical schemes, then mix everything up despite the inconsistencies (Mehra 1982, p. 37). He was an adventurer, what we describe now as a non-linear thinker, a fluid generator of ideas and rapid associations. But Pauli, looking over Heisenberg's shoulder, was worried that he was forgetting the real problems of atomic theory.

In 1925, Heisenberg hit upon what he called the Matrix Mechanics. Starting on his own, and then working closely with Born and Jordan, they succeeded in replacing numbers that represented physical properties, such as the position and motion of the electron in the atom, with numbers that could be measured directly from experiment, such as transition amplitudes and frequencies. The scheme produced useful predictions for the energies of the hydrogen atom, but had little or no reference to underlying physics. It was a Machian theory.

In the summer of 1926, Erwin Schrödinger went out to his family estate, a place where he could relax and think. On his mind was the peculiar fact that particles had some kind of wave-like behavior; electrons, for instance, diffracted through a crystal, producing patterns of constructive and destructive interference typically only seen in waves. And there was the problem of why electrons could only remain stable when occupying certain orbits in the atom.

What if one riddle answered the other?

Growing up, Schrödinger often heard his mother playing the violin. A string on a violin was physically capable of any kind of motion, but only resonant frequencies—pure notes—were sustained by the string for longer than a fraction of a second. Perhaps the electron was a kind of resonant object, able to occupy discrete frequencies in the atom. *Notes*, instead of orbits.

It was a beautiful idea motivated by physical analogy; he sat down to work. He began with a well-known equation in physics for describing wave behavior, the wave equation. Using it, Schrödinger calculated the energy states the electron would occupy in the atom if it obeyed this equation, and solved for the case of hydrogen. He wrote down the result, sat back, and let out a sigh.

It was, in fact, totally wrong.

Perplexed, he reluctantly tried another equation, one that was similar to a heat-diffusion equation. Schrödinger conjectured a static, non-moving cloud of electron density that diffused outward from the atom in all directions, what he called the "mechanical field scalar," resulting in something that might look like fog illuminated by a street lamp. (Later, his equation came to be called the "wavefunction," which is an appealing term, but unfortunately perpetuates something of a myth that the model allows the electron to wave). When Schrödinger recalculated the energies of the electron orbits for hydrogen, it worked.

To account for the different electron orbits, Schrödinger used spherical harmonic functions: mathematical equations that produced beautiful, symmetrical patterns in electron density about the nucleus. The electron, in its diffuse emanation, changes its density to occupy one of these patterns. Each had a different energy corresponding to the electron orbit.

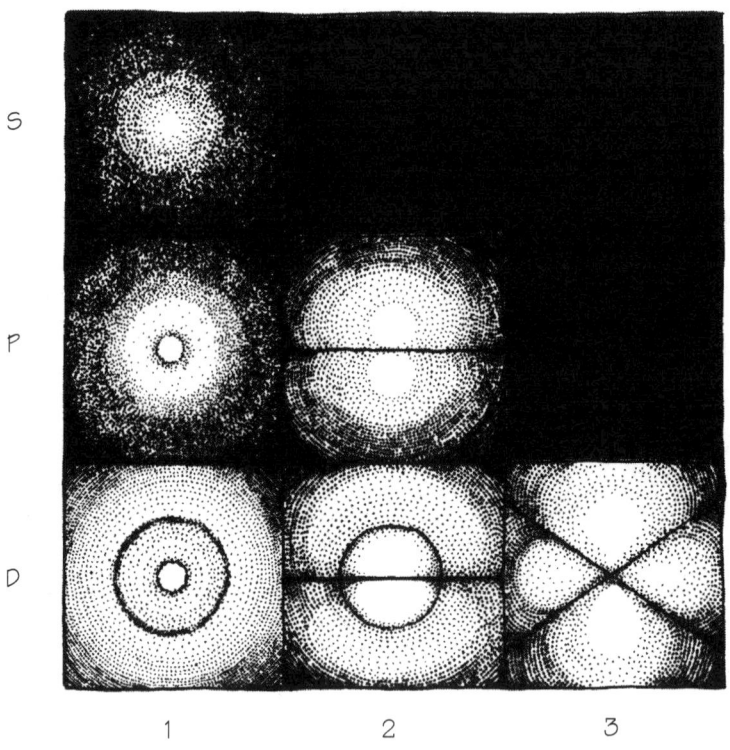

QUANTUM WAVEFUNCTIONS
OF THE HYDROGEN ATOM

SCHRODINGER CONJECTURED A STATIC CLOUD OF ELECTRON DENSITY THAT DIFFUSES OUTWARD FROM THE ATOM, GUIDED BY SPHERICAL HARMONIC FUNCTIONS.

He also found that his model of the atom was mathematically identical to Heisenberg's. Both had arrived at the same theory, but from different motivations. The new theory, which adopted Schrödinger's more intuitive mathematical formalism, became quantum mechanics.

Schrödinger was disappointed that the original equation didn't work; he knew that the true wave equation took a form that would be compatible with relativity theory, while the final version did not.[18]

Quantum mechanics was born twice, from two different philosophical minds, and like parents quarreling over custody of their child, physicists argued over how to use and interpret it.

Schrödinger's model implied that the electron was something of an extended volume charge, partly a *classical* idea. However, that idea was unable to explain a variety of physical phenomena.

Why does the electron not fall into the nucleus? What about electron spin, discovered soon after? Why do electron-scattering experiments make it appear that the electron is in fact a point, rather than a spread-out object?

The group at Göttingen began pursuing a statistical view. In 1926, Born suggested that the wavefunction was describing the *probability* of finding an electron within a range of locations, if you were to measure its location in an experiment (Born 1968). This retained the idea of the electron as a classical point, but one somehow bound within a probability density cloud.

This may sound absurd. But recall that Born sought only an operational definition, not a description of nature. Its purpose was to tell you about a number you might obtain from an experiment. It was an aid to knowing. But this did not stop others from interpreting the theory as a genuine proposal that the electron really was in many places at once.

Regardless of the physical interpretation, let us take a moment to imagine the mathematics that describe a quantum particle in free space.

Pick up a rope and shake it steadily back and forth; you are generating a wave. But give the rope only a *quick* shake; you will watch a single spike travel down the rope. This is not a wave, it is mathematically represented

---

[18] Incidentally, Oskar Klein and Walter Gordon later published the original equation despite its inaccuracies; and it is now known as the Klein-Gordon equation.

by a Gaussian curve, analogous to a wave burst. When it moves, a *group* of waves move. Its velocity is not a real velocity, but a *group velocity*, a merely apparent motion of a concurrently moving group of underlying waves. Some of the waves are building up the burst, and some of the waves are causing it to fizzle out.

If you were a quantum particle, this may give you an existential crisis.

Are you a thing in yourself, or are you merely surfing, for a glorious moment, the collective action of all the waves that compose you?[19]

Describing a particle in this way makes for some weird results. If a wave burst is constrained to a very narrow spike, it has no clear wavelength, and therefore no velocity. If you stretch it out until it has a rhythmic beat, you have a clear wavelength but an unclear position. This is the essence of the Heisenberg Uncertainty Principle, which we will revisit later.[20]

Ultimately, Schrödinger all but disowned the child he shared with Heisenberg. Perhaps it was too statistical, perhaps it had too many conceptual problems, or that it wasn't compatible with relativity. Perhaps its classical analogies didn't pan out, or that it wasn't very predictive of electron orbits beyond the simplest element, hydrogen. Instead of dwelling in the quantum quagmire, Schrödinger continued searching for a better theory.

Einstein, though a promulgator of Mach's views, also openly objected to the path that quantum mechanics took during the 1920s. Heisenberg relayed a conversation he had with Einstein after Heisenberg's presentation of quantum mechanics in 1926.[21]

> Einstein: "But you don't seriously believe," Einstein protested, "that none but observable magnitudes must go into a physical theory?"

---

[19] Schrödinger's equation allows a tiny bit of the particle to extend out to infinity. It is easy to see why many quantum theoreticians, including Bohr, have professed the idea that there is an interconnectedness between all things, that there are no discrete boundaries between a quantum particle and its surroundings.

[20] See Chapter 18.

[21] Although this cannot be taken to be Einstein's words verbatim, it stands as Heisenberg's recollection of Einstein's position on this issue, and is consistent with Einstein's writings.

Heisenberg: "Isn't that precisely what you have done with relativity?" I asked in some surprise. "After all, you did stress the fact that it is impermissible to speak of absolute time, simply because absolute time cannot be observed; that only clock readings, be it in the moving reference system or the system at rest, are relevant to the determination of time."

Einstein: "Possibly I did use this kind of reasoning," Einstein admitted, "but it is nonsense all the same. Perhaps I could put it more diplomatically by saying that it may be heuristically useful to keep in mind what one has actually observed. But on principle, it is quite wrong to try founding a theory on observable magnitudes alone" (Heisenberg 1971).

"BUT YOU DON'T SERIOUSLY BELIEVE THAT NONE BUT OBSERVABLE MAGNITUDES MUST GO INTO A PHYSICAL THEORY?" -EINSTEIN

Although Einstein helped to usher in the Machian revolution in physics, he was, in the latter part of his life, critical of Mach, who "neglects the fact that the world really exists, that our sense impressions are based on something objective" (Heisenberg 1971).

Like Schrödinger, Einstein continued to seek a theory of nature that would unify relativity with a clear vision of the atom.

CHAPTER 4

THE HYDRINO

In which a new model of the atom proves its worth but comes with some surprises; and the author moves to New Jersey.

For three years, Mills's book sat on my shelf while I studied both physics and chemistry. It was not enough to understand Mills's theory, I also had to understand the experiments, so I bridged the cognitive divide between the two departments. I took organic and inorganic chemistry alongside electrodynamics and quantum physics: it was an exhausting schedule, but allowed me to see how the barriers between the sciences are like those arbitrary lines we draw between states on a map.

One benefit of my course load was that I had experience using a wide array of spectroscopic equipment. Having sent in my resume to BlackLight and almost forgotten about it, I left a short message following up about a summer internship position. The next day, I had two messages: one asked me to call back to discuss the possibility of a position; and the next was a job offer. Turns out they needed someone to help take spectroscopic data and assist with various experiments.

Within a few days my girlfriend and I bought a car and set off, crossing the continent for the first time. Arriving in Princeton on a humid summer day, we moved into a small fourth-floor studio on Bell Street, a charming New England street lined with brightly-colored townhouses.[22]

On the day we arrived, Princeton was swarming with cicadas; an insect that emerges from hives beneath the roots of old trees once every seven years, to swarm, mate, and die. The air was filled with a white noise of cicada chirps, and the ground was strewn with carcasses of the fallen. Occasionally one flew into the car and caused much screaming and commotion before being successfully voided out the window.

BLP was outside of Princeton some ten miles, in an area filled with corporate campuses in science, technology, and medicine. The company occupied a laboratory formerly owned by General Electric for the building and testing of satellites. It had a water tower, a high bay, and

---

[22] I would later recognize my street as one of the settings of the movie "IQ" featuring Walter Matthau as Einstein.

a giant vacuum chamber—a cylindrical steel colossus that looked like a Mars base—standing in the back parking lot.

Mills had told the press that he was going to build his first hydrino power plant in that chamber (why anywhere else?) and though that hadn't happened, the chamber was massive and impossible to move, so there it remained.

Mills himself was not as I expected. He was tall (6'6") with an athletic build and diagonal eyebrows. He was excitable, and laughed freely like a child. He was unpretentious; an engineer-scholar; a farmer's son with the brain of Einstein and the drive of Edison; a modern man; a quintessential American.

Mills engaged those around him excitedly in ideas that perhaps a handful of theorists in the world could meaningfully converse on. There was brilliance in his eyes, and no one who ever met Mills could call him a fool. He was also, for the most part, unaffected by the outside world. He had his own funding, a spacious office, a laboratory at his command; an intense working lifestyle; a routine at the gym; a large brick home with a family in Princeton.

When I asked about the skepticism from the community, he shrugged and said it was only a matter of time. He could wait.

During my tenure at BLP, Mills divided his time between theoretical work and directing his laboratory scientists; reading and writing articles; and writing patents. His days were long and he was often in the office on weekends, with his children running around the lobby. It sometimes felt like he lived at the office. This much was certain: he was genuinely excited by his work, and energized by each step forward. He was like a child on a beach, and wanted to share each new discovery with anyone who would listen.

On the shelves at BLP I found a thin copy of the first bound edition of Mills's book. It was published in 1990, called simply *The Grand Unified Theory*. It contained a rough draft of his entire theory, a sketchy account that was meager in comparison to the now several-thousand-page treatise, but contained the solutions to all the fundamental problems that made up the bones of his theory.

Mills's efforts began where Bohr left off, with the problem of radiation.

Only a trickle of lone voices, spread throughout the twentieth century, still spoke about the problem of radiation; the authors often apologizing in their papers for bringing up an unpopular topic, even while making progress.

So long as the electron was a point, it *had* to radiate. And yet, the electron *couldn't* radiate in the atom. The idea of a point ran deep; a point was easy to work with. But there were several problems with point charges–problems we continue to struggle with today. Since a point occupies no volume, the charge density at the exact center spikes to infinity.[23] When the charge density spikes, so does the energy required to keep all that negative charge from blowing itself apart (the so-called "self-energy").

Only if you push the charge into a *singularity*, a point of infinitesimal size, does the problem theoretically go away. But some theorists feel that all this accomplished is to sweep the problem under the rug.[24] Also, the electric field of a point faces all directions at once, a scenario physicists shrug off and call "undefined."

The electron also has the property of spin, and a magnetic moment results from its spinning charge. A point can spin, but since all its mass and charge is contained in a point, it can't have any angular momentum. Without any moving charge, it can't have a magnetic field. There must be some charge some non-zero distance from the center of rotation.

Aware of these issues, physicists turned away from point charges and began exploring the next best thing: spherical shells.

Spherical shells have an intuitive appeal to physicists. They are easy to work with. They are spherically symmetrical. They have volume and a surface area, which means that any charge smeared onto the outside of the sphere has a well-defined electric field, even if the charge density spikes at the surface.[25] Most principles of physics can be illustrated well with spheres or spherical shells; the Swiss astrophysicist Fritz Zwicky even insulted a colleague thus: "He is a spherical bastard: a bastard any way you look at him."

---

[23] We can alleviate this with a mathematical concept in which the total charge of a particle is finite even if it spikes arbitrarily large at the center: this is called the Dirac delta function.

[24] George Goedecke's turn of phrase.

[25] The Dirac delta function allows us to describe the spike in charge density on the surface of a shell or at the center of a point charge.

The first physicists who worked on the spherical shell model were Abraham, Lorentz, and Poincaré (ALP). They explored models that were rigid, deformable, and those that would be compatible with relativity. Almost all classical models of the electron that have received any attention—either before or after the advent of quantum theory—are spheres: spherical shells or solid spheres, oscillating or orbiting, as these are perhaps the only models that physicists have ever found remotely plausible. And there are a number of recurring and interesting problems that arise in their study.

I have already mentioned the mystery of what holds the electron together. A spherical shell ought to blow up like a balloon as the charge repels itself. Physicists often add an extra unknown (non-electromagnetic, and therefore "mechanical") *self-force* that is responsible for keeping the negative charge from blowing apart. Poincaré suggested that there was a pressure from outside the electron pressing in, this became known as the Poincaré stress. Dirac later suggested something almost equivalent, that it is some kind of elastic force. Either way it is inexplicable.

One of the problems discovered with the ALP model was that there may be scenarios in which a force impinging on the shell causes it to accelerate, but the acceleration causes a release of energy as radiation that is subsequently absorbed by the electron itself. This leads to what is called a *runaway state*, an ever-increasing acceleration that continues after the force is no longer applied. If this were to actually happen, the electron would grow in energy (and therefore mass), snowballing as it sped up towards the speed of light.

But such things are impossible; when you hit a pool ball with a cue, it slows down and stops, diffusing its energy into the environment. It doesn't fly around the table with increasing speed until all the balls are in the pocket (wishful thinking aside).

It is possible that this was simply the result of a bad model. When ALP assumed that the electron was perfectly rigid, with an infinite self-force, they perhaps already let a physical violation in the door. Runaway states are that violation having free reign of the house. There was some debate on this matter; apparently the problem persists even if the self-force is finite. Either way, the problem was a sure sign that the model was wrong.

In trying to get rid of this problem, physicists ran into another equally troubling theoretical possibility: the electron could accelerate in response to a force that has not yet been applied. It is as if you lean over the pool table and prepare to hit the ball with the cue, but just before you do, it begins to move. This *preacceleration* seems to violate our most fundamental principle of causality.

In 1938 Dirac looked again at the problem of the classical electron, and found that the period of preacceleration was equal to the time it takes light to cross a portion of the electron. A force impinging on one side of the electron will instantaneously propagate to the whole electron. It was a non-local effect, and any effect that travels at faster-than-light speed must, according to relativity theory, travel backwards through time. Although Dirac was not advocating a classical model, he was apparently willing to rationalize it away. Perhaps, he argued, our conception of space and time ought to be different on so small a scale as within the particle itself. From our macroscopic point of view, we would never experience such a small effect. At present, I will leave it to the reader to decide whether an itty bitty violation in cause and effect is forgivable.

There were also postulated scenarios in which the electron responds to a force, but the acceleration is opposite to the direction the force is applied! This is called *opacceleration*. You lean over the pool table and as you hit the ball, it actually rolls toward your cue, perhaps knocking it out of your hands. This violated Newton's laws, in which acceleration occurs in response to a force, in the direction of the force.[26]

These explorations help us today to define the problem. If we rule out rationalizing away our problems, we know that a successful electron model must be compatible with special relativity; it must hold itself together in a way that we can justify; it must not allow runaway states, preaccelerations, or opaccelerations; it must be able to spin. Theorists also hoped that the model would produce an entirely electrodynamic resistance to motion that would give us Newton's second law on a silver platter[27]. Throughout the 20th century, this line of investigation was in a constant state of neglect, in which even simple variations of the spherical shell model were not fully studied.

But hope glimmered on the horizon.

---

[26] In electrodynamics, the force does not always occur along the exact line in which it was exerted, but this is because electric fields are able to generate magnetic fields that behave in more complicated ways. Still, we are able to track the forces as they move through space, and the acceleration is always in the direction of the force.

[27] We will revisit this idea in Chapter 12.

In 1933, G.A. Schott published a paper which began by describing a simple experiment to demonstrate that it is possible for charge to accelerate *without* radiating energy (Schott 1933).

First you needed to manufacture a uniformly charged spherical shell. Schott suggested that you acquire a very good insulating material such as ebonite, perhaps broken into two halves. Place a metallic sphere on the inside of the ebonite, and another surrounding it on the outside, and connect those spheres to the leads of a battery to give the ebonite shell a uniform charge.

This uses the same principle as a capacitor: if you put an insulating material between two plates and charge up the plates, then remove them, a charge remains on the material.

Next, remove the inner and outer shell from the ebonite and let it hang from a simple wire. Sway the wire in a little circle, while coaxing the sphere to spin as it sways. If the period of the sway and the period of the spin are properly chosen, the sphere will not radiate energy, and it will remain uniformly charged, *forever*, even while it is actively accelerating in a circular orbit.

Schott did not actually perform this experiment. He was a theoretician, after all, and his paper used Maxwell's equations to solve this scenario in theory. He found that the orbit followed by the center of the sphere must be fairly small, less than the diameter of the sphere itself. Excusing himself for "indulging in speculation," and admitting that such things were "out of fashion," he proceeded to suggest that his findings bore on the problem of the atom.

Since the orbits were too small for the movement of the electron around the proton in an atomic orbit, Schott suggested that his findings might directly apply to the structure of the neutron, in which the electron and proton coexist in a much smaller space. In this scenario, the electron would completely surround the proton, and only its center of mass would orbit around the proton.

This discovery was important. It was fifteen years since the last progress in classical atomic theory. Now, for the first time, there was a promising justification for the stability of the atom.

Schott continued thinking along these lines. In 1937, one of his studies showed that not only could he get the radiation to vanish, but the self-force as well, so that the electron needed no extra force to hold itself together.

SCHOTT'S THOUGHT EXPERIMENT - ACCELERATION WITHOUT RADIATION

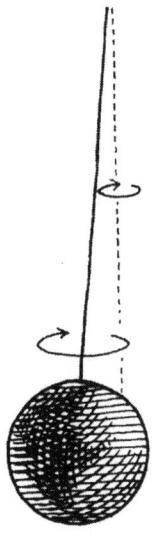

Despite this, Dirac, who retained some interest in classical theory and published a paper on the subject in 1938, continued to insist that quantum mechanics was the *only* option (Dirac 1938).

Another ten years later, Bohm and Weinstein at Princeton found a spherical shell model that could oscillate without radiating energy; that had no preacceleration, and no self-force (Bohm 1948). They also showed that quantization in such a system was straightforward; the electron could oscillate only at certain frequencies. Due to the energies of these oscillations, they suggested that their model could apply to the pion (a quark and antiquark pair), and that the pion could be seen as simply an excited oscillation of the electron.

With an access card into Princeton, I would sometimes spend an entire day digging up these papers from dusty old journals at the library. Following the progression of ideas, I was excited, reliving the discoveries. But obviously the physicists of the day were not; the citations in the intervening years were few, and the gaps in the literature were enormous. I often wondered how many decades had gone by since a forgotten paper had seen the light of day.

On November 17, 1963, George Goedecke, a young professor in the Physics Department at New Mexico State University, was rock climbing in the Organ Mountains. His party was struck by a rock slide; he and another climber were injured: Goedecke had dislocated his hip and hit his head. Two days later, he was carried off the mountain by—as the college newspaper told it—"many willing backs" (Round Up, 1964).

While he was recuperating, his mind turned to the problem of radiation. He had never fully accepted the statistical interpretation of quantum mechanics; he believed that an underlying model was essential. Maybe it was the hit on the head and the subsequent free time to think that allowed his thoughts to wander back to the problem of the classical electron.

He published a paper: *Classically Radiationless Motions and Possible Implications for Quantum Theory* (Goedecke 1964). In it he derived a general, sufficient condition by which an extended charge distribution may be shown to have no radiation, even if it was accelerating (Goedecke 1964). This condition was implicit in Maxwell's Equations, available but undiscovered, for nearly a century.[28]

It was very important that the charge was extended, spread out over a surface or volume. Goedecke used his condition to test a variety of spheres with different charge distributions, some of them spinning. He found that if we assumed the total charge equaled that of the electron, the angular momentum of the distributions was close to that of the electron. Goedecke was obviously excited by his preliminary results:

> Naturally, it is very tempting to hypothesize from this that the existence of Planck's constant is implied by classical electromagnetic theory augmented by the conditions of no radiation. Such a hypothesis would be essentially equivalent to suggesting a 'theory of nature' in which all stable particles (or aggregates) are merely nonradiating charge-current distributions whose mechanical properties are electromagnetic in origin. We certainly do not believe that this paper gives a sufficient foundation for hypothesizing a theory with such profound implications. Rather, we hope that this paper will serve as a foundation and as a stimulus for much further investigation. (Goedecke 1964)

Goedecke was happy with the paper, and his colleagues enjoyed it. In the years that followed, he would continue to publish on the topic and encouraged students to do the same. He found that some nonradiating distributions were free of the kind of preaccelerations, opaccelerations, and runaway states that plagued earlier models.

The radiation condition diffused silently into the general consciousness of the field, but further investigation of electron models took years to show signs of life. Few seemed to understand the potential significance.

---

[28] The condition for no radiation, if not satisfied, is a condition for radiation. Logically this is a biconditional, or "if and only if" statement in which implication proceeds both ways. So it is equivalent to speak of this as a "radiation condition" or a "nonradiation condition".

It was a pet topic pursued by those who were looking to satisfy their curiosity, not a topic of research likely to ensure you fame, fortune, or even tenure. Among them, Philip Pearle, who picked up the ALP model and continued work on it in the mid-1970s, and found that it could not undergo radiationless acceleration. In 1982, he published an extensive review article on classical electron models, and was also quite excited by Goedecke's condition.

In 1984, Tyler Abbott, an undergraduate at Reed College, published a thesis and subsequent paper with David Griffiths. They considered charge distributions such as infinite cylinders, solenoids, and planes, none of which were good models for the electron, but interesting to study in theory (Abbott 1985).[29]

A year later, in 1986, a paper was published by Herman Haus at MIT, who derived Goedecke's condition in a new way, but arrived at similar conclusions. The condition, compactly-phrased, stated:

> *An extended current distribution may accelerate without radiating if it has no light-like Fourier components.* (Haus 1986)

Let us take a moment to understand this important conclusion.

CLASSICAL NONRADIATION CONDITION:

$$J(k,w) = \iiint J(r, t)\, e^{(iwt - ik \cdot r)}\, d^3r\, dt = 0$$

Joseph Fourier was an eighteenth-century scientist and mathematician who showed that any complex waveform can be described by the sum of a series of simple waves. An appropriate analogy can be made with sound: any sustained tone can be constructed from a distinct set of pure notes, like those on a piano. A Fourier component is one of these fundamental waves.

A Fourier *transformation* is a mathematical process that tells you how much of each component you need to build your waveform.

Getting back to Goedecke's condition, if you take a distribution of

---

[29] I had the opportunity to chat with Griffiths about his work. His work with Abbott aside, he was not particularly interested in this area of research and had apparently never thought much about using the nonradiation condition as the basis for a particle theory.

moving charge (a current), you can perform a Fourier transform on the equations that describe its motion. If the motion has Fourier components that are "light-like," that is, synchronous with waves traveling at the speed of light, then the charge distribution radiates; it gives off light of some type.

If there are no fundamental harmonics that are synchronous with waves traveling at light speed, then there is no radiation.[30]

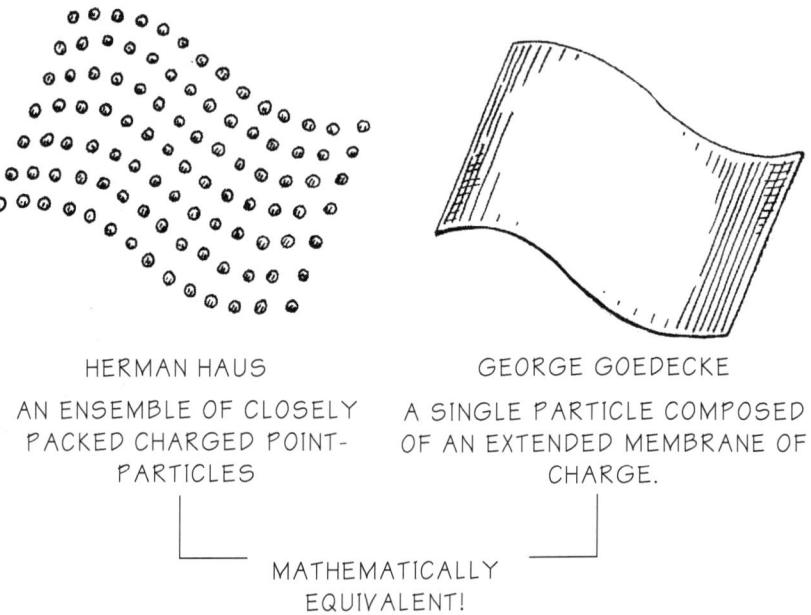

THE CONDITION FOR NO RADIATION

HERMAN HAUS
AN ENSEMBLE OF CLOSELY PACKED CHARGED POINT-PARTICLES

GEORGE GOEDECKE
A SINGLE PARTICLE COMPOSED OF AN EXTENDED MEMBRANE OF CHARGE.

MATHEMATICALLY EQUIVALENT!

Classical electron theory was such a niche topic that even Haus, a professor of electrical engineering, may not have had much familiarity with it. He wasn't thinking about extended classical particles, but rather "ensembles" of point-charges packed infinitesimally close together on a macroscopic scale. Goedecke, however, understood that the nonradiation condition applied only to extended distributions.

After almost a century of small steps, separated by long intervals, physicists had inched closer to a feasible classical model of the electron. The conditions of the problem were well formulated, and sufficient work

---

[30] If this occurs in a medium other than a vacuum, the local speed of light applies, and may result in Cerenkov radiation.

had been done to suggest that a solution was possible. This research yielded a simple and elegant formulation of the nature of nonradiating systems. It was an achievement of theory, but carried with it no fanfare.

When the electron was discovered, the physics necessary to arrive at Goedecke's conclusion was already known. We can speculate that if a high level of interest in classical models had been sustained, this understanding of radiation would have been found much sooner. But quantum theory established a strong grip on the minds of physicists.

Soon the problem of the stability of matter was forgotten. The development of the classical electron was drawn out; the topic was an empty hall in which occasional contributors heard only the reverberation of their own voice decades later.

As the decades went by, electrical engineering and quantum theory diverged. The engineers forgot they were doing real physics, while quantum theoreticians were not willing to admit the possibility that atomic theory had taken the wrong road. They still believed the problems of the Bohr Model were, *in principle*, insurmountable.

Herman Haus was an engineer, and wasn't much interested in atomic theory. He was researching the theory behind the free electron laser. He gave a talk about it to his graduate class and mentioned his paper on radiation. One of his students voiced an interest; Haus handed him a copy.

The student was Randell Mills.

When John Farrell allowed Mills to work out of his small office and laboratory at Franklin and Marshall in 1988, he assumed it would be a short-term accommodation. Mills was developing an idea for an artificial gland that would automatically regulate the body's glucose and insulin, and he needed a lab space.

As it turned out, Mills would spend four years there, working days and nights, often sleeping on the floor. He built MSI prototypes, battled tumors in mice, and speculated on artificial intelligence. Farrell would leave at night with Mills in the lab and find him still working when he came in the next morning.

Mills started obsessing over what he had learned from Haus. Like prior theoreticians who worked on the classical electron model, Mills was drawn to the idea that the electron was a spherical shell instead of a point. But Mills tried something different: he centered the shell on the proton, which had never been seriously considered before.

It was an intuitive move: every physicist knows that the electric field of a uniformly-charged spherical shell is identical to that of a point charge at its center, so long as you are observing it from outside the shell. So, the positive charge of the proton could be perfectly masked by the negative charge of a surrounding spherical electron shell, and outside the shell there would be no field.

Mills was not aware of the obscure early models in which the sphere was oscillating or orbiting; nor was he aware of Goedecke's work. His foundation was Bohr. In the planetary model of the atom, the electron was balanced by two forces: its attraction to the nucleus due to its charge; and its inertia, the outward (centrifugal) force.

Mills knew the electron couldn't be a point, because it would radiate as it orbited along a curved trajectory. But if he spread the electron over its path to form a continuous ring, the math would look very much the same, and it would avoid the radiation drain. And if he took the ring, and twisted it to spread it out over a sphere, again the math would be the same. The result was a continuous extended electron shell, having a radius equal to the well-known Bohr radius of the hydrogen atom.

We might find Mills's model counterintuitive. These rings of current overlap and intersect on the sphere, and yet charge flows through each on paths independent to neighboring rings. Each ring is centered on the nucleus on a *great circle* (with a diameter equaling that of the sphere) allowing the physics to keep the ring balanced. If the electron were a monolithic rotating shell, each path would have a different center, and the physics would not produce a balanced system.

The result was a hybrid idea—a rigid shell made up of individual rings of current. It was (as required by the Goedecke-Haus condition) an extended and continuous distribution. Since the shell was centered on the proton, the proton kept the electron tightly bound to the atom—there was no self-force needed to keep it from inflating like a balloon.

Also, by mathematically describing the pattern of current loops on the sphere, Mills's model could account for the spin of the electron and its unusual behavior in magnetic fields, which required a more complex pattern of motion than that possible due to a monolithic spinning shell. Farrell made some of the first illustrations of the loops that made up the electron shell, showing the pattern Mills described; what Mills had come to call the *orbitsphere* (Mills 2015, Ch. 1).

Mills had good reason to believe that the atom was a continuous sphere. Experiments found that when a beam of light or other particles is fired at an atom, they glance off (scatter) in a pattern expected from a sphere.

A spherical shell also offered an intuitive explanation for the hydrogen atom's excited states. In Bohr's model, the electron could make "quantum jumps" between discrete orbits. Only certain orbits were allowed for each atom, and you never found the electron somewhere between those orbits. But it was never understood how the electron made those jumps.

Resonance effects are ubiquitous in nature. Just like the violin string, a conducting sphere can absorb certain frequencies of electromagnetic waves, acting as a resonator cavity to trap energy as a standing wave. A

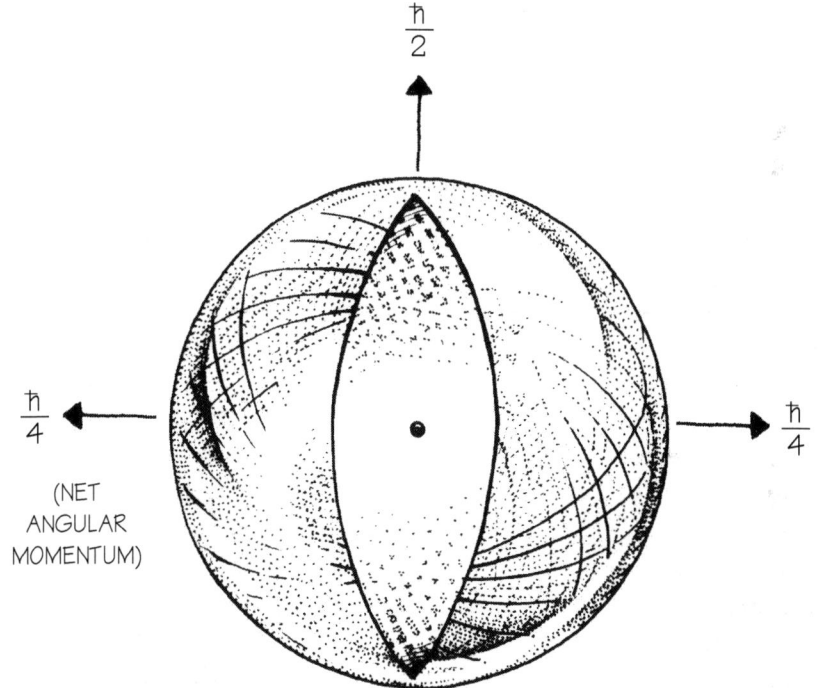

THE ELECTRON ORBITSPHERE

AN ALMOST PERFECTLY THIN SPHERICAL SHELL OF CHARGE, COMPLETELY SURROUNDING THE NUCLEUS, COMPOSED OF AN INFINITE NUMBER OF CURRENT LOOPS FOLLOWING GREAT CIRCLES THAT OVERLAP ONE ANOTHER ON THE SPHERE. THE SHELL IS <u>NOT</u> MONOLITHIC; SPIN EXISTS

ON MULTIPLE AXES! THIS IDEA SETS MILLS'S MODEL APART FROM ALL PRIOR CLASSICAL ATTEMPTS.

spherical shell electron could act in much the same way, but on the scale of the atom, to absorb or emit single particles of light: *photons*. A photon of just the right frequency could resonate in the electron shell, creating an electric field within the sphere, inflating the sphere like a balloon until it reached an excited state orbit. In this state, the photon was captured.

Unlike the "ground" state orbit of the hydrogen atom, the excited state orbits have a captured photon which makes them unstable. They quickly decay within a fraction of a second, releasing the energy that was momentarily captured, and falling back to the ground state (Mills 2015, Ch. 2).[31]

When Mills calculated what the energies of the excited state orbits would be, he found the same relationship that the Bohr Model had found; the same that the quantum-mechanical model had found; the same that, in the early years of the 20th century, Rydberg had seen in the spectral lines of hydrogen. Mills matched our best predictions of the hydrogen atom, but with the first-ever internally consistent model based on classical physics.

"I was extremely excited," Mills told BBC about the discovery, "and there were times when I was driving home and [thought] Oh god. I'm the only one in the world who actually knows of this solution. I should call my friend and tell him. What would happen if I crashed on the road and no one discovered this for another hundred years?" (BBC 1994).

Mills brought the idea to Farrell, they were in close quarters, and would talk into the night. Farrell, a chemistry professor, was an expert on quantum theory, and provided a sounding board.[32]

Mills's model not only calculated the ground and excited states of hydrogen (and other one-electron atoms), but correctly calculated the ground state of helium (and other two-electron atoms); something that, after a century of work, quantum theory could still not do accurately.

Quantum theory was always foggy on how two electrons interacted, but in Mills's theory it became a simple electrodynamic problem. He used a three-term force-balance equation that accounted for the attraction

---

[31] According to Mills, the reason for the instability of the excited states was a radial dipole moment within the atom.

[32] John Farrell felt he had only inadvertently contributed to Mills's line of thought. For their friendship and discussions, as well as his help with figures and editing, Mills listed Farrell as a coauthor on his first book.

FORCE BALANCE EQUATIONS:

HYDROGEN (AND OTHER 1-ELECTRON ATOMS)

$$\frac{m_e v^2}{r} = \frac{Ze^2}{4\pi\varepsilon_0 r^2} - \frac{\hbar^2}{m_e r^3}$$

HELIUM (AND OTHER 2-ELECTRON ATOMS)

$$\frac{m_e v^2}{r} = \frac{(Z-1)e^2}{4\pi\varepsilon_0 r^2} + \frac{\hbar^2}{Z m_e r^3}\sqrt{s(s+1)}$$

LITHIUM (AND OTHER 3-ELECTRON ATOMS)

$$\frac{m_e v_3^2}{r_3} = \frac{(Z-2)e^2}{4\pi\varepsilon_0 r_3^2} - \frac{\hbar^2}{4 m_e r_3^2 r_1}\sqrt{s(s+1)} - \frac{(Z-3)r_1\hbar^2}{(Z-2)r_3^4 m_e}10\sqrt{s(s+1)}$$

between the electrons and the nucleus, the inertia of the spinning electron, and the diamagnetic force produced by the attraction of the two electrons' spins. This caused them to combine into a single shell (Mills 2015, Ch. 7).

Mills had found a winning strategy. In time, it would be expanded, with atoms and molecules falling to his equations effortlessly, replacing all of the overburdened scaffolding of quantum theory.

A new prediction, in science, is the most interesting and salient result of any theory. To derive known phenomena in a different way might have advantages over existing theory, but unless it produces something new, we are hard tasked to find it important.

In the first months of 1989, Mills was working with his new model of the hydrogen atom. He now understood how it absorbed photons to jump to excited states orbits, and for the first time in history, he understood why the ground state of hydrogen was stable: why it would not radiate; but also why the excited state orbits were unstable: how a radial dipole produced by the absorbed photon caused the states to radiate energy quickly and fall back to the ground state.

But was this all the hydrogen atom was capable of?

While studying his luminides, Mills had become sensitive to the sophisticated ways in which molecular reactions allowed energy to be transmitted without the release of light. Energy can produce vibrations (phonons) or be transmitted down the arm of a molecule and be released as bond breakage. Radiation—absorbing and emitting light—is only *one* way to transfer energy.

On at the atomic scale, over very small distances, some interactions allow the direct coupling between the multipole fields of atoms. Florescent lights appear to work as a result of atoms exchanging bits of energy through resonant transfer; manganese atoms becomes luminescent when the Sb_3+ ion transfers energy to the Mn_2+ ion (Lumb 1978).

Resonant energy transfer is also a well-known phenomenon on a macroscale. At MIT, a team of researchers put this physics to new use, to develop a new way of charging electronic devices over distances of up to two meters. They started a company, WiTricity Corp., to commercialize the technology (Joannopoulos 2010).

To demonstrate this effect, you need a device that produces a field with

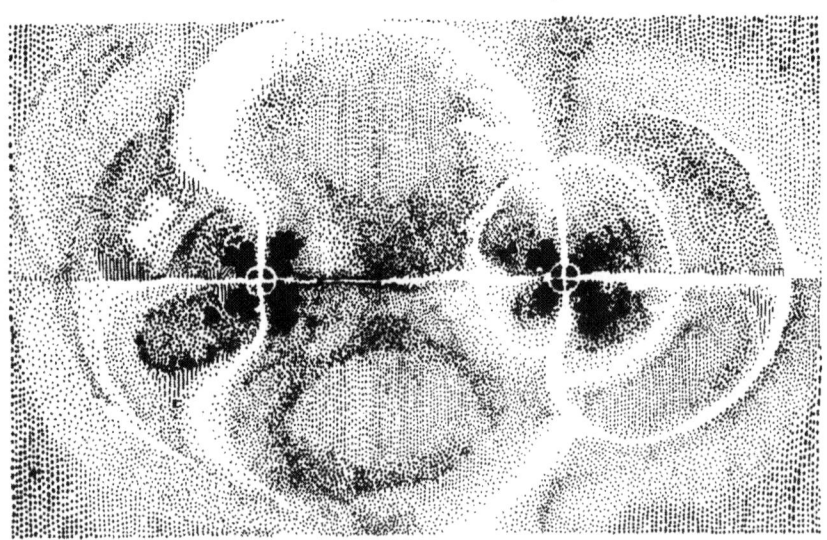

RESONANT TRANSFER

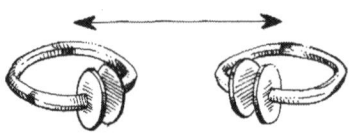

NON-RADIATIVE ENERGY TRANSFER BETWEEN TWO RESONANT STRUCTURES MEDIATED BY THE COUPLING OF THEIR "EVANESCENT TAILS." AFTER THAT IN (JOANNOPOULOS 2010).

periodic oscillation. The electromagnetic field lines (the evanescent tails) diffuse out; if you have a device that responds to this frequency nearby, the two may couple. The field lines will spontaneously change so that they bridge from the first device to the second; energy can flow across the gap, with virtually no loss of energy to surrounding space. This effect is called *resonant inductive coupling* and relies on the interaction of the higher order variations (multipoles) of the electric fields.

Mills wondered if the hydrogen atom could undergo this kind of coupling. If the hydrogen atom collided with a suitable atom—an atom that could resonate with and absorb energy from hydrogen—then it might be possible for the electron in hydrogen to fall *below* the ground state.

He quickly began working out the idea, and calculated that if he was right, there may exist a series of stable orbits, each an integer fraction (1/2, 1/3, 1/4, 1/5 .... etc.) the size of the ground state shell radius (Mills 2015, Ch. 5).

Hydrino State	Energy Hole (eV)	Binding Energy (eV)
H(1/2)	27.2	54.4
H(1/3)	54.4	122.4
H(1/4)	81.6	217.7
H(1/5)	108.8	340.1
H(1/6)	136.1	489.6
H(1/7)	163.3	666.4
H(1/8)	190.3	870.4
H(1/9)	217.7	1101.6
H(1/10)	244.9	1360.5

Hydrino states allowed by the resonant coupling of a hydrogen atom to a suitable catalyst capable of providing an energy hole of m * 27.2 eV. The hydrino atom transfers energy to the catalyst, then decays with the release of light to form a hydrino (Mills 2015, Ch. 5).

Each step down to a lower fractional orbit should release energy in integer-multiples of 27.2 electron volts (eV). Falling to an H(1/2) orbit releases 27.2 eV, but falling to an H(1/4) orbit releases a whopping 81.6 eV per atom: more than what most single-bond-breaking chemical reactions release by a factor of a hundred! Mills found that the electron could potentially drop all the way to the H(1/137) orbit before the currents on the electron shell would need to be moving faster than light to shrink further.[33]

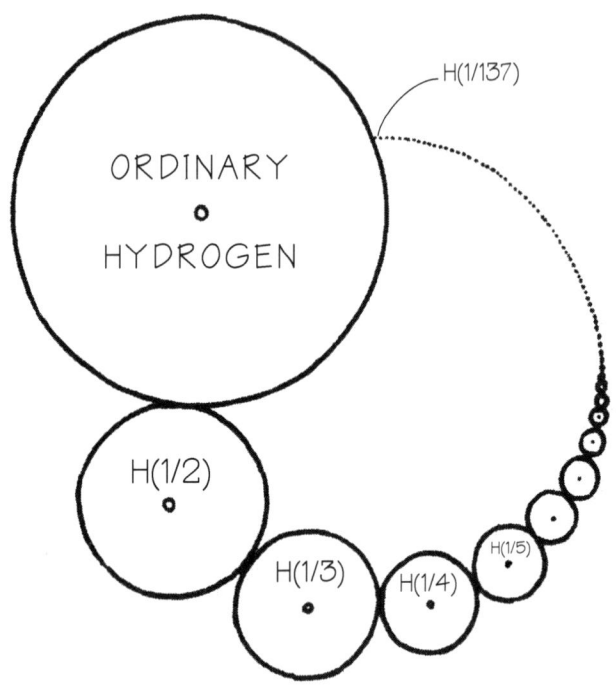

HYDRINO STATES OF THE HYDROGEN ATOM

He called his new shrunken hydrogen atom the *hydrino*.

If they existed, and if he could manufacture them, he had just made the quantum leap from a fundamental breakthrough in physics to a powerful new energy source for mankind.

---

[33] Incidentally, the electron reaches the speed of light when its radius was exactly H(1/137.035), a number of special significance: it is the coupling constant, also known as the fine structure constant or (α), which we will discuss in Chapter 12.

Catalyst	m	Catalyst	m
$He^+ \to He^{2+}$	2	$Rb \to Rb^{7+}$	14
$Li \to Li^{2+}$	3	$Rb \to Rb^{8+}$	19
$Be \to Be^{2+}$	1	$Sr \to Sr^{5+}$	7
$Na^+ \to Na^{4+}$	8	$Sr^+ \to Sr^{3+}$	7
$Ar^+ \to Ar^{2+}$	1	$Nb \to Nb^{5+}$	5
$K \to K^{3+}$	3	$Mo \to Mo^{6+}$	8
$2K^+ \to K + K^{2+}$	1	$Mo \to Mo^{8+}$	18
$Ca \to Ca^{4+}$	5	$Mo^{2+} \to Mo^{3+}$	1
$Ti \to Ti^{5+}$	7	$Mo^{4+} \to Mo^{5+}$	2
$V \to V^{5+}$	6	$Pd \to Pd^{2+}$	1
$Cr \to Cr^{3+}$	2	$In \to In^{3+}$	2
$Mn \to Mn^{4+}$	4	$Sn \to Sn^{5+}$	6
$Fe \to Fe^{3+}$	2	$Te \to Te^{2+}$	1
$Fe \to Fe^{4+}$	4	$Te \to Te^{3+}$	2
$Fe^{3+} \to Fe^{4+}$	2	$2Ba^{2+} \to Ba^+ + Ba^{3+}$	1
$Co \to Co^{4+}$	4	$Cs \to Cs^{2+}$	1
$Co \to Co^{5+}$	7	$Ce \to Ce^{5+}$	5
$Ni \to Ni^{5+}$	7	$Ce \to Ce^{6+}$	8
$Ni \to Ni^{6+}$	11	$Pr \to Pr^{5+}$	5
$Cu \to Cu^{2+}$	1	$Sm \to Sm^{4+}$	3
$Zn \to Zn^{2+}$	1	$Gd \to Gd^{4+}$	3
$Zn \to Zn^{8+}$	23	$Dy \to Dy^{4+}$	3
$As \to As^{6+}$	11	$Pb \to Pb^{3+}$	2
$Se \to Se^{7+}$	15	$Pt \to Pt^{2+}$	1
$Kr \to Kr^{6+}$	10		
$Kr \to Kr^{7+}$	14		

Atomic catalysts capable of undergoing resonant absorption of approximately m * 27.2 eV of energy from a hydrogen atom to produce an H(1/(p+m)) hydrino. For instance, an H(1/1) hydrogen atom (where p = 1) may undergo a transition to an H(1/4) hydrino by transferring 3 * 27.2 eV to a potassium atom, which undergoes ionization to produce K^{3+}. The catalyst may later recover its electrons, and is unchanged in the overall reaction. Hydrinos may then undergo further catalysis, or themselves act as catalysts. (Mills 2000)

New energy is the holy grail of invention, and Mills lost focus on his other activities to dedicate himself full-time to the hydrino research.

He started by making a list of atomic catalysts that could absorb the required amount of energy from the hydrogen atom, 27.2 eV. The catalyst, as the receiver, must be able to expel the energy it absorbs, perhaps by breaking off (ionizing) electrons or breaking molecular bonds; the ionized electrons would carry off the energy kinetically. So any ionization that occurred at (or close to) integer multiples of 27.2 could potentially serve as the catalyst.

The list was long: many of the atoms in the periodic table could be catalysts. Lithium, twice ionized, could catalyze a transition to an H(1/4) hydrino; beryllium, twice ionized, could catalyze a transition to an H(1/2); potassium, thrice ionized, could catalyze a transition to an H(1/4). Ions could also serve: a previously ionized helium ion (He+), if it ionizes again, could catalyze a transition to an H(1/3) hydrino.

Even molecules may serve as catalysts. If gas-phase sodium hydride (NaH) breaks apart, and ionizes one of the sodium atom's electrons, the reaction could allow a transition to an H(1/3) hydrino. And a water molecule, if it breaks up and ionizes the oxygen, can allow a transition to an H(1/4) hydrino (a reaction which will become important later on).

After inducing the hydrino transition, the catalyst is then free to recapture its electrons or reform its bonds later on, so overall it remains unchanged. The only permanent change (a loss of energy) is within the hydrogen atom itself.

Once the catalyst absorbs the necessary energy, the electron orbit in hydrogen is made unstable, and it can then shrink, emitting a photon in the process, to form a hydrino. The hydrogen is permanently altered, forming an atom hitherto unexplored by science.

Mills was still working out of Farrell's lab. He had arrived at a list of catalysts, but not yet begun experiments, when news broke out from the University of Utah that two electrochemists were unveiling a new major energy source of their own.

CHAPTER 5

THE COLD SHOULDER

In which we learn that cold fusion with light water is even more unbelievable than cold fusion with heavy water; and Mills gains some early collaborators in a new frontier of electrochemistry.

On March 23, 1989, the University of Utah shook the world by announcing to the press that two of its researchers—Martin Fleischman and Stanley Pons—had achieved a "sustained nuclear fusion reaction" at room temperature, and that it had been operating for 100 days.

Fusion, the process that fuels the Sun, occurs when two atomic nuclei collide and combine to form a new, heavier nucleus, releasing a large burst of energy in the process. For instance, two hydrogen nuclei may come together to form a helium nucleus. To fuse, the two positively charged nuclei must overcome their repulsion, so fusion occurs at very high temperature and pressure, such as the conditions that exist inside the Sun.

For decades we have been trying to build "hot" fusion reactors, in which we magnetically confine a hydrogen plasma at millions of degrees Celsius in order to compel it to fuse. Billions of dollars have been spent on the attempt.

Fusion is also the phenomenon that fuels the hydrogen bomb: by wrapping a layer of hydrogen around a nuclear fission bomb, the explosion within will cause the hydrogen to fuse, releasing even more destructive potential.

The prospect of "cold" fusion—fusion at room temperature—had been studied for several years prior to the Utah announcement. Steven Jones at Brigham Young University coined the term while investigating something called "muonic hydrogen catalyzed fusion." A muon is a kind of electron, except that it is about 207 times heavier. When it meets a proton, it can form a muonic hydrogen atom, but with a much tighter radius. When two muonic hydrogen atoms combine to form a muonic hydrogen molecule, the electron orbit brings the two protons very close together: so close, in fact, that they occasionally fuse.

Muons are unstable, decaying in a few microseconds, and manufacturing these particles is energy-intensive. So the question is: will a muon catalyze enough fusion events to justify the energy used to manufacture it? Jones found, after years of research, that the answer was clearly no. This kind of cold fusion was a dead end.

Jones then turned his attention to other possibilities. He knew that some metals could absorb hydrogen and facilitate a variety of reactions.

What if fusion could be made to occur on the surface of one of these metals, such as palladium?

Jones scribbled his idea in a notebook years before he got around to testing the idea. When he was finally thinking about giving it a try, by coincidence he was asked to review a proposal by two electrochemists at the University of Utah, who were studying the same concept (Taubes 1993).

Fleischmann and Pons's experiment was simple, and based on a simple electrolytic cell. This was essentially a vessel of water containing two metal electrodes that were attached to a battery; when the battery charged the electrodes, it caused water molecules to split into positively- and negatively-charged ions, breaking water into its components: hydrogen and oxygen. They filled a Dewar with "heavy" water, in which deuterium, a hydrogen isotope with an extra neutron, was used instead of traditional hydrogen.

This made fusion much easier, as the fusion products of helium-3 and tritium both require extra neutrons. The electrode was made of palladium. Deuterated lithium hydroxide was added to the cell as an electrolyte. They claimed to have already produced excess heat that could not be accounted for, and were looking for funding to continue research (Pons 1990).

Jones must have decided that now was the time. He began studying the effect, and accumulated some modest evidence. He saw little heat from his small electrochemical cells, and he detected a very small number of excess neutrons, possibly a sign that a nuclear process was taking place. His little neutron peak was not evidence of a strong reaction of the kind that could be harnessed as a game-changing energy source, but it was something.

Urged to publish and present his findings in order to secure ongoing funding, he set a date to give a talk.

Because Jones had seen Fleischmann and Pons's proposal, there was a clear conflict of interest, and he reached out to them to discuss his results, and even opened the door to collaborate. At least, he wanted to give them the opportunity to publish simultaneously in order to share credit for the discovery.

But Fleischmann and Pons had a very different picture of the situation. They believed that they had found a way to harness fusion for energy-generating potential in a simple, bench-top device. They were only producing modest amounts of excess heat, but they believed that their experiment had make serious heat, resulting in a melt-down event.

Apparently, their experiment, while unattended one night in the lab, produced so much heat as to melt the palladium bar. What likely happened that night was that the palladium had absorbed significant amounts of hydrogen; when the electrolyte began to evaporate, it left the bar exposed to air, and the hydrogen started to off-gas from the bar, recombining with oxygen in the air.

Palladium is very good at facilitating combustion at its surface, and the combustion of hydrogen and oxygen is a powerful reaction (and due to its light weight, one of our best rocket propellants). It could have quickly heated the bar, conceivably melting down or otherwise destroying the bar. Whatever happened, it was a one-time event that occurred without any supervision, and reports of it were likely exaggerated.

They also believed that Jones had stolen their idea, and that if they were to let Jones give a talk on the subject, it would amount to a "public disclosure" that would preclude them from patenting the discovery.

Fleischmann and Pons tried to convince Jones to wait while they completed their research program. They hadn't run important controls. They hadn't detected any neutrons, although they believed they had observed gamma rays from their cells: another important byproduct from the formation of helium. They kept the research secret and hadn't had any other professionals, such as physicists from their own University, scrutinize their findings. They believed they had something, but they were by no means ready to go public.

But at stake was a trillion-dollar energy market. After discussing the situation with patent lawyers and the University, they went public.

Fleischmann and Pons were respected electrochemists, among the best in the world, and had a long history of publishing important research. Their announcement was made officially through the University of Utah, and mentioned that another researcher at BYU had independently confirmed their results: not exactly true, but it had added effect.

The scientific community was optimistic; they had just been wowed by a recent discovery of high temperature superconductors, materials so easy to make that high schoolers were doing so in chemistry class only months later. It stoked the fire of interest and optimism of science. Further, the world was in the midst of an energy crisis. When the press release issued to the world on March 23, 1989, and said that "the world may someday rely on fusion for a clean, virtually inexhaustible source of energy," it struck a chord.

The announcement was a sensation. Dozens of scientists around the country dropped what they were doing to replicate the experiments. The *Washington Post* was laudatory, though some newspapers were more conservative in their treatment. Fleischmann and Pons were instant celebrities.

They had not yet published their results, and in the weeks immediately after the announcement, hesitated to release all of the details of their experiments, although they sometimes answered specific questions. As a result, online discussion forums emerged with scientists sharing bits of information while trying to replicate the findings.

When a preprint of the forthcoming paper spread virally via fax machine, scientists were underwhelmed. Calorimetry, the measure of heat, is a difficult science that requires extremely careful calibration using controlled experiments. These had not yet been done. The gamma-ray peak offered was, by anyone familiar with gamma-ray spectroscopy, an obvious artifact, not a true peak.

They presented no evidence of neutrons being emitted by the cell. In fact, if a nuclear reaction was producing the heat claimed, whomever was operating the cell ought to be dead. If a melt-down event had occurred in the lab, the entire laboratory should have become contaminated with radioactive neutrons. At Los Alamos National Lab and elsewhere, sophisticated neutron detectors were being set up around Fleishmann-Pons cells—surrounded by adequate shielding to protect against radioactive exposure—but they weren't getting any neutrons.

Almost immediately, the story began to melt down under a heap of accusations of scientific misconduct.

By April 30, only a month later, the *New York Times* announced that cold fusion was dead. Later that year, the research advisory board of the US Department of Energy issued a report summarizing much of the work that had been done in recent months: they recommended against any special federal program to fund cold fusion research. It would have to fight its way through traditional grant programs, as it had been doing for years.

Nevertheless, over the next several years, hundreds of journal articles would be published on cold fusion. Research groups sprouted up all over the world. Many groups found nothing, but some found excess heat in careful experiments, heat beyond what could be explained; some researchers found evidence of helium and tritium produced in the cells, but few claimed any evidence of neutrons. When neutrons were occasionally detected, they weren't correlated with measurements of excess heat, and may have been artifacts of experiment. Fleischmann and Pons suggested that the nuclear reactions taking place were without traditional nuclear byproducts.

Those who continued with cold fusion research, pursuing whispers of heat and nuclear byproducts and the dream of limitless free energy, were quickly ostracized from the mainstream scientific community. What momentarily received high praise, was thereafter suppressed. It became an isolated field on the fringe. This made matters worse, as traditional standards of practice and rigor were difficult to maintain under these conditions. The only place to publish was in journals already friendly to cold fusion research, such as the *Journal of Hydrogen Energy, and Fusion Technology*. Few outside this group were paying attention any longer.

When Mills and Farrell heard the news from Utah, they were skeptical, but Mills felt that his own theoretical discovery—made only months prior—could potentially account for the reports of excess heat. Perhaps hydrinos were forming in Fleischmann and Pons's cells, producing heat but no nuclear byproducts.

Mills founded a company, HydroCatalysis Power Corporation, and obtained $155,000 in financing from a small group of investors. Among them were Aaron Martin, Chairman of the Board of Trustees at Franklin and Marshall, who had also subsidized the first print edition of Mills's book, and John Graham, the family accountant for the farm (Stolper 2006).

Mills spent most of the next year on theoretical work before embarking on experiments. He recruited a friend, Steven Kneizys, who had experience with electrochemistry. At first they worked out of their kitchens, with cells made from test tubes. Over the next year and a half they would run over a thousand cells, optimizing conditions for excess heat and (as we will discuss later) looking for tritium, while adjusting conditions and parameters. They ran cells around the clock, manning them all the time, trying to make progress as rapidly as possible. They scaled up cells from 1 to 10 W, then 120 W, ultimately experimenting with a 1 kW capacity cell.

Mills's first patent was submitted in April of 1989 (Mills 1989).

Mills modeled his cells on Fleischmann-Pons-style electrochemical cells, but his was different in significant ways. He used ordinary ("light") water, not heavy water. He used a thin coil of nickel foil as the cathode, not palladium. The anode was a thin coil of platinum wire.

By testing a wide array of different electrolytes containing potential catalysts, he found that the cell reliably produced significant excess heat, only with one of these catalysts. He was particularly successful when he used potassium carbonate in the electrolyte. When dissolved, it released potassium ions (K^+), a catalyst.

If the potassium were to meet a hydrogen atom, it could—according to Mills's theory—absorb energy from the hydrogen atom and release it by giving off three electrons, to allow the hydrogen to transition to an $H(1/4)$ hydrino atom.

Mills and Kneizys calibrated the cell by warming it with an internal heater, as well as changing ambient conditions to see the impact on cell temperature. Then Mills ran identical control experiments substituting a different electrolyte, such as sodium carbonate in place of potassium carbonate.

These controls demonstrated that significant heat was produced only in the potassium runs.

Since the cell was very small, the heat was only on the order of a few watts, but it was still significant and measurable outside the range of error; in fact, thousands of percent above what could be explained by any conventional chemical reaction using the ingredients in the cell. It was also more heat than was being reported from "cold fusion" cells.

On February 1st, 1991, Mills and Kneizys submitted an article describing their experiments, together with a summary of Mills's theory, to the journal *Fusion Technology* (Mills 1991).

Although Mills did not believe he was doing cold fusion, it was natural to assume that his new explanation of the results, together with his improved experiments, would appeal to cold fusion researchers, and push the field in a new direction. So he directed his article to this fact: claiming in the title and in the abstract that his work explained the cold fusion phenomenon, *without* fusion.

On April 25th, Mills held a press conference on the steps of the county courthouse in Lancaster, Pennsylvania. A few local reporters attended. He announced that he had just completed the first round of experiments confirming his predictions, and he would be publishing his experiments

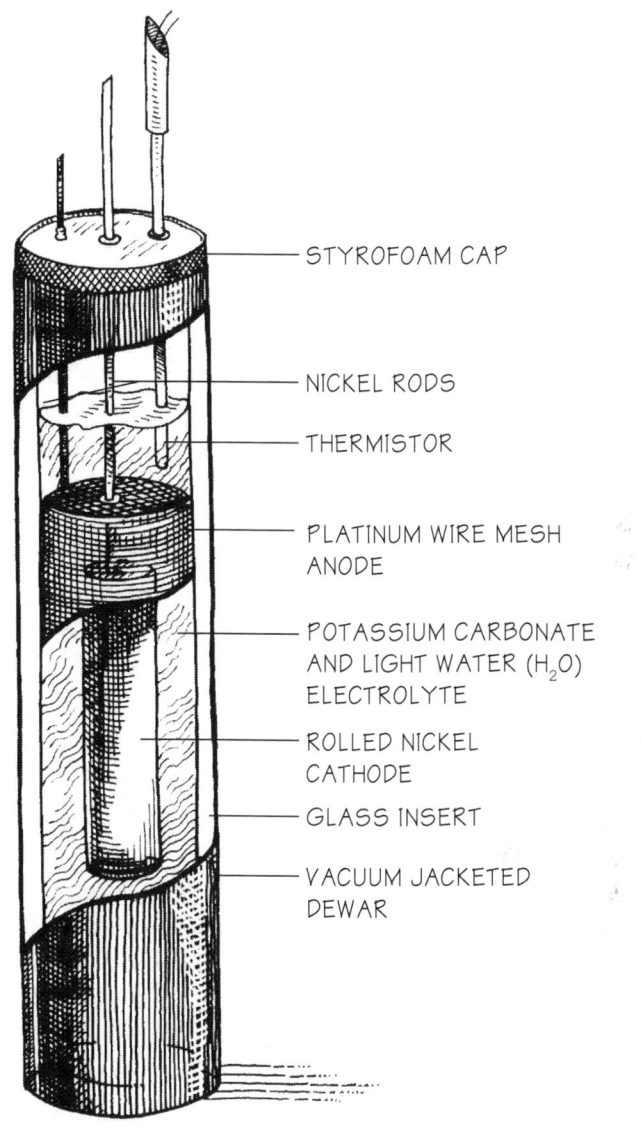

ELECTROLYTIC CELL

HYDROGEN PRODUCED FROM THE ELECTROLYSIS OF NORMAL WATER IS CATALYZED BY POTASSIUM TO FORM HYDRINO ATOMS, RELEASING HEAT THAT WARMS THE CELL. SODIUM CARBONATE SERVED AS THE CONTROL. SIMILAR IN DESIGN TO "COLD-FUSION" CELLS - BUT NO FUSION! AFTER (MILLS 1994).

and data later that month. Mills promised the world a new age of energy abundance that used the hydrogen derived from ordinary water as fuel.

In his article and press conference, Mills cashed in on the possible tie to cold fusion. He even offered an explanation for the neutron emissions reported in some experiments: that a form of hot fusion could be taking place via a mechanism similar to muonic-hydrogen catalyzed fusion but with hydrinos. In hydrino-catalyzed fusion (what Mills called "Coulombic Annihilation Fusion") a hydrino molecule reduces the space between the two nuclei and promotes fusion events.

It was not the dominant energy releasing process, but it could result in some nuclear byproducts. Mills's first patent applications even focused on this possibility.

Mills would later calculate that it was much less feasible than muonic-catalyzed fusion as a power source. One $H(1/15)$ hydrino molecule would have a similar size to a muonic hydrogen molecule, but the hydrino could only catalyze a *single* fusion event, whereas the muon could catalyze *hundreds* of events before decaying. Mills also quickly learned not to mention the phenomena if he wanted to reinforce that he wasn't proposing to do fusion.

Lithium, which was used in the Fleischmann and Pons cell, was a catalyst. As was a three-body interaction between hydrogen, palladium, and lithium. These catalysis pathways could explain why cold fusion cells were producing some heat, even when neutrons were not observed. Mills's catalysts, however, allowed him to do better.

This connection to cold fusion was important. On the same day as Mills's conference, there was a news conference held at MIT featuring Frederick Mayer, a well-known hot fusion physicist. Mayer also had a theory of smaller hydrogen atoms, which he called "hydrons," and unlike Mills, Mayer believed that they were unstable but facilitated fusion.[34]

The next day, Mills's work and Mayer's work were both covered in a *New York Times* article, "Two Teams Put New Life in 'Cold Fusion' Theory;" a story that was also picked up by the *Washington Post* (Broad 1991; Suplee 1991).

Mills knew nothing of Mayer's work, but it was an incredible coincidence. He was flooded with calls.

Mills's media attention was both a blessing and a curse. The next year, Mills was able to raise another $720,000 in venture capital and upgrade

---

[34] Mayer's reaction to Mills's work can be found in Mayer 1991.

from a one room office and laboratory to a larger space in Lancaster. He hired his first full-time employee: Bill Good, a recent graduate of Franklin and Marshall. Good had been working with Mills while an undergraduate, living out of his girlfriend's dorm room and using his own room as a lab to run electrochemical cells. Once, his floor advisor noticed the operation when his door was open, and said: "I am going to pretend I didn't see that." Good would later go on to earn an MBA and become BLP's Vice President.

As he intended, Mills's first article in *Fusion Technology* created a buzz among the cold fusion community. Some of them began replicating his experiments successfully. Among these was Robert Bush, from California State Polytechnic University (Bush 1992, 1994). Another was Vesco Noninski, an electrochemist who was asked by Eugene Mallove (a cold fusion advocate and editor of *Infinite Energy* magazine) to debunk Mills's work, because his success with light water was complicating the cold fusion landscape. Noninski had planned to stay in Lancaster a day, but ended up staying a month, and published a paper on his work (Noninski 1992).

Another was Mahadeva Srinivasan at the Bhabha Atomic Research Center in Bombay, India. Srinivasan had successful results but later retracted them after an unsuccessful later collaboration with Michael McKubra at SRI in Palo Alto, California (Srinivasan 1997).

Reiko Notoya was a research associate at the Catalysis Research Center of Hokkaido University, and held a PhD in electrochemistry. Notoya made an important breakthrough in reducing the amount of nickel required by Mills's cell, using a special electrode made of sintered nickel particles, which gave it a much larger surface area. Notoya presented her results at the Third International Conference on Cold Fusion in October of 1992. She also appeared at MIT but she was unable to get the cell to work during her presentation (Notoya 1993; Stolper 2006, p. 71).

But there was a hitch. Notoya presented her work on Mills's cells not as a demonstration of a *new* phenomenon—hydrino catalysis—that explained the inconsistent cold fusion results, but as *cold fusion*. This was unexpected. After all, Mills's experiments were only successful with certain chemical catalysts, and they used light water, not heavy water, making the idea of fusion a joke: there wouldn't be enough neutrons to make a helium nucleus.

Notoya was not alone. Other fusion researchers also treated Mills's work as cold fusion, not as a new chemical process. In an article about the upcoming International Conference on Cold Fusion to be held in Nagoya in 1992, *Businessweek* ran an article on Mills and those replicating his work. It quoted Robert Bush as heralding Mills's work as "earth shaking... one of the events of the millennium," but noted the disagreements over what was actually going on. Bush's theory was that hydrogen was being fused with potassium to form calcium-40, and believed he had found calcium rising in concentration in Mills-type cells (Port 1992; Fusion Facts 1992).

After the conference, Andrew Pollak, the Tokyo correspondent of the *Times*, wrote about the conference. He didn't mention Mills directly, but said that scientists found light water cold fusion even harder to accept than heavy water cold fusion.

Mills continued to receive occasional favorable press coverage, with articles in the *Wall Street Journal*, *Newsweek*, and five minutes of international TV coverage in a program on cold fusion from the BBC and CBC (Bishop 1992; Focus 1993).

He would reiterate to the press that he wasn't doing cold fusion, but the associations ran deep: his initial announcement in the context of cold fusion; the interest and replications by cold fusion researchers and who continued to refer to his work as such; his own suggested mechanism for hydrino-catalyzed fusion, his publications in *Fusion Technology*, his early patents which heavily cited cold fusion work, and his media attention in articles about cold fusion (Mills 1993, 1995).

Then there was the *Fusion Facts* "Fusion Scientist of the Year" awarded to Mills in 1991; an honor he shared with two others: Robert Bush and Robert Eagleton (Fusion Facts 1992).

Mills's goal was to redirect the cold fusion scientists, but he was being dragged into it.

In 1993, Bill Good was telling a reporter that they were attending the next International Conference on Cold Fusion in Hawaii, when the reporter asked "...but I thought you weren't doing cold fusion?" Something clicked in that moment in his mind. He realized any interface with the cold fusion community would continue to reinforce the connection and confuse the press. They canceled their trip and adopted a new policy of avoiding the whole cold fusion scene.

Twenty years later, Mills has been unable to live down this past. His ties to cold fusion were an initial blessing that became a permanent curse.

Mills found am early collaborator in Thermacore, a spin-off from RCA that produced specialty heat transfer equipment and piping. The majority of its business was contract research, especially for the US Department of Defense. Its founder, G. Yale Eastman, had followed the dramatic arc of cold fusion for several years. When he heard about Mills, a Lancaster local, he decided to get involved.[35]

Eastman was not put off by Mills's theory, but rather intrigued by his model of the orbitsphere as a resonator cavity, since he had worked with resonant cavities as an electrical engineer at RCA. Although not convinced about the theory, he saw that Mills was getting more reliable heat. He arranged for Mills to meet Thermacore's manager of development research, Robert Shaubach, at an ACS regional meeting in 1992. They got along well, and worked out an agreement: Mills would work on basic research, while Thermacore worked on engineering and commercial development.

They got to work. Initially, Shaubach had a difficult time making convincing measurements with the small, low-power cells that Mills had designed the previous year. He asked Mills to design a much bigger test cell. Mills did, and when Thermacore tested the cell, it was able to generate 50 W of "anomalous heat" (Thermacore 1993). Shaubach was excited to be working on a potentially important discovery, but also worried that they had overlooked something. "When we first got the excess energy," Shaubach later told BBC, "we weren't sure where that energy was coming from. So one of the first things we did was run experiments to determine if there was some degradation in the electrodes, in the electrolyte, or if there was a nuclear source, and all of those tests showed that none of those possibilities were likely." (BBC 1994).

As the months passed, the group at Thermacore became more confident in the accuracy of their measurements. They were careful, and larger cells brought more certainty. By March of 1992, Thermacore was running a large test cell that produced 68 W of power from an input of 18 W. That is a *gain* (output power over input power) of 3.7[36]. The cell could run continuously for months on end (Mills 1994).

---

[35] Special thanks to Tom Stolper for this background (Stolper 2006).

[36] The gains reported in this book will ignore the input power required to maintain the conditions of the experiment, such as the ambient temperature of the cell. This is the key difference between a benchtop experiment and a field prototype.

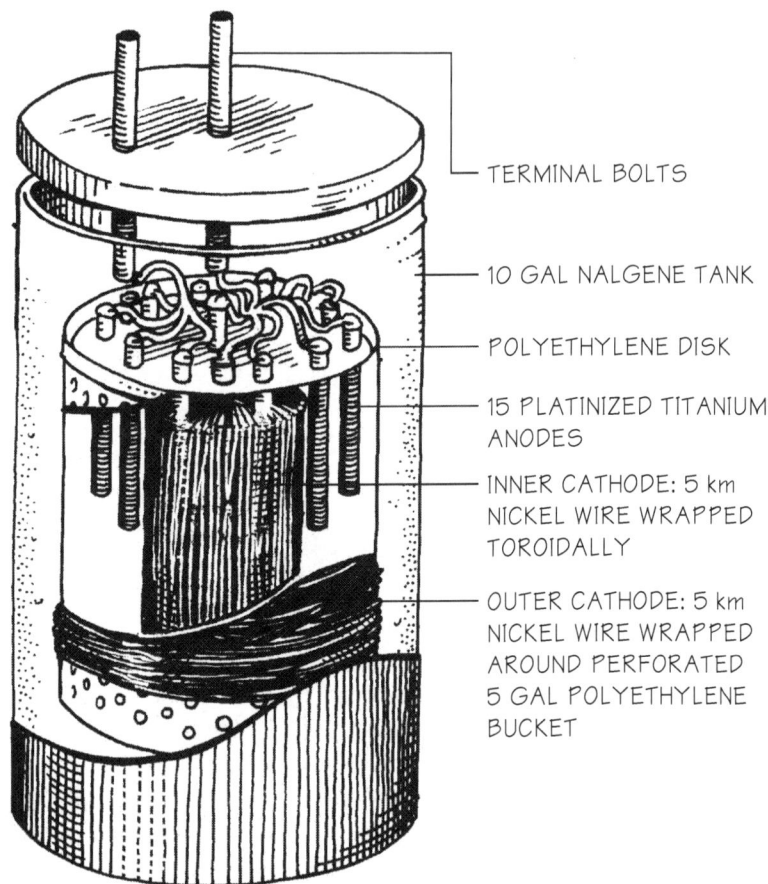

THERMACORE CELL

SCALED-UP ELECTROLYTIC CELL DEVELOPED BY HPC IN COLLABORATION WITH THERMACORE. USED A LIGHT WATER AND POTASSIUM CARBONATE ELECTROLYTE. REPORTED TO PRODUCE 50 W OF EXCESS HEAT, INDEFINITELY - BUT REQUIRED 10 km OF NICKEL WIRE! AFTER (MILLS 1993).

By August, Shaubach was confident enough to give a talk at the annual meeting of the Intersociety Energy Conversion Engineering Conference (IECEC), but he did not present a formal paper. Since they were not eager to see a hoard of competitors rush into the field, they limited their public disclosure to basic information; they answered questions but did not give out all the details. Such was the difficulty of science in the pursuit of coveted technology.

They also felt uncomfortable giving out names of collaborators. The subject had become so controversial that those working at government laboratories felt their funding might be cut if it were known they were working on anything remotely connected to cold fusion. One of these researchers anonymously appeared for the BBC Horizon special on cold fusion. "I have to be careful about the jobs of my colleagues, for instance, and our whole laboratory can suffer from having one individual working who's too far out of the mainstream" (BBC 1994).

Thermacore hoped to develop a small industrial unit to produce low-grade heat. That isn't glamorous, but a low-grade heater would at least demonstrate commercial feasibility, and it could be competitive in a billion-dollar market. Thermacore's best small test cells had demonstrated a gain of 10; and they hoped to produce a scaled-up space heater that could produce 2.5 kW at a gain of 5.

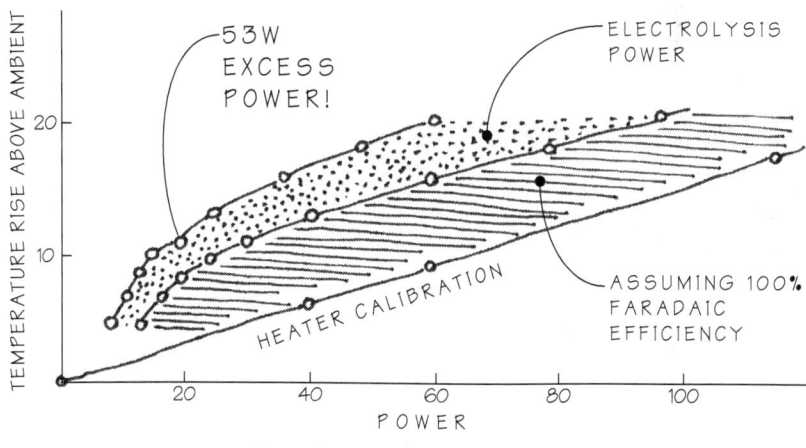

THERMACORE CELL

TEMPERATURE RISE OF THE ELECTROLYTIC CELL DESIGNED BY HPC AND THERMACORE OVER A SERIES OF 9 EXPERIMENTS WITH INCREASING INPUT POWER. AFTER (MILLS, 1993).

The kicker, however, was that the electrolytic cell that produced 50 W of excess heat used 10 kilometers (40 pounds) of nickel wire. The reaction occurred on the nickel surface at a power density of only 2 mW/cm². Even though a single gram of nickel had the surface area of a tennis court, they were unable to design a cell that used nickel more efficiently.

To make the reactor commercially feasible, Thermacore needed 10-100 times more heat output from the electrolytic heater. The new gas-phase cells being developed by Mills held more promise. At the end of 1995, as Mills was moving his laboratory to New Jersey, they suspended efforts on friendly terms, hoping that Mills would eventually return with a better cell.

Thermacore's validation of Mills's early work with electrolytic cells did little to boost Mills's reputation. Rather, the relationship was a constant strain on Thermacore's reputation. This would be a pattern with Mills for another twenty years. And scientists without the benefit of BLP's guidance were seldom able to get far.

Not all researchers who took an interest in Mills's work were successful in replicating Mills's results. Michael McKubra at SRI in Palo Alto, California, was unable to do so. Charles Passell, a manager of the cold fusion program at the Electric Power Research Institute, did a small study and nothing came of it. Neither published on the topic.

Others believed that the excess energy must be due to other reactions within the cell. Since an electrolytic cell used energy to split water, there was always the possibility that the recombining of hydrogen and oxygen could generate a burst of energy. A study by Janis Niedra, funded by NASA, used the Mills-Thermacore cell and found that the excess heat could be explained if one assumed 100% recombination (Niedra 1996). This was much less energy than reported by Mills and Thermacore, and even so, researchers had found that only 34% recombination was typical in this kind of cell.[37] At BYU, another project came to similar conclusions (Jones 1999).

Mills had started with electrochemical cells because they were a good source of hydrogen, and because he had caught the cold fusion wave: it was what everyone else was doing. But electrolytic cells were finicky and difficult to replicate. Only by the mid-nineties did the wildcatting days of on-the-fly electrolysis evolve into a fine art. Control after control could be run, calibration after calibration, until the results were reliable.

Nuanced changes in procedure could result in success or failure. When Chalk River Laboratories was contracted to conduct experiments, they calibrated the cells with internal resistance heaters and changes in ambient temperatures and modeled the heat loss mathematically.

---

[37] See Zvi Shkedi's work at the Bose Corporation (Shkedi 1995a, 1995b).

At first, they had difficulty getting excess power, but in consultation with Mills they were able to pinpoint subtle differences that were initially overlooked.

Laboratory	Work Performed	Reported Gain
Idaho National Engineering Lab	Electrolysis, XPS	8.5
SDIO-Wright Patterson US Air Force Base	Diffusion Cell	?
Chalk River National Lab (Canada)	Electrolysis	1.3
NASA – Lewis	Electrolysis	1.7
Brookhaven National Laboratory	Electrolysis	?
Lehigh University	XPS	N/A
MIT Lincoln Laboratory	Electrolysis	4.0
Pennsylvania State University	Gas Cell	20.0
Ursinus College	Electrolysis	?
Moscow Power Engineering Institute	Electrolysis	2.5
LEPGER[1]	Electrolysis	?
Thermacore, Inc.	Electrolysis	21.0
Air Products & Chemicals	Mass Spectroscopy	N/A
Westinghouse Electric Corp.	Electrolysis	1.5
Schrader Analytical & Consulting Lab	TOF-SIMS	N/A

Collaborators of BLP prior to 1997, with summary of maximum reported gain from calorimetry. (Jansson 1997)

For instance, Mills's cell should not be electrolyzed above approximately 2.5 volts and 1 amp of current. The cell and anode should be washed in hydrochloric acid. And the hydrino gas should be allowed to escape the cell as it evolves. This tireless pursuit of detail allowed Chalk River to obtain a modest 28% excess energy balance with their cell.

Some were successful but unable to continue research, such as Michael Jacox, a research scientist working for the Department of Energy at the Idaho National Engineering and Environmental Laboratory. Jacox felt compelled to give Mills's cells a try, but kept the project in relative secrecy. He obtained three of Mills's large electrolytic cells and began operating them with a pulsed input current. His early results were encouraging, with a gain of 4 (Jacox, 1993; Baard 1999; Stolper 2006).

But in early 1993, as he and his team proceeded with the research, management discovered the operation: "there was a management decision that said we should pull the plug on the whole project and not disclose that we had been involved in the project at all," Jacox later told a reporter (Baard 1999). Despite this, Jacox and his team decided to continue work in what he called a "clandestine operation," to analyze the unusual materials being produced at BLP.

Learning about Thermacore's success, Charles Haldeman, a top engineer at the US Air Force's Lincoln Laboratory at MIT, requested funding from the Advanced Concepts Committee to build and test a Mills cell in 1993. He was given $25,000 to start. Haldeman designed a careful experiment and even built a custom power source. His initial study found excess heat with a gain of 2, enough to convince management to commit another $75,000 to the effort. In the second phase, he found a gain of 10 from an input of 0.5 W.

When presenting his findings to management, he was told there must be some error he was overlooking. Haldeman had no suggestions for what the error could be, and neither did they. He wrote a preliminary report, but retired before it had passed the review process necessary to become final. This allowed the management at MIT to withhold the paper for six years; it didn't see the light of day until 2001 (Haldeman 1995).

Haldeman later told a reporter, "This area is not well understood. There's clearly incontrovertible evidence that there's something going on in the work of Mills and others that certainly deserves further study. It's a tragedy that the politics of cold fusion has prevented science from taking its course" (Baard 1999).

Some wanted to do research, but were disheartened from the get-go at their chances of securing any funding. Luke Setzer, a mechanical engineer at the Kennedy Space Center in Florida (who started the Hydrino Study Group), began talking to the physicists there, but it was clear they would not support it. "One of them kept referring to 'fictional energy' rather than 'theoretical energy.' That kind of language tells me they're already shutting their mind to the possibilities" (Baard 1999).

The bias against Mills's work (as, perhaps, with all bias) was self-sustaining; most feared to be associated with the work; those who had the courage and interest to pursue it were few, and those who obtained confirming results were often put under pressure to suppress the study and stop work; those who persisted in the research were ostracized; those who connected with BLP to collaborate, and especially those who sought to become business partners, became guilty by association.

Others took interest in Mills but maintained tight non-disclosure agreements;[38] a smart move, as these groups could dangle their feet without getting wet.

As electrochemists perfected the art of calorimetry and provided more rigorous analyses of the gases that evolved from electrolytic cells, several researchers began reporting more reliable evidence for the production of nuclear products. In particular, tritium and helium-4 were found and well-correlated with the measurements of excess heat, even though there was no neutrons emitted. This was a mystery.[39]

In early experiments, tritium was a common contaminant of deuterium, which is produced by neutron bombardment in a nuclear reactor. And as the gases from a cell are released, tritium is more likely to remain in the cell and build up in concentration.

Regarding the helium, Mills saw another possible explanation. Since Fleischmann-Pons cells had all the ingredients for some hydrino production, hydrinos (or rather *deuterinos*) ought to be forming in the cells, and combining to form deuterino gas, the heavy equivalent of hydrino gas.

Mills predicted that these molecules would have a similar size to the helium atom, but a higher ionization energy and a lower liquefaction point than deuterium. In short: a deuterino molecule should look an awful

---

[38] I maintain respect for such agreements and reserve my knowledge of undisclosed collaborators for future editions of this book.

[39] See Miles 1991a, Miles 1991b; Chien1992.

lot like the helium-4 atom, but they could be distinguished in a careful experiment.

In one study, a team performed a quadrupole mass spectroscopy analysis of the gases from a cold fusion cell and found a large shoulder on a deuterium peak that they assigned to the hydrogen-tritium (HT) molecule. They made this assignment despite there being no hydrogen present in the experiment. The authors proposed that they had a hydrogen contamination, perhaps due to the fusion process itself (Yamaguchi 1992).

This peak is a good match for deuterino, but, Mills's explanation does not explain the helium peak, and begs the question: were there impurities that could introduce both helium and HT?

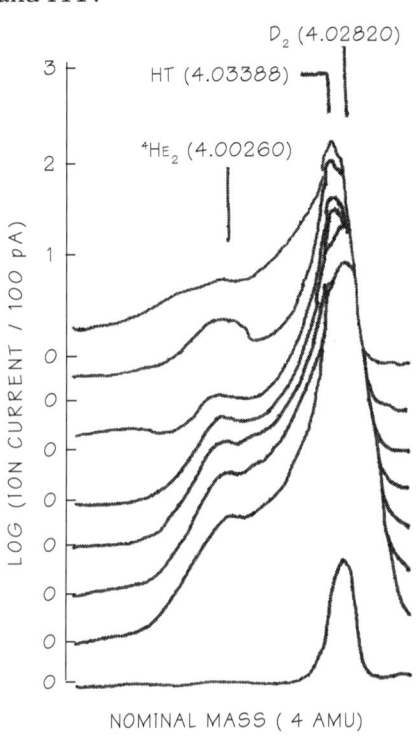

HT OR $D_2(\frac{1}{2})$?

MASS SPEC DATA OF THE GASSES RELEASED FROM A DEUTERIUM-LOADED, MAGNESIUM OXIDE COATED PALLADIUM SHEET. AFTER (YAMAGUCHI 1992).

THE SHOULDER EMERGES WITH TIME TO BECOME LARGER THAN D_2. AUTHORS ASSIGN TO HT - BUT THERE IS NO HYDROGEN!

In 1993, Mills and Good, collaborating with Thermacore, took special pains to isolate hydrino gas in an unambiguous way. The key to doing so was that hydrino molecules have an enormously high binding energy and should not combust with oxygen. So after capturing the gases that evolved from the electrolytic cell, they activated a spark plug in an elastomer bladder to combust them, then put that gas through a mass-spectrometer.

Although there was plenty of oxygen left in the gases after combustion, there was still hydrogen gas: that is, a molecule with the proper mass to charge ratio. And this molecule had a higher ionization potential than traditional hydrogen gas (Mills 1993).

In a study funded by the US Air Force, Thermacore recruited Alfred Miller at Lehigh University to run an X-ray photoelectron spectroscopic study of the hydrogen absorbed on the nickel cathodes; he found that there was a peak at 55 eV that corresponded to Mills's predicted binding energy of the dihydrino (H_2) molecule predicted to be 54.4 eV. Dr. Miller was unable to come up with another explanation for the peak, which raised Thermacore's confidence that Mills's explanation was right (Thermacore 1994). "Over the years I haven't really come across too many things that haven't been explainable" he said to a reporter, "At least if you thought about it long and hard enough."

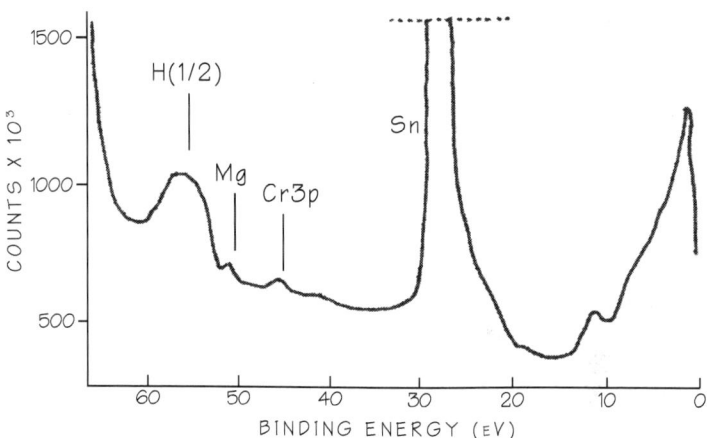

FIRST XPS IDENTIFICATION OF H(1/2)

XPS OF NICKEL FOIL CATHODE MATERIAL. SUBJECTED TO ELECTROLYSIS. A PEAK MATCHING THE 54.4 EV BINDING ENERGY OF THE H(1/2) HYDRINO. AFTER (MILLS, 1993).

John Spitznagel at Westinghouse looked for possible sources of the peak. Although nothing intentionally introduced into the cell could have produced it, potential alternatives included the $3p$ electrons of iron (52.8-57.95 eV), as well as compounds of lithium and osmium (Spitznagel 1994).

Miller, as many who would collaborate with Mills, developed a good opinion of him: "...this is not the equivalent of cold fusion, [Mills] is serious and honest. He may well have ventured upon something" (Baard 1999). Miller, however, didn't want his work to be interpreted as an unequivocal confirmation of Mills's theory.

Mills was always curious if hydrinos or hydrino hydride ions $H^-(1/p)$ could react to form more complex compounds. A few years later, HPC rotary evaporated the potassium carbonate (K_2CO_3) electrolyte from the Thermacore cell at high temperature, and found a yellow-white goo that was a mess of never-before-seen hydrides. They were also able to grow crystals from a precipitate.

In a monumental 26-page paper published in 2000, Mills presented the analysis of dozens of new hydrino hydride compounds and clusters, using TOF-SIMS, XPS, XRD, FTIR, NMR, and Raman spectroscopy (Mills 2000). The authors report finding a new class of inorganic clusters containing novel hydride combinations, such as polyhydrogen molecules with 16, 24, or 25 hydrogen atoms (H_{16}, H_{24}, and H_{25}); alkali hydrino hydrides such as MgH_3, NaH_3, and KH_3; compounds such as OH^-_{23}, CH^-_{23}, NH^-_{23}; and larger hydride clusters that formed polymeric structures such as $KH\ KHCO_3$.

Lehigh University performed the photoelectron spectroscopy (XPS) of the polymeric material, which found significant peaks corresponding to hydrino hydride ions $H^-(1/4)$, $H^-(1/6)$, $H^-(1/8)$, and $H^-(1/16)$. X-ray diffraction was used to analyze the crystals, and found unidentified lattice structures. When Galbraith Laboratories performed an elemental analysis, they found more hydrogen than could be explained if the samples were from conventional hydrides.

Potassium hydrides typically react violently in water, but Mills's material was extremely water-stable. They were polymers, but inorganic: without a carbon backbone. It dawned on Mills that a whole class of compounds may be generated with hydrino, perhaps as wide ranging as that of carbon.

Yong-Xi Li, who performed mass spectroscopy work for Mills at Ricera's lab in Cleveland, was amazed to find inorganic compounds with organic properties. "We totally don't know what's going on. The reason is that I've never seen before these kinds of properties in all my career" (Baard 2006).

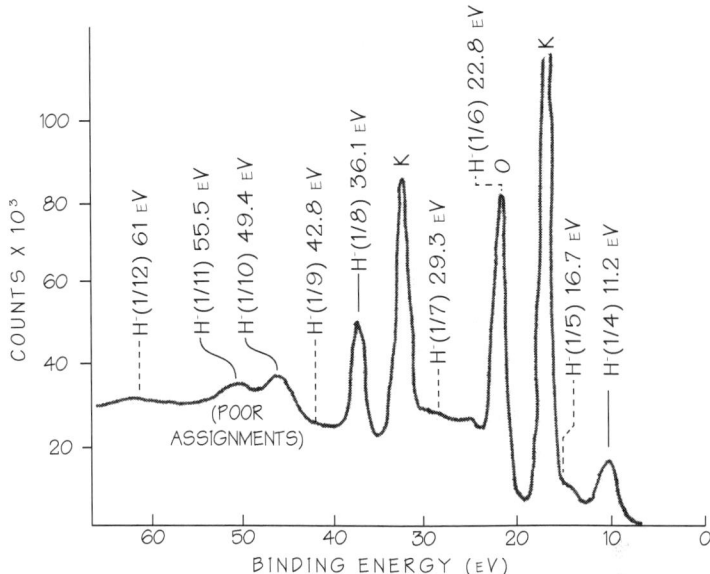

HYDRINO HYDRIDE POLYMERS

XPS SPECTRUM FROM 0 TO 80 EV OF THE POLYMERIC MATERIAL PREPARED FROM THE K_2CO_3 ELECTROLYTE OF A THERMACORE CELL, SHOWING CLEAR PEAKS FOR $H^-(1/4)$ AND $H^-(1/8)$. AFTER THAT IN (MILLS, 2000).

And they had commercial value. Although electric vehicles are now on the market, they are still unable to compete with the versatility of the internal combustion engine. The problem with a mobile energy source is the *gravimetric energy density*, or how many watts can be produced per unit weight. Batteries are heavy, and thus limit how far an electric vehicle can travel before a recharge. One key to the function of a battery is how much energy can be stored in the molecular bonds. Mills's hydrino hydrides have very high binding energies, an order of magnitude more than conventional chemical bonding.

Very high binding energies also means very high chemical stability, and this did not escape the notice of the US Navy. A ship that is rust-proof would save millions of dollars by reducing crews needed to wash the deck. BLP began talks with the Naval Air Warfare Center at China Lake, California, to develop military applications (Baard 1999). The base at China Lake had a long history of participating in some of the most rigorous cold fusion research, so they were open to working with Mills.

BLP even gained a board member, retired vice admiral Michael Kalleres, to help with this process.

Some board members were not too excited by this. They worried that the hydrinos would be classified for national security. One of them urged Mills to refer to energetic materials as potential "propellants" instead of "explosives." Mills is said to have replied: "That would be as if I pointed a duck gun at you and said not to worry, because it only kills ducks" (Baard 1999).

Mills was so excited about producing these materials that he began thinking that there might be more money in materials than energy. A materials factory might be easier to scale up, the properties of substances are easier to validate than heat, there were fewer engineering risks, and the company could hit some high-value markets such as microelectronics. Perhaps energy would be a *byproduct* of materials manufacturing (Newmeyer 2000). It was a new frontier.

Cold fusion was fading from public consciousness, and had been largely debunked in the US. It held on through the '90s through Japanese funding, but by 2000, Japan decided to cut national support for the effort. Cold fusion (or rather, the politically correct moniker: Low Energy Nuclear Reactions, or LENR) had lived out its life cycle.

Mills, however, was still standing, flush with millions for ongoing development.

Eugene Mallove, a spokesperson for the diminished cold fusion community, reflected on the '90s with the acknowledgment that Mills's work had come to greater prominence. Perhaps, he speculated, fusion reactions were also taking place in Mills's cells (Mallove 2000a, 2000b).

Mills had made serious progress, whereas the LENR community had made none. Mills's cells would soon, however, lose their resemblance to cold fusion cells.

The future was hydrogen plasma, and it was *hot*.

CHAPTER 6

THE ELECTRON, OLYMPIAN

*In which we get more acquainted with the
extended electron model, and foray into
low-temperature physics.*

In the summer of 2004, the main lab floor at BlackLight Power was filled with calorimeters and reaction cells under a canopy of cords and water lines. Large foam cubes held water baths for calorimetry, while a row of hot kilns ran twenty-four hours a day, making hydrino hydrides.

Scientists came in and out of the lab, monitoring experiments. Stations were constantly being torn down, reconfigured, rebuilt, replumbed. It was a prototyping facility. When a new type of reaction cell showed promise, testing was accelerated by building a whole line of stations with replicas of the original cell. It was a factory of data, gathered slowly but continuously, day and night, producing results for Mills and his scientists to analyze.

The kilns ran steel reaction cells that had been sealed under an argon-atmosphere, after being loaded with a small crucible of catalyst, such as potassium metal, along with another of potassium iodide (KI) salt. A vacuum was applied for several hours to remove moisture, and hydrogen gas was pumped in under low pressure intermittently over several days, during which the kiln was maintained at 650 ° C. A vacuum would again be applied to the cell, then disconnected from the kiln; after which the kiln was opened up in an argon-atmosphere glove box. Beautiful blue, purple, or green crystalline salts (depending on the reactants) would be removed, labeled and placed in sample containers for later analysis.[40]

Alkali hydrides could trap hydrogen gas in its lattice, but also substitute hydrino ion H$^-$ (1/n) for the hydrogen in the lattice to produce alkali hydrino hydrides. That summer at BLP, my job was to transfer the samples to a quartz tube in an argon-atmosphere glove box; decompose the samples by heating them to a high enough temperature to release the stored gas; then condense the gas into an NMR sample tube suspended in liquid nitrogen. After the gases were collected in the tube, I sealed it with a torch, and took it back to Princeton.

I'm sure it was no coincidence that Mills bought a facility located only a short drive from one of the most prestigious physics universities in the

---

[40] For a description of this experiment see Mills 2000.

world. Even if there was little or no interaction, there were conveniences. We could access the Princeton libraries and purchase time on their equipment, such as the NMR spectrometer in the chemistry building. Not a particularly uncommon instrument, but it was a newer model and well-maintained.

In these samples, we could often see peaks arising from hydrino gas and compounds. Mills had identified hydrides involving a positively charged metal ion (such as K, Rb, Cs, Sr), a hydrino ion, and a positively charged halide (such as F, Cl, Br, I).

Preparing the samples was repetitive and time-consuming, worthy of a new intern. BLP would run dozens of reaction cells in a given week; and I set up multiple stations for decomposing samples. Pulling a good vacuum on the apparatus to remove impurities took time, so even if I worked efficiently, I could decompose and prepare only four or five samples a day. On such days, I found free time. I was given an office cube, and would often use the time to study Mills's theory more closely. It was an ideal situation; I would rarely see Mills while busy in the laboratory, but when at my desk he would often saunter by.

Mills sensed my interest in his theory and would occasionally drop drafts of his latest theoretical work on my desk. A pile quickly formed. I began to look through them and we began to chat more often.

Soon, Mills asked if I could help run some calculations and create some visuals of his work. At first, I fit this around my lab schedule. But by mid-summer, it began to take up more of my time. I kept one foot in the theory and one in the lab. I was busy and enjoying my work.

By the end of the summer, I was asked to stay. I was still a year away from my degree, but here I had an opportunity to do the kind of work that had charged and motivated me for several years.

Mills was asking me to help reinvent our theory of nature.

My decision had already been made.

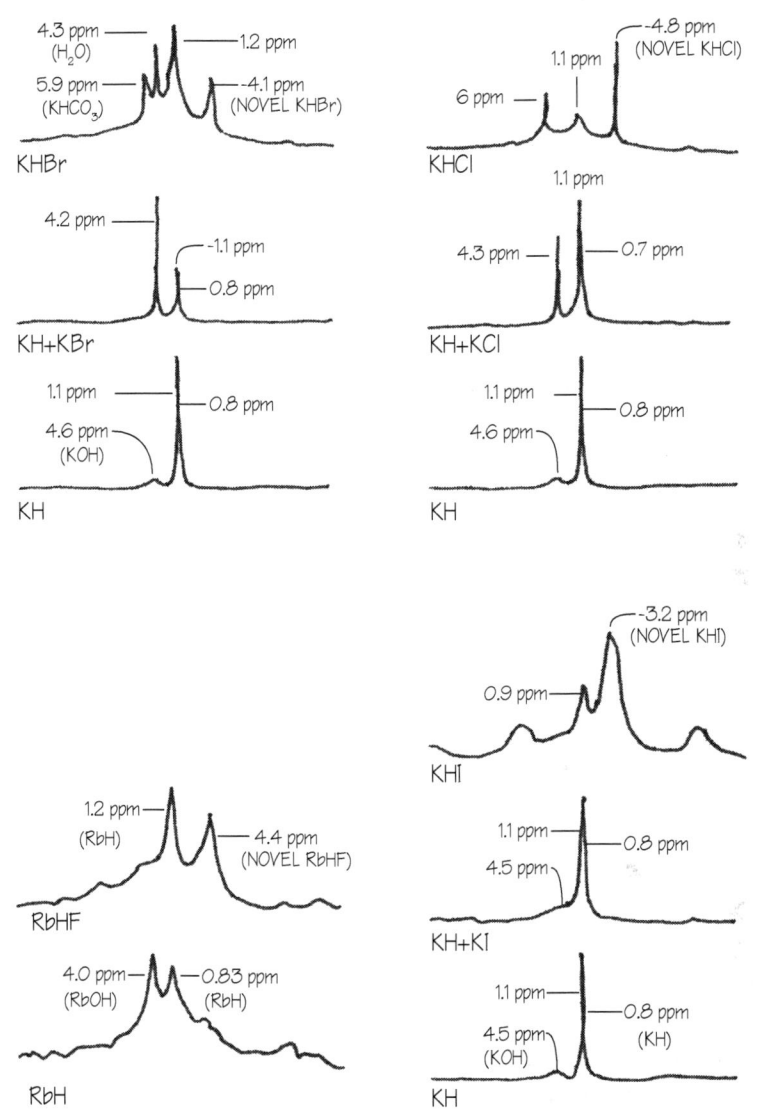

NMR IDENTIFICATION

OF ALKALI AND ALKALINE EARTH HYDRIDES SHOWING DRAMATICALLY UPFIELD-SHIFTED PEAKS OF TIGHTLY-BOUND HYDRINO HYDRIDE IONS. AFTER (MILLS 2000).

Mills's model was compelling because it could visualize physics in a way never before possible. As summer turned to fall, I continued doing calculations and illustrating his ideas.

Our first project was to explore how the electron spins in the atom.

According to Mills's theory, the electron current flows along great-circle loops, overlapping one another on a shell. But this doesn't tell us how the loops are laid out. They could follow any distribution, so long as the net result of the motion produces angular momentum in the needed directions. To match our experiments with electrons in magnetic fields, you need angular momentum along three separate axes.

It was also necessary to sweep out a continuous sphere. Mills accomplished this with his first attempt in the early '90s, but now he wanted to cover the sphere uniformly, a much more difficult problem. Every great-circle drawn on a sphere intersects every other circle at two points, which become points of higher density. We explored pattern after pattern and put them through an algorithm to visualize the results (Mills 2015, Ch. 1).

The loops of charge on the sphere resemble a ball of yarn. Intersections are everywhere. In fact, if there are an infinite number of infinitesimal loops, there are twice as many intersections. David Griffiths once asked me why the charge in each loop doesn't collide with the others. After all, on a macroscopic scale, electric current is made up of little electrons. If two electron beams collide, they repel and scatter. But surely the current *inside* the electron isn't made up of even tinier electrons!

Instead, we need to step back in time to pre-twentieth century physics, before the discovery of the electron, to the notion that an electric current can be an ideal, continuous flow of charge. This continuously flowing charge is wrapped into dynamic surfaces making up the substance of the particle, composing all matter.

I find it a poetic reminder of how physics on one scale echoes on another: it is through the echo, the physics of flowing electrons on a macroscale, that we can understand the flow of charge on the microscale.

I would personally prefer an electron surface in which current wasn't passing through itself at an infinite number of points. If the electron charge did not intersect, it would be something more akin to a vector field, in which each point on the surface has a unique direction and magnitude of current flow. Perhaps the subatomic equivalent of superconducting vortices on the surface of this shell could produce angular momentum along different axes.

As it turns out, there is a theorem (the unfortunately named "Hairy Ball Theorem") that says you can't lay a vector field onto a sphere without causing at least one point on the sphere to stick up in the air—a cowlick on a perfectly combed head of hair. It would be a point with no velocity.[41]

Mills's spin pattern does work; however, there may be other possibilities. Any theoretical solution has tight requirements that it must be stable and in force balance.

A popular topic among those debating Mills's concept was whether the electron shell repels itself. While it was clear that the entire shell would blow up without a nucleus, the issue was whether each infinitesimal point of charge repels each of its immediately adjacent neighbors, to which it is infinitesimally close. Let us call this the problem of self-interaction.

To consider this problem, suppose we were to place a series of point charges on a line, like ants on a log; each one having an electric field that emanates outward in all directions. In this scenario, the point charges would repel.

Next, suppose we were to bunch these particles closer together. The electric fields will start to emanate away from the whole group. The immediate neighbors repel more strongly, but cancel one another out as you get further from the source.

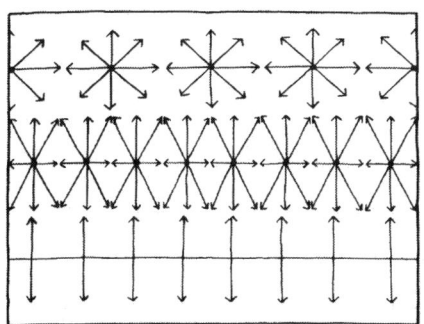

SELF-INTERACTION
IS THERE A PROBLEM?

IF POINT-CHARGES ARE PACKED CLOSE TOGETHER AS TO FORM A CONTINUOUS TWO-DIMENSIONAL SURFACE, THERE IS NO REPULSION BETWEEN NEIGHBORING INFINITESIMALS!

Finally, suppose we were to pack them so close that they form a *continuous surface*.

---

[41] Many physicists starting to digest Mills's model get tangled up in the mathematics of the spin pattern. I recommend putting it off until you digest the larger theory, for the atomic and molecular solutions that flow from Mills's model really only depend on the net angular momentum and magnetic fields.

In this scenario the field between the charges disappears entirely, and instead emanates out from the surface along the normal vector (the perpendicular).[42]

So lines of current within a surface won't interact, but the surface must be infinitesimally thin. Indeed, the surface would have to be two-dimensional! Is this possible? It is hard to imagine, but if you ask me, slightly *less* hard to imagine than a zero-dimensional point.

Mills later recognized that the electron shell must have a thickness due to the curvature of space produced by its mass, a width of only 10^{-43} meters.[43]

To say this number is a *small* is an understatement. It is so small that I struggle to give it human scale. If we take our galaxy and make it the size of a penny, this thickness would correspond roughly to that of a penny in that shrunken galaxy.

I have no idea if this thickness is enough to give us problems. But alas, matter in the universe is stable. It may abide being imperfectly thin.

When the electron becomes *unbound*, and free to move about the world, we wonder how it can be stable. After all, there is no proton in the center holding it together! Every bit of negative charge ought to repel every other, blowing it up like a balloon. Do we need the self-force here? Even Schott had come up with a spherical shell model that does not require a self-force.

Mills found a simple and elegant solution: a spinning disk of charge, with increasing charge (and mass) density as you approach the center. This disk, made up of current loops packed tight like the lines on a phonograph, produces a magnetic field with forces that pull the loops into the center (Mills 2015, Ch. 3).

Properly balanced, the magnetic field in the plane of the disk will counteract the outward inertia of the spinning charge to create a balanced system.

One interesting feature of Mills's electron is that the charge distribution, and the overall radius, depends on the relative velocity at which you observe it. If you fire an electron beam at high velocity toward a target, it will glance off like a point particle, because the radius will have

---

[42] Mills attributes this behavior to Gauss's Law. Some have questioned this interpretation, but it is consistent with the approach taken by classical electron theorists.

[43] If the surface were thinner than the corresponding Schwartzchild radius, it would form a black hole.

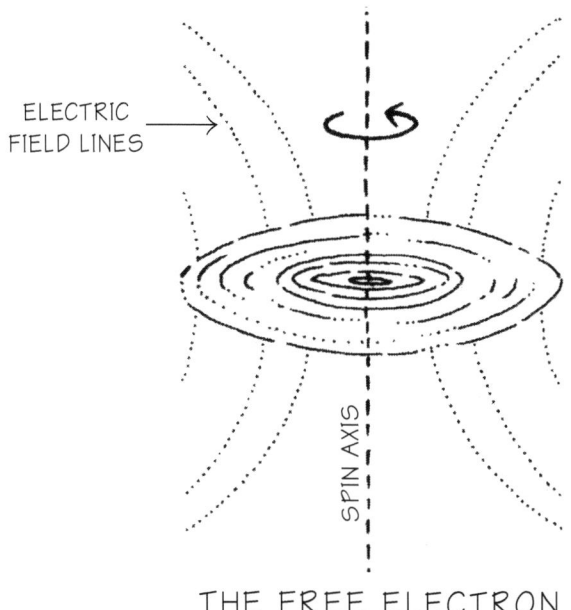

THE FREE ELECTRON

THE FREE ELECTRON IS A ROTATING (MONOLITHIC) DISK OF CHARGE WITH INCREASING CHARGE TOWARD THE CENTER. EACH LOOP OF CHARGE HELPS TO HOLD THE OTHERS IN PLACE. THE ELECTRIC FIELD IS INDISTINGUISHABLE FROM A POINT-CHARGE AT GREAT DISTANCES.

contracted almost to a point. Even today most of our experiments with electrons involves firing them at high velocity to narrow the focus of the beam. In doing so we may make it impossible to see any structure.

Because of its extended nature, the electron can do some amazing things. It can jump over a voltage barrier that it really has no business jumping over.

Quantum theoreticians call this *tunneling* and describe it as a purely quantum phenomena that results from the electron having a small statistical probability of finding itself on the opposite side of a very high barrier.

But quantum theory is still thinking in terms of a point. A pole vaulter may do something similar. He may twist and contort his body such that he gets over the bar, while his *center of mass* goes beneath.

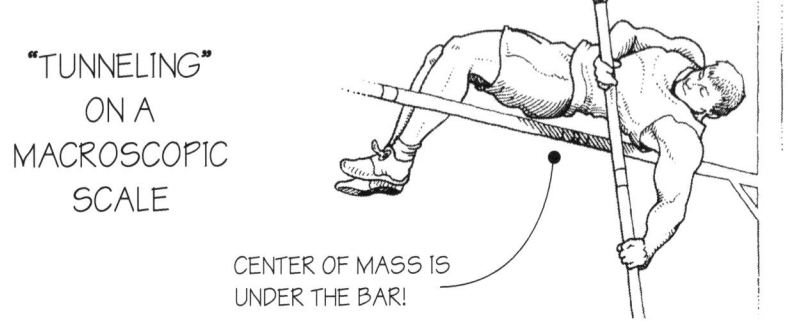

"TUNNELING" ON A MACROSCOPIC SCALE

CENTER OF MASS IS UNDER THE BAR!

That electrons are extended particles also allows them to form continuous planes of charge in a lattice structure, such as that of a metal. When the metal is brought below a critical temperature, the electron becomes superconducting due to the Goedeke-Haus condition (Mills 2015, Ch. 25). Current theory says it has something to do with the pairing of electrons into Cooper Pairs, a theory that earned its authors a Nobel Prize, yet failed to predict the superconductivity of some substances at unexpected higher temperatures.

I prefer Mills's description of the electron to that of quantum theory. But are there any true dead ends, experiments in which quantum predictions utterly fail?

Let us turn now to one of the simplest experiments with electrons, one that may emerge as the death knoll for the quantum century.

———∞∞∞———

In the 1930s, the Russian scientist Pyotr Kapitsa discovered that when helium is liquefied (its liquefaction point is extremely cold, only 4 K), and then further cooled to about 2 K, the Wan der Walls forces between helium atoms allow the fluid to lose all viscosity; it becomes a *superfluid*. Analogous to superconductivity, superfluidity means there is no resistance to motion, and without this natural dispelling of frictive interactions as heat, vortices and vibrations can persist uninhibited. It is an interesting state of matter that won Kapitsa a Nobel Prize.

Forty years later, experimentalists were using superfluid helium cells to measure ion mobility. A vapor of atoms (say, potassium) was introduced to the top of the cell, an electrical discharge or beta radiation source was used to produce ions, and when an electric field was applied to the cell, the ions would move through the superfluid. We can learn something about the size of the ions as they move through a viscous-free environment.

But when the top layer of liquid helium submerged the beta radiation source, unexpected charged species were found migrating through the helium.

In fact, electrons trapped in the helium will open a cavity for themselves, an electron *bubble*. At low pressure, this cavity will have a radius of about 19 Å, about forty times the size of a hydrogen atom. As pressure is increased, the radius decreases.

This makes sense; instead of an electron captured by a positively charged nucleus, the electron is trapped within the van der Waals attractions in the helium. Forces from without, instead of within.

It occurred to some experimentalists to hit these bubbles with sound waves in order to make them pop and release a little flash of light in the process. Since the electron quickly reformed the bubble, the experimenters repeated this every few nanoseconds to track the movement of the electron through the superfluid.

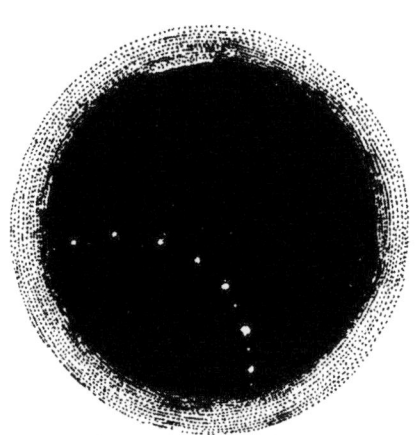

THE PATH OF AN ELECTRON BUBBLE MOVING THROUGH A CELL OF LIQUID HELIUM AT 2.5 K. THE POSITION IS CAPTURED EVERY 31 MILLISECONDS. AFTER THAT IN (MARIS 2008).

Once an electron is excited by absorbing light, it is predicted that it can then relax and dissipate its energy to its surroundings by emitting either a weak pressure wave or an infra-red photon.[44]

The drag that electron bubbles experience as they move through the fluid is a good match for quantum theory's prediction for their size.

However, in 1969, experimentalists found that in addition to the electron bubbles, there were charged particles (ions) moving through the fluid at up to *seven times* the velocity of the electron bubbles.

---

[44] So far, we haven't been able to observe this emission, but chances are good that we will develop an experiment sensitive enough to do this eventually.

A higher velocity means the ions are either a higher charge, or physically smaller.

In 1971, two more unidentified ions were found, each moving through the fluid at their own rates, all faster than the "normal" electron bubble.

Experiments continued, and by the following year, *thirteen more* were found moving through the helium, each with their own unique velocities.[45]

Which mysterious ions were formed seemed to depend on the experimental setup, such as the voltage of the discharge used to introduce electrons. However, whether using a radioactive source or other means of generating electrons, these mysterious particles appeared whenever the experimenter expected electron bubbles to be formed.

Physicists scratched their heads.

Perhaps they were free electrons conducting through the fluid? If so, they ought to travel much faster.

Perhaps they were some kind of impurity? The purity of the helium was improved with no change in results.

Perhaps they were helium ions? These are known to exist in free space, but have a rather short lifetime of only 345 microseconds, whereas these carriers were much more stable, with a lifetime exceeding 10 milliseconds.

There was a final, and perhaps most natural option: perhaps they were some kind of excited state of a one- or two-electron bubble.

Theoreticians explored this option, but unfortunately, excited state electron bubbles were predicted by quantum theory to be invariably *larger* than the ground state at about 19 Å. So they should have a higher surface area and be moving more *slowly* through the fluid, unlike these exotic charge carriers.[46]

Humphrey Maris did some calculation of the shape of the excited state electron bubbles, and found that under certain pressures, the $2p$ excited state could produce a double-teardrop shape with a small waist that could be made to shrink with increasing pressure, eventually *splitting* the electron into two pieces! Maris called these *electrinos*.[47]

---

[45] See Doake 1969; Ihas 1971, 1972.

[46] Despite this, quantum theory can do a pretty good job of predicting the absorption energies.

[47] Physicists seem fond of the "ino" suffix, and the hypothetical electrino is not to be confused with such things as neutrinos or, of course, hydrinos!

In decades of attempts, physicists were unable to split electrons by smashing them together at phenomenally high energies. How then, could a simple experiment with liquid helium split an electron?

It is an unlikely prospect. Some theoreticians tried to rationalize this away, by arguing that even if this were to happen, the two halves of the electron would still be conjoined, even while physically separate, in a quantum entangled state.

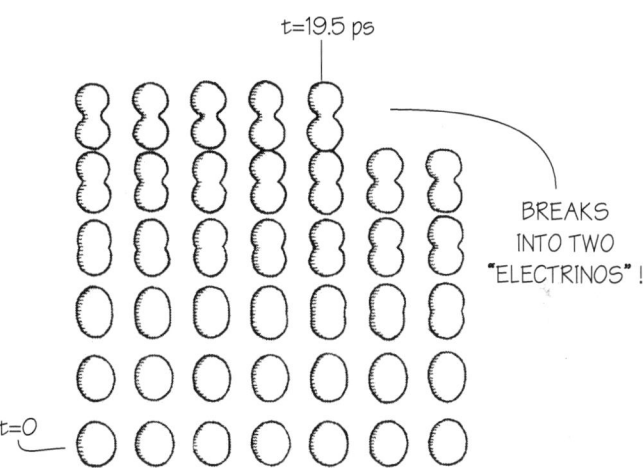

ELECTRON BUBBLES IN LIQUID HELIUM

A SIMPLIFIED QUANTUM MECHANICAL PREDICTION FOR THE SHAPE OF AN ELECTRON BUBBLE AS IT TRANSITIONS FROM A 1s TO A 1p EXCITED STATE. THE THEORY PREDICTS THE ELECTRON SHOULD BREAK INTO TWO PIECES. AFTER (MARIS 2008).

In a 2008 review article, Humphrey Maris lamented: "So far it has not been possible to find any model that can explain the nature of these objects" (Maris 2008). If the ions are indeed electron bubbles, Maris estimated they have radii as small as only 7.3 Å.

When the editor of the *International Journal of Hydrogen Energy*, Professor Veziroglu, heard about this work, he invited Mills to submit a paper on the topic. He thought that Mills's theory might have a good explanation.

And Mills did, publishing in 2000. He found that according to his model, electrons could form orbitspheres in the superfluid. In this state, they could then absorb light much like they did in the atom, forming excited states, except that instead of inflating to a larger radius, they *shrunk*, much like hydrinos (although for totally different reasons), forming bubbles that are 1/2, 1/3, 1/4... etc., the radius of the "ground" state electron bubble (Mills 2000).

Although similar to atomic excited states, the physics of electron bubbles is somewhat different. Let us take a moment to clarify.

In the hydrogen atom, the captured photon that produces the excited state shields the positive electric field of the nucleus, allowing the electron orbitsphere to expand. Whereas, in an electron bubble, the photon forming the excited state shields the negative electric field of the electron itself, causing it to shrink. As it does so, the electron increases in angular velocity and energy.[48]

Mills used his model to calculate the orbits at which the electron bubbles may remain stable. This varies depending on temperature and pressure. Recall that the ability of an extended membrane of charge to remain stable to radiation depends on possessing no light-like Fourier components. But the speed of light in liquid helium is not the same as in free space, and it varies with temperature and pressure. As these properties change in the superfluid, so do the allowed electron bubbles.

And like in the case of the atom, these excited state electron bubbles have angular quantum numbers, which produce a smorgasbord of possible bubbles with different radii. Mills was able to find excited state orbits to match those commonly seen in experiments. The results were stunning; this experiment was one of the definitive tests of Mills's new quantum theory.

---

[48] The physics is also somewhat different than hydrino states, despite the similarity of fractional orbits. Electron bubbles form by the absorption of light, not through a nonradiative mechanism; although they may relax nonradiatively by releasing energy as compression waves in the helium. Recall that during the formation of a hydrino state, the hydrogen atom expels some energy to its surroundings by resonant transfer, placing the atom in a metastable state that quickly decays, with the release of a photon, to a hydrino state. When a photon is released, a resonant mode in the atom is excited that adds to the field of the proton, pulling the electron in. Whereas, in an excited state electron bubble, the field diminishes.

Ion Peak	Maris Estimated Radius (Å)	Mills Assignment (n, l, m_l)
1	19.0	(1, 0, 0)
2	16.8	(1/3, 2, ±1)
3	15.6	(1/2, 1, 0)
4	14.2	(1/4, 2, ±1)
5	13.6	(1/2, 1, ±1)
6	13.0	(1/3, 1, 0)
7	12.3	(1/3, 2, ±1)
8	11.9	(1/2, 0, 0)
9	9.6	(1/4, 1, 0)
10	9.3	(1/3, 0, 0)
11	8.9	(1/4, 0, 0)
12	--	(1/5, 0, 0)
13	--	(1/6, 0, 0)
14	--	(1/7, 0, 0)
15	7.3	(1/100, 0, 0)

"Exotic" ion peaks discovered by injecting electrons into superfluid helium and timing their migration through the fluid under an applied field. Maris estimated their size from their mobility. Mills calculates allowed excited state electron bubbles from his classical electron model (Mills 2000).

Since Mills's publication, later studies found that in addition to a series of distinct peaks, a continuous background of charge carriers with different mobilities were flowing through the liquid helium (Wei 2013). The authors of the study were confounded. But Mills's theory may provide a very good explanation: each burst of light may produce a wide range of fractional electron radii. There are hundreds, even *thousands* of possible states as a function of n, l, and m_l quantum numbers.

Superfluid helium bubbles appear to be a dead end for quantum theory, but Mills's theory provides an excellent explanation, tying together everything that makes Mills's theory great: a good model for radiation and stability, and an explanation for how light is trapped by a particle. The experiment also shows that the electron is a knowable thing, with a shape and size and behavior that is very classical. Together with fractional atomic orbits, fractional excited states of free electrons may mark the end of the quantum century.

During my time at BLP, I enjoyed the feeling of coming into the office to find Nobel Prize caliber discoveries waiting in a pile on my desk.

CHAPTER 7

GREATER THAN FIRE

In which electrochemical cells are given up for the much more interesting gas-phase plasma reactors; and we learn how to detect an invisible atom.

In 1990, John Phillips was 'kidnapped.'

When the cold fusion fiasco hit, many scientists were jumping into the field, especially specialists in calorimetry, who knew the art of measuring very small amounts of heat produced in electrolytic cells.

John Phillips was a materials scientist, who had earned his doctorate from the University of Wisconsin Madison in 1981. His specialty was catalysis, but measuring the effects of catalysis requires careful measurements of heat, so a specialist in catalysis really meant that you were a specialist in calorimetry.

Phillips was an associate professor at Penn State when he was recruited by Stewart Kurtz, a professor there who was creating a Materials Institute and wanted Phillips to be a part of a cold fusion task force. At Penn State, professors were on their own to fund their work through grants, often from the National Science Foundation, and Kurtz assembled his group with the hope of procuring more funding for research. His general interest in cold fusion led him to the work of Mills, an entrepreneur who was funding his research without NSF grants.

Kurtz decided that he ought to introduce Phillips to Mills. After all, Mills could use a good calorimetrist. So Kurtz asked Phillips to join him on what Phillips assumed would be a trip across town. As they pulled onto the highway, Kurtz revealed that they were on their way to Malvern.

That's a four hour drive.

On the way, they had lots to talk about.

Weary with Kurtz's attempts to prepare him, Phillips was delightfully surprised with his first impressions of Mills; he later described Mills as charismatic, charming and extremely intelligent. Mills and his assistant Bill Good had a legitimate lab that was well equipped, and they appeared to be making an earnest effort to make accurate measurements.

Phillips thought it was more likely he would meet a talking giraffe on the streets of Malvern than that he would overturn quantum theory, so he decided to forgo Mills's theoretical explanations and concentrate on experiment.

After all, there was nothing illegal about having a new theory.

Phillips was happy to do the work if he was paid, and believed that he could do a better job than what Mills and Good had already done. His expectation, of course, was that he wouldn't find anything. In fact it was his personal goal to *debunk* Mills's work, something that should have been easy.

The basic chemistry was simple: you needed hydrogen atoms, in the presence of specific atomic chemical catalysts. But electrolysis of water was only one way to produce hydrogen atoms; another is to pass hydrogen gas (H_2) directly over a hot filament. The filament causes the gas molecules to decompose into individual atoms, which maintain a high concentration in the boundary layer around the filament. This implied a reaction cell design using a *gas*-phase architecture, something Mills had already started working on.

Phillips and Kurtz ran some of Mills's electrolytic cells in the early '90s. But by 1995, they wanted to build a gas-phase cell.

Phillips used a steel reaction cell. It was a Calvet calorimeter, equipped with a row of thermocouples in contact with the inside surface of the cell, and another row in contact with the outside surface. The difference in the readings of the thermocouples gives you the heat *flux*, how much heat is passing through the cell.

Into the cell was placed a stainless steel cup filled with potassium nitrate (KNO_3) powder, and a platinum filament was wound around the cup. Feedthroughs in the lid of the cell provided gas lines for hydrogen and helium, and copper wires for the filament. The entire cell was wrapped in a layer of insulation and placed in a 250 ° C kiln.

When the cell heated up, the weak bond that attached the potassium to the NO_3 should break, allowing potassium ions (K^+) to be released in the cell. The filament would split the hydrogen, and you would have both hydrogen and potassium floating around in a narrow region in the cell, providing conditions for hydrino catalysis to take place.

To Phillips's surprise, it worked.

"I always design an experiment to debunk the theory." Phillips explained as he reflected on his early experiments, "and it should have been easy to disprove. I failed to do so."

Phillips found that when hydrogen was introduced to the cell, there was an obvious spike in power output, which did not occur when helium was introduced.

Even after this spike diminished, the heat output from the cell could remain elevated, for hours, even *days;* sometimes it *never* went back to the calibrated baseline unless the cell was flushed out.

This was a head scratcher.

Experiments are expected to produce effects in proportion to their cause; if they don't, there is reason to suspect something is wrong. It is possible that the introduction of hydrogen into the cell changes it somehow, permanently, in a way that we have not discovered. It is also possible that hydrino catalysis doesn't reach equilibrium like a traditional chemical reaction, but that hydrino atoms fall to lower states over time, slowly descending the ladder of allowed states.

There was not a lot of heat produced by Phillips's calorimeter, but within the parameters of the experiment, it was significant, far beyond what could be accounted for by conventional chemical reactions that could occur within the cell.

The chemicals available were few and well understood: potassium, nitrogen, oxygen, and hydrogen. In fact, most of the other known reactions were *endothermic,* not exothermic. They could only *consume* energy and cool the cell.

Phillips estimated that the energy released by the most exothermic reaction possible—that between hydrogen and oxygen to form water—would be about half of a kilojoule. If released over fifteen minutes, it would not even approach the long-term baseline of excess heat output.

When Phillips realized that Mills might be right, and quantum mechanics might be wrong (or at least incomplete), he kept it in perspective. "It really didn't bother me," he told me in an interview, "theory comes and theory goes."

Phillips knew that you couldn't overturn a paradigm of physics on the basis of one experiment alone. You needed to perform similar experiments with different types of calorimeters to be sure of the results. So the logical next step was to try a different experimental set up.

He built and tested a larger cell submerged in a water-bath calorimeter. In this experiment, as the cell heated up, it transferred that heat to the surrounding water. A small fan redistributed the heat throughout the bath, so all of the water in the bath was at approximately the same temperature.

A few digital thermocouples connected to a computer data acquisition system recorded the change in temperature over time. Any temperature rise can be converted into units of energy if you know the total volume of the water bath. These experiments were calibrated to a very high accuracy by placing a heater in the cell.

The water bath calorimeter didn't work; at least, not on the first try.

When Phillips removed the cell from the water bath to look it over, it was clear that the cell had not been kept at a constant temperature; the catalyst had condensed on the side of the cell just as moisture condenses on a farmhouse window in winter. If the catalyst is confined to a surface away from the filament, it isn't active in the reaction. Phillips realized that he would need to keep the cell at a uniform temperature high enough to maintain the catalyst in the gas phase.[49]

Phillips's paid consulting gig for this work was over, and he submitted the report of his current progress. There was no decisive conclusion, but he had just begun. There was no guarantee that the reaction would work with another calorimeter; perhaps there was something in his first experiment he had missed, but he was intrigued enough to move forward.

Mills and Good were happy with his progress. Phillips signed another consulting agreement, and went back to work.

In the 1990s, the engineers at Atlantic Energy were forward thinking; they understood that new technologies often start at the fringes, and several engineers were willing to take the time to investigate new energy claims. Usually the results were negative, and they formed a reputation as something of a squad for debunking.

When Mills came on their radar, Peter Mark Jansson was among those who visited them at Malvern. He found Mills and Bill Good to be competent, intelligent, and well-educated, not the kind of people he expected to see in a scam. He also visited Jon Phillips at Penn State. He realized Mills's claims would not be easy to debunk.

Jansson had been taking graduate courses at Rowan University, working towards his Master's degree, and Atlantic wanted to know if they should be investing in Mills. The executives suggested that Jansson run his own test cells as part of his Master's thesis, and as part of Atlantic's due diligence.

The atmosphere of Rowan was friendly to Jansson's interest. Rowan had just opened its program to graduate studies, and Jansson's was the first

---

[49] For Phillips' reports from this period see Phillips 1996)a, 1996b.

Master's thesis conducted there.[50] His thesis advisers were excited about the project.

In 1997, when Jansson approached BLP (then HPC) about the project, they agreed and offered their cells for Jansson's use. One of his trials was with an 'isothermal' cell experimental design, in which a low pressure cell was maintained at a temperature of 275 °C with an input of 97 W; when hydrogen and three grams of KNO_2 were present in the cell, the heater was then turned down in stages, while a tungsten filament was turned on and raised to 40 W. With the heater off, despite less than half of the input power, the cell maintained its temperature at 275 °C. Something else in the cell must have been producing 50 W of power (Jansson 1997).

Jansson then ran a series of studies on the Calvet calorimeters, to replicate the work Phillips had been doing at Penn State. In three trials, each composed of twelve individual runs in March and April of 1997, he observed an energy production of up to 207 Wh, the equivalent of 278,000 times the most exothermic conventional chemical reaction possible with the ingredients in the cell.

Jansson was not trying to prove Mills's overall hypothesis, but rather show that the phenomena was scalable: by increasing the length of the filament, he was able to increase the excess power in proportion. Effects in proportion to their cause. This was consistent with the idea that hydrino catalysis was occurring directly around the filament, where there was a large population of dissociated hydrogen atoms.

In one experiment, the filament in Jansson's cell broke in the middle of the night, and there was a sudden drop in temperature from 270 °C to 160 °C before the cell began to convectively cool. Either the thermocouples in the cell were somehow coupled to the filament to produce an inaccurate result, or there was an exothermic chemical process occurring in the cell that required filament power, and stopped when the filament broke. Jansson concluded the latter, because the coupling had not been seen in any of the control runs with helium in place of hydrogen.

Jansson was laudatory of Mills's experimental and theoretical work, and in his thesis he reflects on the situation faced by Mills. "Most academicians I have spoken with… are annoyingly critical and pessimistic before even

---

[50] Jansson would later go on to earn his PhD in Engineering from the University of Cambridge and work for both Rowan, the University of Colorado, and Bucknell University.

asking to hear the details of their experiments or supporting data." He also laments that the "cold fusion scandal has created a stigma which has made it difficult for the academic community to perform a complete and unbiased analysis" (Jansson 1997).

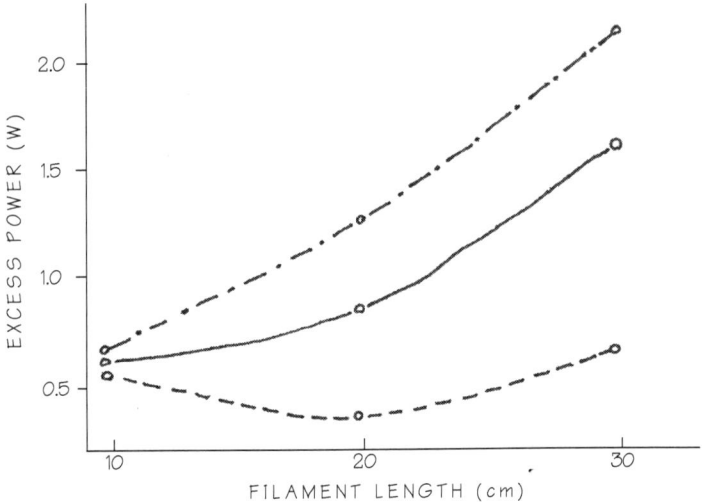

A PLOT OF THREE CALVET CALORIMETER TRIALS CONDUCTED BY PETER JANSSON AS PART OF HIS MASTER'S THESIS AT ROWAN UNIVERSITY. HE FOUND THAT EXCESS POWER FROM A BLP ISOTHERMAL CELL WAS CORRELATED TO THE LENGTH OF THE FILAMENT. EACH TRIAL WAS MADE UP OF 12 SEPARATE RUNS CONDUCTED IN MARCH AND APRIL OF 1997. AFTER (JANSSON 1997).

Jansson advised Atlantic that he believed Mills's work was real and had potential, but there was no clear and immediate path to commercialization, so investment still carried significant risk. Jansson knew that seldom is a new discovery brought to market by the scientist that originated it. Atlantic (which later merged with Conectiv) decided to put about half a million dollars into BLP (then HPC).

Phillips continued to collaborate with Mills, off and on, over the next fifteen years. After ten years as a professor at Penn State, he moved to Los Alamos National Lab. He knew that getting permission to work on hydrino research would take a lifetime at LANL, so he developed a relationship with the University of New Mexico (UNM) where he was appointed as a professor, and where he was allowed to work on hydrino experiments. They even gave him a lab space: a windowless room behind two locked doors. It was obvious that no one else wanted it.

He kept a low profile and didn't talk much about his work. The work was, however, very exciting. In the intervening years, both Phillips and BLP had been experimenting with hydrogen *plasma*.

Plasma is the stuff of stars: a hot, glowing, ionized gas, made up of atoms and molecules bombarded by a gas of high temperature electrons that are joining and ionizing from the atoms while emitting light. Plasmas may glow brilliantly at specific wavelengths due to their temperature and chemistry.

Phillips knew plasmas; for years he had investigated materials produced by plasma deposition. A plasma is a good way to keep hydrogen gas decomposed into individual hydrogen atoms in a broader volume than just at the surface of a filament or dissociator.

When Mills swapped out a gas-phase reaction cell for a transparent Pyrex vessel or quartz tube, you could see a plasma form in the cell. It began to glow with the emission of violet, visible ultraviolet (VUV), and extreme ultraviolet (EUV) light. Excess heat was strongly correlated with the formation and sustaining of a plasma.

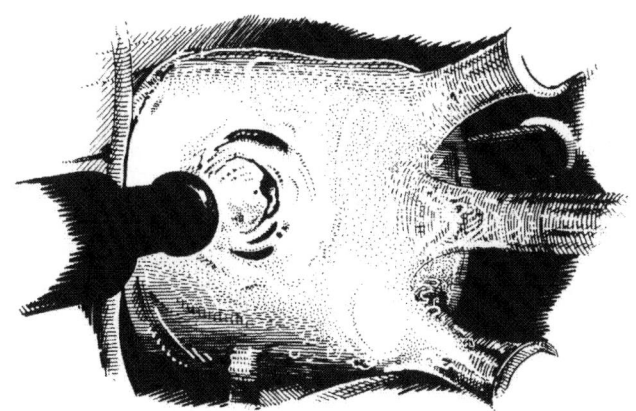

BLP PLASMA CELL

In collaboration with Mills, Phillips and his postdoctoral associate, CK Chen, ran some tests on hydrogen and hydrogen-argon plasmas. They found excess power, but too little to confidently issue a paper. Later, Chen went to work with Mills, who was jumping whole-heartedly into the field of plasma physics.

In 2000, BLP submitted a monumental paper describing a set of 138 experimental trials, demonstrating EUV light emission and excess energy from plasma cells containing hydrino catalysts (Mills 2000d). They tested different combinations of gases, filaments and dissociators.

Though Mills was refining a new, proprietary energy source, he was open about his experiments and felt that it was important to continue publishing.

To mark a new era, Mills renamed the company from HydroCatalysis Power Company to BlackLight Power, Inc. (BLP). Mills's triangular logo, dating from his first book publication in 1990, acquired a deep violet glow that emanated from the edges. And with the name change, a small percentage of all incoming calls were requests for purchasing blacklight bulbs, the kind that makes your white socks glow in a dark room.

Mills found strong emission of hydrogen in the Lyman α series for cesium metal catalyst, but not sodium metal catalyst. He found strong emission for strontium metal, but not magnesium vaporized from a foil. Mills also found strong emission when the mesh was treated with a potassium carbonate solution (in 10% hydrogen peroxide), but not sodium carbonate.

We should note that according to the theory, sodium may be a potential catalyst with an $m = 8$ to produce an H(1/9) hydrino, but plasma physics is a messy business and that reaction may not work under experimental conditions. More important is the general conclusion that the reaction taking place is chemically selective.

Overall, in this study Mills found strong emission from the catalysts given below.

$Ba(NO_3)_2$	$RbNO_3$	$NaNO_3$
K_2CO_3	$KHCO_3$	$RbCO_3$
Cs_2CO_3	$SrCO_3$	$Sr(NO_3)_2$

Catalysts found to produce very strong hydrogen Lyman alpha line emissions in a Mills hydrogen plasma cell. The cell typically used a tungsten filament with a titanium mesh dissociator soaked in the catalyst solution. The cell was typically operated at 700 °C at 300 mTorr of pressure. (Mills 2000d)

The gas-phase cell included a cylindrical titanium or nickel mesh screen, at the center of which was a tungsten coil. The screen was a dissociator, splitting hydrogen molecules into constituent atoms, while tungsten was the filament, a source of heat and electrons, both of which are required to keep the plasma going. The titanium was soaked beforehand in a solution containing a catalyst, such as potassium carbonate, resulting in a thin layer on the mesh that vaporized as the cell heated up. The cell was typically run at very low pressure, making the plasma easier to maintain. In addition to hydrogen, helium or argon could be introduced as well, which seemed to aid the reaction due to its catalytic activity, but only so long as it remained a small percentage of the overall gas mixture.

From a commercial standpoint, gas phase reactions are a better way to produce energy than electrolytic cells. There is no solvent. The reaction occurs in a volume instead of on a surface, allowing more chemical activity to occur in a smaller space with fewer costly materials.

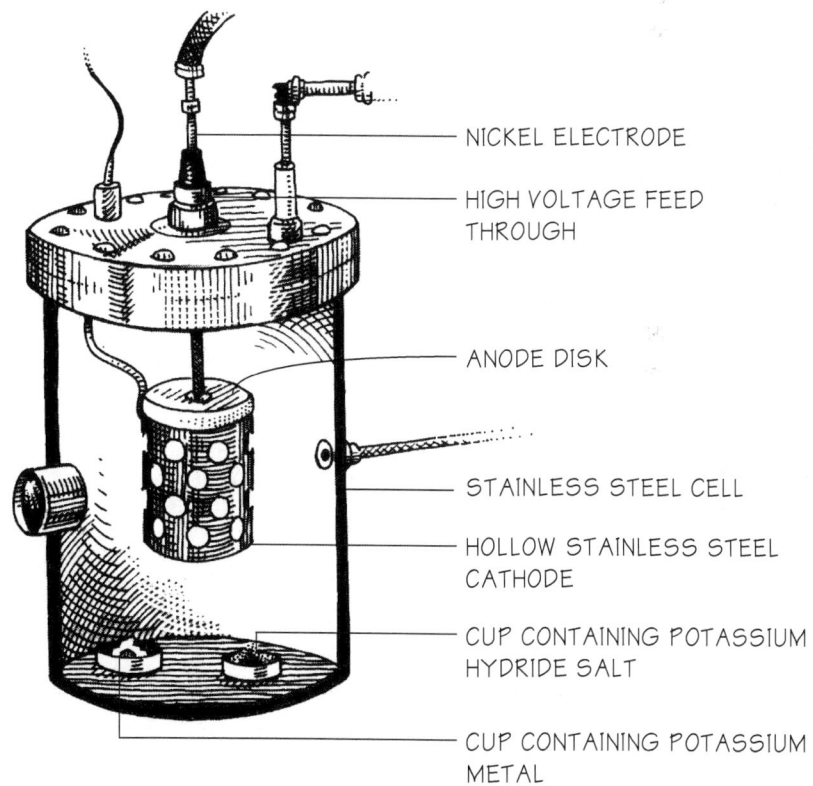

HOLLOW CATHODE DISCHARGE PLASMA CELL

Mills felt that if he was going to build a generator, it would be with gas-phase cells. By 2004, when I came to work for BLP, electrolytic cells were still running, but they were clearly a thing of the past. Only one refrigerated case of cells was left, for demonstration purposes, and it was largely ignored.

Instead, BLP was experimenting with a variety of plasma cell configurations, including those described above; water vapor plasmas in a quartz tube heated by an Evanson microwave cavity, or plasmas with internal electrodes used to generate radio-frequency capacitively coupled plasmas, or direct-current discharge plasmas.

Over the next ten years, BLP would become a publishing machine, releasing sixty papers in peer-reviewed scientific journals that described the heat, light, spectroscopy, and new compounds of the various configurations of the plasma cell, as well as commercial applications, such as heating, lighting, and lasers.

Others began to notice.

Johannes Conrads was director of the Institute for Low-Temperature Plasma Physics[51] at the Moritz Arndt University in Greifswald, Germany. He had started researching plasmas in 1959, he had taught at Princeton and consulted with NASA, and was among the most respected plasma physicists in the world.

Mills met Conrads while he was on contract in the states, and in December of 1998, he asked Conrads and his team to perform an investigation of mixed hydrogen and potassium iodide (KI) plasmas with a hollow cathode discharge. They would do several on-call experimental studies for BLP, resulting in at least two publications in 2001. Convention might have that the INP would be included as coauthors, but at this point they were merely providing contract services, and were likely cautious about becoming entangled in BLP's crusade prematurely. Instead, they were thanked in the acknowledgments (Mills 2001a, 2001b).

Conrads was intrigued by the results of his work with Mills and began his own set of experiments. He found that if the voltage applied to the cell was turned off, there was a residual glow that lasted far longer than in

---

[51] Institut fur Niedertemperature-Plasmaphysik (INP) e.V. Friedrich-Ludvwig-Jahn-Strasse, 19, 17489, Greifswald, Germany

conventional hydrogen plasmas: two full seconds, or about 10,000 times longer than the millisecond rate at which the measured electric field falls to zero. This was unique in his experience. If the electric field wasn't directly creating the plasma, something else must be going on.

The blue and white emission from Conrad's cell included Lyman α and β lines of hydrogen (very energetic excitations of about 10.2 and 12.1 eV) which were over 20 times hotter than the measured temperature of the free electrons in the plasma. He concluded that the electrons could not possibly be exciting these states in hydrogen through collision. He was left with the result that some *chemical* reaction must be occurring in the cell which itself was a source of heat and light.

Conrads knew that such high energies were possible in a variety of conditions: three body collisions only occurred at very high pressures; multiphoton absorption required gigawatts of input power; and excitations by electrons required very high electric fields.

None of these matched the conditions of the cell.

In addition, identical conditions with sodium carbonate in place of potassium carbonate produced none of this phenomena, showing chemical selection in the plasma.

In 1999, Conrads presented his findings alongside Mills at the American Chemical Society. During his presentation he said: "Something from the Mills cell is releasing energy, and remarkably high energy, that is clear." The temperature required to excite the hydrogen lines seen in the spectroscopic results was 15-20,000 ° C. It was the first time he had *ever* seen a chemical process excite the Lyman α emissions.

A true experimentalist, he stopped short of saying his work completely verified the hydrino hypothesis: "None of my experiments so far is falsifying Randy's theory, but unfortunately none of my experiments is verifying it, either."

Conrads retired from the Institute in 2000, and when he asked to be allowed to use its facilities to continue his hydrino plasma research, he was denied. Rebuffed, he found a new home at the University of Bochum to continue work, and finally copublished with Mills in 2003 (Conrads 2003).

The vocal critics of Mills claimed the hydrino could not exist because we already knew everything there is to know about hydrogen, but plasma physics was still a cutting edge science. New experiments were performed with hydrogen plasmas that had experimentalists scratching their heads. Since at least 1987—several years before BLP began playing with plasma cells—there had been reports of an unusual phenomenon.[52]

In any plasma, atoms are moving and bouncing around at high energy while they are absorbing and emitting light. This light depends on which energy level in the atom is being excited, which in turn depends on the temperature of the plasma, and the light usually falls on a specific frequency.

When atoms are at high temperature, therefore moving quickly in the plasma, these lines broaden, because they are Doppler shifted in all directions. Researchers had noticed that in pure hydrogen and mixed hydrogen plasmas, the Balmer series of lines were becoming unusually broad.

It appeared that the hydrogen in the plasma was *far more energetic* than the other gases in the cell, such as argon or helium. Hydrogen, of course, is a very light element; if it collides with a heavier atom, the hydrogen will bounce off like a ping pong ball hitting a baseball; so we expect it to be moving faster than anything else.

However, even if you take this into account by calculating the mass ratios of the atoms, it still appears that the hydrogen in the cell can be up to *ten times* hotter than anything else in the plasma.

Some experimentalists noticed this, but didn't publish the results because they had no explanation for them. Others took the data seriously and began a dialogue in the literature, seeking to explain the phenomenon within the confines of conventional theory. They hypothesized that the electric field between the electrodes was accelerating hydrogen atomic and molecular ions (such as H^+, H_2^+, and H_3^+), which were then splitting apart, imparting additional energy to free hydrogen atoms. Hydrogen was then colliding with other gases in the cell to excite the Balmer lines.

This might make sense if you point your spectrometer between the electrodes at the center of the cell, because charged species are being accelerated there. The experimentalists did this, and assumed their model was correct. They didn't see any reason to try to disprove their own model, because there was no reason to think that they were wrong. Also, in some

---

[52] See references in Phillips 2007.

conditions, hydrogen does only exhibit broadening between the electrodes. They didn't go looking for conditions in which it didn't.

But BLP discovered that you can point the spectrometer at the end of the cell, far away from the electrodes, and you could find the same broadening. If the hydrogen atoms were being accelerated by the field between the electrodes, they ought to have lost their excited temperature long before they reached the end of the cell, their excited states decaying by the time each atom moved only a fraction of a centimeter through the plasma. It also appeared that the broadening was the same from any axis one looked, which was unusual because the charged species would only be accelerated in one direction, from the anode to the cathode. When experimentalists noticed this, they hypothesized that fast hydrogen is bouncing off of the cathode in equal quantity to that being directly accelerated.

Yeah, that is a bit of a stretch.

From 2003 through 2009, Phillips and BLP conducted a series of studies of increasing scope and sophistication. They studied a wide range of gas mixtures and pressures, while taking spectroscopic data from many different places in the cell. To avoid any cathode reflection effects, they even used pin-electrodes in a DC discharge cell.

BLP produced a long list of phenomena not explainable by the field acceleration model:

- They found that the highest hydrogen temperatures in the cell were not the charged species that could be directly accelerated by the field, but neutral atoms. These were present far away from the electrodes, up to 15 cm away, and often at highest temperature at the point where hydrogen gas was being injected into the cell.
- They found fast hydrogen moved both parallel and perpendicular to the electrodes.
- They found that the gas ratio mattered, and over many studies were able to optimize the production of hot hydrogen with a mixture containing about 5% argon.
- They found that the temperature of the electrons in the plasma and the excitation temperature of the atoms were very close, both around 1 eV, showing that the rest of the plasma was at an equilibrium temperature, but the population of hydrogen atoms was twenty times hotter.
- BLP actually found *three* populations of hydrogen, one cold

population that was likely the new hydrogen entering the cell, one due to hydrogen that was at the same temperature as the other gasses, and one very hot population. BLP could even optimize the conditions until the very hot population represented 99% of all the hydrogen in the cell.

¤ They also found that by changing the gas mixtures, they could eliminate the effect. Argon was a catalyst, and the hydrogen/argon plasma was up to 150 times hotter than the same ratio in a hydrogen/xenon plasma.

This was all very weird.

The only way to explain it is if there was some kind of chemical reaction occurring in the cell. The reaction involved hydrogen, producing heat and light. But the reaction could occur even in a *pure* hydrogen plasma, which was consistent with Mills's theory: a three-body collision of hydrogen atoms can provide the energy transfer required to catalyze hydrino. Whatever the reaction was, it wasn't conventionally understood.

The light emissions from the plasma cells added another potential application to hydrino technology. Since the emissions were strongest in the ultraviolet, a hydrino plasma bulb could be an effective light source for niche markets such as scientific instrumentation. BLP found a superstar gas mixture of 77% hydrogen and 23% strontium produced a bright plasma that could be initiated at only 2 V and maintained at 0.008 W. Other plasmas with sodium, magnesium, or barium required a hundred times more initiation voltage and thousands of times more power to maintain. Adding a small amount of argon dropped the maintenance power in half (Mills 2002c, 2002d, 2003b).

The line emissions from the plasmas were also strange. Hydrogen emits light due to the electron falling from excited state orbits, and spectroscopic series can be assigned to which state the line falls to. The $n = 1$ state produces the Lyman series; the $n = 2$ state the Balmer series, and the $n = 3$ state the Paschen series. This is all well known.

Typically, for a gas at any given temperature, there will be more atoms in lower states than higher states. This is called the Boltzmann distribution, and is a result of pure thermodynamics.

However, in Mills's plasmas, something was causing the population of these states to *invert*, so that there were more hydrogen atoms in excited states than lower states, and this inversion was sustained for long periods.

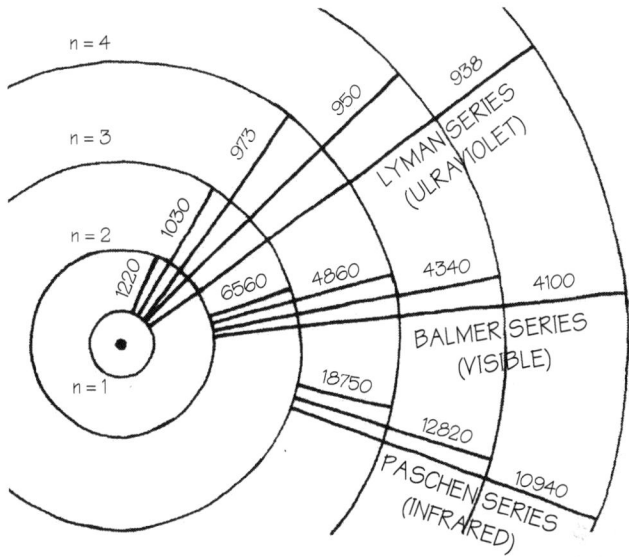

HYDROGEN EXCITED STATE TRANSITIONS (Å)

Interpreting the inverted Boltzmann distribution literally, you might think that you were looking at a *negative* temperature, though this could not be the case. The distribution was not due simply to thermodynamics, it was due to a chemical process.

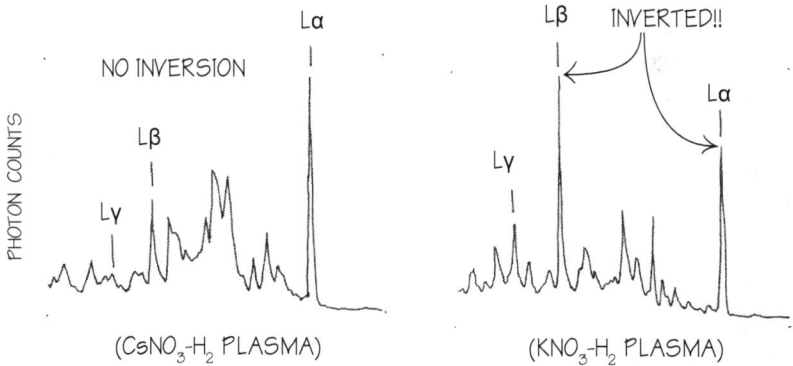

EXAMPLE SPECTRA (900-1300Å) OF CELL EMISSION FOR TWO RESONANT-TRANSFER PLASMAS. BOTH SHOW EMISSION IN THE LYMAN SERIES; THE RIGHT SPECTRA SHOWS SUSTAINED INVERSION OF THE LYMAN SERIES. AFTER (MILLS 2003).

In one study, BLP studied a water vapor plasma. Since water was easily heated with microwave radiation (the reason why microwave ovens are good at heating up food), they placed an Evanson cavity around a thin quartz tube, and a water vapor gas mixture was flowed through the tube. Water here acted as both the hydrogen source, and the catalyst. Once it got going, hydrogen and oxygen would split, and oxygen would become available as a catalyst.

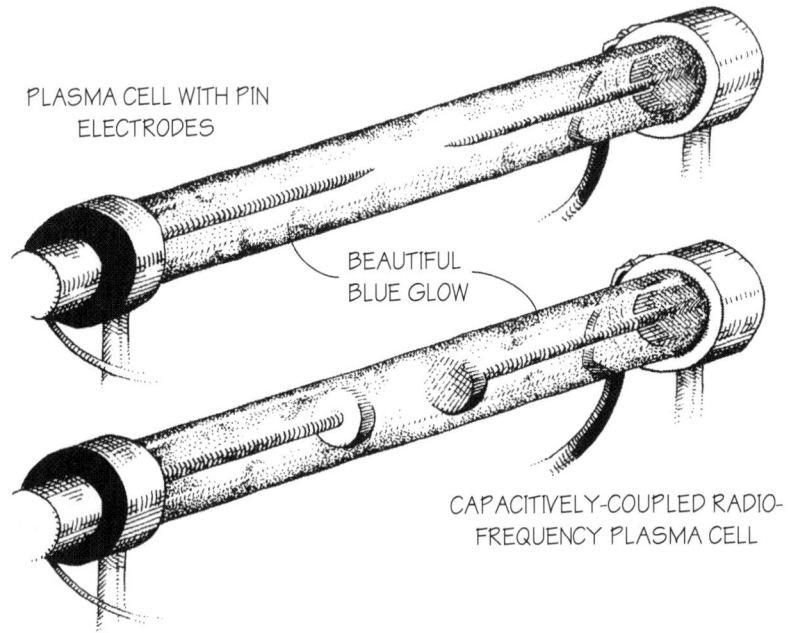

The emissions that resulted were capable of being sources for new, short wavelength lasers, from infrared to blue and even violet. Red lasers were common, but blue lasers had proven difficult to make. You have to superheat a confined plasma in order to get atoms to jump to the desired excited state energies. This was a complex and bulky technology, not suited to small applications. So BLP's plasmas could be competitive. BLP was able to make this work with KNO_3, $RbNO_3$, and $CsNO_3$ catalysts.[53]

All of this was consistent with hydrino catalysis. Hydrino atoms that formed in the plasma cell needed a way to exhaust their energy, and could do so either by emitting light, or by colliding with another atom and

---

[53] For studies on inverted populations see Mills 2003c, 2003d, 2003e.

jettisoning off the other atom in the collision, generating "fast" (or "hot") hydrogen.

Phillips felt that he had laid the issue to rest with a very robust experiment (Phillips 2007). Nevertheless, there was push back from established plasma physicists, resulting in at least two comments in the literature (Phelps 2005; Sisovic 2005).

Phelps, who had studied hydrogen plasmas since at least 1992, calculated that a 10% variability in the microwave power source could explain the effects if the device was not properly calibrated (Phelps 2005).

Phillips replied with more details of the calibration procedure and pointed out that a 10% effect would have to exhibit itself only in the Mills-type (resonant-transfer) plasmas, and not in the control plasmas, and do so every time consistently, in an almost "anthropomorphic" way. Phillips, an experienced plasma physicist, had carefully calibrated his power source to within a 1% accuracy.

Although he was already a highly cited chemical engineer, Phillips had great difficulty getting his articles published in the most relevant journals. In one case, an editor wouldn't even send his manuscript out for review because they were afraid that if the reviewers recommended publication, the journal would be embroiled in controversy.

Phillips also had trouble posting his theoretical work regarding Mills's theory on the arXiV preprint site (it was deemed "not appropriate"). But he did eventually publish a series of experimental articles in respectable journals (Phillips 2004, 2007, 2008), among them, the *Journal of Applied Physics*.

Phillips was an outside researcher with a comprehensive study that invalidated previous theories for excessive hydrogen line broadening in plasmas. It showed that conventional theory could not account for the phenomena. Everyone expected the *JAP* article to be a hit. When asked about it, James Viccaro, editor of the *JAP*, told a reporter: "the paper underwent formal review and was accepted for publication based on review. The findings are quite interesting and the reviewers found them relevant to the field. I'm actually kind of interested to see what happens now, when the news hits. ...I guess we are sticking our necks out, but I can't just reject it because I have some preconditioned thinking about it. He made it through fair and square, he answered all the questions" (Baard 2002).

Phillips had been smart to keep a low profile, but now it was blown. After publishing his paper in *JAP*, he was approached by the Dean of the College of Engineering at UNM, Joseph Cecchi, who had gotten an earful about Phillips's work from Phelps.

Cecchi asked Phillips to stop work, with the excuse being that perhaps hydrino was a pollutant, or had some other unknown biological side effects. It was clear to Phillips that he was looking for any excuse. But Phillips agreed, because he had already finished his experimental project. He had carried the research as far as he could.

With some tongue-in-cheek humor, he agreed to Cecchi's request with the comment that, "it was wonderful to meet another scientist who thinks hydrinos are real." Cecchi balked defensively in a long email. Phillips was amused.

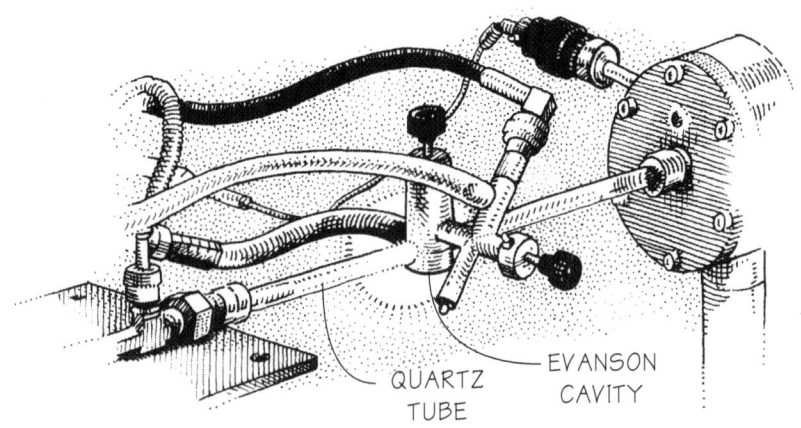

MICROWAVE PLASMA CELL

APPARATUS FOR ACHIEVING A LOW PRESSURE, WATER VAPOR PLASMA INITIATED AT ROOM TEMPERATURE. OXYGEN ACTS AS THE CATALYST. BEAUTIFUL VIOLET LIGHT EMISSION REVEALS A SUSTAINED, INVERTED BALMER SERIES.

When cold fusion hit, Peter van Noorden, a nuclear medicine physician in Rotterdam, decided to set up his own experiments to test for radiation from the Fleischmann-Pons cell.

He found none, but he did notice that the electrolyte would sometimes heat very quickly, which was strange. Perhaps *something* was going on.

After a 1997 ICCF meeting, he was finally unsatisfied with a nuclear explanation. He remembered learning of Mills's interpretation from the BBC documentary, and kept up with Mills's work for a few years, eventually questioning Mills over the phone. He asked for details of experiments, and Mills was always open and quick to respond. Mills even sent him hydride samples for van Noorden to have tested with NMR.

In 2000, van Noorden and a group of plasma physicists went to Bochum to see Conrad's cell. They were impressed, and when they returned, van Noorden scheduled an appointment with Gerrit Kroesen, a renowned plasma physicist at the Technical University at Einhoven with an expertise in low-pressure plasmas. Kroesen had a good professional opinion of Conrads and told a reporter "if he said that anomalous effects occurred, you can be sure there was no nonsense involved" (Eijk 2005).

Van Noorden suggested that they apply for a grant from the Netherlands Agency for Energy and the Environment (NOVEM), which was offering €100,000 grants for the study of new energy technologies. The grant was awarded, and Kroesen built a cell matching Conrads's setup. When they were ready to light up the cell, they invited Conrads into the lab. They gathered around, injected hydrogen into the cell and turned on the filament.

> Conrads increased the current in the coil, but nothing happened at first. He asked if we could apply more heat. Unfortunately we weren't able to. "Then we shall just have to wait," said Conrads. Then, at some point, we actually saw a bright white plasma that seemed to form by means of an unknown chemical reaction between potassium and atomic hydrogen. (Eijk 2005)

The plasma didn't form in a control run with sodium. Kroesen regularly saw plasmas formed by high electric fields produced by high voltages, but here was an experiment with only 50 V across the heating coil. "It is unlikely that the weak electric field of the heating coil was the cause of the plasma" he told a reporter (Eijk 2005). BLP was used to seeing the plasmas activate at a power level thousands of times lower than plasmas consisting of non-catalyst combinations of mixtures (Mills 2003b).

As Conrads had noticed before, Kroesen found that when they switched off the heating coil, there was a residual 1-2 second glow. This is about how long it takes for the coil to cool such that it can no longer maintain

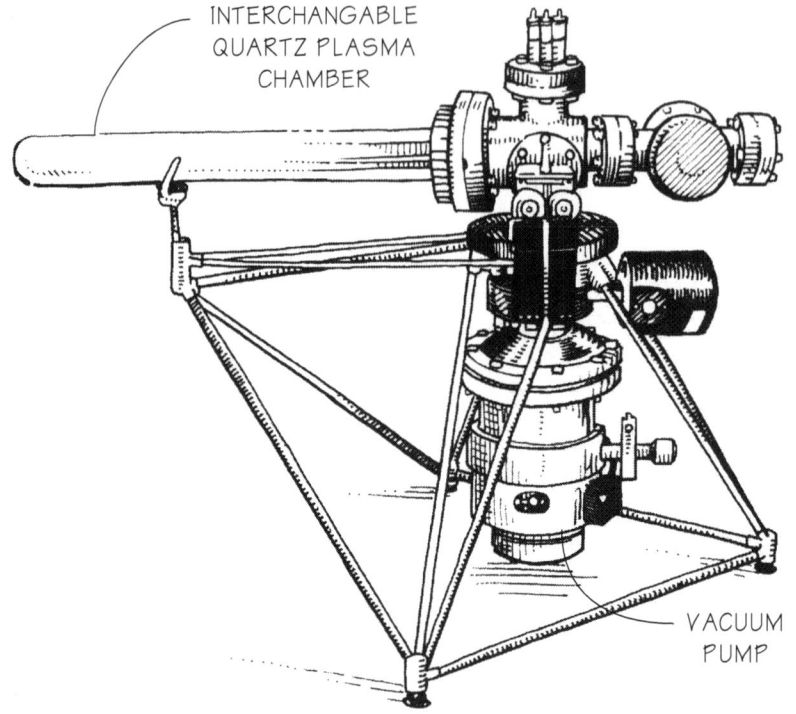

KROESEN'S TEST CELL

a population of dissociated hydrogen atoms in the cell. This indicated that the source of the plasma was chemical, not due to the electric fields.

In March of 2005, Kroesen invited Mills to speak at a convention at the Center for Plasma Physics and Radiation Technology at Lunteren. Mills presented his findings and corroborating results by Conrads and Kroesen, and was up half the night chatting with scientists and reporters about the theory.

One attendee, Wim Ubachs, a professor of spectroscopy at the Free University of Amsterdam, attended the convention to see Mills present. He told a reporter: "If we assume the spectrum isn't *faked*, it is certainly odd that spectral lines are found in the extreme ultraviolet region and that none of the elements present in the plasma are radiating at that wavelength." But Ubachs was skeptical, and expected to find some artifact of the spectrometer causing the lines (Eijk 2005).

As part of the grant, Kroesen and his team in the Applied Physics department carefully modeled the shape of the broad Balmer α emission line to ensure the broadening was due to Doppler shifting, not other artifacts such as the diffraction grating of the spectrometer. They were able to measure the temperature of the hydrogen in the plasma, confirming work by Mills and Conrads, and published in 2005 (Driessen 2005).

Like electrolytic cells, plasma cells could be fussy. In Kroesen's experiments, they were able to achieve this line broadening ten times in three separate experiments. But when the filament broke down and was replaced, it didn't work.

Van Noorden's attempts to get other theoreticians interested in Mills's work met the usual barriers. He approached Gerardus 't Hooft who had won the Nobel for his work on electroweak interactions in quantum theory. After sending him material and approaching him at a conference, 't Hooft told van Noorden "that is not how we do physics" and angrily stormed off.

Others who Van Noorden had gotten interested in hydrino research were afraid to pursue it openly lest they jeopardize their careers. The Netherlands is not a large country; 't Hooft would hear of it.

Mills's plasma cells produced heat and light beyond what could be explained with conventional chemistry; they activated at never before seen low voltages; and they emitted light in unique ways. But Mills also found that he could manufacture unusual materials.

In 2003, BLP published that it had created a hydrogenated silicon coating that they found to be 1500 times more stable to oxidation than a silicon surface treated by hydrogen fluoride, as was typically done in the silicon manufacturing industry (Mills 2003, 2004).

They also found that their microwave plasmas were vapor-depositing polycrystalline diamond films, another unexpected application of hydrino chemistry (Mills 2003g, 2004b, 2005b).

Mills may have found potential spin-offs in niche applications of lighting and lasers, silicon manufacturing and polycrystalline films, and the potential for an entire class of unexplored materials, but the millions of venture capital rolled in for one purpose: to produce *power*, a trillion-dollar annual market.

So BLP tried scaling up the plasma cells. If you could produce heat continuously, in sufficient quantities, you could power a steam cycle, just like a coal-fired power plant. The conversion efficiency was high (80%)

and could be implemented in large-scale power plants. But equipping a prototype plant was an expensive proposal for so controversial a technology.

Mills also felt that hydrino power was a better fit for a decentralized power infrastructure, and explored options that would be feasible in this model. One option was to directly convert the kinetic energy of the plasma into electrical energy with plasmadynamic conversion (PDC). In this situation, two electrodes would be immersed in the plasma, one of which is an electromagnet. The potential difference between the electrodes would generate a voltage through the plasma that extracts kinetic energy. In 2002, Bob Mayo at BLP developed a demonstration device (Mayo 2002).

Mayo built two versions: a DC discharge plasma cell, and a microwave plasma cell. The latter performed better, and Mayo was able to extract 220 mW at a conversion efficiency of about 19%. It was the first time power had *ever* been extracted from a small, chemically-assisted plasma.

BLP also experimented with a gyrotron. In this scheme, the plasma would be subjected to a magnetic field causing the electrons in the plasma to orbit along circular paths. Although the electrons may have a range of temperatures, and thus a range of velocities in the plasma, once the gyrotron gets going, a feedback loop forces each electron into an orbiting radius that allowed it to match the other electrons at a consistent angular frequency, the cyclotron frequency. As the electrons circulate, they release radiation with a highly monochromatic wavelength, which could be easily captured with an appropriate resonator (Mills 2000e).

Neither of these concepts went forward to commercialization, possibly because neither, like the Thermacore cell, could deliver the power density needed to be a robust energy source. Mills knew that hydrino catalysis could be the most powerful energy source on the planet, and he was driven not just to make something minimally adequate for a small market such as low-grade heat, but a commercial superstar.

In 2005, the hydrino officially entered science fiction fame.

In the Canadian series *Andromeda*, there was an alien crew member capable of transforming herself into a kind of miniature sun. Her name was Trance Gemini. In Season 5, the crew of the *Andromeda Ascendant* was saved from disaster by Gemini, but in the process, she scattered the crew across space and time.

Trance Gemini was found by one Captain Derrega, an executive of a local shipping fleet, who hoped to exploit her secrets.

> DARREGA: ...Ten years ago, when she was found disoriented and wandering through the forest, and we discovered her metabolism was a form of hydrino fusion, I began to have a vision. That a way could be found to harness that energy, and perhaps someday power my entire fleet.

Dillian Hunt, Captain of the *Andromeda*, who was sneaking out of sight, overheard the conversation and added, under his breath, "at *least*."

CHAPTER 8

SPHERES, ELLIPSOIDS, AND THE VOID

*In which the architecture of nature gives us
a panoply of beautiful structures.*

I was excited by my work with Mills. I was learning the theory in the proper way, by using it, while challenging myself mathematically, learning to code more complex algorithms, producing more beautiful graphics, and a few times a day I would tromp across the building to Mills's office to chat about the theory. Mills was always enthusiastic, and I was likely the only one in the office with whom he could discuss it on a daily basis.

There was years of work to catch up on; since his first slim volume in 1990, he had expanded and re-published the book several times. And I had the fortune of catching Mills in a fairly intense phase of ongoing theoretical development. He was energized to develop new solutions to old quantum mysteries, and there was much left to be done.

Mills had modeled the electron in the hydrogen atom as a thin extended membrane of moving charge, a spherical shell surrounding the nucleus that remained stable to radiation even while the currents circumnavigating the sphere were in a constant state of acceleration.

But what happens with heavier elements, with more electrons surrounding the nucleus?

The great failure of quantum theory was describing the interactions between electrons, the forces that cause them to organize themselves in the atom.

The electrons in the helium atom pair up and occupy the same orbit. Although both electrons are made up of negative charge, and therefore repel, the charge of the inner electron only partially shields that of the nucleus, so the outer electron still feels a remaining positive charge. And the electrons are attracted magnetically due to their spins, just as two loops of electricity attract one another if they are circulating in opposite directions. This attraction helps pull them together, in a single shell, one electron infinitesimally larger than the other.

In nearly a century of work, quantum theory could not solve the energy of the electron orbits of helium exactly. But Mills's equation, as we first saw in Chapter 4, was a simple force balance equation with three terms, one for the attraction between the proton and electron, one for the outward inertia of the electron's motion, and one for the diamagnetic attraction between the electron spins. Its solution matched the energy of the ground state of helium exactly (Mills 2008, 2015, Ch. 7).

Solutions flow naturally from a good theory. It also reveals old theories to be what they often are: cumbersome, inflated, and ineffective.

For example, in quantum chemistry, the extent to which an inner electron shields the charge of the nucleus on the outer electrons is called "effective nuclear charge" and determined by stand-alone rules (Slater's rules), suggested in 1930. According to these rules, electrons shield the nucleus by about 35%, unless we are talking about helium, in which case we make a special exception: 30%.

If electrons are overlapping clouds of electron density, the conceptual and mathematical complications are daunting, and we are forced to use these rules of thumb. But Mills' electron produces a physical rule that is very clean and simple. Each electron completely shields one proton for all outer electrons, and that's it. Another reason to love spherical shells.

Slater's rules have become something of a fudge factor and their values can be manipulated arbitrarily in order to get the right answers. In the realm of theoretical derivation, you ought not to take anything for granted. We want clear physical reasoning at every step of our process, not rules justified only by the results they obtain.

Mills's equation not only allowed him to calculate the ionization energy of the ground state of helium, but the excited state energies, something quantum mechanics only recently calculated with some degree of accuracy. In helium we have not one, but two electrons in the atom that can be excited to larger orbits. And like hydrogen, there are hundreds of these energies that have been measured.

In these calculations, theoreticians have always been between a rock and a hard place. If the electron was considered as a quantum object, it was a spread out region of electron density that overlapped other electrons in mysterious ways. But when it was considered classically, like a particle, physicists had to solve a *three-body* problem: two electrons plus a nucleus, all interacting with one another. Three body problems may not have a clear analytical solution. Typically you need a good computer to solve such problems in small steps. Calculate the forces, move the objects slightly, recalculate the forces, and so on. The bodies may orbit each other forever without getting back to where they started.

Mills's nested shells, however, simplified this calculation to a force equation along one dimension, along a straight line, as if we took all three particles and stuck them on a skewer, allowing them to move only inward or outward along the skewer.

Helium is a relatively uncommon element on Earth due to its lightness and tendency to diffuse out of the upper atmosphere, but it is the second most abundant element in the universe after hydrogen. This is because it is relatively easy to make in stars. Fusion can occur in a star only half the size of our Sun.

The diamagnetic force that keeps the two electrons paired is so strong that helium forms a very small electron shell, about half the size of the hydrogen atom. This strong shell means helium is unhappy about giving up an electron to form a bond with another atom, so the element is inert.

It is for this reason that helium occupies the last column of the periodic table, which it shares with neon, argon, krypton, xenon, and radon, collectively called the noble gases, all of which have a highly stable, filled outer shell of electrons.

As a result of their inertness, this was the last series of elements to be discovered, and among the most difficult to isolate. Indeed, helium, derives from *Helios* (the Sun) and was first observed in the spectrum of the Sun before it was found on Earth. (Hydrino, smaller and much more inert, has proven even more difficult!)

The next atom in the periodic table, lithium, with three protons and three electrons, has two electrons paired comfortably. The third electron forms a new, concentric shell, at a larger radius, as the other alkali metals in the periodic table. This electron is easy to strip, and in nature the alkali metals seem to prefer it gone, so that the atom becomes a positively-charged ion, which, when combined with a negatively-charged anion, is good at forming salts.

The next atom, Beryllium, adds another electron to the outer shell. The atom after, Boron, forms yet another shell, although it is not like the others: it does *not* have a uniform charge on the surface. It has regions of high and low charge density forming symmetrical patterns, called spherical harmonics. There are an unending series of harmonic modes— the simplest with two patches of vibration, the second, four patches, the next, eight, and so on—described by equations also used by quantum theory.[54]

---

[54] Spherical harmonic variations in charge density also come about in excited states.

MODULATION FUNCTIONS
(SPHERICAL HARMONICS)

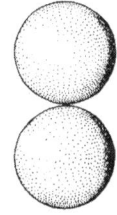 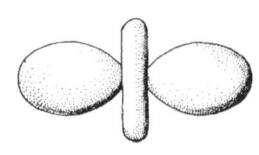 

QUANTUM THEORY: SPATIAL LOBES REPRESENT PROBABILITY OF FINDING AN ELECTON AT EACH POINT

HIGH

 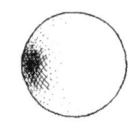 

LOW

MILLS: VARIATIONS IN CHARGE DENSITY ON THE SURFACE OF THE ORBITSPHERE

Electrons form these patterns in order to pack more electrons into a single shell that can remain closer to the nucleus. In the series of elements from boron to neon, the six electrons pair up into three pairs of conjugate spherical harmonic patterns. Each pair uses opposite patterns of high and low charge density, and each pair is oriented to each of three axes.

The shells that have only two uniform electrons and only spin-pair are called s shells; those with six electrons are p shells, and those with eight are d shells, and so on. Each shell is called an _atomic orbital_, and they form a largely predictable series throughout the periodic table.

This series is why the periodic table expands awkwardly as you go down the rows. As you get farther away from the nucleus, it becomes more favorable to pack as many electrons as you can into a single shell, so shells from higher atomic orbitals are recruited for this task. As such, the properties of the outer electron shell changes, and we need to insert large swaths of new atoms which do not have identical reactivity to those on upper rows.

The structure of atomic orbitals through the periodic table is well known from experiment. And spherical harmonics are also well known;

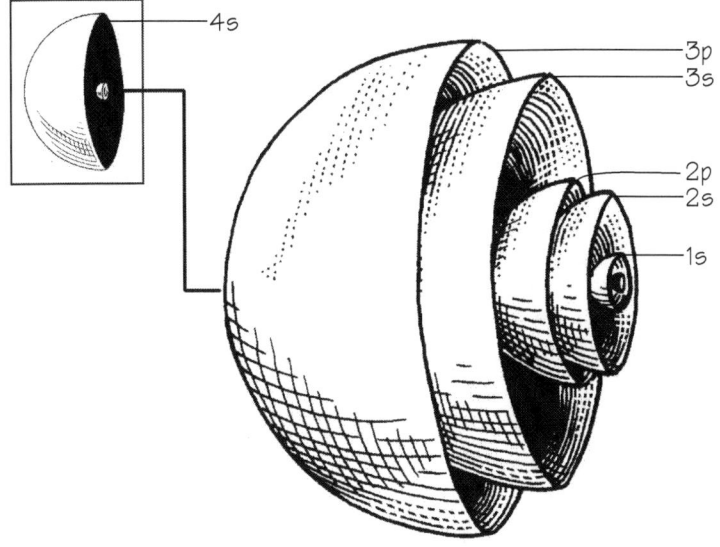

MULTI-ELECTRON ATOMS

ATOMIC ORBITAL SHELLS (s, p, d, f...) ARE CONCENTRIC ORBITSPHERES EACH HOLDING ONE OR MORE ELECTRONS. THE CHARGE DISTRIBUTION ON s-SHELLS IS UNIFORM, BUT OTHERS REQUIRE MODULATION BY SPHERICAL HARMONIC FUNCTIONS. THE RADII OF EACH SHELL IS CALCULATED FROM FORCE-BALANCE EQUATIONS.

quantum mechanics uses them to predict features of chemical reactivity. However, instead of the three-dimensional spatial patterns of probability density described by quantum mechanics, Mills's spherical harmonics are charge density variations confined to the surface of a sphere.

Another difference between quantum mechanics and Mills is that in addition to the *angular* variations in density, that change as you spin around, quantum mechanics had *radial* variations in density that changed as you go outward from the center. These radial functions do not exist in Mills's model; instead, the radius of the outer electron shell provided a discrete size to each atom.

Again, we find that Mills's theory eliminates more rules of thumb. The Pauli Exclusion Principle states that no two electrons can occupy the same atomic orbital, and the same spherical harmonic pattern, and the same spin, at the same time. Why is this? Because nature rejects it as an energetically unfavorable position.

Another, Hund's Rule, gives us the order in which the electrons will fill the different atomic orbitals. In Mills's theory, this is pure electrodynamics: electrons will always occupy the least energy configuration.

Mills raced ahead with his theory in the early nineties, solving the structure of boron, carbon, nitrogen, oxygen, fluorine, neon, sodium, magnesium, aluminum, silicon, phosphorus, sulfur, chlorine, argon, potassium, and calcium (Mills 2015, Ch. 10, 2005). He calculated the energies necessary to strip off every electron from every one of these atoms (calcium has twenty), plus cations of the rest of the atoms in the periodic table up to twenty electrons. His hundreds of solutions matched experiment to fantastic accuracy – typically five significant figures, which is within experimental uncertainty.

The only limit implicit in Mills's simple equations was the propagation of error due to our experimental measurement of the physical constants of nature. The more accurate we know the fundamental constants, the more accurate our predictions will be.

This results were so good, so perfect, that Mills was told by statisticians that they could never hope to produce so good a fit to the physical data through pure mathematical means. It was, in a manner of speaking, *statistically* indicative of truth.

I made quick work of taking Mills's solutions and arranging them into the first-ever periodic table showing the true size and structure of the atoms; a graphic that was bound to appear in chemistry textbooks for… well, for *forever*. I looked it over.

If you go down a column, the same number of electrons are in the outer shell; when you go across from right to left, the atoms get smaller because the electrons are more tightly bound, so they are more stable. Stability is a function of energy which is a function of size. And the more stable, the more likely an atom will be to fill its outer shell by *gaining* electrons from a bond, so we call these atoms more *electronegative*. The easiest atoms to steal an electron from are those that have a single electron in a large orbit by itself, like the alkali metals in column two; these are *electropositive*.

Mills's solutions, unlike quantum theory, were also compatible with special relativity. As you walk up the periodic table to higher elements, the magnetic fields of all the outer electron shells begins to squeeze the inner orbitals, which draw nearer the nucleus. As they do so, they must preserve their total angular momentum, so they spin faster. For heavy elements, the spin becomes relativistic. When corrected with relativity, Mills's solutions actually *improved* marginally.

This is all what we would expect from a good theory. Schrödinger himself expected a good theory of the atom to be compatible with relativity. He knew the Schrödinger equation was not, and he was never happy with it.

With such great success at predicting energies, why did Mills stop at calcium? After all, he was on a roll. He could have kept going through all the elements, but he had largely exhausted the supply of experimental data that our species has amassed. If he solved the 40-electron atom, he would only be able to compare his 40 ionization energies to just a few reported numbers. There is little point in rote calculation unless you have experimental data with which to compare. And he had launched so far beyond the abilities of quantum mechanics, that doing more would be the theorists' equivalent of beating a dead animal.

Mills's solutions were simple force-balance equations made up of a few terms: the attraction of the electron to the nucleus, the outward inertia of the electron's mass, the spin-pairing force, and terms describing the diamagnetic and paramagnetic forces between the electrons, by which the electron shells attract and repel one another. Seeing the patterns in these forces, Mills was even able to create a single equation for *all* the energies of the first twenty electron atoms. Theoretically Mills's equation could be--and someday will be--extended to all possible atoms.

When I began to realize Mills might be right, not just about the hydrino, but about everything, it meant his work was vastly more important than anything else happening in the world of science and technology and I was among the few people in the world who understood this.

With this realization came a pressure of opposing the majority, and the creeping doubt that perhaps I was missing something obvious, that I was the fool.

Yet the alternative described by quantum theory did not seem real to me. I believe that nature is, at its root, simple and knowable, an incredible, beautiful geometric order on all scales, what Einstein once called the "perfect structure."

At what point does a model convince us that it is physically true of the world? How many numbers must we match from experiment? How simple must it be? How clearly predictive? It seems hard to believe that there could exist a more rigorous test for a theory than that met by Mills's model. And yet, the model is almost unknown. How many people must *believe* a theory for it to be true?

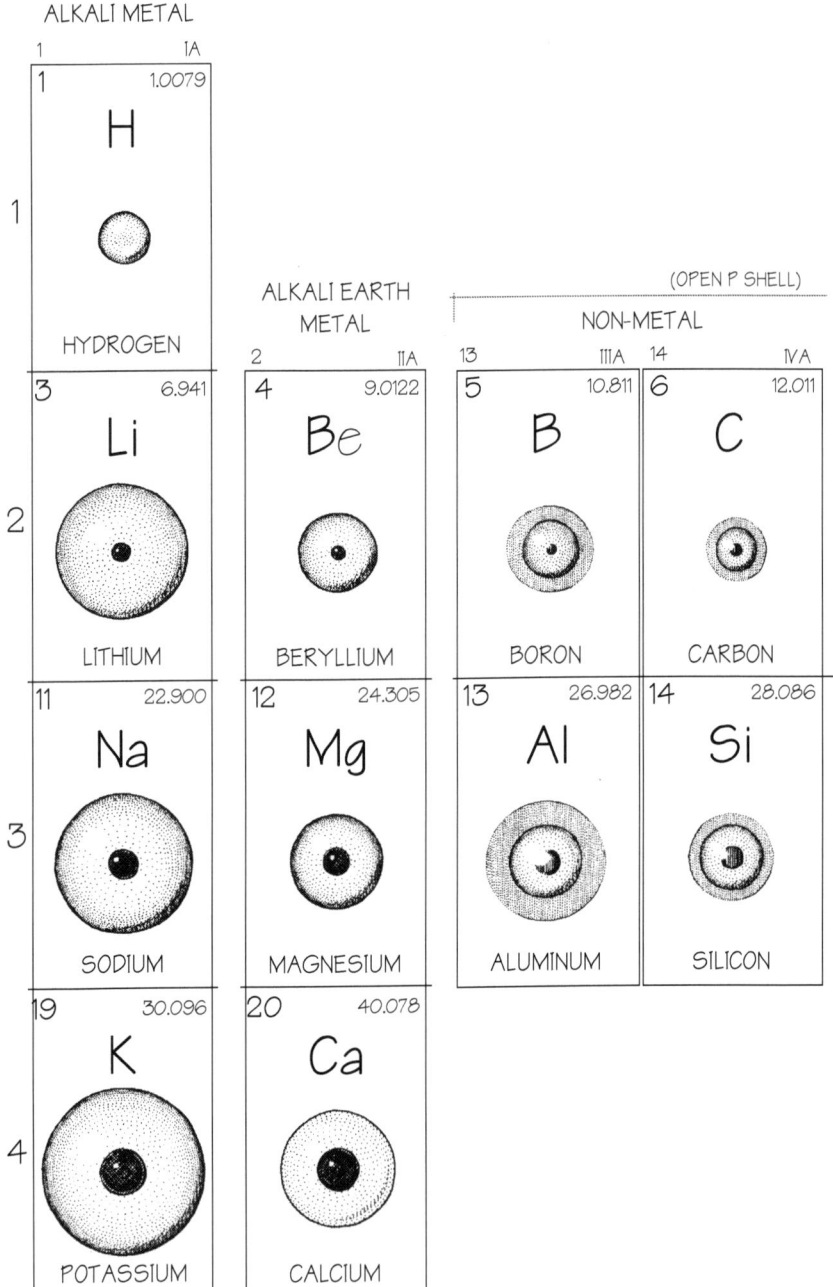

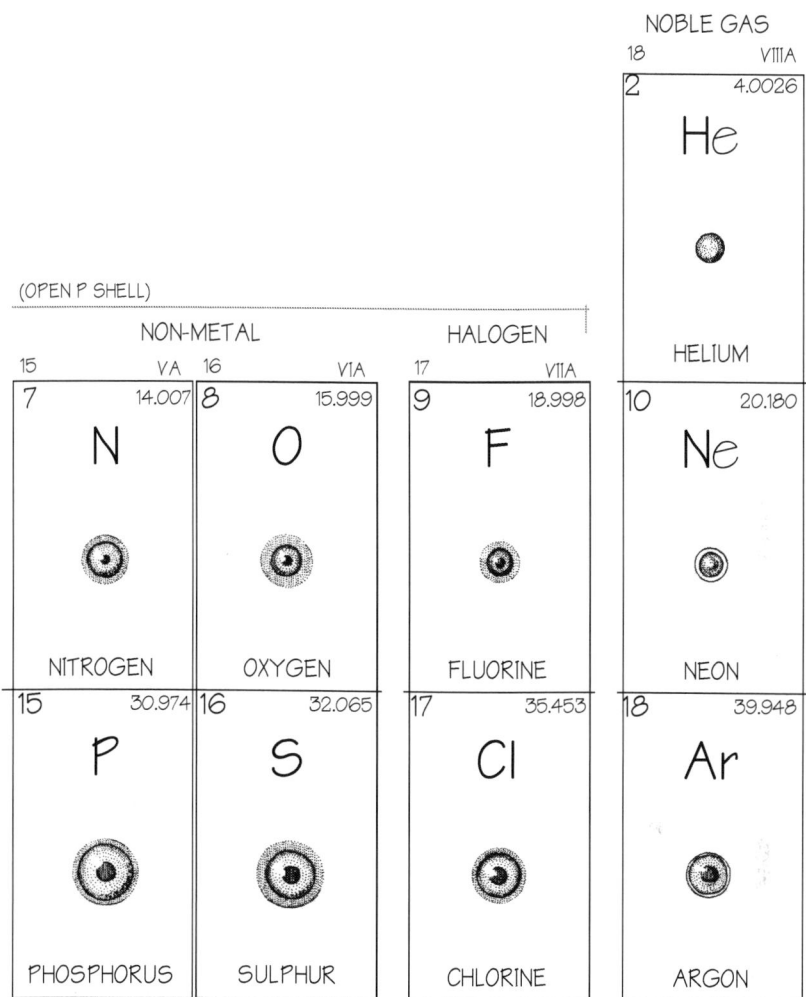

THE ARCHITECTURE OF THE ATOM

PARTIAL PERIODIC TABLE FOR THE FIRST 20 ELEMENTS. ATOMS ARE SHOWN TO SCALE, WITH ACCURATE INTERNAL STRUCTURE OF ATOMIC ORBITAL SHELLS. PREDICTED IONIZATION ENERGIES OF ALL ATOMS AND IONS MATCH EXPERIMENT TO VERY HIGH ACCURACY WITH SIMPLE FORCE-BALANCE EQUATIONS. THIS IS HOW THE WORLD IS BUILT. AFTER (MILLS 2015, CH 10).

Looking down at Mills's periodic table, these questions floated in my consciousness. But it seemed to me that the universe had answered for me. Truth is independent of our metrics; it cares not whether a civilization accepts it; truth demonstrates itself to the open mind.

In the fall of 2004, Mills was looking for something new.

His manuscript was already a thousand pages long, filled with results that quantum theory had been unable to achieve in eighty years. The ionization energies of atoms, the state lifetimes and line intensities of hydrogen, the excited states of helium, the prediction of a smorgasbord of hydrogen atom properties with a theory that was both internally consistent, and intuitively coherent. And of course, the hydrino.

Another problem Mills solved was the structure of the hydrogen (H_2) molecule. This simplest of molecules, containing two protons and two electrons, was a fairly intuitive extrapolation from the case of the atom. Just as a charged spherical shell is equivalent to a point charge at its center, a charged *prolate spheroid*, a sphere elongated about its major axis, is equivalent to two point charges, one at each focus. Unlike the case of the atom, however, the prolate spheroid has regions that are closer to the protons, and thus regions with greater congregation of charge; it is not uniform.

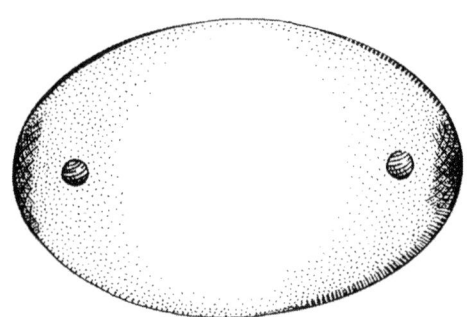

THE HYDROGEN MOLECULE (H_2)

MILLS'S THEORY DESCRIBES THE MOLECULAR BOND AS A PROLATE SPHEROIDAL SURFACE OF CHARGE COMPLETELY SURROUNDING THE NUCLEI, WHICH LAY AT THE FOCI. CHARGE ACCUMULATES NEAR THE ENDS. AFTER (MILLS 2015, CH. 11).

Mills's new model for the electron allowed him to construct a force balance equation and calculate the bond distance, energy, and vibrational constant of the molecule, something quantum mechanics had never done easily, or well. It also gave a clean explanation for bonding; the build-up of charge density on the ends brings more of the electron charge closer to the protons, reducing the total energy of the system (Mills 2015, Ch. 11;, 2004).

FORCE BALANCE EQUATIONS:

FOR THE HYDROGEN MOLECULAR ION (H_2^-)

$$\frac{\hbar^2}{m_e a^2 b^2} D = \frac{e^2}{8\pi\varepsilon_0 ab^2} D \qquad a = 2a_0$$
$$b = \sqrt{3}\, a_0$$

FOR THE HYDROGEN MOLECULE (H_2)

$$\frac{\hbar^2}{m_e a^2 b^2} D = \frac{e^2}{8\pi\varepsilon_0 ab^2} D + \frac{\hbar^2}{2 m_e a^2 b^2} D \qquad a = a_0$$
$$b = \frac{a_0}{\sqrt{2}}$$

But it was a proof of concept. What of more complex structures?

Mills embarked on a program that would, over the next several years, *double* the length of his overall manuscript.

Only a year after Schrödinger published his equation, Walter Heitler and Fritz London attempted the first quantum mechanical calculation of the hydrogen molecule. They discovered that even for this simplest of all molecules, the equation became a ten-term behemoth, as it must track the movement of the electrons, the nuclei, and the forces between them. Such an equation was impossible to solve, even after some simplifying assumptions.

But late one afternoon in 1927, Heitler awoke with a vision: "the picture before me of the two wave functions of two hydrogen molecules joined together with a plus and minus and with the exchange in it." He quickly called a friend, Fritz London, and the two developed a method for understanding bonding from the point of view of probabilities.

In statistics, two probabilities don't add, they multiply. So if we use the statistical interpretation of the wave function, there is a spike in electron density between two atoms, called the *exchange integral*.

This early calculation produced a number that was about 71% of the actual value of the hydrogen bond strength. Not great, but it was a start. The method became what we now call the *valence bond theory*. This idea did offer some useful descriptions of molecular structure. Recall that atomic orbitals may contain spherical harmonic distributions of charge density. Since an *s* orbital is spherically uniform, it will not bond as strongly as a *p* orbital which has polarized regions of charge density on either side. In a double bond, the *p* orbitals are thought to contribute, and if they do, we expect the bond to be unable to rotate, which is indeed what we see for ethene's carbon-carbon double bond, for instance. However, it isn't perfect. We might expect that bonds, following the orientation of *p* orbitals along each axis, would be 90° to one another. While this occurs for some octahedral coordination compounds, we do not see this in most of organic chemistry. Instead, they are tetrahedral.

Linus Pauling considered this dilemma and found that if you add together *s* and *p* atomic orbitals, creating a hybrid *sp* orbital, you get a good prediction of tetrahedral geometry. The probability density of the combined orbitals spikes along observed tetrahedral bond angles.

To make a molecular orbital, you combine atomic orbitals by adding instead of multiplying. Since there are a potentially infinite number of atomic orbitals for each of the two atoms involved in a bond, you choose a small set of relevant atomic orbitals that you think will play a role in the bond. This is called the *basis set*. Typically you start with the outer orbitals, and include more as needed. But how much of each atomic orbital do we incorporate in the bond? By mathematically playing with the percentage until we find the lowest-energy solution. There are qualitative rules you can learn for approximating this for small molecules, and what arises is the idea that there are bonding orbitals as well as antibonding orbitals, arrangement of possible bonds that actually weaken the bond.

To do a molecular orbital calculation for the hydrogen molecule, we start by adding together the atomic orbitals of each hydrogen atom. We start with the simplest *1s* orbital (in which the electron density is spherically symmetric) but find out that this does not give us a good answer, so we start blending it with some of the other non-symmetric atomic orbitals, and eventually arrive at an answer that is about 85% correct.

Well, we are better off than before, at least.

Now, we need to distort the electron density further by taking into account how one of the electrons is distorted by the presence of the other electron, and the other nucleus. These calculations are enormously complex: a 13-term equation was used by Rosen to achieve 99.4% accuracy, and in 1960 a 50-term equation was used to match experiments to multiple significant figures. In all, it took 34 years of work for a community of quantum theorists to produce an accurate calculation for the *simplest molecule* in nature.

With this kind of complexity inherent in even the simplest calculations, getting good numbers for very complex structures was, at least until recently, at a computational impasse.

Suppose we go about it differently. Take the experimental bond energies of fifty molecules, and fine-tune our basis set to predict them correctly. Then, use these results to predict other, similar molecules. This technique is called semi-empirical because it relies on knowing the answers to many similar problems in order to predict the answer to any one problem. And 'predict' ought to be in scare quotes here. After all, by relying so heavily on experimental data we are not making first-principles predictions, directly from theory.

If the physical meaning of a theory is in limbo, the calculations don't really lend support to the theory. Imagine we were to theorize that electrons are really very small wizards engaged in very small battles. As the wizards cast spells on one another they inadvertently lock themselves into perpetual death grips (chemical bonds), freed only when they come near enough to other wizards that can release them. All chemical bonding, perhaps, is due to this aggravated community of microwizards.

Semi-empirical predictions do not constitute a validation of quantum theory, because there is no step in the process that validates the theory itself. Any theory with enough parameters to map onto trends we see in experimental data is sufficient to make predictions.

But semi-empirical techniques are not completely useless. If you want to make a guess at the heat of formation of an unknown molecule, looking at many other molecules and incorporating the experimental data for structure and energies will allow you to do so.

However, this will in no way constitute a defense of your theory, even if through the agonizing process of recursive manipulations of many variables you get, in fact, a perfect guess.

AN ALTERNATE INTERPRETATION FOR THE SUCCESS OF THE SEMI-EMPIRICAL TECHNIQUES OF QUANTUM CHEMISTRY.

In 1960, the US federal government established the Aerospace Corp, a research and development laboratory with the goal of providing support primarily to the Department of Defense. Within the Industries division, a fair amount of basic research was done, justified by a vague relationship to national security.

On contract to Aerospace was Sid Benson, a professor who went back and forth between the University of California and Stanford Research Lab. Sid was a friendly and gentlemanly man who loved coming up with short rules for chemical properties and reaction kinetics. He was interested in anything that would fit on the back of an envelope, and was considered by his peers and graduate students as something of a walking handbook of thermochemical data.

Sid was not interested in the *ab initio*[55] methods of quantum chemistry. They were too cumbersome, and computers at the time were too slow to provide theoretical bond energies more accurate than about 1 kC/mol, which made a difference in many applications. In collaboration with a

---

[55] "From the beginning" or from theoretical principles.

graduate student, Jerry Bus, Sid had developed a frightfully simple method of calculating the bond strengths of molecules: pure addition.

The strength of any bond in a molecule will vary depending on which two kinds of atoms are bonded, and what configuration those two atoms are in. We refer to this configuration as a *functional group*: a piece of a molecule consisting of an atom at the center along with its attached bond types and terminal ligands.

Take, for instance, a bond between two carbons atoms. Each carbon is a different group; the carbon could include only hydrogens (a methyl group), or a double bond to an oxygen plus another hydrogen (an aldehyde group), or to another carbon and two hydrogens (an alkane group). Each of these configurations influences how the two carbons in question interact, and the strength of their bond.

Benson was looking for a quick way of estimating heats of formation (the energy needed to make a molecule from its constituent pieces). Bonds between atom types vary widely depending on context, so the next best solution would be to look for patterns in the bonds between functional groups. By surveying heats of formation for thousands of molecules, he was able to systematically distill the energy associated with each bond between functional group types. What he found was pretty reliable numbers that can be used to easily predict most organic compounds.

In short, by cutting the umbilical cord that connected the empirical techniques to quantum theory, he was able to get a highly predictive scheme (Benson 1958). This result was later updated and expanded in collaboration with Norm Cohen, a chemist also on contract to Aerospace (Cohen 1993).

Benson's scheme had the advantage of being computationally simple, indeed, accessible even to a second grader. The total bond dissociation energies of a molecule that has never been experimentally studied can be found by adding up the energies of each of its bonds, extracted from a table. It is at least as effective, and often more so, than the most accurate techniques available to a quantum theorist.

This group additivity method is empirical, and it isn't trying to say anything about nature. It doesn't care about theories. It works, and that is what is most useful to chemists.

The fact *that* it works probably means something.

Bonds, it seems, are oblivious to what is happening beyond one or maybe two atoms away. If electrons were fuzzy spread out regions of probability density stretching across a molecule, like a fog clinging to a stream bed, we ought to see the larger structure having more of an effect on the smaller structures. But instead, electrons seem highly localized to specific places, and can be assembled into larger structures like building blocks.

Perhaps the world of the quantum is much less complex than we were led to believe.

MILLS'S THEORY DESCRIBES THE MOLECULAR BOND AS A PROLATE SPHEROIDAL SURFACE OF CHARGE COMPLETELY SURROUNDING THE NUCLEI, WHICH LAY AT THE FOCI. CHARGE ACCUMULATES NEAR THE ENDS, AFTER (MILLS 2015, CH. 11).

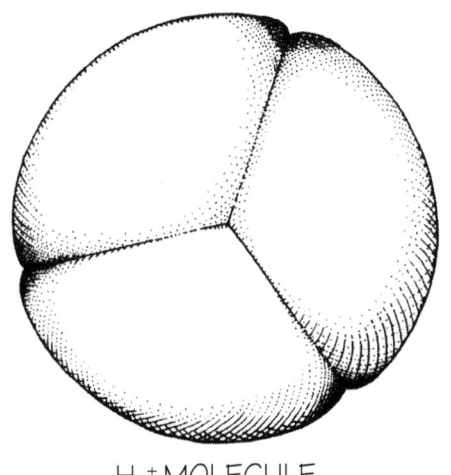

H_3^+ MOLECULE

H_3^+ IS COMPOSED OF THREE INTERSECTING PROLATE SPHEROIDAL SHELLS. AFTER (MILLS 2015, CH. 13)

Mills's solution to the hydrogen molecule was simple: the force balance equation had three terms, and it matched experiment to very high accuracy. It allowed Mills to calculate the bond energy, bond length, and rotational and vibrational constants.

The leap from the Mills's atomic theory to the foundation of his molecular theory was straightforward, and immediately successful.

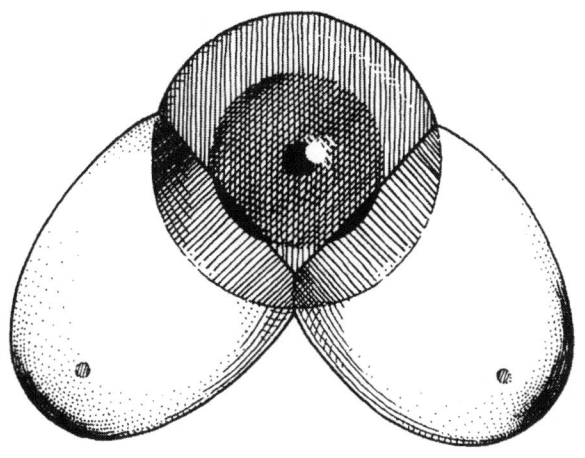

WATER (H$_2$O)

THE PROLATE-SPHEROIDAL HYDROGEN BONDS TERMINATE AT THE SURFACE OF THE OXYGEN ATOMIC ORBITAL SHELL. AFTER (MILLS 2015, CH. 13).

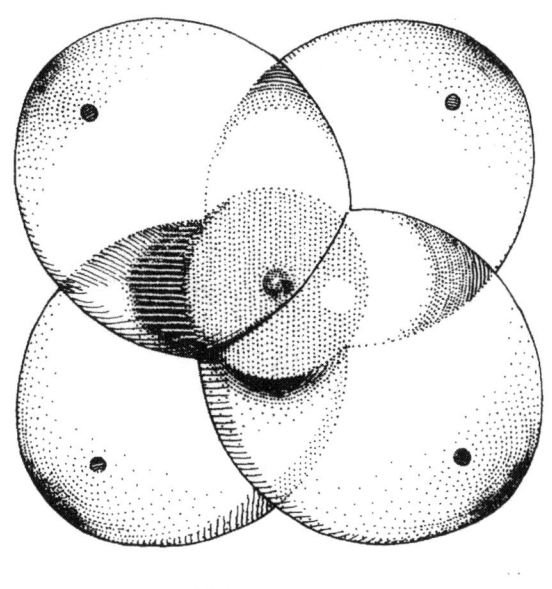

METHANE (CH$_4$)

When Mills started working on more complex molecules, he was excited to be leaping into the unknown. We began gathering data on the next simplest molecule, H_3^+, a structure in which two electrons connected three hydrogen atoms in a triangle. As Mills thought about it, he juggled (as always) his time between theoretical work and managing experimental work in the lab. Some days later he dropped the solution to H_3^+ on my desk.

The result was a literal extension of the H_2 solution: each pair of hydrogen atoms were joined by a prolate spheroidal bond, with nuclei at the foci. Since they were rigid surfaces of charge, they could not pass through one another, but instead bridged between one another, forming a single shell (Mills 2015, Ch. 13).

A week or two later, Mills solved the OH molecule and the water molecule, H_2O. Mills found that the molecular orbtal shells attached to the outside of the atomic orbital shell, and the bond's charge density spread over the spherical outer surface. The inner atomic orbitals of oxygen were much smaller than the outer bond and did not participate in bonding. But the outermost two shells—the *2s* shell and *2p* shell—did something unusual. Under the influence of the bonds, they merged to the same radius, essentially combining. They became what Linus Pauling described as a hybrid orbital, with a charge distribution that was a percentage of each atomic orbital, validating Pauling's calculation decades before. Since a build-up of charge density on the atomic orbital repelled the bond, the geometry of the water molecule came out with a slightly non-ideal tetrahedral geometry at 105 degrees.

Mills continued, marching forward through more complicated molecules such as NH, NH_2, NH_3 (ammonia), CH, CH_2, CH_3, CH_4 (methane), and so on. By the end of the year, he had solutions for dozens of small molecules, and his calculations continued to yield excellent results, for bond distances, energies, and angles. He had clearly found a winning strategy (Mills 2015, Ch. 13).

An important part of this process was finding good experimental data with which to compare numbers. Our calculations produced numbers with very high precision, typically five decimal places, and we needed the best data with which to compare.

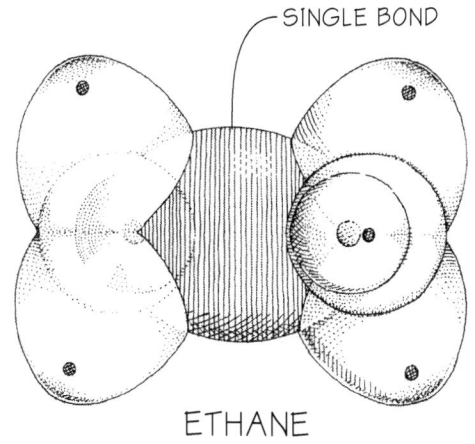

ETHANE

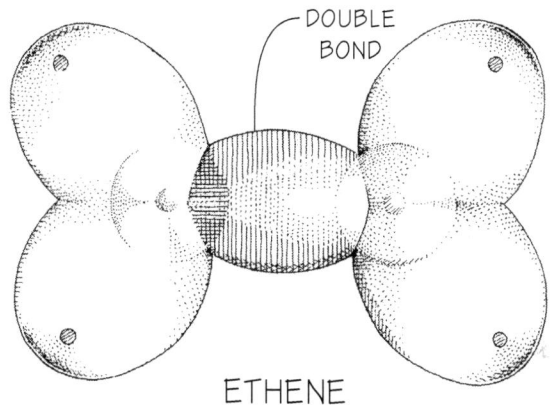

ETHENE

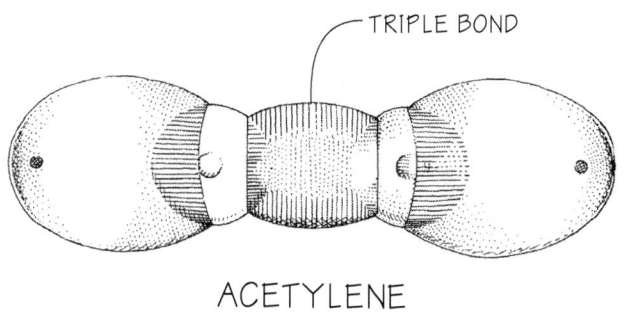

ACETYLENE

Typically, a scientist will rely on *The Handbook of Chemistry and Physics*, a giant tome that lists a wide array of experimental data. But I quickly learned to distrust data obtained there because it was often long out-of-date. I specifically recall one case in which the number had been averaged from two divergent experimental numbers from the 1940s. There had been no attempt by the publisher to update it or point out that it was a poor guess.

Textbooks, in fact, rarely cite their sources for experimental data, a practice that seems to have resulted in common misconceptions over the true values of some parameters. In our hunt for the best data, we began to dig up the latest experimental papers, eventually hundreds of them, compiling our own reference guide of thermochemical data. As a result of our efforts, I would trust the numbers cited in Mills book over any other reference.

Next came larger molecules, such as chains of carbon atoms (alkanes, alkenes, alkynes). It was at this point that Mills quickly realized that the bond strength and distance was influenced almost exclusively by the two functional groups joined by the bond (Mills 2015, Ch. 14).

For instance, the total bond energy of a fifty-carbon chain was the standard carbon-carbon bond times forty-eight, plus two carbon-methyl bonds. Mills could easily write down an equation for alkane chains of unbounded length.

This principle held true as he solved more kinds of molecules. Soon, Cohen and Benson's group additivity theory came to our awareness. Perhaps electrons are *not* delocalized throughout a molecule, but localized to individual bonds. There were exceptions to this rule: occasionally bonds would interact beyond one or two functional groups away, such as in the case of conjugated bonds or aromatic bonds, but these cases could be uniquely described.

Mills found that two fundamental equations could describe almost any functional group; one gave the energy, and one gave the geometry, and with them he was able to describe any situation. As the new molecule solutions poured in, I built models of each for illustrative purposes. This work slowly eclipsed my laboratory work; I was working with Mills full time.

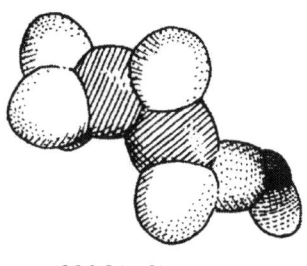

PROPANOL

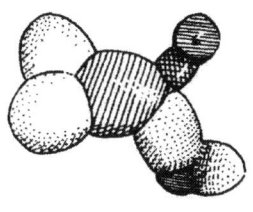

ACETIC ACID

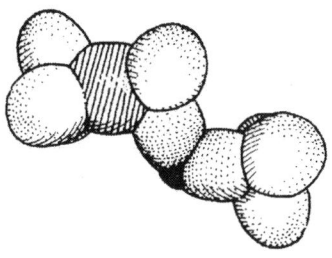

ETHYL METHYL ETHER

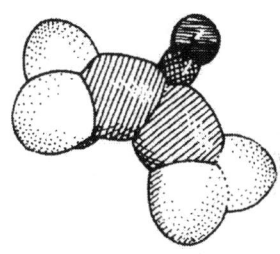

ACETONE

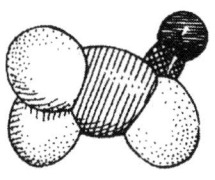

ACETALDEHYDE

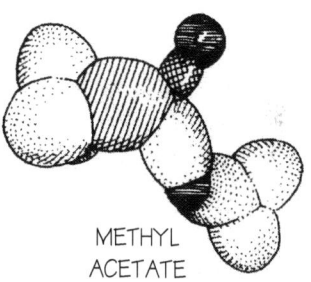

METHYL ACETATE

EXAMPLES OF ORGANIC MOLECULES

IN MILLS'S THEORY, FUNCTIONAL GROUPS ARE SEMI-INDEPENDENT UNITS, FROM WHICH MOLECULES OF ARBITRARY SIZE AND COMPLEXITY MAY BE COMPUTED EASILY.

My three-month internship had become a year, then eighteen months. In addition to atomic and molecular visualizations, Mills asked me to model lattice structures, metals, superconductors, and create animated visualizations of hydrino catalysis and new reactor concepts. These visuals appeared in scientific papers, articles, bounced around in the blogosphere, and even the news press.

I animated flying into a potassium atom as if on board Carl Sagan's *Ship of the Imagination*. I showed how electrons ionized, their behavior in magnetic fields, in molecular reactions, and absorbing and emitting light. The mathematical workbook used to aid in this work became three hundred pages. Additionally, in my free time I worked through Mills's atomic solutions to understand their logic, and experimented with new electron current patterns.

But I could wait no longer to return to school without having to reapply for admission. So I promised to continue working remotely and returned to the West Coast. My relationship with BLP continued, I would wake up for early calls from the East Coast, stagger out of bed in my pajamas, and slump into my desk chair. Working from home was peaceful and productive, and after a few hours of work I would shower and set off for class.

The molecules Mills was solving became larger and more complex, and although I quickly learned how to handle the geometry of intersecting prolate spheroids, it made sense to take the next step. One morning Mills called; he wanted to build a molecular modeling program to utilize his growing database of solutions.

So Mills started a subsidiary company, Millsian Inc., to carry out the project. Overseen by Bill Good, we started hiring programmers in Portland, Oregon and in New Jersey.

At first our goal was simply to visualize molecular structures, and we started from scratch with no knowledge of how to make a molecular modeling program; drawing the geometry of the spheroids from the parameters of the bonds according to Mills's theory. It would be a beta, a proof of concept.

Later, with the aid of Wangshen Xie and Amit Makwana, we rewrote the program with a sophisticated internal data structure. With this under-the-hood work we were able to solve complex problems, such as contorting the molecule into its most natural state (its lowest-energy conformation), fusing multiple rings that shared atoms, color-coding the surface of the molecule to show precisely the amount of charge at every point, and calculating dipole moments.

I remember plowing through organic chemistry as a student, trying to keep track of a steadily expanding vocabulary of structures and functional groups. But it wasn't until I went through the long process of manually constructing the geometry of hundreds of compounds that I began to get an intuitive sense for them.

Later, as the software began to take shape and was doing more of the work autonomously, we would struggle to keep up with the larger, more complex molecules that Mills was solving, calling on his database of functional group solutions.

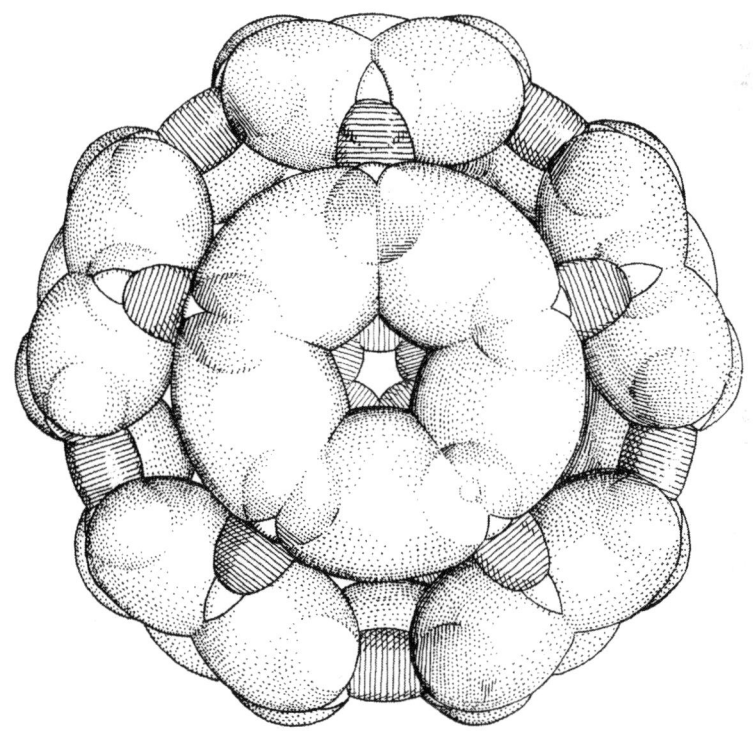

CARBON FULLERENE (C_{60})

COMPOSED OF 60 CARBON ATOMS JOINED BY 5 AND 6-MEMBERED FUSED RINGS. AFTER (MILS 2015, CH 17).

Among the most interesting structures was the C_{60} fullerene, a sphere made of carbon atoms, the structure consisting of alternating five- and six-membered rings. It is the same pattern as that found on the shell of a turtle; its subtle curvature is allowed by the angles of the connection points. In our illustration, the width of the bonds clearly show where the single and double bonds are located in the structure.

One morning, I began forcing the new fledgling software to construct the phosphate backbones of the DNA molecule. It took perhaps two days of work, a task that now takes the software microseconds; my efforts were the modern equivalent of those poor souls who once wrote code in assembly language. But I came away from it with an intimate knowledge and memory of the structure and geometry.

The phosphate strands, joined by a ladder of base pairs, spiral around one another in a double-helix. Seeing the structure visualized with Mills's theory was not just a milestone for our software, a satisfying culmination of a year of development work, but an extraordinary experience of beauty.

The strands seemed to be dancers, spinning, their energy and momentum thrusting them outward, a free arm flying through the air, the other locked with that of their partner.

Yes, I think I fell in love with the DNA molecule in that moment. Nature, in all her indifference to human life, is beautiful; in the abstract form of her physical architecture we find reflections of our own memory and experience.

Practically speaking, the ability to represent the exact distribution of charge on the surface of the molecule is a *huge* leap forward from the approximations of quantum mechanics that are available in today's molecular modeling software.

Mills's theory should allow us to better predict chemical reactivity, and better predict how proteins fold. It should aid drug-discovery programs aiming to find molecules that fit reactive sites. These are improvements that I expect will allow great leaps in the pharmaceutical industry in years to come. Large biomolecules such as proteins and DNA pose less of a computing burden if you know exactly how their charge is distributed, if we know what they are, down to the last electron.

Life, down to the last electron.

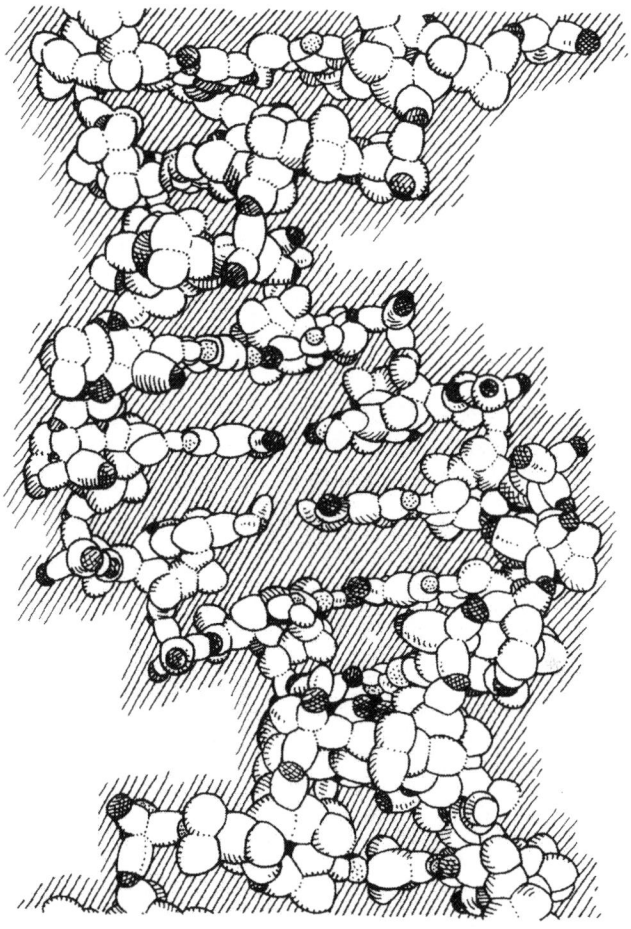

LIFE: DOWN TO THE LAST ELECTRON

DNA SHOWN USING MILLSIAN SOFTWARE. THE EXACT LOCATION OF EVERY ELECTRON IS KNOWN - AS WELL AS THE EXACT CHARGE DISTRIBUTION PROFILE ACROSS EVERY BOND!

There is a view held by some philosophers that we can explain the nature of a complex organism only by narrowing our focus to its biochemical activity, this is called *reductionism*. But I think the problem is more complex; living beings exist in a complex environment, often a social one, and there are behaviors that some call *emergent* properties of a being: those that can only be understood as a kind of collection action of an organism or group.

But biochemical activity is what allows an organism to exist. Each molecule performs a task, and each one is itself animated by the collective behavior of the functional groups within it. These, in turn, are made of interlocking ellipsoidal membranes of charge, able to interact and exchange electrons. It is a purely physical process, but an animate one as well, determined by electrodynamic laws. And these laws that guide our most basic nature allow the encoding and transmission of information on a biological scale, allowing cells to be aware of their environment, the first step towards consciousness. Now that we understand the rules, we can trace their effects upward through the chains of complexity and causality that give rise to life and intelligence.

If we were to trace our lineage back through the ages, over billions of years, we would likely find a single kind of life from which all of life on Earth evolved. But if we were to go back further, tracing the evolution of that first microbe, we would find more remote ancestors: those replicating molecular strands, perhaps cousins of RNA, wrapped in a fatty bubble adrift in the early ocean. They were structures with no purpose, no awareness; they replicated only because that was the consequence of their existence.

We are all children of the Earth; more deeply, we are children of physics. Before we had the will to live, physics gave us the means.

Mills's foray into molecular physics had expanded his already large manuscript by another thousand pages, and his solutions covered the broad spectrum of molecules, including organics and organometallics, coordinate compounds, the allotropes of carbon (graphite, diamond, and fullerenes), compounds of silicon, aluminum, tin, and boron, ionic bonding, covalent bonding, and the bonding that occurs in metals, semiconductors, and superconductors.

He was a machine, a force of nature in himself, believing perhaps that he could overwhelm the scientific community by brute productivity. Or maybe he was just having too much fun to stop.

Two particular publications came from the project. In one, we compared our numbers against Hartree-Fock theory (ignoring more advanced computations such as electron correlation). We found that the quantum method, which was output from standard modeling programs, gave horrible numbers, with errors often in the tens of percent, whereas our numbers rarely matched less accurately than a tenth of a percent (Mills 2010, 2011). The evidence that Mills had hit upon the correct theory was as overwhelming for molecules as it was for atoms.

There came a day, when I was working on complex polycyclic aromatic compounds, that I was unable to find data on their energies and geometry. Mills had, again, exhausted the experimental data that mankind had amassed (now for molecules instead of atoms) and the process came to an end. All told, Mills had confirmed his functional group solutions with over eight hundred molecules, spanning all classes of compounds.

He had once again left quantum mechanics in the dust.

In my experience, the fear of opposing the majority was only a minor note within the excitement, a desire to know more, to be a part of the change. I would leave the library and go for a walk, up through the access stair to the roof of the physics building to lay prostrate in the middle of the day. If I got involved early, would it make a career, a financial future, a life?

I enjoyed my time with Mills, but already my thoughts were searching. I had a strong will to invent, to create, to be my own entrepreneur. I believed in my work with Mills, yet I filled my free time with an eclectic range of personal creative projects, from coding algorithms to writing fiction. I experimented with my own interests and abilities. And I rediscovered my interest in architecture, my imagination freshly fueled by the beauty of nature's geometry.

In fact, while in high school, I had also been accepted by the Philadelphia School of Architecture. Perhaps it was no mistake that in my work with Mills I had gravitated to visualizing and communicating complex structures.

I began to ask myself: what if we could use the beauty of nature, its simplicity and engineering purity, to build cathedrals for man? I imagined a roof of thin ellipsoidal shells floating above a hypostyle hall, the joints punctuated by arcs of light.

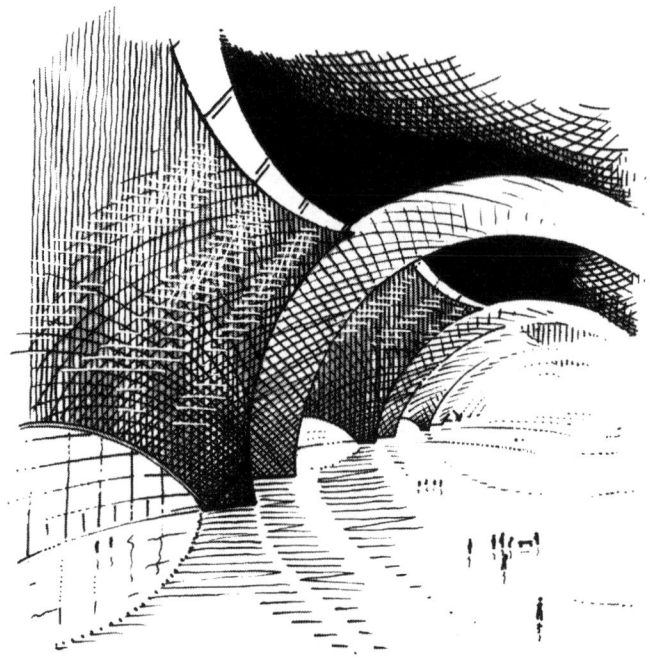

THE CATHEDRAL OF THE ATOM

I wrapped up my degree at Reed, and again leapt into the unknown, on a career trajectory that no one understood, least of all myself, and to what end I couldn't tell.

While in graduate school for architecture, I continued to work with Mills remotely. By the time I graduated, the Millsian project—now online with a few hundred beta users—had achieved a proof of concept, but was going back into dormancy. The funds that supported the project would need to be renewed, some of the employees were moving on, and Mills himself had put blinders on; he felt that he was closer than ever to a commercially feasible reactor.

Meanwhile, the scientific world seemed no more interested in his upheaval of quantum chemistry than it had in his upheaval of quantum physics. The project, ripe for a major sale to a molecular modeling or pharmaceutical giant, would become another important invention languishing on the back burner as the search for hydrino energy went on.

CHAPTER 9

SOUTH OF THE SOUTH POLE

In which the APS spokesperson makes some blog posts; and the United States Patent Office trips over itself.

Robert Park was a tenured professor of physics at the University of Maryland who spent the latter part of his career as something of a guardian angel of American science. As the director of public information for the American Physical Society in Washington, DC, he spoke out against junk science in all its forms, both in congressional hearings and in books, condemning everything from homeopathic remedies to crank inventors with modern perpetual-motion machines.

Perhaps no one had so thoroughly characterized the mind of the modern junk scientist as Park. His book *From Foolishness to Fraud* reported on the behavior and personalities of its subjects, whose synthesis of charisma, showmanship, and religious fervor often sold the promise of infinite energy sources to unsophisticated laymen (Park 2000).

One of Park's favorite subjects was a man named Joe Newman, a charismatic, self-educated "inventor" who developed a motor that, he claimed, converted the mass-energy of a copper coil into useful power. Having gathered a large crowd at the Superdome, Newman demonstrated by driving a Newman-engine powered car around the stage to the loud cheers of his psychologically captive audience. He even wrote a book in defense of his ideas.

Park had long known about Mills; as early as the 26th of April in 1991, days after Mills's first press conference, Park made fun of the announcement in his online column "What's New." When Park glanced at Mills, he assumed he was seeing another poor soul captivated by cold fusion.

Ten years later, in the midst of Park's discussions of Newman and other cranks, Park devoted a small, three-page segment of his book to Randell Mills, in what became the single most damning quote on Mills in the scientific community. In it we find this:

> Scientists reacted to Mills's claim exactly as they had to Joe Newman's–they ignored it. In the first place, there was really nothing to react to. His "theory" reminded me of my thesis advisor's comment when I referred to

my first scientific paper as a "theory." "It's a theory," he said gently, "to the extent that it was done with a pencil." Nor had Mills offered any experimental evidence for his claim. (Park 2000)

Park had made his career on persecuting junk science, and to do so he extended a healthy effort: he attended paranormal conferences; he traveled across the country to attend parking-lot presentations by crank inventors peddling their products; he waited around for hours in the hot sun to be herded into tents to hear speeches and claims of psychic powers; he went all the way, and his portraits of junk scientists are compelling.

But Park didn't exert himself in Mills's case. By 2000, Mills had published several papers offering experimental evidence for the hydrino.[56] To acknowledge this research complicates the situation considerably: something that might call into question the history of negative remarks Park had made on Mills's work in his blog.

Mills was a complicated case, and it was possible that to Park, the most effective way to treat Mills was to do so *casually*. After all, Park had learned that if a reputable scientist takes up the project of rigorously refuting a case of junk science, it (ironically) often gives a sense of *validity* to the junk scientist. When Newman's engine was being debunked by a commission from the patent office, Newman was happy to tell the press. So Park must step very carefully around subjects such as Mills. Give Mills too much attention, and the press would take notice. Completely ignore him, on the other hand, and the press might think they were discovering an unknown genius.

The trick was to drop your subject into conversation once or twice, nonchalantly, with a slight chuckle. Wave off the so-called 'science' as childish nonsense. After all, fraudsters are common. Crack a joke ("Honey, I shrunk the hydrogen atom!") and you have achieved the desired effect: you scared off the press and biased anyone newly approaching your subject *without actually accusing him or her of anything*. An accusation, after all, is a noose. It opens you up to the need to be rigorous and thorough.

Mills was running a business funded with tens of millions in venture capital, and he was not afraid of protecting his interests through litigation. Park would need to come clean and run a disconfirming study of his own. That would take effort, and funding, and if the unthinkable happened—if the results came back positive—you would have to be ready to deal with

---

[56] Including Mills 1991, 1993, and 1995.

that. Better to avoid the risk. Park was sure Mills was wrong, or wanted Mills to be wrong, or both.

Peter Zimmerman, an adviser to the US Defense department and a friend of Park's, appeared on the Hydrino Study Group online forum, almost daily, for years. There he maintained a constant presence of skepticism. Like Bob Park, he had the knack of writing off Mills's theoretical arguments as being full of childish mistakes. He criticized but never attempted to replicate experimental data. I often wondered what could possibly motivate his activity there.

While still a PhD student, Zimmerman's thesis adviser, a Nobel Laureate, was bombarded with letters from the public proposing discoveries claiming to overthrow modern dogma. He made these a challenge for his graduate students to debunk on a monthly basis, and Zimmerman had gotten hooked on the exercise. Mills was especially gifted at Fourier math, which gave Zimmerman no end of grief to follow. Another challenge.

The Hydrino Study Group had been mentioned in the press as a forum for scientists to discuss Mills's work, and I felt that the result of the activity of Zimmerman, and others like him, was to dissuade new visitors to the forum from taking Mills seriously. This may not have been intentional. Insinuation and satire can be more effective than accusation. One 1999 blog post, which had a very high online search ranking for a decade, was in fact a satire about "doofusino" theory.

Soon after Park's *Voodoo Science* was released, Mills disclosed his plasma cell and became a publishing machine. As Mills's research partners and scientific publications spiked, the best strategy of critics was *not* to pose a direct confrontation.

Mills was getting collaborators to confirm the unusual characteristics of his plasma cells, and the patent disputes made something of a story.

In 1999, Eric Baard published a series of articles for *The Village Voice*, quoting supporters and detractors. Reading these articles, you could believe that Mills was a fearless visionary confident enough to go against mainstream science. Although the articles got a lot of people interested, they also made public off-the-cuff critical remarks by Nobel Laureates, and in the end, sparked as much criticism as support.[57]

When the opinions of Michio Kaku, Philip Anderson, Paul Grant of EPRI, and Bob Park became public, BLP's board became concerned and asked the company lawyers to issue letters requesting that they stop making defamatory comments in the press about BLP.

Park, of course, handed a copy to the American Physical Society and the story ran in *Nature* (Reichhardt 2000).

The threat of legal action is intimidating. Fighting a libel charge can be expensive in court. BLP attorney Michael O'Hayre told a reporter "we're not interested in stifling any free and open debate," but the letters could be perceived as challenging free speech and victimizing physicists.

Although Park lied about Mills's experimental work in his book, he did acknowledge when pressed by *Nature*, "the issue is not whether their stuff is out there for review. The issue is whether anybody believes it, and whether people who don't believe it have a right to say they don't believe it" (Reichhardt 2000).

Park was now the public victim of BLP's censorship, instead of visa-versa. In my opinion, the maneuver was a net loss to BLP's reputation. A lesson to step lightly at the fault line between business and science.

A new scientific theory ought to be engaged by the scientific community. Experiments by many parties should confirm or disconfirm predictions, as a pathway to acceptance or rejection of the theory. There must be intellectual engagement.

Park's efforts helped accomplish one thing: to ostracize Mills from the scientific community without opening the floor to debate.

The patent office is not the ideal forum for the judgment of scientific truth. But it does have a reputation to maintain; a reputation to pass patents that demonstrate legitimate technologies. Mills's ability to patent his work prior to it being accepted as legitimate by the scientific community would, predictably, set off warning bells.

After the successful granting of BLP's first patent, the next was due

---

[57] Baard, reflecting on his reporting of Mills, revealed to me that he had once been ordered by an editor to remove an expert source who was positive toward Mills, and replace with a source who was negative. When he refused, the article was taken out of his hands. This was unique in all of Baard's publishing career.

to issue as patent number 6,030,601 on February 29th, 2000. But on February 17th, Jeff Melcher received a notice informing him that the patent application was being withdrawn from issue to allow the reopening of prosecution, as requested by the Director of the Special Program Law Office, signed by Frances Hicks (Hicks 2000).

When Melcher inquired, he was instructed to speak with Esther Kepplinger, who told Melcher that Mills's technology was based on cold fusion and perpetual motion; and that if they had allowed the patent to proceed, it would have incited (as Melcher recalled) a "firestorm."

A firestorm from whom? Kepplinger would not say; it appeared to Melcher that she was implying there was some kind of warning from an outside source that there would be some commotion if the patent proceeded.

Kepplinger did say that the patent had come to her attention by Gregory Ahronian—an outsider of the patent office known for his public attacks on US patents—although she later refused to confirm this fact; instead she insisted that it didn't really matter how the patent came to her attention, and that she was never pressured to deny the patent (Simenauer 2000).

Melcher knew that if an outside source was aware of Mills's patent application, it was unusual and probably illegal. Outsiders were not supposed to be aware of applications in progress.

In June of the prior year, there had been a memorandum issued by the office instructing examiners not to answer questions about applications to the press (USPTO 1999). But from the sounds of it, someone at the office had received a call from someone with clout.

It was odd that the rejections of Mills's patents were not authored by either of his examiners, Stephen Kalafut or Wayne Langel. It was also odd that the justifications for the rejection were somewhat vague. After Kepplinger's initial citing of "cold fusion" and "perpetual motion," on March 22, 2000, a statement was issued that the patent was withdrawn due to "violation with the laws of chemistry and physics." And still later, it was cited that the patent was not specifically in compliance with the Schrödinger Equation (Melcher 2001).

A good way to annoy a lawyer is to swamp them with a plethora of moderately synonymous justifications.

Kalafut and Langel told Melcher that the rejections were drafted by an undisclosed committee of examiners and directors, established to conduct a behind-the-scenes prosecution of the case. They suggested that this group consisted of Vasudevan Jagannathan, a physicist, as well as (individuals for whom I have last names only) Tsang, Massie, Griffin, and director Jacqueline Stone.

When Kalafut and Langel had asked Jagannathan about the spectroscopic data showing evidence in favor of hydrinos, he is reported to have dismissed it as "a bunch of squiggly lines," revealing that he may not have had the background necessary to interpret the chemical spectra (Brewer 2001).

BLP filed a suit in the US District Court. A judge ordered the patent office not to make any decision on the case until the trial in June. Meanwhile, the patent office rejected two other applications: Mills's artificial intelligence patent, which was handed to a new reviewer (after a year of work) and quickly rejected, and another on a hydrino power plant (Baard 2000).

Mills was attempting to patent technology that he had conceived but not yet invented, and the office may have been correct to dismiss this kind of patent. But the patent office didn't have a specific or consistent justification for the eleventh-hour withdrawal.

Keven Baer, the official council of the office, tried to make the case that Kalafut and Langel were simply swamped and didn't have time to properly review the patent, or that they had been pressured to approve it and let it out the door. Baer also suggested that Mills did not have the credentials to make the discovery he did; a somewhat amusing turn of logic. And to make matters worse, the patent office claimed it had "lost" the file when they ruled on the application: something almost unheard of (Baard 2000).

In a discussion of the rationale for preventing a false patent, Baer explained that if a bad patent were allowed, it could prohibit someone else from patenting the discovery claimed by the bad patent. This particular point by Baer can be understood in the context of patent law: if someone successfully patented a technology (for example, that cures cancer) but never had a clear demonstration of the technology, then when someone eventually does come along with something that actually cures cancer, it could technically be prohibited by the prior patent.

But Baer's remark would play on any inventor's fears. Was someone else trying to patent hydrino technology? Mills, perhaps overly paranoid, thought so.

Langel eventually asked his group director, Jacqueline Stone, if he— as the examiner—had the authority to grant Mills's patents. Stone said no, and instructed him, against common practice, that he must get the approval of his superiors.

So Langel went to his supervisor, Stanley Silverman. Silverman was clear in his position, without even looking at the data, that "allowance is not an option." Silverman even suggested that Langel make it look like he was in favor of full rejection. But Langel, instead of going through with the charade, removed himself from the case. Unfortunately, this meant that the assignment needed to go to a new examiner.

Silverman later reformulated this encounter by saying he took Langel off the case because Langel didn't have the technical expertise to review the patent.[58]

With the changing justifications and obfuscations, and the lack of a clear authority or decision maker, Melcher and fellow attorney Jeff Simenauer wanted answers. They formally requested a full written disclosure of the personnel involved in preparing the rejections. It was more than wanting to lay blame; they effectively could not proceed until they knew *who* they were required to address to continue the process.

But the PTO was silent. Mills told a reporter "We intend to fight this all the way to the Supreme Court and enlist whatever resources it takes in Congress and industry to rightfully win this" (Baard 2000). Indeed, after several months of silence, BLP enlisted the help of five current and former US Senators to write letters on their behalf. Among these were Ron Wyden, Max Cleland, Jon Corzine, and Robert Torricelli. They also tried to reach Donald Evans, Secretary of the US Department of Commerce, and Johnnie Frazier, the Office of Inspector General (Allen 2003a, 2003b).

But the patent office refused to give out information, citing that the case was currently in litigation and therefore confidential. Later, when pressed, the PTO insisted that the individuals responsible for the rejection were not "germane" to the litigation.

On February 21, 2003, Oregon Congressman David Wu sent his Senior Legislative Assistant, Ted Liu, to the patent office to attend a meeting. Wu was no doubt informed by his constituents at PacifiCorp, who had invested in Mills. There, Douglas McGinty, the PTO Quality Assurance Specialist, stated that the examiners on record indeed had full authority to review BLP's scientific data and issue patents as appropriate.

---

[58] It made me wonder, if this were true, why was Langel put on the case to begin with?

He said there had been no secret committee working behind the scenes. Langel was actually in attendance at this meeting, and he said if that was the case, he would issue the patents on the spot (Allen 2003).

During the investigation, Melcher found an online blurb for a speaking engagement posted by Peter Zimmerman (Zimmerman 2000). In it, Zimmerman mentions that his department and the patent office "have fought back with success" against claims such as hydrinos.

When Melcher and Simenauer tried to contact the State Department, they were directed to a Mr. Thessin, who, after insisting that the matter was closed, agreed that they could go ahead and contact Zimmerman. Melcher immediately did so, but *during* the conversation Zimmerman received an email from Thessin advising him *not* to answer questions regarding the case. However, the email came too late, and Zimmerman had already spilled the beans.

Zimmerman insisted that he, and the State Department, in fact had nothing to do with Mills's case, but that he had learned about the patent battle from a friend, Robert Park.

Park had told Zimmerman that he had a contact in the patent office, a person who he didn't name, using the pseudonym "Deep Throat." Apparently, Park had given his contact a call to sound an alarm on Mills's patent. It may not have been a threatening call, it may not have been an illegal call, but Park was bound to know someone in the PTO.

Indeed, Park even gloated about this publicly in his online column. On September 5, 2002, Robert Park boasted:

> Prompted by an outside inquiry (who would do such a thing?) the patent director became concerned that this hydrino stuff required the orbital electron to behave 'contrary to the known laws of physics and chemistry. (Park 2002)

By 2004, after repeated attempts to get information, there was no reaction to BLP or any of the inquiries by the five US Senators.

BLP formally filed suit against James Rogan, the Director of the PTO. In the process of the suit, the court admitted that *no one involved in the withdrawal had actually reviewed the patent* (BLPvRogan 2002).

Nevertheless, the court decided that the withdrawal was reasonable, and a last-chance procedural measure to observe the PTO's mandate to issue viable patents. Kepplinger acted under the belief that the application "had not been adequately examined" and this was part of the director's rights and responsibilities.

BLP filed an appeal, but the decision was confirmed.

A patent is not a scientifically meaningful object. And yet, the PTO does have a responsibility to issue viable patents, and it ought to give individual examiners proper support and oversight, especially when dealing with difficult or potentially controversial cases.

This case raises some important questions.

- Why was an outside source *needed* to alert Director Kepplinger that the PTO was about to issue a controversial patent?
- Why were the examiners on the case not made part of the upper-level decision making process, utilizing their years of work?
- Why all the secrecy?

In 2006, a memorandum was leaked from the PTO that described something called the "Special Application Warning System," (SAWS), a program within the PTO meant to flag patents that have a subject matter of special interest. Among them: perpetual motion machines, antigravity devices, room-temperature superconductors, faster-than-light signals, or other potential violations of physical laws; anything that might generate extensive publicity, or that contains objectionable or derogatory subject matter, or that might cause environmental or personal harm, or compromises national security.

Until the 2006 leak, even experienced patent lawyers had never heard of the SAWS designation. Then, in 2014, a Freedom of Information Act Request released 43 pages consisting of memorandums outlining what ideas were subject to the SAWS (Siehndel 2014). The list was long, including additional topics such as HIV vaccines, human cloning, stem cell research, anti-aging cures, engineered microorganisms, intelligence enhancers, anti-global warming devices, nanotechnology, and so on. Among them the topic: "Cold Fusion, 'hydrino' reaction, or magnecule as an energy source or any other production of excess heat outside known chemistry or physics" (Siehndel 2014).

Once a SAWS patent had been identified, a panel convened to scrutinize it. The patent could only be issued after the SAWS designation was been removed.

If the SAWS program was in effect in 2000, it is possible that Mills's patents were, at the last minute, found to be subject to a SAWS designation, and the obfuscation was to keep SAWS under wraps.

It is also possible that this program didn't exist at the time, and it was just the blundering of the PTO's handling of the case. Maybe SAWS *was* the office's response to the hydrino saga.

In any case we ought to ask: why all the secrecy surrounding SAWS?

I am not arguing here that Mills's subsequent patents should have been issued. I think the patent office must be careful when dealing with new technologies based on new science.

However, the patent battle was a microcosm of Mills's reception by the wider scientific community. His work was rejected because of ignorance and insinuation, as well as the inability to be open to the possibility that he was right.

Park spoke of how the path from foolishness to fraud is thin: that by the time you discover your own foolishness, you are too entrenched in your position, psychologically and otherwise, to back out from clear evidence to the contrary. As Mills and his team of scientists at BLP were publishing their one hundredth journal article; as independent groups in America and Europe were successfully validating Mills's experiments; as important predictions of Mills's theory were confirmed by outside scientists, Park kept the story simple: "they have nothing to sell but bullshit" (Park 2008).

In the fifteenth century, the philosopher Francis Bacon had an idea. It was a new, cutting edge, even disruptive concept. He envisioned centers of learning in which individuals were dedicated to the pursuit of scientific understanding on a full-time basis; they gathered, shared knowledge, even peer-reviewed one another's discoveries, which were disseminated among the community in the form of letters.

The scientific community has evolved to become a world-wide bustle of activity by researchers in universities, institutes, and industrial labs, conducting conferences, peer-reviewing publications in the form of articles and textbooks; issuing grants, fellowships, and scholarships to develop new talent. But perhaps uniquely with regard to Mills's work, the scientific community has not performed one of the functions it was responsible to provide: to vet new ideas, to conclusively confirm or disconfirm new evidence in a timely manner to allow scientific and technological growth.

Due to this, individuals who were not equipped to deal with the scope of Mills's ideas or evidence have repeatedly been tasked with determining, almost autonomously, whether Mills was right, in the context of a decision that had a large impact on how Mills's ideas were perceived by the scientific community.

I believe that only when the normal mechanisms of scientific communities *fail do their job* do these kinds of situations occur.

In 2008, BLP submitted two patents to the UK Patent Office, one describing BLP's plasma reactors, and another describing hydrino lighting and laser technology.[59]

Deputy Director P. Marchant was tasked with determining whether the patents complied with patent law. Section 1(1)(c) required an invention to "be capable of industrial application" and Section 14(3) required that the inventor "disclose the invention in a manner which is clear enough and complete enough for the invention to be performed by a person skilled in the art."[60]

The original examiners of the applications had decided that the hydrino was unknown to science and therefore (implicitly) did not exist. Since the invention relied on the hydrino, the invention was obviously not capable of industrial application because it wouldn't work.

If you are thinking that this was something of a roundabout justification, I agree, but there was no explicit clause in the patent law of the US, UK or EPO that dealt specifically with questions of scientific fact, even though Mills's inventions relied on such questions.

Marchant reasoned that a new theory proposed by an applicant need not be accepted as true by the scientific community. Yet, it was important to not grant frivolous patents. So he proposed a slightly less demanding requirement: "I will therefore make the assessment on the basis that it should be more probable than not that the theory is true if I am to allow the applications to proceed."

Mills had submitted 114 papers for Marchant's analysis, but he did not have the background necessary to study them. Of the 114 papers, 79 of these had Mills as a principal or coauthor, so Marchant threw these out.

Of the remaining 37 remaining papers, Marchant then threw out those which included commentaries or declarations from scientists regarding

---

[59] Applications GB0521120 and GB0608130.
[60] See Marchant 2008a, 2008b, 2009.

theoretical calculations or experimental results that were in some way solicited by BLP.

The remaining 15 papers were by authors other than Mills, largely from the early or mid-1990s regarding first generation electrolytic and Calvet cells. Many of these were produced under contract to BLP, or by groups in financial connection to the research. These groups included Rowan University, Keith Keefer, Philips and Kurtz from Penn State, Chalk River Labs, Thermacore, Westinghouse, Moscow Power Engineering Institute, and Idaho National Engineering Laboratory. Further, noticing that the authors of these experimental papers generally abstained from making theoretical claims, Marchant was not convinced that they were evidence for Mills's theory.

So, setting aside the actual science, Marchant had to place his trust in the general opinion of the scientific community. When a new idea is proposed, one likely to be true but one that has not yet been accepted by the community, what would we expect to see?

Marchant reasoned that we should see evidence for traction: we might see lots of academic papers by various researchers on hydrinos; conferences fully or partially dedicated to hydrinos; scientists working in various countries; original contributions by independent groups; evidence of incorporation of hydrinos into mainstream theories; more serious reporting by the press; and discussions in textbooks and popular science books.

While Mills made inroads into many of those categories, the sum total was not, in the eyes of Marchant, significant when compared to the sheer scope of Mills's proposal.

> One would expect that activity be in proportion to the importance of the new theory. The present theory threatens to overturn substantially the whole basis of our current understanding of fundamental physics and it would consequently be expected to create a huge amount of speculation and work of this sort if it had any degree of credibility. (Marchant 2008)

In short: if Mills's work is not a modest advance, but a great leap, why haven't we all heard about it before? The assumption is: if something *is* great, we will all hear about it *very soon*.

This was my view of the world at the age of eighteen, when I walked into Wheeler's office. My belief, deeply but naively held, was that the community of scientists could recognize something potentially game-changing, be inspired by it, throw down their current projects and ferociously pursue it, like a swarm of bees descending on a threat, with the goal to confirm or disconfirm it.

This is, in fact, what happened with the announcement of cold fusion. Within months, experiments had debunked the claim all over the country.

But this poisoned the well. When Mills went public, only a small trickle of activity occurred on the sidelines, by scientists who were intrigued enough to pursue the research even at the potential cost of their careers. When they found confirming results, they were afraid to publish, their academic journals were afraid to publish, the author's institution was afraid to be listed alongside their authors, and when they finally were published, they were ignored.

When these scientists collaborated with BLP, their results were believed to be tainted by business interests. When they funded their experiments with BLP's venture capital, they were guilty by association. When they went on record in defense of certain experimental results or theoretical calculations, it didn't matter.

Ironically, only in the closed doors of conference rooms, in which investors put their own money on the line, was the experimental data the focus.

Marchant correctly concluded that there was substantially no acceptance of Mills's theory, that scientists considered it implausible, and that Mills's work had never gotten "off the starting blocks for inclusion among the group of such theories which might eventually turn out to be valid." He decided that it was likely that Mills's theory would not turn out to be true, and rejected the application.

In 2011, Michael Rimmer reviewed the series of decisions made in BLP's patent cases in the US, UK, and European Patent Office (Rimmer 2011). He argued that patent examiners must be "vigilant and skeptical" and careful to weed out applications like BLP's.

Like the others, he is a lawyer, unable to read a scientific paper, so assumed that BLP's work was perpetual motion, and even fraudulent. Rimmer missed the real issue that underlay the problem: how should patent-granting institutions treat new technologies that are based on new science?

Until there is a *scientific* process, not simply a judicial one, the next great discovery may face similar barriers.

The patent dispute shows us what happens when the system breaks down, and we give decision-making power over the truth of a new scientific theory to an individual, or to a very small group who are not equipped to accept the responsibility.

Wikipedia is another example. I deeply support a free and open forum for the sharing of knowledge, functioning on the same principle as that of the wider scientific community: knowledge by consensus, the truth of the many. But in cases of polarized controversy, we still have some work to do.

I first began to edit the Wikipedia article on BLP in 2001 by adding summaries of Mills's theories and experimental work. The online encyclopedia was still new, and the article was sparse. But over time, conflict swelled. It changed focus, it changed categories ("Physics" "Pseudoscience" "Protoscience" or "Fringe Theories") and sometimes the article would just disappear for months.

Every article on the Wikipedia has a "talk" page where editors discuss the material. Here the battle commenced between believers and skeptics; the talk page could have filled a book all on its own, but it was clear the skeptics maintained control, allowing the article to become, essentially, a BLP negative publicity ad.

I occasionally made attempts to seed the article into a more encyclopedic structure. I didn't want to see it become laudatory, nor did I want it to rely on the off-hand remarks quoted in the *Village Voice* over genuine scientific data. But my attempts were in vain; my contributions dissolved into the ether, cut and pasted and editorialized.

By 2008, any edits that were not clearly critical of BLP, regardless of their factual content, would be reverted within minutes of posting, usually by one of only a few editors.

Welcome, I thought to myself, *to the age of crowd-sourced knowledge.*

Some years later, I made a renewed attempt. I focused my efforts on the goal of offering one crucial fact that could drastically alter the perception of Mills in the article (and thus, in the wider scientific community). The crucial fact? That Mills and his team had published *over a hundred* experimental papers in peer-reviewed scientific journals. After all, the question: "Is it published?" is the first question we ask of any scientific proposal. This is not a value judgment of any kind, it is simply a fact, but with huge implications: Mills was pursuing traditional outlets for his research, and on an ambitious scale, with papers spread over two dozen well-read journals. It would also beg the question in the article: was anyone responding to his actual *research*, or were they responding only to what had been said about Mills in the popular press?

Wikipedia seeks to be a tertiary source, which means that it cites secondary sources, which in turn discuss original source material (papers, technical reports, and so on). Direct citation of any original works by any Wikipedia article is frowned on, and any conclusions made in the article from primary sources is considered original research, not appropriate on the Wikipedia. However, in the lack of good quality secondary sources, primary sources may be used with caution.

Scientific journal articles are considered the most reliable of Wikipedia sources, and a primary source may be used to make "straightforward, descriptive statements of fact" that can be verified by anyone without specialized knowledge.

Jimmy Wales, founder of Wikipedia, was asked about his encyclopedia's stance on neutrality. He seemed to appreciate the problem, and said:

> It isn't appropri ate for us to try to determine whether someone's novel theory of physics is valid, we aren't really equipped to do that. But what we *can* do is check whether or not it actually has been published in reputable journals or by reputable publishers. 2016 (Wales)

Despite my attempts, and the apparent intent of the founder of the Wikipedia, I could not get even a single sentence inserted into the article mentioning the existence of BLP's publications, even after I forced the issue with a 90-item linked list on the talk page that allowed quick access to the scientific papers. Ironically, my attempts caused a notice to appear at the top of the article warning readers that the article may be *biased* because it was being edited by someone who was suspected of being closely associated with the topic.

Aware of the issues that controversial topics produce, the Wikipedia created a process for arbitrating disputes that allows multiple tiers of appeals to a kind of Wikipedia Supreme Court. This process begins with a significant minority voicing a complaint, yet imposes barriers that bias the process from the start. Anyone closely associated with a topic (which sometimes translates to: anyone who might know something about it) is asked not to participate in editing, and anyone who gathers other editors to the article to mount a minority opinion is engaging in "collusion."

In short, I could get into arbitration if I started a conspiracy.

Wikipedia is obviously aware of the problem that controversial topics pose. BLP may be unique in this category because it is controversial but little understood; it is a topic with a bad reputation in the popular press, but a strong presence in the scientific literature. The article became a genuine reflection of how BLP is perceived in the wider scientific community. But to accept this as the purpose of an encyclopedia is a sad statement on how our society perceives objective truth. The Wikipedia has become such a strong engine of disseminating ideas that controversial ideas must be treated more carefully, for the article will immediately begin to influence the perception of the topic[61].

Good policies are in place; they need only be followed. Wikipedia asks its editors to strive in good faith to provide complete information. Articles should avoid stating opinions as facts, and neither sympathize nor disparage the subject. It should represent all significant viewpoints that have been published by reliable sources, and in the lack of reliable tertiary sources, it should allow primary ones. These ideals were thrown under the bus in the article about Mills.

At the end of the day, I advised BLP to find reputable scientists who could survey their body of scientific literature and produce review articles that would become good secondary sources, and a pathway to understanding by the wider scientific community.

Whether due to lake of interest or lack of effort on the part of BLP, nothing like this has yet emerged; Mills preferred to write his own review articles.

If you are an idealist, there may come a moment in your life in which you are no longer willing to wait for someone else to bring about change.

Our scientific community is vast; it has already far surpassed Bacon's vision, and it is still growing. Yet we are still learning how to do science, and learning how to communicate.

Perhaps we will see another kind of online encyclopedia for original research, in which detailed review articles emerge spontaneously from the

---

[61] Despite all my trouble to get somewhere within reaching distance of neutrality in the article, the existence of the article alone has irked some, who believe that such topics represent an attempt by crank theories to gain credibility.

small contributions of individuals. Perhaps we will see scientific papers organize like threads in a talk forum. Perhaps e-books will be crowd-source annotated to reflect the latest knowledge.

We need to extend Bacon's vision for a digital age.

CHAPTER 10

THE SEMMELWEIS EFFECT

What infectious pathogens, ice-age floods, and hydrinos have in common.

In 1824, Johann Klein assumed duties as director of the laying-in hospital at the Allegemeine Krankenhaus, the General Hospital of Vienna, which was part of the University. Right away he reinstated several practices that were on the books as part of the medical school curriculum but had fallen out of practice. Among them, teaching with autopsies of real cadavers, and having students conduct thorough (in fact, unnecessary and tortuous) examinations of women in labor.

Childbed fever was a constant presence in the Vienna ward, but when Klein was made director, cases skyrocketed, and sustained high levels during the twenty years of his tenure. We know this because Vienna was one of the first hospitals to keep detailed records of patients, although the practitioners had not yet learned to analyze the data. We know that in 1846, at least 459 women died of childbed fever.

The next year, the young Ignaz Semmelweis became the new assistant of obstetrics.

In *The Doctor's Plague*, Sherwin Nuland MD has written an examination of the case of Semmelweis, who I first introduced in Chapter 1 (Nuland 2004)[62]. I have found that although everyone knows the story of Galileo being forced to recant by the church, Semmelweis is virtually forgotten; at best, a legend that floats behind more familiar faces like Pasteur. So I am dedicating a chapter to retell the story of Semmelweis, to bring his face out of legend.

When Semmelweis arrived at Vienna, he surveyed the carnage and embarked on a personal mission to identify the cause of the disease. The laying-in hospital was a convenient place to experiment; it was separated into two divisions: the First Division was used for training medical students, the Second was run by midwives. And the First had a *much higher* incidence of fever. Mothers giving birth in the streets were better off than those unfortunate souls in the First Division.

---

[62] Although Nuland's book is not the only available source for information on Semmelweis, I enjoyed the interpretation of an MD. I direct readers to Nuland's book for references and further reading.

Semmelweis was among the first to carefully review patient records in order to test the many wide-ranging theories for the cause of the disease. He found no strong correlations between incidences of fever and such vagaries as the weather. But the two divisions offered a controlled clinical experiment on a silver platter, and he began to study the differences in care between them. He also began spending more time at the autopsy table, analyzing fever victims, to learn what he could.

Pathology, the understanding of disease through observation, was a new science. A friend at the hospital helped train Semmelweis, but in a fate of irony, the same friend pierced his finger during an autopsy of a fever victim, and died. When Semmelweis performed the autopsy, he saw many of the signs of childbed fever, and theorized it was the same disease. Perhaps invisible "cadaverous" particles had entered his bloodstream, perhaps the same that were being carried to expectant mothers on the hands of physicians and students.

The tragedy became a serendipitous moment of illumination.

Semmelweis instituted new procedures: everyone entering the ward was required to wash their hands in a chloride of lime, a solution that was effective at removing odors. If students had gone to the morgue, they were banned from the clinic for the remainder of the day. Within a year, Semmelweis pushed down deaths due to fever to a level matching that of the Second Division.

When a patient came in with an infected knee, and another with advanced breast cancer that had ulcerated and was draining pus, childbed fever again shook the entire ward. This led Semmelweis to develop a refined distinction between a disease contagious through air, and that transmissible by touch. He took steps to keep such patients from infecting the others. It could be carried on the hands of nurses from one patient to another, and even by bedding.

Semmelweis was having great success with his efforts, and exactly why his two-year assistantship was not renewed by Klein is not known for sure. But with Semmelweis gone, cases of the fever returned, just as before.

When I was still in high school, I began to take an interest in philosophy, and signed up for a course at the local community college. Noticing my interest, my high school librarian, Susan Schmidt, handed me a copy of Thomas Kuhn's *The Structure of Scientific Revolutions*, and asked me what I thought about it.

Kuhn is famous for his historical analysis of the progress of science, in which he proposed the idea of a *paradigm*, a universally-recognized scientific achievement that for a time, provides a coherent set of model problems and solutions for a field of study (Kuhn 1970).

A paradigm is a way of thinking about a problem: in the words we use, in how a problem is framed, and how we go about solving it.

The physicians of Semmelweis's day were, like all of us, a product of their time, of the historical events and discoveries leading up to their moment in history. They were in the midst of a scientific revolution, diligent about making careful observations but often proposing speculative theories that were difficult to test. They were, in short, still learning how to hypothesize.

During an autopsy of a childbed fever victim, an infected whitish fluid would be found in the womb and throughout the body. Was this some kind of stagnant back-up of the fluid that normally issued from the uterus after a delivery? This notion had its roots in the ancient corpus of Hippocrates. Eighteenth-century physicians speculated that the causes could vary from "too great a thickness of the blood," to "grief and other passions of the mind," even to drinking cold water. Or, perhaps, it was breast milk that had somehow been forced away from the breast.

Semmelweis's discovery that a disease could be caused by particles carried from one patient to another, but the disease would otherwise not be contagious through air, is one of many examples of a new paradigm. It was an idea that would uproot the normal practice of science, replacing old methods with new, and force practitioners to reconstruct and reevaluate previous theories and facts. To do so, they had to be willing to look at the world afresh, and learn a new language.

The arrival of a new a paradigm produces an abrupt moment of punctuated change, forcing scientists to evolve quickly, as life itself does in periods of stress or opportunity.[63] Many scientists resist the change, clinging to prior theories and practices, like those unadaptable organisms fated for extinction.

The first time I read Kuhn, at age 16, I couldn't understand why one way of thinking should be fundamentally different from another. After all, if you are thinking *rationally*, there is a common language between paradigms of thought. A perfectly rational scientist would soberly climb the rungs of scientific knowledge, giving no more credit to a theory than

---

[63] See one of my favorite books, *Wonderful Life* by Stephen Jay Gould for a discussion of the evolutionary theory of punctuated change.

was due, always ready for new ideas to come along with greater explanatory power, always willing to absorb the necessary concepts with patience.

But later I began to realize that Kuhn was saying something important about human psychology, applicable even to scientists familiar with the scientific method.[64] In short, we aren't rational. Psychologists have noticed that there are many ways the human mind can err. Among these errors is the biased interpretation of data in favor of a particular theory. We call this *confirmation bias*.

This may present in a variety of ways. Once exposed to a theory, our ability to test it is qualified by several irrational tendencies.[65] We pay more attention to evidence that is in support of our theory than to evidence that disconfirms it, even if there is an equal amount of both. And what we pay attention to, we will inevitably remember better.

We are also more likely to interpret data as being in favor of a theory, even if that data is completely ambiguous. We are more likely to find fault with evidence and arguments presented against our theory, and more likely to turn a blind eye to mistakes and omissions in the evidence supporting our own. And once we have a theory in hand, we are less likely to seek out alternatives.

While it is clear that all of this is *irrational*, it is not clear that it is *bad*.

It is human nature to build theories from supporting examples, to make leaps of imagination that go beyond the evidence, and only cross them out when we find disconfirming examples that are overwhelming. If we try to build theories on disconfirming evidence, we have a rather hard time doing so, especially in a new areas of study (Tweney 1981). Perhaps this is why we are cognitively designed to pay less attention to disconfirming cases.

Sometimes scientists must keep the faith despite evidence weighted against them. Einstein waited patiently for two years as observatories reported that they had seen no bending of light around the sun during a solar eclipse, as predicted by his new theory of gravity. Then, an observation in 1919 by Sir Arthur Eddington did confirm the theory. When a student later asked Einstein what he would have done if the results turned out

---

[64] Also see Popper 1959.

[65] For further reading see Tweneny 1981, pp. 113-130, 171-174; Gilovich 1991, pp. 49-72; Lord 1979.

negative, he said "Then too bad for the observations; my theory is right anyway."[66]

Despite our cultural love affair with the idea of creativity, new ideas immediately make many of us feel uncertain. We have to ask ourselves if a new idea is really practical, and we like to think of ways in which it is somehow deeply flawed. Think of how the latest gadget unsettles us when it changes our behavior or how we socially interact; we always assume that it must contain some lurking instrument of our society's downfall. This makes it difficult for us to even recognize when useful advances have been made (Mueller 2012).

Age plays a big role. Our brain goes through several growth stages early in life; during these, we create our own value system and personal view of the world. As we age, our knowledge locks into place ("crystallizes") so it becomes more difficult to learn new things or revise old beliefs. What we gain in experience we also lose in adaptability.

And so, perhaps, those most susceptible to resisting new ideas are those at the top of their profession, those incumbents of knowledge, who ascended from past achievements, perhaps even those innovators who established the current paradigm of thought.

Klein's refusal to believe Semmelweis was not simply a disagreement over a scientific paradigm. It was wrapped up in tensions in the medical school between the young practitioners, pitting those who were committed to the new methods of rational pathology, with those of the old guard such as Klein.

These were in turn wrapped up in larger tensions outside the hospital walls: the revolutions of 1848, partially driven by student uprisings. When the students formed themselves into a corps called the Academic Legion, Semmelweis proudly wore the uniform in his duties, which must have angered Klein.

Further, Semmelweis's conclusion that physicians were literally carrying death on their hands was more than some could bear. One physician spoke out in support of Semmelweis's views; but without taking proper precautions, he delivered a child to his favorite niece who subsequently

---

[66] This tale is a somewhat apocryphal one told by Ilse Rosenthal-Schneider many years after Einstein's death.

died from the fever. Grief stricken and filled with guilt, he committed suicide.

Could Klein admit that in the decades of his practice he had been responsible for so much death and heartbreak? Semmelweis faced his own demons, admitting that he must have caused an inordinately many cases due, ironically, to the time he spent on the autopsy table in search of the cure.

Although Semmelweis's progressive peers were receptive to his discovery, and even defended it at meetings and in writing, Semmelweis himself had little aptitude or interest in participating in a community of science. He hated writing; he dragged his feet on performing controlled experiments with animals. He did not look for his contagion under the microscope. He believed the results of his theory were as clear as day in the performance of his ward, and that was enough.

As a result, inaccurate interpretations of his method spread among physicians, leading to confusion, and then loud criticism as other physicians were unable to properly replicate his results.

Klein also had a pet theory that a new ventilation system installed in the clinic, around the same time Semmelweis made his discovery, caused the decline in cases. Regardless, without Semmelweis managing the ward, cases of fever again spiked. About Klein we may only say that some men are willing to allow any horror so long as they don't have to face a new reality with eyes open.

Over the course of years, Semmelweis continued to perfect his techniques, virtually eliminating cases of fever from his clinics, often while meeting fierce resistance from administrators and even staff. This changed him as a person; as a younger man he was likable, but now he was angry and overbearing, which didn't make it easy for anyone to work with him.

While at the University of Pest in 1855-1856, Semmelweis allowed only 2 women of 514 to die of the fever. When his assistant sent a report of this to a medical journal, it was published with the following editorial note:

> We thought that this theory of chlorine disinfection had died out long ago; the experience and the statistical evidence of most of the lying in institutions protest against the opinions expressed in this article: it would be well that our readers should not allow themselves to be misled by this theory at the present time. (See references in Nuland 2000)

When Semmelweis did finally write a full account of his discovery, it was a poorly organized tirade of over five hundred pages, a scientific treatise mixed with angry letters directed at individual fellow practitioners. Few bothered to read it. Instead, it became a target of ridicule.

Ignaz, we now believe, was doomed to tragedy, as he may have had an early onset of Alzheimer's (although this is in debate). At the age of fifty he was committed to an institution, and after only two weeks was beaten to death for resisting the guards. His body was returned to the hospital at Vienna, to lay on the autopsy table where he had worked for so many years.

A few years later, Louis Pasteur started to look into the microscope.

Perhaps I was naive to have such faith in our individual use of reason as the great arbiter of ideas. We do better in groups, in scientific communities where the good ideas can be slowly distilled from the bad, where many researchers with different backgrounds perform experiments and theorize, and then come together to share knowledge and argue over the best explanation.

It seems that the best atmosphere for creative scientific work is when there is much fluidity in the environment; institutions such as the Rockefeller Institute (now University) are loosely structured with teams moving between interdisciplinary lines; relying on heterogeneity and intense interaction among peers in neighboring professions, to pool talents to solve problems in innovative ways (Hollingsworth 2004).

We might also conjecture that scientists who move across disciplinary lines do so without the indoctrination of the new territory. They may be less susceptible to perpetuating old ideas.

While organizations like the Rockefeller are highly responsive to fresh points of view, those working in academic departments within large universities have comparatively low creative output. With some exceptions, physics departments in particular tend to pursue traditional, long-standing problems in their field, using the same tools that were available to previous generations; digging along the same trenches.

All of this allows me to look somewhat compassionately on aging professors such as Wheeler, who tossed aside Mills's book. He had a long career within an academic department that prized itself on good teaching rather than good research. His project was to digest and filter twentieth century physics, feel out its interrelationships and history. Wheeler wrote his own textbooks on every topic, compiling and commenting on the work of others to express his own route to understanding.

To accept the hydrino, Wheeler would first have to learn a great deal about chemistry and plasma physics, then unravel and revise his life's work.

For some, the prospect might be an opportunity to burn with the flame of new understanding. Others might take it as a demonstration of the futility of their life's work.

I have fond memories of Wheeler also. He could be very compassionate to students, even those who were struggling. Despite his belief that my interest in Mills was crazy, he wrote a good recommendation for my application to BLP. He also had a hidden, lurking sense of humor that he rarely let show: if you followed him through the stairwell after a class, he would cluck like a chicken. Everyone loved and revered him.

When I returned to Reed after eighteen months at BLP, I was consumed by the question of how to communicate new ideas in science. I felt that before I moved on into the world of architecture, I needed to resolve my old demons.

How could I reach the Nick Wheelers of the world? Was it a social problem, a psychological problem, a philosophical one, or merely a scientific one?

I came to believe that, perhaps, a paradigm is influenced as much by the basic assumptions and philosophical influences that underlie our ideas as the science itself; branching points on the path to knowledge; choices made, years ago, their reasons forgotten.

We are born into this world, and we implicitly accept it because that is what we know. Did anyone remember why quantum mechanics came to be? Even Nick Wheeler was given the same world; he did not know a time before quantum theory. Few, perhaps, understood that physicists abandoned classical physics too soon, with important avenues left unexplored, while under the spell of philosophical ideas that were deeply flawed.

To bridge from one paradigm to the next, to upset Nick Wheeler's view of the atom, would require going to the root of the matter.

For the remainder of my time at Reed I studied philosophy. In my hundred-page thesis I explored the early history of quantum theory, the philosophical influences of Mach, and sought a full understanding of the nature of scientific theories (Holverstott 2007). I felt the project would close the door on the part of my life with Mills, but in fact, it set me on the path to this book. I have yet to find out whether *this* book finally closes that door, or opens yet another.

Perhaps my efforts are frivolous. It may be the younger generation who impel their professors to move into the next paradigm of thought. In the end, it will be they who replace them.

We can find other cases similar to that of Semmelweis in the history of science; I am aware of two cases in the twentieth century in the field of geology.

In 1912, a practicing meteorologist with a PhD in astronomy, Alfred Wegener, proposed the theory of continental drift. He was not a geologist, and he called on evidence from a wide array of fields including paleontology, zoology, geophysics, and cartography, all of which lent support to the idea that the continents were once joined in a massive supercontinent.

The reaction was fierce; it is said that Wegener's own father, a geologist, read his theory and advised him to stick to meteorology. One critic, T.C. Chamberlain, wrote: "If we are to believe in Wegener's hypothesis we must forget everything which has been learned in the last 70 years and start all over again" (Legrand 1988).

Despite the abundant evidence Wegener had collected for his theory, he had a big problem. He imagined that the continents must be something akin to ice-breaking barges smashing their way through oceanic crust. What force could be so powerful as to move them? Wegener could only speculate when he introduced his hypothesis. Unfortunately, he died while on an expedition in Greenland.

It was many years before his theory was developed into a mature understanding of plate tectonics, by which thermal currents in the Earth's crust slowly push the continents over millions of years.

In J Harlen Bretz we find another clear case. In *The Rebel Geologist*, John Soennichsen has written about Bretz,[67] who is the kind of man we would pay to see on the silver screen.

Bretz was a curious and avid field geologist who was intrigued by the gashes of exposed basalt that could be found in the landscape of eastern Washington State. These scablands were host to steep-sided river

---

[67] Soennichsen has also written field-guides to the scablands, which I have used in my family expeditions.

gulleys, channeled and interlocking ancient streams, with now sun-baked remnants of waterfalls that were many times the size of Niagara Falls, yet where nary a trickle of water exists today (Soennichsen, 2010).

Bretz took his students on expeditions to the scablands, traversing thousands of miles over rugged terrain to map these features. By his second visit, he had reached a conclusion which appeared, on its face, to be absurd.

The region must have been carved out by a massive flood, unlike anything that has been seen by civilized man. A flood where waters towered hundreds of feet, for miles around, turning a dry plateau into water as far as the eye could see; that reversed streams to deposit backwards sand bars high upstream; that filled basins until they overflowed at many places; that cut entirely new gulleys as it leaped over barriers from one stream to the next; that pushed large boulders far from their point of origin; that produced gargantuan plunge pools; and that destroyed the landscape on a biblical scale on route to the Columbia River.

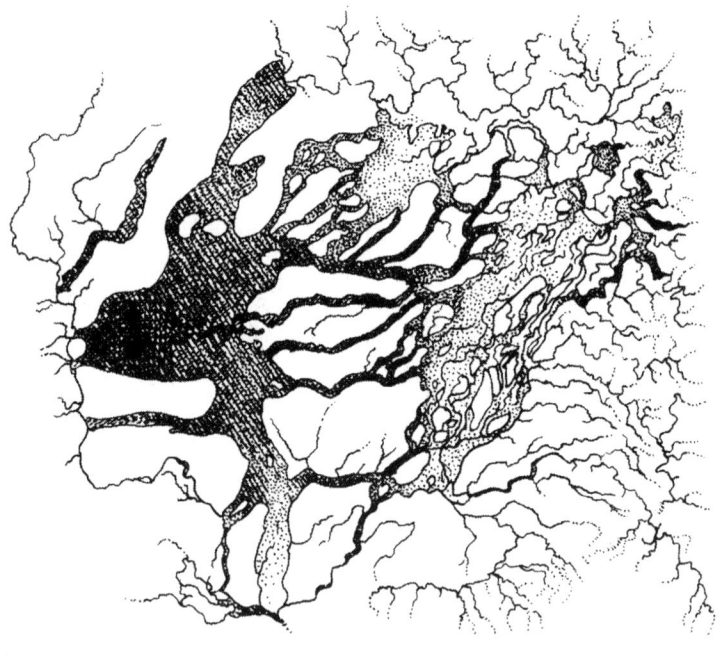

A MASSIVE FLOOD

THE EASTERN WASHINGTON SCABLANDS - EVIDENCE OF THE DESTRUCTION OF THE LANDSCAPE ON A BIBLICAL SCALE. IN 1927 THE USGS OFFICIALLY DENOUNCED BRETZ' THEORY AND IT WAS DECADES LATER UNTIL THE THEORY WAS ACCEPTED.

The theory was not just new; it seemed to go against paradigmatic, philosophical assumptions in geology at that time: that the geologic processes that shaped the Earth in the past were the slow, evolutionary result of processes that were ongoing in the present, not unlike evolution of plants and animals.

Geology, after all, was a science struggling to free itself from the Creationist myth that the world had been created in six thousand years and was shaped by a series of divine catastrophes. And here comes a new theory of a great flood.

Bretz's theory was first published in 1923. The initial result was little more than an uncomfortable silence on the part of the geology community, who felt little need to take Bretz seriously until there was some plausible origin of all that water.

In 1927, the United States Geological Survey (USGS) invited Bretz to speak, but, in a cruel move, only to officially denounce his hypothesis to his face. Bretz, however, continued publishing on the topic for a decade, while the community of geologists came to think of him as something of a fool.

Eventually, another geologist, J.T. Pardee, found evidence for a great prehistoric lake in Missoula. At that time the lake was at the base of the great Cordilleran ice sheet, and had a volume equivalent to one or two of North America's Great Lakes. If this lake spilled all of its contents at once, such as in the breaking of an ice dam, it could have unleashed the water needed to carve the scablands.

Bretz was something of an Indiana Jones geologist, donning khakis and a shovel; leading students on expeditions and encouraging them to reach their own conclusions. Bretz often argued with fellow professors about the value of this field work. His peers taught from books, less often from life; they wanted geology to be a respectable academic profession.

It was not surprising that few of Bretz's peers undertook the strenuous effort of touring the scablands, although this did not prevent them from offering their own theories. When, decades later, some of them did visit the area, they were quick converts to the theory.

J.T. Pardee in fact had visited the scablands before Bretz, in 1921, and likely came to conclusions that were likely similar. He didn't speak out about his thoughts, perhaps due to the fact that his superior at the USGS, W.C. Alden, discouraged him from doing so.

I wonder how many discoveries in the history of science were delayed, either because their discoverers were afraid to speak out, or they were discouraged—or suppressed—by an authority before they could be made known.

Pardee did eventually become an open ally of Bretz but focused his efforts on Lake Missoula. There he found ripples, the kind you might see on a stream bed, except they were fifty feet tall and five hundred feet apart.

Acceptance of the great flood hypothesis took an extraordinary amount of time. Not until the 1960s did college textbooks finally mention his work. But Bretz lived a very long life, and at the age of 97 finally received the Penrose Medal (the geologist equivalent of the Nobel Prize). Too weak to make the trip, his daughter received it in his honor.

How are we to understand these cases in the history of science?

While each is unique, common to them is a fierce *prima facie* ("on its face") opposition to the new idea, accompanied by an unwillingness to closely examine and weigh the available evidence, followed by a delay of decades before the theory is accepted.

There is no doubt that theories need time to come to fruition. The accumulation of a wide array of evidence by the community eventually pushes us into acceptance, like a chemical reaction coming to completion. But sometimes this process is protracted beyond all reason.

I have already introduced the idea of the '*Semmelweis Effect*,' a term already suggested to be a knee-jerk negative reaction to a new idea. To genuinely reflect the case of Semmelweis, it is the fierce and seemingly irrational resistance that meets some paradigm-shifting proposals, due to a variety of factors, some intrinsic to the proposal itself (such as its state of development or status of confirmation), others due purely to contextual, external factors.

Randell Mills appeared on the scene at the *worst possible time* for proposing a new source of energy from hydrogen: immediately following the cold fusion fiasco.

Although Mills had something genuinely new and different, there was enough confusion to produce a lasting stigma. While finding a receptive audience in the early cold fusion research community, his attempt to steer them in a new direction just made matters worse.

There is a joke often heard that a piece of bad science must have been done by an MD. With degrees in chemistry and medicine, Mills had the wrong credentials. And instead of going into academia, he was excited to develop new technologies in the commercial world. This affected how others saw him and his work: suddenly there was reason to doubt that he was sincere.

It is worth pointing out that in biomedicine it is common for major discoveries to quickly fall into a pipeline for commercialization. But it is almost unheard-of for a new widget to go hand-in-hand with a fundamental breakthrough in theoretical physics. It hasn't happened in a long time. So long, in fact, that our modern physics community hasn't had to deal with it. Physics still lives in an antiquated past in which the Einsteins and Edisons are working in separate rooms, and often in separate decades.

Authority can also play an important role. The USGS in the twentieth century had a strong official position, despite the fact that they represented only the opinions of a small group. The General Hospital in Vienna, in Klein's time, was an institution with strong bureaucratic ties and a top-down hierarchy.

Likewise, Robert Park became the official voice for the American Physical Society, and when he spoke, his voice carried. He nested his accusations in his unique brand of passive aggressive humor, and went unchallenged because he was in an honorary position of authority.

Regardless of skepticism from physicists, Mills's technology was so potentially profitable that he did not need the National Science Foundation to fund his research, and instead raised large sums of money from interested individuals and funds, enabling him to continue slow, careful research with a handful of PhD scientists.

However, twenty years later Mills has still not completed his task, despite having told the press repeatedly that he was only a year or two away from a commercially-feasible reactor. This gave skeptics the freedom to sit back and wait, perhaps indefinitely, for the technology to emerge.

The economist Albert Hirschman noticed that sometimes, underestimating the creative effort required for a major new undertaking is the only way we can be motivated to undertake it. Once we have invested ourselves financially and otherwise, we are forced to solve the myriad creative challenges that arise, and these solutions bring us more value than we could have anticipated. Hirschman called this *The Principle of the Hiding Hand.*

Mills vastly underestimated his own project, and his investors likely did the same; although I suspect few of them believed that the timeline for commercialization could really be as short as what Mills told the press.

Could he have funded the project with a more realistic timeline? Before a billion dollar initial public offering could be realized, he had to demonstrate that the theory itself was valid, and that the technology could be commercialized in an economical way. Either task alone would have been a tremendous feat, but he needed to do both in a scientific community intensely hostile to his project.

Mills was also in complete control of the execution of his project. Whereas most corporations allow the board of directors to hire and fire management, Mills had set up his corporate bylaws such that he had full authority to toss out his board without so much as a meeting to discuss it. Mills went through at least three boards of directors, each made up of major movers and shakers in finance and energy; he took their advice when he wanted it, and parted ways when he didn't.

Sometimes, this closed doors. Brand name companies seriously interested in collaborating with BLP were rebuffed by the terms he offered for licensing and profit sharing; terms that some directors also felt were unreasonable. Mills developed a reputation of being difficult to work with, and those who knew the type kept their distance.

But Mills's technology was also without precedent: a trillion dollar invention. No one had ever attempted to do what Mills was doing, and he was so far ahead of his peers in his research program that perhaps he saw little value in 'giving away the farm' to sign on with a name brand who would ask him to do the bulk of the remaining work anyway.

Perhaps, what Mills needed most, but did not feel the need to seek out, was to be surrounded by high-level creatives: not merely experimentalists, specialists, or those who could check his math, but partners and collaborators with whom he could share the creative load. This may have been the hidden value of 'giving away the farm,' to be surrounded by a team of brilliant people who could accelerate the process of scientific discovery.[68]

Unlike Semmelweis, Mills *was* willing to look through the microscope. However, such was the bias in the scientific community that his early papers would only be accepted by specialty journals dedicated to hydrogen

---

[68] I would be surprised if there were more than a handful of people on each continent who could have satisfied this criteria.

energy and fusion research, instead of those dedicated to fundamental discoveries in physics. He climbed the ranks of reputable journals in the chemical sciences slowly and with great difficulty, and by the time he was publishing in top journals, his papers were sweeping and robust and, perhaps, worthy of the Nobel Prize, but they were still ignored.

In 2011, the editors-in-chief of the *European Physics Journal D* published an important paper by Mills, but felt it necessary to add a comment that addressed the wider context:

> The Editors-in-Chief of the *EPJ D* wish to clarify that [this] publication... is in no way an endorsement of the authors' "hydrino" hypothesis by the Editors of the journal...
>
> ...Despite the reservations about the "hydrino" hypothesis expressed by some members of the scientific community, we decided that, after ensuring that the paper passed all necessary refereeing procedures (review by two independent senior members of the academic community), we should publish this paper rather than silence the discussion by rejecting it. We view this as the most effective way to stimulate scientific discourse, encourage debate, and engage in a meaningful dialogue about what is admittedly a controversial postulate.
>
> We would therefore like to invite the scientific community, opponents and proponents of the "hydrino" hypothesis alike, to send us their comments and views. (EPHD 2011)

Certainly no academic publisher would touch his book. While at BLP, I submitted it to several important academic publishers, which, in retrospect, was massively naive.

Another apocryphal comment sheds some light on this process. When Mills and John Farrell submitted a paper showing how the EUV lines observed in interstellar space match hydrino transitions, Mills included a massive tract of theoretical material to provide background for the claims, but the paper was rejected. When Farrell slimmed it down and resubmitted it without the theoretical tracts, the referee of the article is said to have replied: "The author has explained interesting scientific data with a novel and completely unsubstantiated theory of atomic structure. This theory, if true, would completely overthrow all of quantum mechanics. This seems quite unlikely. I strongly recommend this work not be published."[69]

Perhaps Mills's work was too big to be compacted in the form allowed by most journals; the one that tolerated it the most was *Physics Essays*, Mills's outlet for theoretical work, in which he was sometimes allowed fifty pages or more. Because Mills had so much material to reiterate before he could even begin to discuss the relevance of his research, his papers could be a chore to read, with large swaths of important background material occurring again and again.

Mills nevertheless worked outside the mainstream, surrounded by a small and rotating group of colleagues and collaborators, most of whom were competent specialists in niche areas of laboratory work with less interest in digesting the full theory. When Mills collaborated with those at the top of their profession, such as Conrads, they were guilty by association, subsequently ostracized by their peers and their work ignored.

As the search for hydrino energy was drawn out year after year, Mills tackled every new question that arose regarding his new theory. Solving the hydrogen atom was not enough, could he solve heavier atoms? Still not enough, could he solve molecules? What about the physics of semiconductors and superconductors? What of particles and gravitation? The expansion of the universe? Dark matter? Black holes?

Mills loved to work on these problems, but as with any creative thinker, he hoped his advances would capture the attention of the scientific community. For this he offered a ransom of his intellectual effort, seldom equaled in history, the mental equivalent of the gold of the Incan Empire. The "hiding hand" of the undertaking was that before hydrino was even brought to market, Mills had a highly-developed, novel physical theory to present to the world.

It is almost unimaginable to physicists of today, that one man could single-handedly overturn a century of physics. Science in our century is big, and collaborative. Nobel Prizes are rarely awarded to a single individual anymore, and experiments that produce new physics are expected to cost billions of dollars. We shoulder these costs, and argue it could not have been otherwise. But every new idea is born in a single mind, and dollars do not necessarily equate to discoveries.

---

[69] This may not be the exact wording, as this was communicated to me second-hand by John Farrell.

When I asked Mills about these things, he simply said that he enjoyed being the first one to solve problems with the theory, and he enjoyed the freedom BLP had to work without competitors.

The world isolated him, perhaps, but not disabled him.

I did not throw Mills's book into the trash as I left Wheeler's office, and sometimes I wonder why my instincts led me to continue. By nature, I am a rather independent person, energized by opposing the majority, ambitious in my desire to be creative and successful. I was young and curious, with no reputation at stake, and perhaps better than average insight into human nature.

But I also learned of Mills at the right time, before I was invested in an established theory. I am simply among the first of my generation to look on Mills's work with fresh eyes, and to find in it truth, and delight.

CHAPTER 11

THE BLACKLIGHT ROCKET ENGINE

In which an aborted NASA study offers a glimmer of hope for the future of manned spaceflight.

In the weightlessness of space, a droplet of burning fuel forms a beautiful glowing sphere. Without gravity, its shape is determined by its surface tension. Since only the surface is exposed to oxygen, the combustion time of the sphere is useful for learning about the reactions taking place.

As part of his doctorate in Mechanical and Aerospace Engineering, Anthony Marchese sent a series of microgravity combustion experiments up with the Space Shuttle Columbia. The project made Marchese something of an expert in thermal measurement. So in the fall of 1996, when he joined the new engineering department at Rowan University, just a stone's throw from Princeton, he was asked to help out with the Master's thesis of Peter Jansson. Jansson had shown positive results with BLP's isothermal cell and Calvet calorimeters. Later, Marchese couldn't help wondering if the reaction could be used for rocket propulsion.

We went to the moon in a journey of only three days. But what about Mars? It is a thousand times farther away than the Moon. How do we do it?

Until the late nineties, NASA didn't have a real plan for Mars. We had dreams of a space station and a Moon base, and a Mars mission seemed a little too ambitious. This changed when someone outside of NASA, Robert Zubrin, developed a Mars mission plan that was feasible with 1969 technology. The keystone of the plan was harvesting the Martian atmosphere for fuel, which would dramatically reduce the amount of propellant we would need to send a ship to Mars. Less propellant, less weight, less money.

The Martian atmosphere is primarily carbon dioxide (CO_2), and catalytic processes allow it to be converted into methane, oxygen, or carbon monoxide, which can be used in combination with hydrogen to produce rocket propellant. This would require an energy source, but the cost of transporting a small nuclear reactor is far less than the cost of transporting rocket fuel.

It would also require (in the case of methane) carrying some hydrogen to Mars from Earth, at least until we learned how to exploit Martian sources of hydrogen.

Whereas previous concepts for the Mars mission require assembling vast tankers of fuel in Earth orbit, the new proposal allows Mars to be reached with one or two Saturn V rockets, the same that went to the Moon.

Shaken up by the proposal, NASA produced a series of mission studies with only a few changes to Zubrin's plan.

A manned journey to Mars using conventional rockets would likely take at least 150 days of interplanetary travel, and the trip home at least 110 days. This assumes that we would correctly utilize windows of time in which Earth and Mars are in favorable alignment. These mission opportunities occur in cycles, a favorable trip to Mars every two years, and a favorable trip home about a year and a half later, giving an astronauts 450 days to explore a planet (NASA 2009).

In general, trip times could be reduced only if we accelerated to a higher velocity on route, but this would come at the cost of needing to decelerate on approach. If we add together the acceleration and deceleration required, we end up with a number that propulsion experts call the δv, the *total* change in velocity experienced by the spacecraft over its entire journey. This is a useful number because the amount of propellant needed is directly related to the δv, not necessarily to the total distance or duration of the journey.

Zubrin also suggested we aerobrake using the Martian atmosphere to reduce fuel needed for deceleration. A craft would sweep through the atmosphere on a series of elliptical passes. Of course, a wrong turn might mean a fiery death. NASA preferred to avoid risky moves, and changed the plan accordingly.

A long interplanetary journey is not unlike that of a tour of duty on a space station, but the astronauts would be outside the Earth's protective magnetosphere, and more exposed to solar flares and cosmic rays. A shorter trip would always be preferable.

And what about the outer planets? Using conventional rockets, it could take *years*. It is clear that mankind needs options beyond 1969 technology that can get us there and back again.[70]

---

[70] For outer planet trajectories see Petropoulos 2000.

Propulsion systems can be roughly broken down into two categories.

First, you have combustion with chemical propellants, which can deliver the high thrust needed to escape a planet, but only for a short amount of time before being exhausted. These are high-thrust but considered low-performing because they have a high ratio of fuel weight to total thrust produced.

Second, you have drives that cannot provide high thrust, but instead can provide low thrust over long periods of time, with higher performance. These drives may be useless for leaving a planet's atmosphere, but they actually outperform chemical propellants over the course of a long journey through space. They are low-thrust, but high-performing. Such drives require a source of energy, such as solar or nuclear, which is used to heat up ionized gas that is then ejected from the craft to create thrust. One of the high-performing options that NASA is considering is a cluster of four nuclear thermal rockets (NASA 2009). But such drives would only be useful in interplanetary space, whereas chemical propellants would handle the high-thrust demands of ascent and descent.

The performance of space-based drives are measured primarily with specific impulse, or I_{sp} (in units of seconds) which tells you the ratio of the exhaust velocity to the pull of Earth's gravity. Chemical combustion, with high-thrust but low-performance, has a specific impulse of about 500s.

By contrast, the Dawn Space Probe that went to the asteroid belt was high-performance but low-thrust; using energy collected from solar panels, it ionized xenon and applied an electric field to accelerate the ions, generating thrust. It had a specific impulse of over 3000s, but was designed to be operated continuously at low power.

These drives were state of the art, but they are not the future of manned space flight. High performance, low-thrust drives would not substantially reduce trip times for astronauts, even if they allow reductions in cost and weight. A Mars mission would still require 900 tons of spacecraft and fuel to be lifted into orbit on at least 5 heavy-lift boosters. Getting to Mars with established technology is possible, but expensive.

To make it in space, we need a drive capable of both high and low thrust, and capable of matching or surpassing the performance of the best ion drives. These were the issues on Marchese's mind when he applied for a grant to study the BlackLight Rocket Engine.

In 1998, NASA created the Institute for Advanced Concepts (NIAC); a program with a budget of about four million dollars, formed for the purpose of acting as an independent source of far-out but potentially revolutionary aerospace concepts that could dramatically affect future NASA missions in the long term. The NIAC solicited proposals, evaluated them with peer-review, and awarded small grants to fund the early stages of research. The program would award a number of Phase I grants typically around $50-75,000 for use over 6 months. On completion of the Phase I grant, researchers could apply for a Phase II grant, with funding up to $400,000.

The NIAC was where science fiction met science fact. Over the years of its operation, the NIAC funded studies on such concepts as the Space Elevator, a vertical tether to allow the transport of payloads into low-earth orbit; the Mars Entomopter, a flying machine that mimicked insect flight; concepts for an ultra-light space telescope array capable of taking high resolution images of extrasolar planets; concepts for genetic engineering of life for survival on Mars; Moon base radiation shields; cryoprobes for exploring liquid lakes beneath the ice shields on Mars and Europa; and antimatter propulsion for interstellar journeys, among many others.

The much-loved program ran only until 2007 before closing, but was soon replaced by the NASA Innovative Advanced Concepts program (also using the acronym NIAC) which would serve a similar purpose in providing a high-level entry point for scientists outside of NASA to work on broadly applicable technologies for future NASA missions.

For the 2002-2003 funding year, Marchese teamed up with Peter Jansson, who was now an Associate Professor of Electrical and Computer Engineering at Rowan, as well as John Schmalzel, Chair of the department and thesis adviser to Jansson's Master's project, to propose studying the applicability of BLP's new plasma reactors for propulsion.

Marchese imagined a journey to Mars that would take only forty days. Such a mission would require an enormous amount of acceleration and deceleration (a very high δv), and would be nearly impossible with chemical rockets. Dozens of heavy-lift launches would be required just to assemble the propellant in low-Earth orbit, and the payload delivered to Mars would be microscopic by comparison to the weight of fuel consumed. A specific impulse of 1000s would not be enough. What was really needed was one in the range of 10,000s (Marchese 2002).

They made some calculations. The energy release from a hydrogen atom catalyzed by a helium ion to an H(1/3) hydrino releases 108.8 eV. From that we have a theoretical maximum specific impulse of a hydrogen-helium thruster of 21,000s, assuming all of the hydrogen is hydrino-catalyzed. The exhaust velocity from this rocket would be 207,000 m/s, 40 times that of a hydrogen oxygen chemical rocket!

Marchese argued that a BlackLight Rocket Engine could provide a high performance drive ideal for long interplanetary journeys to Mars and the outer solar system. And his analysis caught the attention of the NIAC review panel. His proposal was selected, along with fifteen others, for a Phase I grant.

When Marchese was first asked to help out on Jansson's Master's thesis, he visited BLP, and found a small operation with just Mills and Good. When Marchese returned to consult on the rocket, he was impressed to see that BLP had amped up with 20 people and millions in the bank.

Marchese remembers Mills, in typical fashion, excitedly talking a mile a minute. And although Marchese had a PhD, he was not an expert in quantum theory. He would focus on experiment. In Marchese's final report, he judiciously avoids the theoretical argument: "regardless of the theoretical explanation, the experimental data suggests that these plasma systems have unique characteristics that warrant further exploration for propulsion applications" (Marchese 2002).[71]

Marchese, like John Phillips, had the attitude of an experimentalist. While working on the project, he would occasionally get calls from friends asking why he was involving himself with Mills. He would explain that he felt the purpose of science is to refute something if it is wrong, and if it isn't, build upon it and do better.

Let the data talk.

"I have not been one to explore anything beyond the fringes of science until this point in my career, and I may never do it again" he told a reporter (Baard 2002). He felt that even though Mills was not accepted by the scientific community, he had raised serious money by convincing the

---

[71] In a Nature news feature interview, Marchese commented that he "doesn't buy all of BLP's claims" a comment that might imply criticism of Mills's model, but in my phone interviews with Marchese it was clear that he never felt himself equipped to comment decisively on the theory (Reichhardt 2002).

science advisers of hedge funds. That's something.

Marchese's first order of business was to verify that BLP plasmas were really working the way they had been described in the literature. At BLP, he and his team walked through several experiments. These were not intended to be independent replications, but were performed at BLP, on BLP equipment, with the help of BLP scientists.

However, it gave Marchese's team an opportunity to see things for themselves and modify experiments to characterize the plasmas. After completing this due diligence, Marchese told the press he was as confident as he was ever going to be that there was no fudging going on. "For me not to continue with this study would be unethical to the scientific community," he said (Baard 2002).

BLP scientists had designed its cells to produce heat, but Marchese needed *thrust*. While you could design a cell to convert heat into thrust, it couldn't give you a higher specific impulse. Better to use the plasma itself as the exhaust gas.

In collaboration with BLP, Marchese designed two test configurations.

The first was an adaptation of a successful hydrogen/neon plasma cell. BLP's cell contained a disk anode and a hollow cathode assembly that included a chamber and tube bundle, with the gas inlet positioned on the side of the cell. When running, the hydrogen and catalyst mixture is injected into the cell; the gas diffuses through holes in the chamber and into the tube bundle. In this type of cell, the plasma forms between the anode and cathode.

In Marchese's modified version, the gas inlet was fed directly through the chamber, so all the gas must pass through the tube bundle and out through a supersonic nozzle. This nozzle, as in other rockets, pushes the gas to a small point and forces it to escape in only one direction, thereby producing thrust. But it quickly spreads at its base and minimizes friction on the walls of the nozzle.

To test the cell, Marchese and his team had to build vacuum chambers with integrated spectrometers. They needed to measure the exhaust velocity, and to do so they would spectroscopically analyze the emission plume to detect the Doppler shift of known emission peaks.[72] Marchese could have used one of BLP's spectrometers, but it could only approximate the exhaust velocity within 2700 m/s, which proved too low a resolution

---

[72] Another option would have been to build a test stand capable of measuring very small amounts of thrust, but they chose not to go this route.

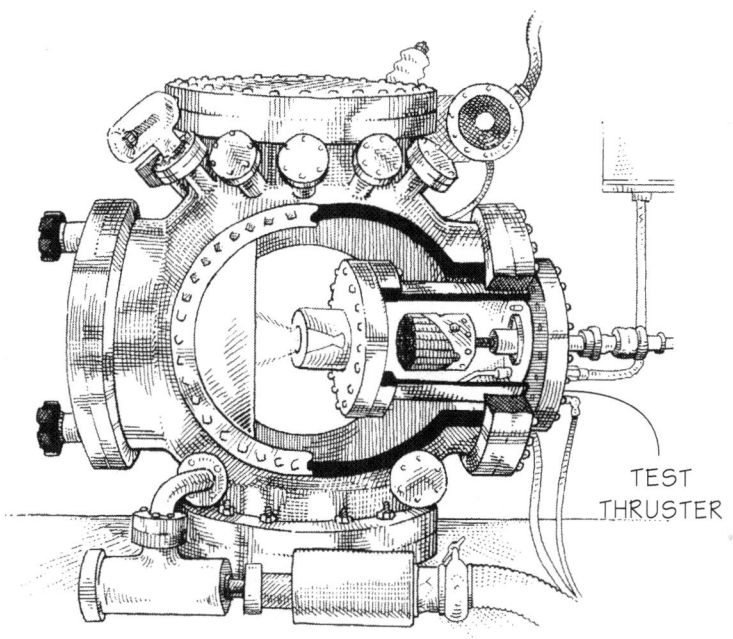

PLASMA THRUSTER TEST CHAMBER

SHOWN WITH A TEST THRUSTER ADAPTED FROM BLP'S HYDROGEN-NEON PLASMA CELL WITH A HOLLOW CATHODE ASSEMBLY. THE CELL WAS REDESIGNED TO ALLOW GAS TO FLOW THROUGH THE CHAMBER AND TUBE BUNDLE BEFORE PASSING OUT THE SUPERSONIC NOZZLE. AFTER (MARCHESE 2002).

to be useful. Instead, Marchese had to estimate the exhaust velocity indirectly from the temperature, pressure, and flow rate of gases into the thruster. Doing so produced an estimate of 5,000 m/s, which is similar to a hydrogen-oxygen reaction.

If Marchese's math was right, he had a thruster that used hydrogen and helium (an inert gas) to produce as much thrust as hydrogen and oxygen. That would be amazing.

However, it was not backed up by direct measurement, so Marchese's data was inconclusive.

Utilizing BLP's ongoing research into microwave plasmas, Marchese also chose to fabricate a second prototype, a microwave plasma thruster. This consisted of a gas inlet feeding into a quartz tube, which passed through a microwave cavity, and then through a custom nozzle. The nozzle was in fact the only modification to BLP's prior microwave experiments.

Unfortunately, complications with the experimental setup prevented Marchese's team from measuring the exhaust velocity. The fiber optic probe that was intended to measure the Doppler-shift of the exhaust plume was catching reflections from around the cell and from the thrust chamber itself. A highly resolved measurement could not be made; they would need a larger, redesigned chamber, and a new technique more suitable to low-pressure systems

---

The project received some press from BLP's favorite reporter, Erik Baard. When asked about it, Marchese admitted that "something interesting, something unexplained is happening in [BLP's] cells" (Baard 2002).

Marchese perhaps suffered from trying to do too much with a limited timeline and budget. While he was able to construct the highly sophisticated and expensive test chambers needed for the project (often by obtaining expensive parts for a fraction of their cost, or with matching funds from Rowan) he did not have time to modify and rebuild these chambers before the completion of the study. Still, when he looked at what he had done, he had the impression that he had gotten much more done than the other Phase I projects.

Science is not cheap. The NIAC may have dangled its feet in BLP technology, but despite optimistic (though not conclusive) findings, the Phase I grant was not renewed. And it was not for lack of interest that Marchese moved on, but rather that ever-present force in modern science: the lack of funds.

CHAPTER 12

THE FULCRUM OF PHYSICS

*In which we learn how a particle is born,
and how a black hole dies.*

On March 5th, 1995, the 400 or so physicists working at the Fermilab Tevatron Collider published, at long last, the discovery of a new fundamental particle: the *top quark*. The three-kilometer loop of the proton-antiproton collider had cost over a hundred million dollars to construct, and the discovery was hailed as a triumph for the prevailing theory of particle physics: the *Standard Model* (Campagnari 1997, p. 138).

Quarks come in two varieties: those with a charge of 1/3, and those with 2/3; these are the building blocks of the protons and neutrons that make up the nuclei of atoms. Physicists had been searching for the top quark (2/3 charged) ever since the late seventies, when they discovered the bottom quark (1/3 charged). Since quarks seemed to come in conjugates of 1/3 and 2/3, they knew they were looking for a "top." And of course, since all particles are born in pairs, the top quark would be born along with its antiparticle, the anti-top quark (different than the bottom quark!), with an opposite charge but the same spin and mass.

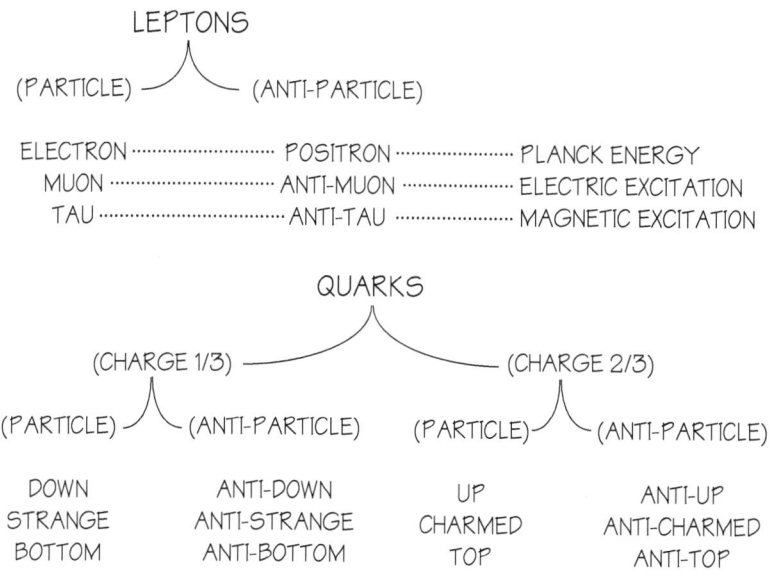

The Standard Model predicted the existence and charge of the top quark but it did not give a good prediction of its *mass*. Mass was a free parameter in the theory. So we had to go looking for it.

To do that, we needed to slowly turn up the energy of our particle accelerators, looking for the top to emerge. The heavier the particle, the more energetic the collision needed to manufacture it. But no one believed that the top quark would be so *heavy*.

Only a few months before the discovery, Mills made his own prediction of the top quark mass at 186 GeV, which is pretty close to the now accepted experimental value of 173 GeV. When I mentioned this prediction to my professors, my excitement was met with indifference. It was many years until I would understand why.

The first experiments searching for the quark mass were performed at the PETRA collider starting in 1979, using high energy collisions between *leptons*: electrons and positrons. This found no top quark below about 45 GeV.

Next, the CERN collider came online at Fermilab, able to collide *hadrons*: protons and antiprotons, which had a mass over a thousand times that of leptons, a key advantage in producing high energy collisions. These experiments found no top quark up to 91 GeV. In 1988, Fermilab's Tevatron collider came on line.

If you were a hydrogen atom unfortunate enough to be chosen for a round at the Tevatron, you would feel something like Chevy Chase's character in *Nothing But Trouble* as he is tossed on the "Bonestripper," a roller coaster ride followed by certain death.

A preaccelerator brings you up to 750 keV, whereupon you get launched through a straight shot linear accelerator, going 400,000 keV by the end of the stretch. From there, your electrons are stripped off, leaving you a naked proton, at which point you are flung into the Booster, a 150 meter diameter ring that accelerates you to 8,000,000 keV. From there you pass into the Main Ring, a kilometer-diameter ring of conventional magnets that brings you up to 150,000,000 keV; whereupon you are injected into the Tevatron, a ring of cryogenically cooled, superconducting magnets that bend and focus your beam while you accelerate to up to close to 1,000,000,000 keV! And of course, the finale: a head-on collision with an antiproton traveling the same velocity in the opposite direction; producing an annihilation event with a phenomenal release of energy.

Energy is conserved in all its forms, whether in the kinetic energy of motion, or the energy of electromagnetic fields, or that contained in the rest mass of a particle. The energy from the collision is released as photons—particles of light—which then transform into a cascade of new particles. We hope that among the fragments is an intermediate particle that will survive just long enough for us to notice it before it decays into something else. If we have a good theoretical understanding of the decay pathways, and we are able to measure the masses of the products, then we can reconstruct the mass of whatever new particle blipped in and out of existence.

Two teams developed around the Tevatron Collider. Doing simultaneous studies they raced for the goal. The analysis was difficult, and required them to test background assumptions for decay processes. At one point, a false positive at 40 GeV was announced by one of the teams. Finally, in 1995, both teams settled on a top quark at a mass of about 175 GeV. This was over 40 times heavier than the bottom quark, and about as heavy as an atom of gold.

The physics community was thrilled with the discovery but burdened now with the question of why nature had made the top quark so damn heavy.

Theory had followed experiment; every time a new lower bound was placed on the particle's mass, theoreticians produced new numbers with higher masses. In the final months before the discovery, theoreticians were working hard on what I feel are best described as semi-empirical *prediction-clouds*: scatter plots with hundreds of predictions for the particle mass, given different parameters in their models, which were incorporating the latest data from the colliders. It was no surprise that when the mass was finally revealed, it fell somewhere within the cloud.

Although no one expected to win a Nobel Prize for predicting the quark mass, many believed that the discovery was a great achievement for the Standard Model, a theory that would have received equal praise if the top quark had been another hundred times heavier and cost another ten billion dollars to find.

Perhaps it was a magnificent achievement of experimental science, of mankind's technological and scientific prowess, our modern equivalent of the pyramids of Giza; but it was not an achievement of *theory*.

Rather, we ought to let it inspire us to make a better theory. This was what the particle physicists promised they would do once they had more data.

So many theoreticians were chasing the top quark mass that it really means nothing, within the context of this activity, to be told that *someone* had predicted the top quark mass. Mills published only shortly before the discovery, mere months, so he was confident that the particle mass would not be below his prediction. This was something of a safety net. If he had made the prediction earlier, it would have been a bigger deal.

But Mills equations were, by nature, very different from what was being done by quantum theoreticians. Having solved the structure of the electron for the first time, he then went about solving other subatomic particles. It was a natural extension. Mills assumed that *all* matter is built on the same model: extended membranes of charge.[73]

The result was a new model for particles (we might call it the "Mills Model") and it can calculate what the Standard Model cannot: the particle masses.

Let's take a look at how he did it. It will take us into the heart of Mills's theory, and bring us finally to the problem of unifying the forces of physics.

Imagine we were to take Mills's spherical electron, and with the turning of a dial, make it shrink. It begins at the radius of the hydrogen atom, although there is no proton at the center. And as we turn the dial, it contracts, passing the H(1/2) hydrino radius, the H(1/4) hydrino radius, and so on. Since the shell is made up of flowing currents that follow great-circles, as the shell shrinks, the currents must speed up to conserve angular momentum, just as an ice skater spins faster when she pulls in her arms.

Suppose we turn the dial down as far as it can go. We find that there is a notch at which the dial stops turning. Why? Because at this point, the electron is orbiting at very near the speed of light. Try as you might, the dial will not budge.

We have reached the smallest possible radius for an electron orbitsphere.

Ever since the discovery of the electron, physicists have sought a unified theory of matter. When classical theorists such as Abraham, Lorentz, and Poincaré (ALP) first began to consider classical models of the electron, they imagined how a (monolithic) spherical shell model would behave in a purely electrodynamic world, and wondered if we could explain

---

[73] While this delivered on Goedecke's conjecture, it did not "explain" the existence of Planck's constant.

Newtonian mechanics only with electrodynamics.

They reasoned as follows: suppose we exert a force on a spherical shell. It accelerates in response, but the acceleration of charge will cause the whole distribution to release energy as radiation. As this occurs, the radiation produces a recoil in the particle that dampens its motion. This is called the *radiation reaction*.

ALP theorists hoped that the radiation reaction would give us a Newtonian force law. After all, if we want a unified theory of matter, we need a connection between *charge* and *mass*. Both are substances that imbue particles with powers. Charge acts through the forces of electricity and magnetism, whereas mass acts through the forces of mechanics and gravitation.

The theorists had a glimmer of hope: the radiation reaction produced an equation that was proportional to acceleration! But it wasn't quite right. It had an extra factor of (4/3).

RADIATION REACTION FORCE: $f = \left(\frac{4}{3}\right) m a$

— NOT IN NEWTON'S LAW!

The term for mass (m) in the above equation is not a Newtonian mass, but an electromagnetic interpretation of mass. We know from Einstein that mass and energy are interconvertible by a factor of (c^2) and we also know that energy may be stored in electric and magnetic fields, like the build-up of energy between the plates of a capacitor. The ALP model stores energy in the particle by squashing it down to a radius in which the energy stored in the electric fields (by the charge repelling itself on the sphere) equals the energy equivalent of its mass (m).[74]

In an earlier chapter, we discussed the many problems associated with the classical particle. It must be stable to spontaneous radiation and stable to perturbations; it must be extended, and have real angular momentum; it must not repel itself and blow up like a balloon; it must be free of the problems of preaccelerations, runaway states, and opaccelerations.[75]

In 1977, someone discovered that we can satisfy many of these conditions if we assume that an electromechanical particle is of a certain minimum size (Levine 1977). In fact, the radius of the spherical shell needs to be at least:

---

[74] See Jimenez 1999 or Pearle 1982 for a good overview of this topic.
[75] See Chapter 3 and 4.

CLASSICAL ELECTRON RADIUS: $r_0 = \left(\frac{e^2}{mc^2}\right)$

what is known in the literature as the *classical electron radius*. At this radius, a force impinging on the particle will propagate through the particle at the speed of light, causing a change in motion that is free of problems with causality or locality.

And this radius also happens to be the point at which the energy trapped in the electrostatic fields of the sphere equals (m), the rest mass of the electron.

Is this merely a startling coincidence, or does it say something important about nature?

Levine posits:

> In effect, classical electrodynamics is a consistent theory only in describing the motion of charges with a characteristic charge radius greater than the classical radius. (Levine 1977)

In other words, classical theory just might work after all. We just need to finish construction on the house abandoned by the early model-builders of atomic theory; stud by stud, girder by girder. And it might turn out to be more beautiful than we imagined.[76]

In Mills' theory, the current in the electron reaches exactly light speed at only a hair past 1/137th of the Bohr radius of the hydrogen atom, at precisely 1/137.035.

Incidentally, this number has special significance: it is the *coupling constant* (also called the *fine structure* constant) denoted by the symbol α. This constant is something of an honorary physical constant, since it can be expressed as a combination of other constants. But it seems to come up everywhere, causing Feynman to remark the following:

> It has been a mystery ever since it was discovered more than fifty years ago, and all good theoretical physicists put this number up on their wall and worry about it. (Feynman 1985)

In Mills's theory it represents the bottom of the barrel; there are no hydrino states beyond H(1/137) for this reason, and Mills refers to

---

[76] In 1911, John Nicholson had the idea that the proton must be very small, on the assumption that its mass was electromagnetic in origin (Kragh 2010, p. 41).

the H(1/137) state as the true "ground state" of the hydrogen atom, to appropriate the term (Mills 2015, Ch. 28). It is Mills's equivalent of the classical electron radius, but actually larger by a factor of α.

Let us get back to our thought experiment. We turn our dial down as far as it will go, shrinking the orbitsphere down to H(α). Suppose there is a digital readout of the stored electromagnetic energy of the electron; when the dial stops moving we find that we have reached precisely 511 keV, or the energy equivalent of the electron's rest mass.

This we intended.

But something unexpected happens here, something magical, something almost unbelievable.

Not only does the *electric* field energy equal 511 keV, but so does the *magnetic* field energy, produced by the moving charge; likewise the energy calculated by the Planck-Einstein equation, using a wavelength corresponding to circulating charge on the sphere; and finally, what Mills calls the spacetime-metric energy produced by the electron's mass: they all simultaneously reach 511 keV.

Mills seems to have found a physical state of matter in which the equations that govern the stored energy of various forces of nature converge onto a single value, as if all the forces of nature are reflections of the same image.

Although we have known since Einstein that mass and energy are equivalent, mass has always been a separate relic of the Newtonian age. Suddenly, it is staring us in the face, with a smile, having removed the antiquated mask to reveal something very electromagnetic beneath. Perhaps mass and charge are, in fact, a singular substance; it is the world that underlies sensation, it is the substratum of existence, or (to borrow from the ancient Greeks) the *arche* from which the architecture of the world is built.

Mills believes that it is in this state that an electron is *born*.

The creation of matter from energy is, in many ways, the fulcrum of physics. To describe the moment of creation, you have to know everything.

In general, particles with mass are born as twins (a particle and antiparticle with opposite charge, such as the electron and positron), created from a photon during pair production. We watch it happen in supercolliders, but it was first seen in a cloud chamber.

In 1948, Patrick Blackett captured an image of a high energy photon moving through a chamber filled with a supersaturated vapor; as it did so, it produced a stream of ionized particles (a vapor trail) and allowed him to track the path of a photon as it split into a particle and antiparticle.

The reverse process, the annihilation of an electron and positron back into a photon (in fact, a high energy gamma ray), also occurs.[77]

Because energy is conserved, when a photon undergoes pair production, the total mass-energy of the particles it creates must be less than or equal to its own energy (the difference being imparted to a third body). In the case of the electron-positron production, the photon must have an energy of at least 1.022 MeV since each particle has a rest mass of 511 keV. This does not include any kinetic energy that the electron and positron carry away, although this will generally be small by comparison.

A photon with an energy greater than 1.022 MeV is like a biological cell impregnated with the urge to divide. When a photon hits the upper atmosphere of some planet and slams into an atomic nucleus, something happens. It makes the leap, and become matter.

Why, and how, this miracle occurs is the great mystery of physics.

Just like an electron is made up of rings of ideal electric current; so too (according to Mills) are photons made up of rings of ideal electric and magnetic field lines.

Suppose we were to ride one of these field lines *inside* the photon as it undergoes pair production. At the moment of transformation, the field line is absorbed by space into a ring of flowing current. This might happen, by analogy, the same way that an LC circuit (one with a capacitor and an inductor) can absorb electromagnetic waves. Except that space is the circuit, with its two fundamental constants, vacuum permittivity and vacuum permeability, giving it a natural frequency at which it is able to absorb fields and transform them directly into electric currents (Mills 2015, Ch. 28).

The particle may be, for an infinitesimal moment, what Mills describes as a transition state, an intermediate between matter and energy. It exists only as the rings of field lines are absorbed, but a lot happens in that moment.

---

[77] Sometimes a positron and electron can come together and briefly form a combined atom-like structure, called *positronium*, but this state quickly decays and produces an annihilation event.

The newborn charge breaks into opposite charges, positive and negative. These attract, yet to form a particle and antiparticle pair, they must accelerate away from one another to overcome their attraction. They must reach an escape velocity that allows them to split.

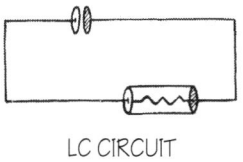
LC CIRCUIT

At the moment that this occurs, and for reasons that I do not fully understand, Mills suggests that the fabric of spacetime bends around the particle, perhaps allowing each particle to accelerate away from its conjugate at the needed escape velocity.

A particle is born.[78]

Mills employs the Lorentz transformations from relativity theory, which govern length contraction and time dilation for fast-moving objects, to describe this process. A special relativistic contraction of *space itself* occurs around a particle, resulting in length contraction and time dilation of space, but radially, out in every direction. This relativistic contraction spreads as a spherical wave front in all directions, giving rise to *gravitation*.

When a particle and antiparticle come back together and undergo annihilation, producing a photon once again, the process occurs in reverse. The relativistic correction is undone, expanding space; pushing it out, so to speak.

In this way, Mills stumbled across a new conservation law in physics, the *conservation of spacetime*. Space can be contracted and relaxed, but cannot be created or destroyed (Mills 2015, Ch. 29, 32).[79]

When Mills calculated the required escape velocities between particle and antiparticle pairs, he was able to derive their *mass*. He was able to determine the masses of fundamental constants from the other physical constants of nature and the forces that govern them.

And this tells us which particles are possible in this universe, because particles can only be created if all the energies of the particle work out correctly during particle production.

In nature we see three kinds of particle for each family. An electron, for instance, can also exist as a middle-weight *muon* or a heavy-weight *tau*, particles that we might think of as excited states of the electron. Like

---

[78] This bending is itself limited by the speed of light, as will become important in a moment.

[79] This will become important for understanding why the universe is expanding, as we shall discuss in the next chapter.

excited states of the hydrogen atom, they are unstable and quickly decay back to an electron.[80] But unlike atomic excited states, they have additional mass. According to Mills, the muon is an excitation of trapped electric field energy during particle production, and the tau is an excitation of trapped magnetic field energy. Both may be calculated.

The same applies to each family of quarks: The charge 1/3 quarks are down, strange, and bottom; strange corresponds to electric, bottom to magnetic. The charge 2/3 quarks are up, charmed, and top; charmed corresponds to electric, top to magnetic (Mills 2015, Ch. 36-38).

With Mills's equations, the fundamental particle masses became derivative constants. This was the grand achievement of his model.

LEPTON MASSES:

ELECTRON: $m_e = \left(\dfrac{\hbar\alpha}{\sec c^2}\right)^{(\frac{1}{2})} \left(\dfrac{c\hbar}{2G}\right)^{(\frac{1}{4})}$

MUON: $m_\mu = \left(\dfrac{\hbar}{c}\right)\left(2Gm_e(\alpha\sec)^2\right)^{-(\frac{1}{3})}$

TAU: $m_\tau = \left(\dfrac{\hbar}{c}\right)\left(2Gm_e(2\alpha^2\sec)^2\right)^{-(\frac{1}{3})}$

In July of 2012, the scientific community was again abuzz. The Large Hadron Collider at CERN was hunting for the latest particle, the Higgs boson. It was a particle important to the Standard Model's picture of nature, according to which, the universe is permeated by a scalar "Higgs field" that gives rise to the particle and gives mass to all other particles.

But Mills's theory did not require another family of fundamental particle. So as anticipation was building among scientists around the world, Mills stated publicly that the Higgs would not be found. I even encouraged him to do so, to take advantage of a potential opportunity. But soon, rumors started to circulate that scientists *had* found something. That July it was announced that they had found a neutral, spin-zero particle at an energy of about 126 GeV.

---

[80] The tau actually has enough energy to decay into a quark-system.

When Mills went back to the drawing board, he calculated that it was possible to produce higher energy resonances that correspond to the Z, W, and Higgs bosons. In typical style, Mills equations were frightfully simple.

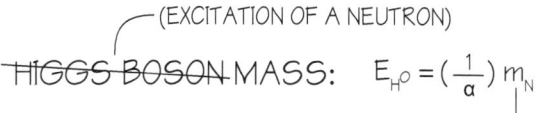

Mills interpretation was that the Higgs was an excited resonance of the neutron; the Z and W particles were excited resonances of the muon. Excited neutrons at 126 GeV had nothing to do with the Higgs field and had no role in imbuing other particles with mass, as believed by current theory. Mills argued that the Higgs field had, in fact, never been independently observed in nature.

There can only be as many particles as there are excited resonances, and in the case of the basic leptons and quarks, these are a direct result of the forces of nature that can act within a particle during production. There are particles due to electric and magnetic forces, are there not particles due to gravitational forces?

The mass of a particle due to a gravitational excitation would need to be extremely high; in fact, it would need to be a quantity known as the *Planck mass*. In current quantum theory, if two point-like particles with the Planck mass were to meet, they would spontaneously form a black hole. The event horizon of the black hole—the point at which light cannot escape from the particle—would be equal to the particle's wavelength.

It was believed that for an extended particle theory, no such mass limit exists. However, in Mills's theory, an extended particle with circulating currents has intrinsic limitations due to the speed of light. For a particle and antiparticle to be created from a photon, the particle must be able to *escape* the antiparticle.

In the case of a Planck mass particle, the velocity needed for escape is too high: it is the speed of light. Just as the speed of light (or equivalently, the speed of gravity) is a speed limit for the universe, so too is the Planck mass the weight limit for any particle.

Instead of transforming into matter, a photon with an energy equivalent of the Planck mass pair is caught in an eternal struggle, two proto-particles circling one another in a matter-energy hybrid state.

This has some fascinating implications.

When a star goes supernova, the leftover core of heavy atoms may be dense enough to collapse in on itself, overcoming the repulsion between nuclei, and creating a black hole. This is where quantum theory gets a little murky, because we don't have a theory of quantum gravity. We can only presume that matter collapses in on itself forever, reaching a point we call a *singularity*.

We could also presume that black holes will grow forever until the end of the universe. We had no clue how a black hole might die. But the Planck pairs might change this story.

In Mills's theory, electromagnetic forces resist the collapse: there is never a singularity. And if the core of the black hole is sufficiently dense, matter can be squeezed so tightly that it can annihilate directly into Planck pairs, matter back into light, side-stepping the requirement that a particle meet an antiparticle to annihilate.

We might imagine how it could happen. A heavy star falls into a black hole in a screaming band of light, causing the black hole core to reach a critical mass. It detonates, with a burst of matter at the center evaporating into Planck pairs, emitting a shock wave of expanding space. The black hole erupts.

A flash of light. It spreads in a spherical front with the brightness of a million suns, and destroys everything within a distance of many light-years. Its light will outshine its galaxy and be seen for billions of years. A black hole *annihilates*.

We observe events in space that may fit this description: they are called *gamma-ray bursts* (GRB).

These sudden flashes are a hundred times more energetic than a supernova; releasing as much energy over twenty seconds as our Sun gives off over its entire lifetime. Astrophysicists speculate that they may be due to the merging of two neutron stars. They are without a doubt the most luminous events in the universe. They are also somewhat rare. In our galaxy, it might happen a few times in a million years.

When we track the particles that fall on Earth from space, we find incredibly energetic cosmic rays, whose origin is unknown. Perhaps they originated in a supernova, or the merging of neutron stars, or perhaps a black hole annihilation event.

GRBs are so powerful that if one occurred nearby in the galaxy, it could result in a mass extinction event. An event as far as 6,500 light-years away could, scientists believe, quickly deplete the ozone layer, cause acid rain, and cause the Earth to cool dramatically. In 2004, it was suggested that such a burst could have been at least partially responsible for the extinction that killed off most of the world's marine species at the end of the Ordovician period, about 443 million years ago (Melott 2004). The author estimated, based on their estimate of the natural rate of their occurrence of GRBs, that we ought to expect a dangerously close gamma-ray burst about once every 500 million years. Apparently we are due.

These tremendous outbursts represent an enormous amount of matter being released as energy. According to Mills's theory, this should push out space in a strong pulse. In an early draft of this manuscript, I speculated that we may be able to observe gamma-ray bursts due to black hole annihilations with gravitational wave detectors.

Shortly before publication of this book, it happened.

On September 14, 2015, physicists at the Laser Interferometer Gravitational Wave Observatory (LIGO), located jointly at Hanford, Washington and Livingston, Louisiana, detected a gravitational wave for the first time (Abbot 2016).

The LIGO is made up of two arms at right angles. Lasers bounce through these arms, and then combine at the center. As a gravitational wave passes through, it compresses space along one axis but not the other, allowing the two lasers to interfere.

LIGO found a signal that occurred in less than half a second, made up of a series of waves that amplified and then quickly reduced. It turned out that this waveform matched what was predicted by general relativity for two black holes spiraling into each other and merging. The event likely occurred a billion years ago.

However, shortly after the discovery was published, there was another surprise. The Gamma-ray Burst Monitor on NASA's Fermi Gamma-ray Space Telescope was, serendipitously, looking at the right part of the sky, and picked up a gamma-ray burst almost immediately after the gravitational wave (Connaughton 2016).

The burst had a 0.4 second delay, which may be about how long it took for light from a billion years ago to be absorbed and emitted by intervening gas and dust. Only *gravity*, it seems, travels at true light speed through any medium and across billions of light years of space. Perhaps physicists of the future will say that light moves at *gravitational* velocity.

Yet, two merging black holes should *not*, according to current theory, release light.

Mills's theory tells us that any process that releases a tremendous amount of light should also release a gravitational pulse. Perhaps this event was the merging of black holes in an unusual situation that produced a jet of gamma rays. Or perhaps it was a black hole annihilation.

It would be nice if a black hole were not the end of the road for matter in the universe, if each hoard of matter, collected like dragon's gold, will eventually be redistributed throughout the cosmos, used for new planets and stars, and new life.

Yet these events may be the arbiter of the age of biospheres and civilizations. Most of the complex life on Earth evolved in the last 500 million years. How many biospheres live long enough to build an intelligent brain? We may one day be swept from this universe by a hellfire that is impossible to predict or see coming.

The Planck pair is matter and antimatter, bound together, unable to break free, unable to complete the transformation from light to matter. Yet it enables catastrophe on a cosmological scale.

I call it the *Lazarus* particle.

A GAMMA-RAY BURST

THE MOST LUMINOUS EVENTS IN THE UNIVERSE. THIS ONE WAS OBSERVED ON FEBRUARY 28, 1997. AFTER (COSTA 1997).

In a classic episode of *Star Trek*, the enterprise met Lazarus, a twitchy, melodramatic man who was pursuing his evil twin from a parallel universe made of antimatter. When Kirk stumbled into the other universe, he found that the Lazarus there was intelligent and mild-mannered; it was Kirk's Lazarus who was the madman, pursuing the other across time and space, willing to risk the destruction of both universes to kill him.

Thankfully, the good Lazarus hatched a plan to trap the other in a tunnel between the two universes, where they were destined to struggle at each other's throats for eternity, until time itself came to a stop.

When Kirk protests, the good Lazarus calmed him with the wise words:

"Not too high a price to pay for the protection of two universes."

WHAT OF LAZARUS?

In a unified theory of physics, we seek a single explanation for the basis of all physical phenomena. Perhaps it is a single force law that underlies all the others, a single equation of motion for all matter. This was how Heisenberg imagined it. But forces are interactions between substances, and it is possible there are multiple kinds of substances with different behaviors. We would prefer there to be only one kind, but that is not a *necessary* condition for unification. More important is an account of all the basic kinds of stuff in nature and how that stuff behaves and transforms.

Einstein wanted a theory of matter that was correct and complete. But we also seek integration, such that the theory makes sense as a whole. Accounting for transformations between substances brings us to the common denominator in all of physics: *energy*. It is through calculations of energy that we discover and describe forces, and it is through the physical constants of nature that we convert between the energy of different kinds of forces.

In Mills's theory, we are left with very few substances in nature. Mass and charge, electromagnetic fields, and spacetime itself. There is also the hybrid mass-energy state of a particle the moment it is created, what Mills calls the *transition state orbitsphere*. A Lazarus particle may be in this state. And *gluons* may be hybrid states as well. Mills describes these as massive photons that can be captured by quarks much like an electron can capture a photon to jump to an excited state. When they are captured, the quark captures the magnetic flux of the gluons to make a neutron.

Before Mills, we had four forces of nature: electromagnetism, gravity, and two nuclear forces including the *strong* and *weak* force. The latter two are really failures of quantum theory to understand the physics of particles; the theory is unable to calculate the energy balance of the neutron's binding energy or its beta decay.

Mills's theory sidesteps both the strong and weak forces by accounting for the stored electric and magnetic energies, and the release of kinetic energy and changes in the gluon fields during these physical processes (Mills 2015, Ch. 39).

We are left with the force of electromagnetism, and the force of gravitation which, arguably, is a close byproduct of electromagnetism. I find serenity in the knowledge that the equations of the unified field theory we have so desperately sought in the twentieth century are Maxwell's equations, which have been with us all along; in fact, for 150 years. Crude experiments by candlelight in dusty rooms obtained the equations that govern the universe.

Newtonian mass is also a byproduct of electromagnetism, but not by way of a radiation reaction. Such forces apply only to charged particles, and we need an understanding of inertia that applies to neutral matter as well.

Mills's explanation is more fundamental than that, almost pointing out that we have solved the problem already, with Einstein's matter and energy equivalence. Mills's model for particles is entirely electromagnetic and obeys relativity theory. Because relativity requires that energy is added to a body as it accelerates, the force resisting the acceleration must be in proportion to the energy added to the system (Mills 2015, Ch. 34).

If I state these things simply, it is because I wish only to introduce what Mills's theory says about the world, in the hope of creating a conceptual scaffolding. I am a poor philosophical commentator on the works of greater minds.

Perhaps Mills has unified physics. If so, humanity now stands on the edge of knowledge and looks out with desire to the darkness of the unknown. Where do we go from here? Is the unified theory the end of physics?

I do think the next generation of physicists will follow Mills's theories to new ends. They will go into the darkness with sight that lasts to the end of their nose, but they will move forward, and they will learn something new.

CHAPTER 13

THEORY AND PRACTICE

In which theoreticians and experimentalists are not on speaking terms.

WIZARD OF WATTS

"BLACKLIGHT POWER SAYS ITS INTRODUCING A REVOLUTIONARY ENERGY SOURCE - AND IT WON'T LET THE LAWS OF PHYSICS STAND IN ITS WAY" (GUIZZO 2009).

While developing plasma cell technology, BlackLight went under the radar. In 2002, Mills told a reporter: "I've been avoiding the media because we've gotten hit pretty hard there. But we've been publishing academic papers at a remarkably steady rate. I love this work—we're not slowing down." (Mills 2002).

The next spurt of press was in 2005 and 2006. BLP had collaborators in Europe, two quantum theoreticians had entered the debate, and two professors at the University of North Carolina (UNC) at Ashville had started speaking out.

Kert Davies was in his third year as Research Director at Greenpeace, attending a conference on hydrogen power, when the man sitting beside him asked "Ever worry about assassins from Saudi Arabia?"

The man, Michael Sabel, was a business development consultant based in Washington, DC, who BLP had hired to help reach out to a network of businessmen, organizations, and scientists. The two got chatting, and Sabel told him about BLP's work. Davies was intrigued; here was a potential solution to not just cheap energy, but climate change; with a value far outweighing what could be calculated purely in monetary terms.

Kert had an ongoing relationship with University of North Carolina; scientists there were studying the presence of mercury in human hair as part of a push against coal power. Among them was Rick Maas, chair of the Department of Environmental Studies at UNC. Kert told him about BlackLight and asked if he would like to join him on a trip to the facilities. He agreed.

Maas and Davies were impressed by BLP, the people, and the experiments. Davies thought to himself that it would be quite an elaborate ruse to fake science at this level, and no one was shaking them down for funds.

Maas understood the chemistry and experiments but needed help with the theory, so he recruited a friend from the physics department, Randy Booker, a radio astronomer. They followed up with a visit in May of 2005 and spent a week there, investigating five experiments. Maas told BBC:

"We went in with a healthy amount of skepticism" (Matthews 2005). He and Booker expected BLP to be secretive about their work, but were pleasantly surprised that they were very open about their experiments and results. They were given free rein in the lab to oversee and modify experiments. They conducted water bath calorimetry and line broadening studies with plasmas.

By the end of the first week, Maas was awestruck: "We found very strong evidence for the existence of hydrinos, and significant net energy gains of 2-40%. ...There's no way—unless you didn't want to believe it—that you'd not say you were convinced" (Matthews 2005).

Davies felt that "If it's wrong, it will be proven wrong. But if it's right, it is so important that all else falls away. It has the potential to solve our dependence on oil. Our stance is cautious optimism" (Jha 2005).

Maas told the *Guardian*: "All of us who are not quantum physicists are looking at Dr. Mills's data and we find it very compelling. Dr. Booker and I have both put our professional reputations on the line as far as that goes" (Jha 2005).

Having captured their interest, BLP asked them if they would like to consult on a long-term basis. Maas would validate experiments, and Booker would validate Mills's theory. They would be paid for their time, and their expenses would also be covered. They agreed (Jakab 2006).

Booker and Maas were complementary personalities. Booker was quiet and solitary; when he wasn't scanning for formaldehyde signals in the star-forming regions of our galaxy, he was happy to sit in his office pouring over the details of Mills's theory. Maas, however, was very outgoing, well spoken, and comfortable with attention. He was gung-ho about BLP and the potential of the technology. Mills and Good realized that Maas would be the kind of ally that could make a big difference in the scientific community. He could advocate passionately and recruit collaborators.

In December, only days after we last saw him in the office, Maas fell ill. He had a serious health condition, and when Bill Good and Michael Sabel heard that he was sick, they were prepared to pull out all the stops to get Maas on a commercial jet and fly him to another hospital. But it was too late, Maas was lost; he was only 54. I understand that Maas was preparing write a book about BLP. In place of his project, I hope this will serve.

Over the course of the next several years, Booker would continue to do theoretical work, going to BLP once or twice a year. Over seven years of work, BLP paid Booker a total of about $10,000, enough to allow him to make room in his schedule from time to time. He felt that he was coming at the project objectively and patiently, unaffected by the rather modest financial ties.

Booker was careful and meticulous in his analysis of Mills's equations and found they were extremely good at matching experimental data, such as atomic ionization energies. He occasionally signed statements to that effect for BLP's use. Occasionally he found small mistakes. Beyond that, Booker never tried to use Mills's theory to solve new problems; never used it as a working tool for innovative contributions. While he was happy to testify to his efforts, he was not a theoretician, he was not the type of personality to make waves in the scientific community. Perhaps, someday, he would teach a course on the subject.

Booker once sat down with a professor in the chemistry department who didn't like Mills. As he soberly tried to explain the theoretical underpinning of the hydrino states, the professor stood and threw up his arms. "You just can't do that." he said, exasperated. He was unwilling to go any further.

"Perhaps," Booker told me, "you just need to have an open mind."

The momentum that Davies had built up nearly died with Maas, but Davies continued to work internally at Greenpeace to make BLP a bigger issue. He brought the executive director and climate policy director up to BLP for presentations, and tried to get some positive stories to run in the press. At the end of the day, there was little they could do but wait and hope for BLP to crack the nut.

In 2005, Andreas Rathke was working at the Advanced Concepts Team in Noordwijk for the European Space Agency (ESA) when he was asked by the Italian aeronautics firm Alenia to look into Mills's work. Before spending money on experiments, the ESA decided to have Rathke scrutinize Mills's theory. Although Mills had received off-the-cuff criticism from physicists since 1991, none had published a scientific paper scrutinizing Mills's theoretical work; Rathke was breaking an embargo.

The paper was short, and focused on the first two or three pages of Mills's thousand-page treatise. Rathke tried to follow Mills's derivation of his model of the electron from a general wave equation postulated on the first page. He concluded that Mills's model was "inconsistent, and in particular does not contain solutions that predict the existence of hydrinos." And having arrived at this conclusion, he stopped there, omitting any further discussion (Rathke 2005).

When Rathke's article arrived, we felt that he had completely missed the point. Rathke was, after all, thinking along quantum mechanical lines, and expecting a single equation to express everything we know about the electron. Although Mills's treatise began with the wave equation, he had used boundary conditions and classical physical laws to model how the electron moves. The periodic motion of the electron in the atom only had the vaguest resemblance to a wave.

I have found other physicists, even those solidly grounded in classical electron theory such as George Goedecke, to be at a total loss with Mills's logic on the first two pages. A quantum paper might begin by postulating an equation for the motion of a particle, but a paper on classical electrodynamics begins by postulating a physical condition.

> **Quantum theory**: "Let us postulate the following equation for the motion of a particle..."
> **Classical theory**: "Suppose we have a rigid spherical shell of charge..."

Mills was confusing both the classical audience and the quantum audience, not making it clear which paradigm he stood in. Most theoreticians—likely Nick Wheeler included—likely dropped the manuscript by page three. Paradigm jumping is hard. Mills finally omitted the wave equation, and changed the name of his theory from the "Grand Unified Theory of Classical Quantum Mechanics" to that of "Classical Physics." Which did not have the same ring, but it was less confusing.

Rathke also briefly considered whether hydrino states are allowed in quantum theory. He pointed out that sub-ground states are not square integrable, with the result that the orbits cannot be successfully described using the statistical interpretation of quantum mechanics.

Yes, he was talking about point particles in a probability density cloud.

I feel this kind of criticism is akin to a Creationist stating that evolution cannot be true, because 5,000 years is not enough time for animals to evolve.

Although Rathke's paper struggled to understand Mills's theory, it did open the floor to debate. Mills wrote a rebuttal, but after receiving it, the editors of the *New Journal of Physics* decided to wait to co-publish it with a counter-rebuttal from Rathke. Of course, it never came. So, as with the many manuscripts that were slowly fighting their way into press, Mills posted it online and went looking for another outlet, eventually publishing an expanded 54-page paper in *Physics Essays* (Mills 2007c).

Rathke was aware of Mills's experimental work, and told a reporter "I think there is indeed some interesting plasma physics. However, the explanation for the high plasma temperatures will most likely lie in conventional plasma dynamics" (Matthews 2005). Not surprisingly, after his brief dismissal of Mills's theoretical work, the ESA decided not to support research on the topic.

Jan Naudts at the University of Antwerp had also been following the plasma developments by Kroesen and others, and began to take seriously the possibility that hydrino atoms were real. Plucking a long-lost equation (the Klein-Gordon equation) from early quantum theory, he found that there may exist at least one hydrino state, and that the issue had not been seriously studied. He concluded his paper by pointing out that until these calculations were performed "there are no serious arguments from quantum mechanical theory to reject the existence of the hydrino state" (Naudts 2005).[81] It is clear that Naudts thought the hydrino could be absorbed into the quantum cannon, but the hydrino state from the Klein-Gordon equation would not explain the unique signatures of each of the fractional orbits that Mills had found in experiments.

Naudts felt that Rathke's article "was clearly incomplete, and even misleading" (Matthews 2005) and told a reporter: "Either the hydrino exists, in which case we have to accept a small correction to the textbooks on quantum mechanics, or it does not exist, in which case we have to find better arguments to explain why it does not exist... Nothing is decided yet, but I think it is time to fill the holes in our theoretical understanding of the hydrogen atom."

Rathke rebutted that what Naudt was proposing was "known in the literature and had previously been discarded as unphysical" (Dume 2005). ...Let's get this straight: a *theoretical* rational for new *experimental* data must be wrong because... physicists eighty years ago rejected it on the basis of *experiment*. I don't think the Klein-Gordon equation is salvation for a quantum hydrino, but yeah, that's circular reasoning.

---

[81] Recently, an article surfaced that suggested fractional-integer orbits of the hydrogen atom may be acceptable in quantum theory. (Bas 2015)

Theoreticians gonna theorize; experimentalists gonna experiment. While quantum theoreticians thought up reasons why the hydrino could not exist, BLP and collaborators continued finding evidence that it did.

Peter Jansson, who had conducted his Master's thesis on Mills's cells as part of Atlantic Energy's due diligence, was back at Rowan University. He had earned his doctorate at the University of Cambridge and was now an Associate Professor in the Electrical Engineering department.

Both Rowan and Princeton are near to BLP, and by all means, BLP *should* have been collaborating with Princeton, a world leader in plasma physics and a center for hot fusion research.

However, Princeton had a reputation to maintain, not only with regard to quantum theory, but with regard to their commitment to fusion. Rowan, by contrast, was not a high-profile institution, nor was it even a graduate institution. But the scientists there were legitimate, respected professionals who were willing to work with BLP, especially if BLP could fund the research. You can easily shuttle between BLP and the campus in a twenty-minute drive.

BLP was looking for outside groups to independently replicate their evidence for hydrino compounds. Using long-duration closed cells, BLP was able to obtain hydrino trapped in KCl and KI salts. And by condensing the gases from a series of helium-hydrogen plasmas, BLP was able to find NMR signatures for a series of hydrino peaks, published in 2007 (Mills 2007).

Hydrino State	Peak
H2(1/2)	3.47
H2(1/3)	3.02
H2(1/4)	2.18
H2(1/5)	1.25
H2(1/6)	0.85
H2(1/7)	0.21
H2(1/10)	-1.8

BLP's assignment of peaks from a series of ^1H NMR spectra of helium-hydrogen plasma gases condensed with liquid nitrogen and dissolved in $CDCl_3$. Peaks at 7.26, 4.63, and 1.57 were due to $CHCl_3$, H_2, and H_2O. (Mills 2007)

In 2009, Rowan repeated some studies of KCl and KI salts. They used a stainless steel cell with a nickel screen, and placed a small crucible containing some potassium metal and KCl. The cell was inserted into a kiln, elevated to high temperature, and hydrogen was fed into the cell at low pressure.

In another experiment, they added some dry Raney nickel to a crucible. This is a powdered Nickel with a very high surface area, valuable as a surface to catalyze reactions. In the same cell they placed another crucible with potassium metal and KI salt. After some hours, the cell was removed from the kiln, dismantled in an argon atmosphere glove box, and the colored salts in the cell were sent out for solid NMR analysis. They were also bathed in a solvent and transferred to a quartz tube for solution NMR analysis (Mugweru 2009a).

A NMR spectrometer is essentially a large superconducting electromagnet that can exert a very strong magnetic field. The field is dialed up and the nuclei of atoms in a compound will resonate with it, absorbing and emitting light. Each atom has a unique signature that is affected by nearby atoms; hydrogen is a highly NMR resonant atom, so it can be seen very clearly. Since the atoms of a hydrino molecule are closer together than those in a hydrogen molecule, their proximity should create enhanced shielding, resulting in an upfield shifted signal.

Rowan found peaks that were indeed shifted upfield from the corresponding peaks for ordinary alkali hydrides, salts that have hydrogen positioned in the interstitial lattice, KHCl and KHI. They were led to conclude: "We cannot assign negative upfield shifted peaks to any known compound from the literature" (Mugweru 2009a). They also found peaks corresponding to the H(1/4) hydrino atom, and in some cases, the H⁻(1/4) ion.[82]

Rowan also conducted a neutron diffraction study showing that there were interstitial atoms in the KH and KI lattice, and conducted an XPS study of KHI, finding two new peaks that did not match anything else in the literature, but matched Mills's prediction for H⁻(1/4).

---

[82] The H_2(1/4) hydrino molecule was found via the associated peak at 1.2 ppm in both solid and liquid NMR samples of KHCl, and at 1 ppm (solid) and 1.258 ppm (liquid) NMR samples of KHI. The H⁻(1/4) ion was found at -4.5 ppm (solid) in KHI, but Rowan failed to find the H⁻(1/4) in liquid NMR that BLP reported at -3.79.

Just as early symptoms of a disease may be benign and unnoticed, evidence for new phenomena may present long before a theory is found to explain it.

Hydrogen is everywhere, and it would be surprising if hydrino went completely unseen for a century. We have already seen that excess heat in electrolytic cells and excessively hot populations of hydrogen in plasma cells may be explained by hydrino formation, but is there any evidence in the literature for hydrino compounds?

In a 2007 study, lithium hydride (LiH) and lithium nitride ($LiNH_2$) were ball-milled at high temperature and analyzed with NMR spectra collected at different points in time. The team recorded a peak at 1.06 ppm that grew as time progressed, but they couldn't explain it. The authors commented that the origin of the peak "remains unclear and requires further investigation" (Lu 2007). Lithium is a catalyst, and as LiH heats it will split apart and produce free hydrogen and lithium that could enable hydrino catalysis. Mills suggested the peak is caused by the H(1/4) hydrino.

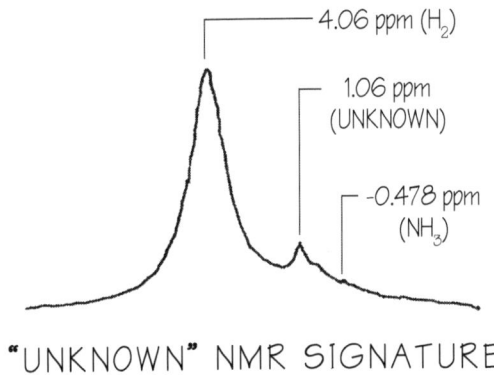

"UNKNOWN" NMR SIGNATURE

EXPANDED NMR SPECTRUM OF AN LiH + $LiNH_2$ MIXTURE BALL-MILLED FOR 180 MINUTES AND LET REST AT HIGH TEMPERATURE FOR 4 HOURS AT 180 °C. AFTER THAT IN (LU 2007).

All molecules vibrate and rotate, and the hydrino molecule is no different. Since the distance between the two atoms in a hydrino molecule is much smaller than in a hydrogen molecule, it has a different moment of inertia. A simultaneous jump in a rotational state and a vibrational state, a *rovibrational* transition, will absorb light at unique energies, and we ought to see this in a series of peaks.

In 2007, BLP released a study showing these transitions in $H_2(1/4)$. They performed an experiment using a gas mixture of argon with only 1% hydrogen, maintaining the plasma with an electron gun, and capturing the light with an EUV spectrometer (Mills 2007b). This clearly showed a series of rovibrational transitions corresponding to the P branch of the v = 1 → v = 0 vibrational transition.

BLP not only saw these lines *in situ* in a plasma, but was also able to excite these rovibrational states in hydrino gas molecules trapped in an alkali hydride crystal (Mills 2011).

But these lines were found in the literature. In 1998, a team was developing a new UV light source. By exciting otherwise unreactive noble gases with an electron beam at low temperature, the team hoped to cause atoms to combine into short-lived excited dimers, or *excimers*, decaying with the release of UV light. The team developed a new ultra-thin silicon nitride foil window that allowed electrons to pass into a gas but kept the gas temperature low, well suited to excimer formation. The team experimented with argon, krypton, and xenon noble gases, using both ultra-pure gas and standard gas with some natural contaminants.

In the argon spectrum, there was a clear series of lines in the unpure gas. The authors noted them as "additional impurity lines which could not yet be unambiguously assigned" (Ulrich 1998). They were a match for Mills's assignment of the rovibrational spectrum of $H_2(1/4)$. Perhaps, hydrino occurs naturally whenever suitable catalysts are present, and even in pure samples of hydrogen gas. After all, collisions between three or more hydrogen atoms provides the energy sink needed for hydrino catalysis.

Hydrino is hard to find, because it is *dark*. The electronic jumps between orbits are forbidden, which is unique in nature.[83] But hydrino can be easily seen with NMR, a *nuclear* excitation. The nucleus of an atom is affected by the orbiting electron, and the radius of the electron has a strong effect. We might say the NMR peaks are "high grade" data, they are very sharp singlets, indicating that the hydrogen atoms are well isolated.

But there is another kind of nuclear resonance. Since both the nucleus and an electron have spin, and a resulting magnetic moment, a hydrogen atom can absorb a photon by switching the relative orientation of the proton and electron's magnetic moments, jumping from a parallel to an antiparallel orientation. This results in an energy shift we call the *hyperfine structure*, also called *spin-nuclear coupling*.

---

[83] We will revisit this feature of hydrinos in the next chapter.

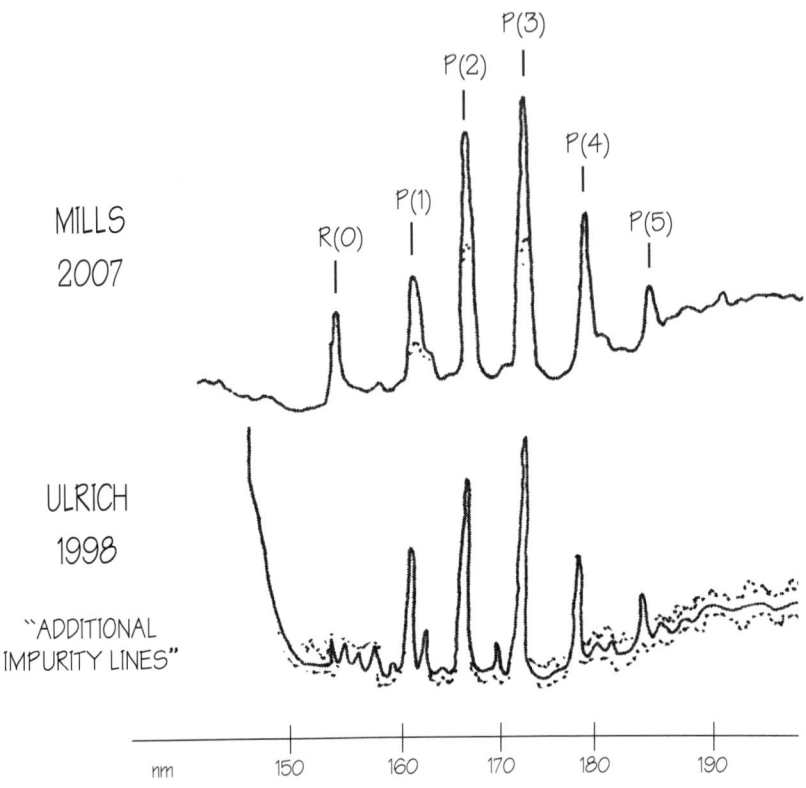

UPPER: (EXPANDED) SPECTRUM OF AN ELECTRON BEAM MAINTAINED PLASMA OF ARGON WITH 1% HYDROGEN. MILLS ASSIGNS TO THE P BRANCH OF THE $H_2(1/4)$ MOLECULE FOR THE VIBRATIONAL TRANSITION: V = 1 TO V = 0. LINES MATCH MILLS' PREDICTION OF VIBRATIONAL TRANSITION OF 8.25 EV WITH A ROTATIONAL ENERGY SPACING OF 0.241 EV. AFTER (MILLS 2007).

LOWER: (EXPANDED) ELECTRON BEAM EXCITATION SPECTRUM OF THE THIRD CONTINUUM OF ARGON WITH STANDARD PURITY GAS, SHOWING WHAT THE AUTHORS DESCRIBE AS "ADDITIONAL IMPURITY LINES WHICH COULD NOT YET BE UNAMBIGUOUSLY ASSIGNED." AFTER (ULRICH 1998).

Mills calculated that the spin-nuclear coupling of the H(1/4) hydrino should produce an absorption peak of 21.4 cm^{-1}. This matched a small peak seen in the far infrared absorption spectrum of very cold molecular hydrogen gas in a study by a doctorate student in 1993 (Wishnow 1993).

Ed Wishnow built a multireflection cell to hold hydrogen gas, which was injected after it was cooled with liquid helium. A beam of infrared light was passed through the chamber and bounced between mirrors at either end of the chamber to increase the path length. The mirrors were curved, allowing the beam to refocus at each reflection, and built-in controls allowed the operator to manually adjust the mirrors as they cooled and deformed. The spectrum was recorded with Fourier Transform Infrared Spectroscopy (FTIR).

In interstellar space, hydrogen gas is very hard to see. Cold, dense clouds of molecular hydrogen that are shielded from nearby stars do not have enough energy to jump to vibrational excitations, and because of the molecule's symmetry, it can't undergo pure rotational transitions. Wishnow was looking for peaks corresponding to weakly-bound dimers of hydrogen molecules. Maybe his results would help us find hydrogen in space, or understand the environments on Neptune and Uranus.

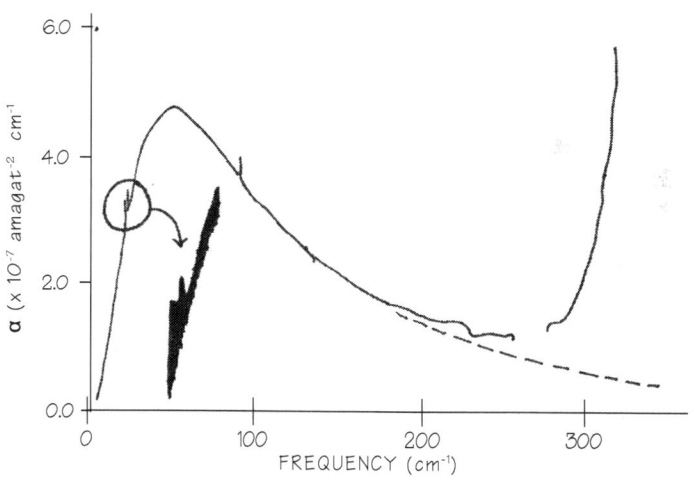

HYDRINO HYPERFINE STRUCTURE ?
FAR-INFRARED ABSORPTION SPECTRUM OF CRYOGENICALLY-COOLED HYDROGEN GAS IN A MULTI-REFLECTION CELL. MILLS IDENTIFIED THE PEAK AT 21.4 cm^{-1} AS THE HYPERFINE STRUCTURE OF THE H(1/4) HYDRINO. AFTER (WISHNOW 1993).

Mills's peak was small, and it only showed up in the 25 K spectrum but not the 35 K one. This might have been due to the ability of isolated hydrogen atoms to survive at 25 K but not 35 K, at which temperature they are more likely to combine into a molecule.

Wishnow didn't notice the peak at the time, but it did appear in two independent spectra. However, in both, it was at the very limit of the spectrometer's capabilities, and in one plot it was almost exactly at the cut off. Wishnow didn't notice it until I pointed it out.

We often don't see what we aren't looking for; psychologists call this *attention bias*. Even if Wishnow did notice the unusual peak at the time, he didn't have a compelling reason to think it was important.

As yet another important piece of evidence for the hydrino, Mills hopes to repeat this experiment. We should see the peak amplify with gases released from hydrino catalysis. But the experiment may need to be redesigned to offer better resolution in the frequency range in which hydrino peaks should appear.

These serendipitous studies show that we tend to ignore unexplained data. After all, experimental science is a messy business. A leaky seal, an improper vacuum, a contaminant upstream in our sourcing of materials or gases, any of these can result in unexplained artifacts. Only if an artifact lingers through multiple trials, after attempts to eliminate it, do we bless it with the status of being real. In which case, we may call it out as "unknown," and relegate it to a footnote.

Perhaps we should pay more attention to footnotes. It is the realm where data that is unexpected, weird, or potentially incompatible with existing theory goes to die.[84]

Who will go to the lengths necessary to hunt down mysteries and flush them out? Who will change focus, divert their experimental goal from achieving a desired outcome to an open-ended process of discovery? Who risks time and energy on the unknown? It is normal to assume there is nothing unexpected in our world until persuaded—perhaps forced—to think otherwise.

An experiment is usually assumed to be a targeted act of confirmation or disconfirmation, or an act of characterizing a specific phenomenon. But it is also an act of observation, an open-ended experience of perception. The next paradigm of thought may come from a bunch of squiggly lines in otherwise unambitious research.

---

[84] Just checking to make sure you are checking the footnotes.

New theories can move and shake science by changing our focus. We don't wait to make a serendipitous find, we predict. The hydrino is elusive; it left only a whisper in a century of chemistry, and was discovered by a theoretician before conducting a single experiment.

Without the theoretician, perhaps the hydrino would have come to focus eventually, at the locus of interwoven threads of unexplained data, by some experimentalist who refused to allow even the slightest artifact of experiment go unexplained, who was willing to trust her senses over the theories of her forerunners.

In fact, astronomers are even now searching the skies for something they know is there, but cannot see. They are looking for a type of matter that does not absorb and emit light in normal ways. They are looking for matter that is *dark*.

CHAPTER 14

THE HYDRINO UNIVERSE

In which we learn how to find an invisible atom.

Some problems in science present as beautiful mysteries that inspire poets and college students huddled in close conversation in coffeeshops at the twilight hours: the nature of gravitation, or that of consciousness. Some problems are nuts-and-bolts problems that carry little glamor, but must be solved in due time by some dedicated individual.

And some problems in science are of the kind that we just want to go away.

In 1933, Fritz Zwicky, a Swiss astronomer and professor at Caltech, began studying the Coma cluster, a nearby group of more than 800 galaxies swarming like gnats on a summer evening. In the middle of his paper, he brought up an issue that concerned him.

FRITZ ZWICKY

Zwicky measured the angular velocity of the galaxies in the Coma cluster at something between 1,000-2,000 km/s. He then calculated the mass of the galaxies based on their brightness. Using the same laws that govern the orbits of planets around the Sun, he then checked his numbers to see if they all made sense.

Unfortunately they didn't. Based on the mass and distances between the galaxies in the group, they should only have been moving at something around 80 km/s! Unless the Coma cluster was about to disintegrate, throwing its galaxies out into space in all directions, Zwicky was underestimating its mass by a huge margin. He was led by the results to speculate:

> ...the average density in the Coma system would have to be at least 400 times larger than that derived on the grounds of observations of luminous matter. If this is confirmed we get the surprising result that dark matter

is present in much greater amount than luminous matter. (Zwicky 1933)

There was more stuff out there, and it was "dark." But what was it?

A few years later, Sinclair Smith found the same thing in the Virgo cluster. The average speed of a galaxy there was 1200 km/s, but after calculating the mass, it came out about 200 times what Hubble had estimated a few years earlier based on the luminosity (Smith 1936). Smith guessed that the missing mass was large clouds of gas forming halos around galaxies, or floating hidden in intergalactic space. While small inconsistencies between theory and experiment are acceptable and even encouraging, huge inconsistencies make us groan. Most astronomers completely ignored the issue, and it would take another fifty years for the community to take serious interest. Zwicky was obviously disturbed by it and embarked on a one-man decades-long hunt for the missing matter. He never found the source, but he did find intergalactic clouds of dust and gas bridging between galaxies.

More evidence continued to pour in. In 1940, J.H. Oort was studying the rotation of NGC 3115 (the "Spindle" galaxy), oriented edge-on to us about 32 million light years away. He found that just above the equatorial plane, the light tapers off dramatically, down to about 10% of its starting value, but the mass holds about constant. At the outer edge, the amount of mass is 250 times what we *ought* to see (Oort 1940).

Twenty years later, two scientists at Princeton stumbled upon the same issue closer to home. Our neighborhood cluster of galaxies, the Local Group, is orbiting too quickly to be reined in by the mass we can see, most of which is held by the two local heavyweights, the Andromeda Galaxy and our Milky Way. The astronomers speculated that the enormous amount of missing matter was likely clouds of gas, mostly hydrogen but some helium, surrounding the galactic halo (KahnWoltjer 1959).

In 1964, Vera Rubin joined the Department of Terrestrial Magnetism (DTM) at the Carnegie Institute in Washington, DC. After two years of studying quasars, an intensely competitive topic, she cast around for something that nobody else was working on, and that could be done on smaller telescopes. She wanted a nuts-and-bolts problem.[85] She chose to study Andromeda, our close neighbor in space at 2.5 million light years. Her goal was to study the movement of stars, to a level of precision that no one had done before. Because Andromeda was so close, she would be

---

[85] For excellent further reading I recommend Panek 2011.

able to measure the movements of stars not just in the suburbs, but in the rural outskirts of the great spiral.

To do so she needed a spectrograph that could detect the subtle Doppler shifts in the positions of well-known atomic spectral lines; these shifts tell us how fast a star is moving. Using a spectrograph invented by her office mate, W. Ford, she could reduce exposure times for her observations by a factor of ten. She could take more, and better, data. Ford and Rubin used two observatories in Arizona, taking turns looking through the telescope. By 1968, they were able to plot the angular velocity of the stars in Andromeda, from the center to the outer edge, at a level of resolution never before done.

When Rubin and Ford plotted the results, they expected to find a diminishing curve, of the kind that Copernicus used to place the order of planets in the solar system, according to which the farther a planet is from the Sun, the longer it takes to make a complete orbit. This makes sense as gravity diminishes with distance. Ford and Rubin expected the stars around Andromeda to steadily drop off in their galactic year the further they were from the center.

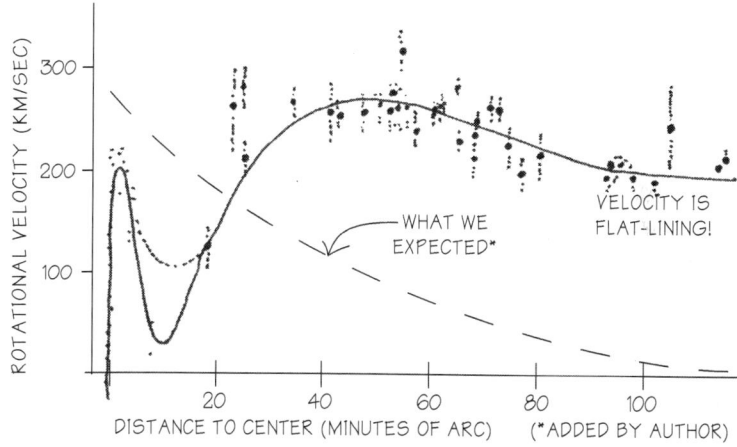

ROTATIONAL VELOCITIES OF THE ANDROMEDA GALAXY FIT TO A CURVE, REPORTED BY RUBIN AND FORD IN 1969. IT WAS EXPECTED THAT THE ROTATION CURVES OF GALAXIES WOULD FALL OFF DRAMATICALLY AT THE OUTER EDGE; INSTEAD, THERE IS NEAR-CONSTANT DISTRIBUTION OF VELOCITIES. AFTER (RUBIN 1970).

Instead, the curve was *flat*. The stars in the metropolis of Andromeda's central bulge, those in the suburbs, and those in the rural outskirts were all moving at nearly the *same* velocity (Rubin 1970). Even at the rim of visible stars in the disk, the curve didn't show any sign of dropping off.

Soon they were joined by Morton Roberts at the National Radio Astronomy Observatory who was studying Andromeda in the radio wavelengths, and took data far beyond the edge of the galaxy's visible spiral. He found the same thing: the velocity profile was flat as far out as he could see.

Perhaps it was the same problem Zwicky had seen with the Coma Cluster, and Smith with the Virgo Cluster, and Oort with the Spindle Galaxy. Over the next decade, every galaxy studied had a flat rotation curve. Astrophysicists ran computational simulations of the dynamics of galaxies to study their motion. *If* our theory of gravity is correct over large scales, the whole Andromeda galaxy—as with perhaps most galaxies—is surrounded, submerged, and stabilized by enormous halos of unseen matter that increase in ratio to visible matter as you move outward from the center of the disk. This dark matter gives off very little or no light, yet represents not just *some* of what is out there, but the overwhelming majority of matter in the universe, perhaps *ten times* what can be seen (Ostriker 1974).

These results were incredible, and astronomers received them with incredible hostility; some thought that Ford and Rubin were ruining their career by pursuing it. Dark matter became the source of arguments at conferences. But eventually astronomers had no choice but to accept the overwhelming evidence that there was a serious problem.

With a visible sigh, they began to theorize.

What could dark matter be? Perhaps objects that emit little or no light, such as black holes or remnants, Jupiters or brown dwarfs, white dwarfs or neutron stars. Astronomers looked for these Massive Astrophysical Compact Halo Objects (MACHOs) in the galactic halo by studying how their gravity bends light from galaxies beyond, but didn't see enough of them to explain so much missing mass.

Perhaps the particles are hot: moving at relativistic velocities through the galaxy. Or maybe they are cold: moving at the same rate as the rest of matter, but only weakly interacting with it. For the love of acronyms, astronomers call these Weakly Interacting Massive Particles (WIMPs).

RINGS OF DARK MATTER
(DETECTED BY GRAVITATIONAL LENSING)

Perhaps neutrinos, once thought to be massless, do have mass. Neutrinos interact so little with matter that trillions of them pass through you every second, so even a very low mass would mean a huge contribution to the weight inventory of the universe.

Perhaps the missing mass is made up of theoretical but never before seen particles such as "axions," "neutralinos," or a supersymmetric particle called the "sneutrino." Or perhaps there is something fundamentally wrong with our theories of gravity or inertia. After all, evidence for dark matter is indirect. Some suggested that we modify Newton's theory over long distances to explain the mass discrepancy (Milgrom 1983). The problem with *dark* matter is that we have nothing to go on. Do we modify theory or invent particles? What restraints are there on the speculations of the imagination?

Dark matter seems to be everywhere we look. Perhaps one way to learn more about it is to look where dark matter *isn't*.

Let me briefly digress. We experience time on a characteristic human scale. A starfish on the beach appears to barely move. But time-lapse film shows that starfish are active, even social creatures. We need to alter our experience of time to truly observe a starfish. A time scale even longer is that of a redwood tree, or a continent, or a mountain. Galaxies live in *cosmological* time, and if we alter our perception to match, we find an equally social existence.

Galaxies often collide over millions of years, their stars interpenetrating and intermingling in a kind of cosmic mating ritual. The gravitational maelstrom of these encounters can often spin off a small eddy of stars that becomes a new galaxy, a cosmic birth. These young dwarf galaxies carry off stars, dust, and gas that originated in small regions of one or both of the parent galaxies, as if we had drawn the sample out with a syringe.

A GALACTIC COLLISION
...AND A COSMIC BIRTH

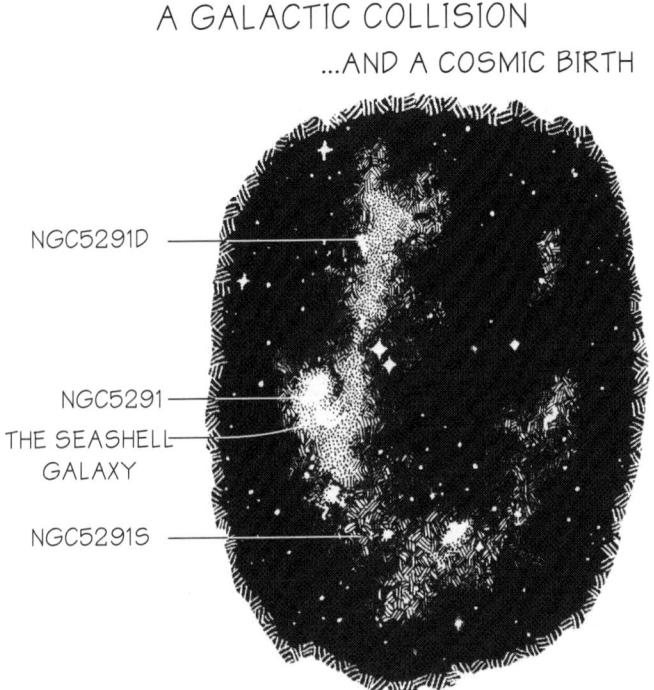

A GALAXY COLLISION SURROUNDED BY A CLOUD OF GAS CONTAINING DWARF GALAXIES. THE DWARFS WERE FOUND TO CONTAIN ONLY TWICE AS MUCH DARK MATTER AS NORMAL MATTER. THE AUTHORS SUGGEST THAT HYDROGEN IS THE MOST NATURAL CANDIDATE FOR DARK MATTER. AFTER (BOURNAUD 2007).

Frederic Bournaud noticed that most theories predict that dark matter surrounds galaxies in large halos. So he went looking for a good syringe to obtain material in the galactic interior, and found NGC5291, a galactic collision surrounded by gas-rich collisional debris, including several dwarf galaxies.

He found that these galaxies contained only about twice as much dark matter as luminous matter (Bournaud 2007). This matter must have resided *within* the disks of spiral galaxies as well as in the halo. Perhaps it is normal stuff, able to form stars much like normal matter.

We appear to live in a hydrogen universe. Of the matter that we can see, about 95% is made up of hydrogen. And what isn't trapped in the inferno of a star lingers as clouds of gas throughout the galaxy. Bournaud speculated that the most natural candidate for dark matter (we might say the *least* imaginative possibility) is hydrogen. Hydrogen is difficult to trace directly, so we estimate its existence via emission lines from carbon monoxide (CO). Bournaud suggested that either the missing hydrogen is very cold, less traceable with CO lines, or there is a "sizable fraction of cold H_2 not traced at all by CO." The amount of hydrogen in the dwarf galaxies needed to be about three times that already detected via the CO line.

To be undetectable, hydrogen gas must be extremely cold, only a few degrees above absolute zero. But the hydrogen observed in these dwarfs was *warm*, over 400 K. Other gases seen also appeared to be quite warm.[86] If hydrogen is the most natural assumption for the identity of dark matter, why the hell can't we see it?

On June 7, 1992, Stuart Bowyer watched a Delta II rocket lift off from Cape Canaveral. It was carrying the Extreme Ultraviolet Explorer (EUVE) satellite, the result of twenty years of work by him and a team of graduate students at the Center for Extreme Ultraviolet Astrophysics at the University of California Berkeley, in collaboration with NASA. For the first time, astronomers would have access to emissions from space within the band of wavelengths between 10-100 Å, what Bowyer called the "last frontier in observational astronomy" (Bowyer 1994).

For many years, astronomers believed that the effort would be futile. The Earth's atmosphere absorbs EUV light, making ground-based

---

[86] For a review of this topic I recommend Elmegreen 2007.

telescopes unusable for those wavelengths. And any light reaching a space-born telescope would still need to pass through the gas that permeates interstellar space in all directions. Observing in the EUV was also difficult, for logistical reasons: new mirrors had to be developed that could focus EUV light without absorbing it, that could be exposed to space without glass windows, and would be stable at extremely cold temperatures.

Prior to 1992, unable to convince his peers that an EUV satellite was justified, Bowyer applied for smaller grants to launch sounding rockets into the upper atmosphere, each of which had five minutes of observing time on each flight, and tested key equipment for later space missions while gathering useful data. Suffice it to say, when he looked into space, he saw EUV light, including sources hundreds of light years away, from white dwarves to stars with highly active corona. Space was more transparent then anyone thought. The EUV Explorer would allow astronomers to count thousands of EUV sources across the sky.

One of these sounding rockets was launched on April 22, 1986, from White Sands, New Mexico, at ten minutes after midnight. Bowyer, with graduate student Simon Labov, bundled three EUV spectrometers into one rocket, each designed to detect different wavelengths. They would not point at individual stars, but take light from broad regions of space to capture the diffuse background radiation. Theoretically, this could tell us something about the interstellar medium (ISM).

Their findings were published in 1991. In addition to a very strong Helium II peak at 303 Å, the diffuse data had found peaks at 99 Å, 178 Å and 635 Å (Labov 1991). Labov and Bowyer searched the literature for these peaks and found that they were near lines for highly ionized states of oxygen, silicon, neon, or iron.

The most likely source for the 635 Å line was oxygen V, though the actual known line is 629.7 Å. Other lines they expected to see from a very hot gas of oxygen were not present, so the emitting oxygen must have been from a very specific temperature. It must have been between 250,000 and 450,000 K.[87]

The instrument was less precise for shorter wavelengths, but no peaks were expected from a hot oxygen gas corresponding to the other peaks at 99 Å and 178 Å. The best match for the 99 Å line was a series of iron emissions at one million degrees, and the best match for the 178 Å line

---

[87] There is also a helium excited state transition at 625 Å, but that is 10 Å off the mark, so less likely.

was iron emission at 4-6 million degrees, all at highly ionized states.

Seeing three wildly different but highly constrained temperatures of gas exist in interstellar space generated more questions than answers, and Labov and Bowyer pointed out that the evidence was, after all, indirect. They couldn't think of any plausible alternative to explain the lines, except a thermal one, the emission of a hot gas.

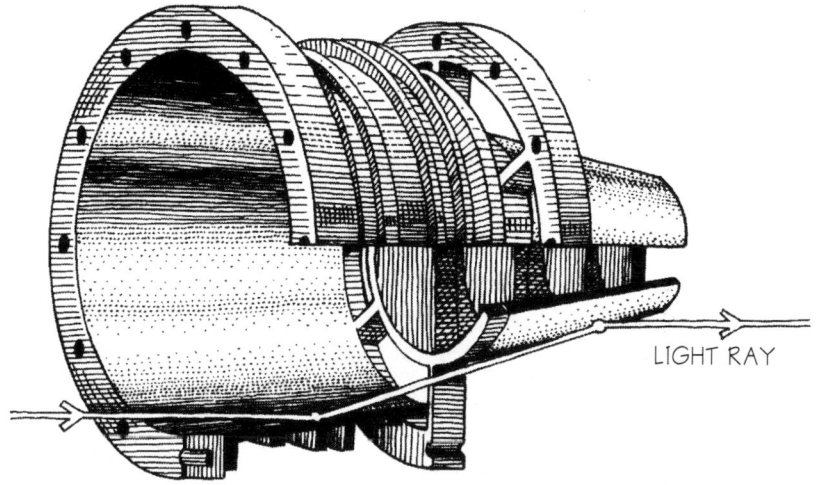

SEEING IN THE EXTREME ULTRAVIOLET

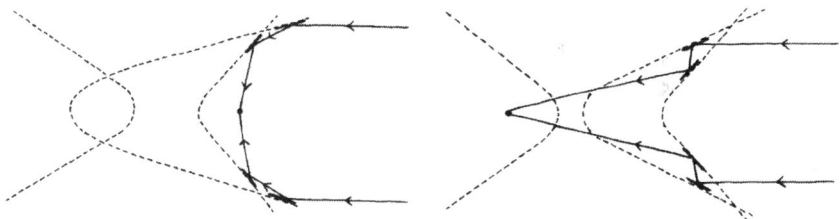

ABOVE: EXTREME ULTRAVIOLET EXPLORER TELESCOPE WITH A GRAZING-INCIDENCE COLLECTOR, AFTER (BOWYER 1994). BELOW: GEOMETRIES FOR GRAZING-INCIDENCE AFTER (BARSTOW 2003, P. 12).

When the Extreme Ultraviolet Explorer launched in 1995, it conducted a follow-up search for diffuse EUV background radiation in the interstellar medium (ISM). It was not specifically designed for diffuse observations, but it had the most sensitive equipment yet in space. It could do wide angle observation and subtract foreground sources to obtain background noise more likely due to diffuse sources. It found a clean spectrum with broad emission lines at 304 Å, 537 Å, and 584 Å, but none of the unexplained lines picked up by the earlier spectrometers on the sounding rocket (Jelinsky 1995; Vallerga 1998).

Two experiments, two different results.

Commenting twenty years later, Bowyer felt that although all astrophysical data must be statistically significant to be published, most of it is overturned by later research. Perhaps the previous lines were merely artifacts. Or perhaps they were real, but this didn't bother him either. Space is filled with stellar processes that result in distinct environments. One emission may be due to a cataclysmic variable star. Another a white dwarf. The source is out there. We just don't know what it is.

We have also found X-ray radiation in galaxy clusters, emitting from what astrophysicists could only guess is a gas at 93 million degrees (Sanders 1996).

The mysteries piled up. Astronomers noticed that our solar system lives in an interstellar cloud of gas, within a much larger, lower density cloud called the Local Bubble. Much of the gas within this bubble was ionized, which was surprising. To split an electron from a proton in the hydrogen atom, it must absorb a photon with an energy at least in the ultraviolet (at 912 Å), but perhaps higher frequencies (lower wavelengths) in the EUV, X-ray, or Gamma-ray range. Since EUV emissions are quickly absorbed by interstellar gas such as hydrogen, the source for these emissions needed to be widely distributed across the sky.

The best explanation is that our bubble was produced by a supernova explosion some millions of years ago, which also perturbed the ionization ratio (Barstow 2003). But we see the same thing throughout the galaxy. If point-sources such as stars, nebulae, or supernovae are the source, they are not widespread enough. Could dark matter be the source of hydrogen-ionizing emissions? If so, then we should find that the distribution of hydrogen-ionizing sources throughout the galaxy should match the distribution of dark matter needed to keep the galaxy stable as a large, flattened disk halo. And indeed, it matched well (Sciama 1990).

So we are looking for a particle that is dark but also decays with a high-enough energy to ionize space gas. In 1990, D.W. Sciama suggested that a neutrino mass around 28 eV could decay to produce a peak in the diffuse background UV (Sciama 1990). But when astronomers looked, nothing was found (Davidsen 1991).

By 2001 when I was a college freshman, the hydrino had started to diffuse into the background consciousness of the field. Early in my first year of Chemistry 101, a professor showed us an image of the excited state energies of hydrogen, and joked as an aside (with a reference that probably I alone in the class understood) "somebody thinks that there should be a bunch of lines down here, but there aren't any."[88]

There had been some talk about Mills among the chemistry department staff. An emeritus professor gave me a stack of monthly issues of the *International Journal of Hydrogen Energy*, containing some of BLP's papers. He had marked them up with questions about details of the experiment, like a thesis instructor might. I enjoyed looking through his comments.

Another professor suggested that the reaction might be dangerous: if it used hydrogen and potassium, what would stop it from blowing up the world's oceans? This didn't worry me, because if it were possible, it would make the existence of Earth's oceans after four billion years unlikely.

It is often overlooked by those newly approaching Mills's work that according to Mills's theory, hydrinos *don't have electronic excited states*. No quantum jumps from a hydrino ground state to a hydrino excited state. No absorption or emission of light. The electron is *locked* in its orbit, unless it participates in more catalysis. Otherwise, it can't be seen.

This is unknown in nature. All substances absorb and emit light of some frequency. The molecule H_3^+ is an exception because it will break apart before it accepts enough energy to form an excited state.

As Vera Rubin was fond of saying "Nobody told us that all matter radiated. We just assumed that it did" (Panek 2011).

So how do we see an invisible atom?

In 2003, BLP published an article in the *Journal of Applied Physics (JAP)* (Mills 2003e). This was a good journal, and widely read. In it, Mills and Parish Ray at BLP studied a plasma with 98% helium and only about 2% hydrogen. They wanted to see emission lines from the hydrogen, so only a tiny bit of hydrogen was used; just enough to emit lines without the rest of the gas in the cell absorbing the light before it made it to the spectrometer. In this experiment they saw a series of peaks they assigned to the formation of hydrino.

---

[88] If memory serves, the comment was made by Arthur Gladsfield.

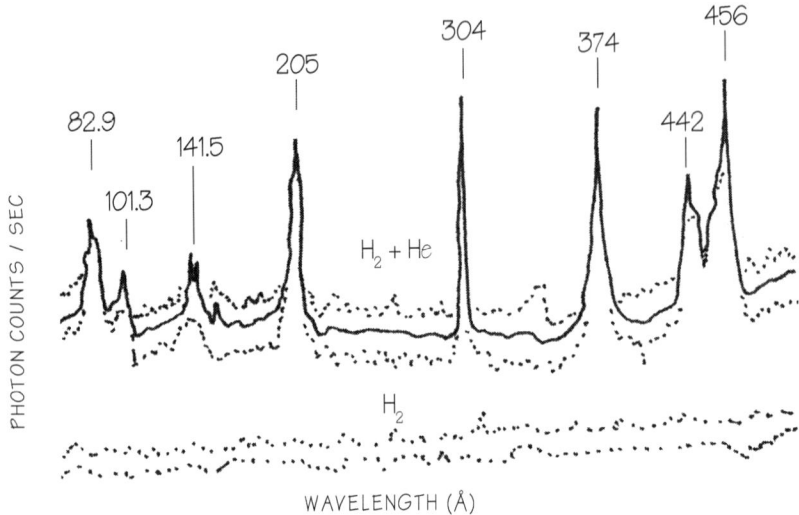

EUV EMISSIONS FROM A HYDROGEN PLASMA

THE EUV SPECTRA OF THE BLP'S MICROWAVE PLASMA CELL CONSISTING OF A 98% HELIUM WITH 2% HYDROGEN MIXTURE RECORDED AT 1 TORR PRESSURE, VERSUS A PURE HYDROGEN CONTROL (HELIUM CONTROLS WERE ALSO PERFORMED). NOVEL EMISSION LINES FROM HYDROGEN WERE OBSERVED THAT CORRESPOND TO HYDRINO TRANSITIONS. AFTER (MILLS 2003E).

A helium atom with one missing electron (He⁺) has an ionization energy of 54.4 eV, which can act as a catalyst to allow a transition to a H(1/3) hydrino. The hydrino must collide with the helium ion, which resonantly absorbs energy from hydrogen and expels it by shooting off an electron. This doesn't result in an H(1/3) hydrino yet, but rather a temporary ("metastable") state H*(1/3) that then quickly decays to form the hydrino. When this last step occurs, light is emitted in the EUV range. If the plasma is optically thin, our EUV spectrometer can detect that light, giving us a window to the act of creation before the hydrino atom goes dark.

And in addition to catalysis by helium, Mills predicted that hydrino atoms, once formed, could further catalyze hydrino formation, in what Mills called *disproportionation* reactions. The frequencies of light emitted by hydrino catalysis form what we might call the Mills series.

The interpretation of peaks that Mills and Ray found was not entirely straightforward. The H(1/7) peak was weak, and appeared only as a shoulder on the H(1/8) peak. The H(1/4), H(1/6), and H(1/8) peaks were scattered from helium, so one must subtract from the line the energy of exciting an electron in helium from the *1s²* to *2p¹* orbital. BLP found the following peaks corresponding to the table of hydrino transitions: 456 Å, 304 Å (scattered), 205 Å (scattered), 130.3 Å, 141.5 Å (scattered), 101.3 Å and 82.9 Å.

The *JAP* wanted to be sure that Mills had exhausted all other possibilities for these peaks, so the paper discussed possible atomic and molecular states of hydrogen and helium that could exist in the plasma, even with little probability of being there. Nothing worked.

Some of these peaks, you may notice, are familiar. The 303 Å line was assigned by Labov and Bowyer as a helium II emission, but there was no corresponding 256 Å helium II line, so BLP proposed that the 303 Å line was substantially due to the H(1/3) to H(1/4) hydrino transition. The 99 Å peak was assigned as a million-degree cluster of highly ionized iron peaks; BLP assigned it as the H(1/6) to H(1/7) transition at 101 Å. And the 179 Å peak, another assignment to iron, matched the predicted H(1/4) to H(1/5) peak, although this line was not seen in BLP's plasma experiment. When BLP asked for Labov and Bowyer's data, they also found a possible peak at 82.9 Å and assigned it to the H(1/7) to H(1/8) transition. And there was a faint artifact at 130.2 Å that may have been an H(1/5) to H(1/6) line.

The 635 Å peak might simply have been explained by scattering of the 303 Å peak from helium. Taken together, the EUV data from 1990 in combination with replications in the laboratory may offer some evidence for the existence of hydrino in interstellar space.

Emissions at exactly 912 Å are also produced by hydrino formations, but like those that sit on the 303 Å peak, these are masked by other plausible interpretations. The collision of two H(1/2) hydrinos forming an H(1/3) and an H⁺, as well as the collision of an H(1/3) and H(1/4) hydrino producing an H(1/5) and an H, both produce photons at 912 Å, exactly the energy released by the binding of an electron and proton to form hydrogen. This peak could be easily assigned, and therefore ignored, by those searching for dark matter.

Peak (Å)	BLP	L&B	q
635.0	(not observed)	O V (629.7)	3 (Scattered)
456.0	Yes	(not observed)	2
374.0	Yes	(not observed)	4 (Scattered)
303.0	Yes	He II	3
205.0	Yes	(not observed)	6 (Scattered)
179.0	(not observed)	Fe	5
141.5	Yes	(not observed)	8 (Scattered)
130.2	Yes	(faint)	7
99.0	Yes	Fe	9
82.9	Yes	(faint)	11

Comparison of lines found in Labov and Bowyer's diffuse EUV background data from a sounding rocket launch in 1986 with those found in BLP's 98% helium / 2% hydrogen plasma cell. Also shown are assignments by each author. q in the reaction indicates multiples of 13.6 eV which are released by hydrino transitions (Labov 1991; Mills 2003c).

Since space is filled with low density gas, especially hydrogen and helium, these emissions in the EUV rarely travel far. EUV astronomers have found windows: directions we can look in space that have very low gas densities (called the "column density"). Since we observe ionized hydrogen in space, the source of these emissions must be distributed broadly across the sky. In short: hydrino formation could be happening everywhere, ionizing surrounding gas as a result of turning hydrogen into hydrino, which becomes totally transparent to light, yet continues to catalyze over time, emitting ongoing flux with wavelengths of 912 Å and lower.

But what of the 1995 data from the EUVE? This showed a peak at 303 Å, easily assignable to He II, but only if the gas in the interstellar medium was at a specific temperature in which the other He II peak at 256 Å did not appear. Otherwise it could have been partially due to the H(1/3) to H(1/4) transition.

The EUVE data also showed a broad peak at 584 Å with a soft shoulder at 537 Å, both potentially helium peaks. Mills was only able to match this feature many years later, with EUV spectra from explosive hydrino formation (which we will discuss later) that produced a spectrum peaking at about 584 Å, corresponding to a plasma with a blackbody temperature of 5,000 degrees. A plasma, mind you, that contained *no* helium (Mills 2015).

Finally, the 1995 data also showed a broad band of continuum radiation that increased below 150 Å, where the data range of the spectrometer cut off. We will have to wait until the next EUVE satellite to interpret this; it could be hydrino-produced continuum radiation, such as the 160-110 Å band produced by the H to H(1/4), or H(1/5) to H(1/6) transitions. Or, it could be something else entirely.

Is dark matter actually hydrino? It seems to fit every feature of the problem.

- ¤ Hydrino atoms and molecules are *dark*, incapable of electronic transitions unless being created or destroyed during hydrino-catalysis.
- ¤ Hydrino gas cannot be traced the same way as hydrogen gas, but ought to be found wherever hydrogen gas exists.
- ¤ Emissions from hydrino formation provide a mechanism for hydrogen and helium ionization across wide swaths of the sky.
- ¤ It explains diffuse EUV and soft X-ray background without requiring there to be weird populations of gases at highly specific, extremely hot temperatures.
- ¤ Hydrogen is the most abundant element in the universe. The next most abundant element? Helium, which, when ionized, is a catalyst.

Whip up a universe, start with a lot of hydrogen, add a pinch of helium, and shake for a few billion years. You may end up with lot of hydrino on your hands. And as I've mentioned before, even without helium, three-body collisions of hydrogen atoms can catalyze hydrino. Three-body collisions are rare, but we are talking *billions* of years. Everything becomes likely given enough time. And hydrinos are also effective catalysts. The reactions will produce a diffuse glow of EUV and soft X-ray light throughout the universe.

Hydrino is telling us, in its own way, that it is out there.

Recently, a team of scientists decided to look for one of the theoretical candidates for dark matter, the "sterile" neutrino, which has a predicted decay energy somewhere between 2-10 keV. They didn't even need to acquire time on a telescope. Instead, they went fishing in a pile of existing data.

X-ray data can be detected by large telescopes equipped with spectrometers; among these are the XMM-Newton, ASCA, Chandra, and Suzaku telescopes. The team borrowed the spectroscopic data from these telescopes' observations of 73 galaxy clusters. (*A galaxy cluster* contains dozens of galaxies, each galaxy containing hundreds of billions of stars.) Then they "stacked" the spectra, using well-known atomic emission peaks to align the data at different redshifts. This had the effect of amplifying any real signals and diminishing random noise.

They expected to find their neutrino in a narrow band between 2 and 10 keV, and indeed they found a small blip at about 3.57 keV (Bulbul 2014). The line was extremely faint; and almost impossible to see when glancing at the full spectrum dominated by strong, well-known emission peaks. It would be lost in the noise if you analyzed any one spectra with the human eye. But taking all the data together, the blip emerged.

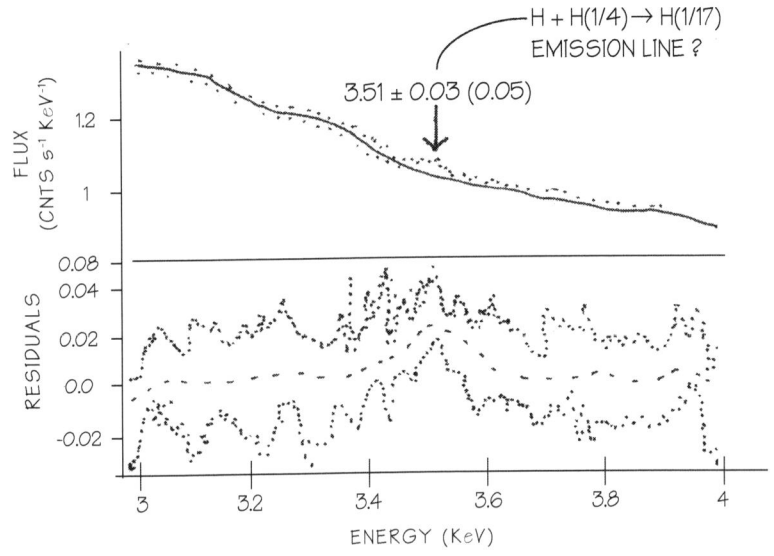

DARK MATTER SIGNATURE?

3-4 KEV BAND OF THE STACKED XXM-NEWTON SPECTRUM OF 73 GALAXY CLUSTERS SPANNING A REDSHIFT OF 0.01-0.35. THE FEATURE AT 3.57 KEV COULD NOT BE EXPLAINED BY KNOWN THERMAL EMISSION LINES. MILLS SUGGESTED IT WAS DUE TO THE HYDRINO-CATALYZED REACTION OF H AND H(1/4) TO FORM H(1/17). AFTER (BULBUL 2014).

The blip was most interesting because there was no known corresponding atomic line. While you could theoretically produce *any* emission line given the right circumstances (say, a plasma with two different gas temperatures out of thermal equilibrium) chances are low that something of this nature is happening literally everywhere in the universe. The authors of the study were excited. Perhaps this was the signature of dark matter?

Mills certainly thought it was. A collision between a hydrogen atom and an H(1/4) hydrino could undergo catalysis to generate an H(1/17) hydrino. The reaction would produce an X-ray emission as a band of continuum radiation with a cutoff at 3.4816 eV.

That's pretty close.

CHAPTER 15

THE ETERNAL TIDE

In which we discover that the universe is accelerating in its expansion, and may be really quite old.

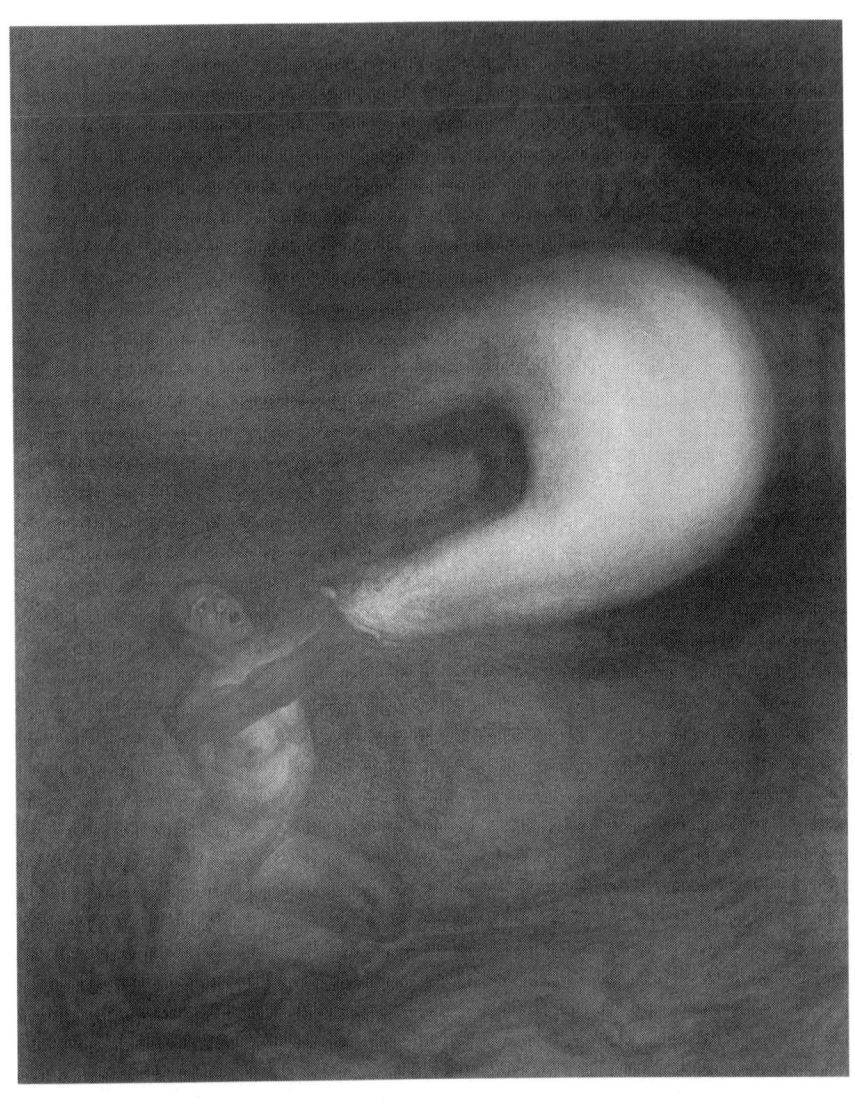

GOD RELEASING STARS INTO THE UNIVERSE
MICHAEL NEWBERRY. 1.5 x 2.1 m, OIL ON CANVAS.

In the summer of 2002, I lay on a beach at dawn, beneath a golden sunrise that electrified the air and merged with the sand and the tan of my own skin. After a swim I trekked back up through narrow streets, passing a wall of stone, and then another, as the pavement became cobble stones beneath my feet, and I entered the heart of the Old Town of Rhodes, once a Medieval fortress. On an overlooked side alley, projecting a little over the road, was a small two-story studio.

It looked over the old town with a view that captured the gentle sweep of the landscape. On this morning, as others, the many colors and textures of Greece began to awake, with a light that has inspired artists for a millennia.

The interior of the studio was still twilight. The floor and stucco walls were textured and imperfect like a Rembrandt painting, and on them hung large canvases, from which light and color emanated even at this early hour, their forms discernible in the morning darkness. Among the works of my friend and host, was the painting *God Releasing Stars into the Universe*.

The idea had emerged from a series of charcoal studies engaged to express feelings of loss and mourning. Charcoal is a sensuous medium that gave poetic expression to the inner being of the subjects, with a light that lifted from their hands and caressed their skin; a light of healing. In one study, the figure was on his knees, arms up, with peaceful waves radiating from his hands and open mouth in an act of ultimate release.

And from the work came the premise for the monumental nude, in which the river of light emanating from the man becomes an explosion of color and texture with depths that carry the eye. Looking into it you can believe that all of this, the nebulae, the stars, the galaxies, their sweeping arms of gas and dust tying them into the luminescent fabric of the world, could have come from an overwhelming act of love and intense desire; a need to fill the void.

Just as with the charcoal, the light from the figure's hands becomes an energy of creativity being released; a powerful expression of self that turns loss into renewal that consumes death and gives life. The artist Michael Newberry was exploring not a biblical theme, nor even a mythological one, but a human one, perhaps that which gave rise to the mythology, the feelings that inspired the first wanderer who spoke of the creation, of the beginning, and imagined it as hollow emptiness shook by a breath of life that renewed all in its wake.

Perhaps the world was born this way; perhaps it was not a benevolent force but purely the physics of the world, expanding like a tidal wave, leaving the fertile motes that shaped themselves, over thirteen billion years, into all of this. It is a beautiful idea, and not only for the sake of beauty is it believed. But in this chapter we will explore an alternative that has its own beauty; not a violent creation but the calm of a breath that draws in and sighs out, the foam of the Aegean washing over the shore of an unending time. I speak of the *oscillating* universe.

On the scale of the cosmos, gravitation rules. Yet gravity is owned not by stars or planets, nor even the grains that compose them, but the subatomic particles that compose the atoms of the grain. And here is where mystery lurks. Gravitation has never been understood in quantum mechanics, and the depth of our ignorance was made clear when we discovered that gravity does not rule the heavens unchallenged; there is another phenomenon combating it. And where there are *two* forces, oscillation can exist.

When Newton published his Law of Universal Gravitation in 1687, the law was a powerful tool to describe not only the parabolic arc of cannon fire but the elliptical orbit of the planets. In conjunction with his laws of mechanics, Newton felt that he had created a grand unification, bringing together separate spheres of heaven and earth under one set of natural laws.

His laws were unchallenged but for one observation. By the naked eye, stars do not move. They seem balanced in equilibrium, what Newton likened to making "not one needle only, but an infinite number of them... stand accurately poised upon their points." Why then does the universe not fall in upon itself, overcome by gravitational attraction?

Newton knew that if the laws in his treatise were universal, the book within which they were written would fall to the floor animated by the same force that pulls the Moon to the Earth, and the Earth to the Sun, that guides the moons of Jupiter and the rings of Saturn; that animates even the asteroids and comets, whose eccentric orbits take them far beyond sight. Yes; gravitation would act even between the stars, crossing immense distances, diminishing in strength but not in potency. Like the will of God, the rational physics of the world acts with equal power over all things and with the same inevitability.

Late in life, perhaps exhausted by the ultimate limitations of his own great scientific creativity, he added to his treatise: "And so that the systems of the fixed stars will not fall upon one another as a result of their gravity, He has placed them at immense distances from one another."

Telescopes continued to improve, many based on Newton's design.[89] As they did, our understanding of the order of the heavens took a leap. Astronomers discovered small, foggy shapes, called nebulae. In time we separated them into two groups: first, there were clusters of dust and gas that were perhaps newly-forming solar systems like our own (we continued to call these nebulae, which are relatively close to us in the universe); and second, there were structures, often spirals, that were phenomenally far away, galaxies with billions of their own stars, what Kant poetically called "island universes."

To distinguish among these groups, we needed to perceive distances accurately. We knew that the farther we were away from a star, the dimmer it would appear. However, stars vary considerably in their brightness. A dim star might very well be closer than a bright star.

It turns out that nature gives us a wonderful benchmark: there is an unusually bright type of star called a Cepheid. These stars have a pulse, getting brighter and darker in a regular rhythm, and their frequency is correlated very well with their brightness. We know this because we've measured the distance to Cepheids with independent methods. View a star in June, and again in December, and the position of the Earth in its orbit around the Sun will give us a slight shift in apparent position, much like having two cosmological eyes spaced apart the diameter of Earth's orbit. We call this *parallax*. It works well for stars that are nearby, but becomes more difficult for those that are distant.

If we know how bright a star like a Cepheid should be, based on our observations of local Cepheids, then we can calibrate the apparent brightness to calculate how far away it really is. It becomes a standard candle. In 1929, the American astronomer Edwin Hubble used Cepheids

---

[89] In which a bucket of light reflects from a parabolic mirror to the eyepiece.

to show conclusively that nebulae—stellar nurseries—are nearby, whereas galaxies are far beyond.

Galileo was the first to find that the band of light that crosses the night sky was made up of uncountable stars, forming the plane of our own spiral galaxy; in which our Sun orbited with billions of others like motes of ice in the rings of Saturn. Perhaps we remain aloft in the heavens for the same reason the Earth does around the Sun, carried by momentum, but in an orbit that takes 250 million years. Perhaps the motions of astronomical time are too slight to observe.

But we have only removed the problem one step. What keeps the *galaxies* aloft?

Having established a first estimate of the distances between galaxies, Hubble then turned his attention to the question of how they move. Hubble took advantage of the Doppler shifting of light waves: if the source was moving toward us, light would be shifted to higher frequencies (to the blue); if moving away it would be shifted to lower frequencies (to the red). Subtle shifts in the light spectrum of some galaxies allowed Hubble to estimate their motion.

Let us pause the historical reel here. Before Hubble announced how galaxies move, our theory of gravity gave us two possibilities: either the galaxies in the universe were falling toward one another, or they were hurtling quickly enough through intergalactic space to remain in equilibrium, like the moons of planets, planets of suns, and suns of galaxies.

What Hubble *did* find, no one expected.

Hubble discovered that almost all galaxies we can see are red-shifted. They are therefore moving *away* from us. Any direction he looked in space it was the same: galaxies flying away at a fantastic clip. By this logic the universe as a whole must be expanding. And the farther away the galaxy, the faster it is receding!

This is called Hubble's Law; and the ratio between distance and speed appeared (at least at first approximation) fixed. It gave us a new physical constant: Hubble's constant.

Are we at some special center of the universe, away from which everything is moving? A great universe-sized fire cracker exploding in all directions, with the astronomically unlikely result that we are at ground zero? Unlikely. Some galaxies are in fact moving toward us. But more likely is that all galaxies are on average moving away from all others. We don't believe we are quite that special, this is often called the *Copernican Principle*.

Let's illustrate with a little experiment.

Suppose you blow up hundreds of balloons. After catching your breath, you corral them into a pile in the center of a large room. Suppose you are then able to seal off the room and slowly evacuate the air. As you do so, the balloons are going to get bigger, because the pressure of the air inside each balloon will want to equalize with the pressure of the surrounding air. As the air pressure drops, the balloons will inflate. As they inflate, they will start to push each other apart. If you pick two balloons from the pile that are next to one another, you will find that they are moving apart slowly. However, if you pick two balloons on opposite ends of the pile, you will find that they are moving apart very quickly, because they are being forced apart by dozens of balloons inflating between them. If you choose any individual balloon, you will find that all others are moving away from it at speeds proportional to distance.

Place a galaxy at the center of each balloon, and you have a model of our universe. Galaxies close to us are moving away more slowly than galaxies further away. Whatever may be causing the expansion, it must be happening everywhere we look. We are being carried outward on the wind of an expanding space, animated by an unknown force so powerful that it overwhelms gravity.

The news would certainly have swept Newton off his feet.

When Einstein proposed his refinement to Newton's theory, he likewise assumed that the universe is static. In a desperate attempt to reconcile this observation with his theory, he introduced into his equation for gravity a new factor, the "cosmological constant" which would, over long distances, counteract the force of gravity and allow a static universe to exist. When Hubble made his discovery, Einstein lamented that it was the greatest mistake of his career, and removed the term from the equation.

Einstein knew, in retrospect, that he had not been true to his own method of theorizing. Einstein liked his theories to bloom logically from a single idea. When he tacked on an extra, purely empirical constant, it marred the purity of his ideas. Without the constant, Einstein would have bravely predicted a few possibilities for how the universe could exist, and remaining static was not one of them.

A universe that obeys General Relativity, without the cosmological constant, must be doing one the following:
1. Be collapsing.
2. Be expanding, but decelerating at such a rate that it will eventually fall back in on itself and collapse. This is a "closed" universe.
3. Be expanding, but decelerating at such a rate that the universe will never collapse, but drift outward, for all time. This is an "open" universe.

In all of these possibilities, gravity dominates. There are no other forces that can act on this scale. And in all of them, the universe is either collapsing, or decelerating.

Before Hubble's discovery, other theoreticians had already begun to discard the cosmological constant and explore the results.

Among them was Georges Lemaître, who thought about what might happen if the universe shrank to a very small region of space. In his writings, Lemaitre speculated that as the universe collapses, the only forces potentially capable of stopping the collapse are nuclear forces such as the strong force. At which point the universe would then be "comparable to a colossal atomic nucleus," (Lemaître 1933).

To expand from this point of collapse would require an incredible opposition to gravitational forces; Lemaitre could imagine it only as an explosion, fueled by a force of unimaginable magnitude; an act that would set galaxies and stars in motion for billions of years to come. It was perhaps fitting that Lemaître was a cleric, and found a fitting metaphor in Genesis: *let there be light*. Fred Hoyle, critical of the idea, inadvertently coined it in a radio interview: "the big bang."

But the big bang was just an idea, prompted by our theory of gravity. There was no proof of any kind, except that the universe was expanding.

In 1964, engineers at the Crawford Hill site of Bell Telephone Laboratories were calibrating a new radio astronomy telescope. They detected a low-level background radiation and assumed it was an artifact, because they observed the same signal no matter which way they pointed the telescope. After several efforts to eliminate the noise, they finally accepted it as real; space, it seemed, hummed with low-level static (Penzias 1965).

And as it turned out, a low-level cosmic background radiation (CMB) was predicted by Ralph Alpher and Robert Herman sixteen years earlier.

They had reasoned as follows: If the universe began as a giant fireball, the temperature and pressure would be so great that protons and electrons would not form atoms. Instead, it would be a gas of unbound particles. These would scatter light at almost all wavelengths, so the early universe would be opaque.

Only when the universe had expanded and cooled would electrons and protons form hydrogen atoms that absorb light only at discrete frequencies. At that moment universe would suddenly become transparent, and light would escape out into space. The light would sail outward in a great front, and as the universe continued to expand, the light would lose energy and shift to the red over billions of years, until it produced a noise with a blackbody spectrum at only a few degrees Kelvin.

The static in our telescopes was the residual buzz of the big bang, and our best evidence that it happened at all.[90]

More evidence comes from the most distant images ever taken of the universe.

In long exposures of otherwise dark regions of space, we are able to see light from galaxies billions of light-years away. The further we look, the further back in time we see, like paging backwards through a photo album. We can see back to the infancy of the universe, though not to its birth. And when we look, we see a higher percentage of youthful galaxies. A young galaxy, like a young solar system, will have a lot of dust and gas and may be irregularly shaped. It will also be full of young stars, and as a result it will tend to emit light in certain wavelengths, specifically the infrared. Star formation appears to have peaked about 10 billion years ago.

Based on this evidence, the big bang theory is accepted by the majority of physicists as the best explanation of the origin and evolution of the universe. It wasn't until the end of the century that the theory began to break down, in ways that we will explore soon. When Mills started thinking about cosmology, big bang theory was enjoying comfortable unchallenged prominence.

---

[90] There are slight variations in the intensity of the CMB, which is thought due to the imperfection of the explosion, leaving more matter here, less there. The CMB also revealed an overall pattern due to the movement of the Earth through space on a galactic scale.

Problems in physics form a dense interconnected web; if you solve a fundamental problem in one area, it will likely ripple outward and impact others.

Previously we learned how, according to Mills, the creation of a particle and antiparticle pair from a photon requires spacetime itself to contract, producing a gravitational field around the particle. And when a particle and antiparticle meet to annihilate back into a photon, or during any process in which part of a particle's mass is released as energy, spacetime is relaxed.

Spacetime pulls in and pushes out, and overall, it is conserved.

This is a strange notion. Spacetime is not stuff, but void. Yet it does have a metric, a mathematical description of how objects may move within it. Mills's new conservation law meant that at the end of the day, this pushing and pulling of spacetime, this creation and destruction of gravitational fields, must come out right.

And, it is an epiphany.

Look up at the night sky, and what do you see? Small glimmering dots. Stars are the universe's factories, enormous fusion engines that digest matter and produce light. To conserve spacetime, each fusion event pushes out space a very little bit; our Sun alone (a relatively modest star) fuses 620 million metric tons of hydrogen per second, refining it into helium, and releasing the balance of mass as energy. There are hundreds of billions of stars in our galaxy alone, and hundreds of billions of galaxies in the universe; at least the ones we can see.

Mills hypothesized that universe is not simply coasting from a primordial explosion, but *actively* pushing itself out. Stellar fusion, the most abundant physical process in nature, provides an explanation for why the universe is expanding, and it needs no big bang (Mills 2015, Ch. 32).

Mills continued to extrapolate from this idea. Over billions of years, the fires of the universe will burn, expanding space. Stars will grow old and die, perhaps explode as supernova, their remnants forming new stars (like ours), which will live out their lives, as their host galaxies slowly drift out on the spacetime wind. This goes on. Matter becomes scarce, and dominated by heavier elements of the ash of stars. Neutron stars will cool, ancient supermassive black holes will grow fat and annihilate in violent bursts; galaxies will shrink, dim, and grow dark. The last stars will be outposts, wavering candles in a vast expanse of emptiness. The expansion stops. The universe will reach its maximum size: about 312 billion light years across, about 22 times larger than it is today.

THE UNIVERSE

AT THE LARGEST SCALE WE KNOW. EACH DOT IS A CLUSTER OF GALAXIES.

(YOU ARE HERE)

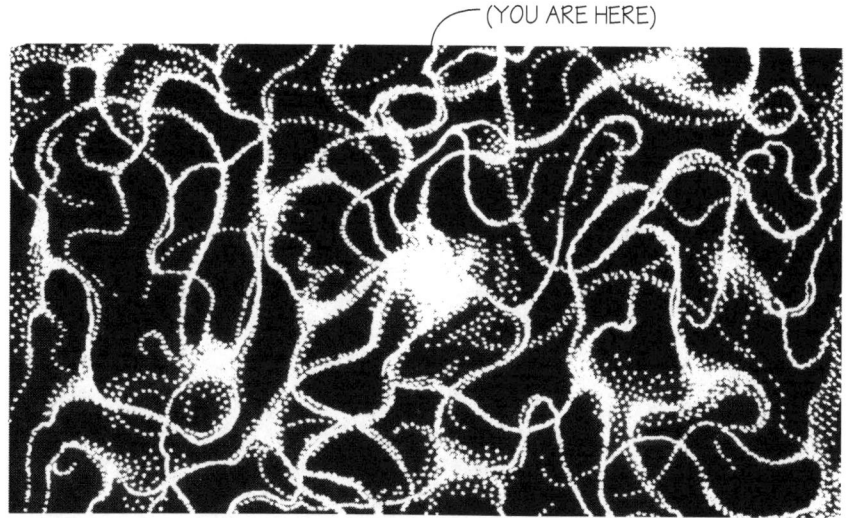

A YOUNG UNIVERSE - ABOUT 14 BILLION YEARS OLD
THE UNIVERSE IS HOT AND ACTIVE. SPACE EXPANDS RAPIDLY DUE TO STELLAR ACTIVITY.

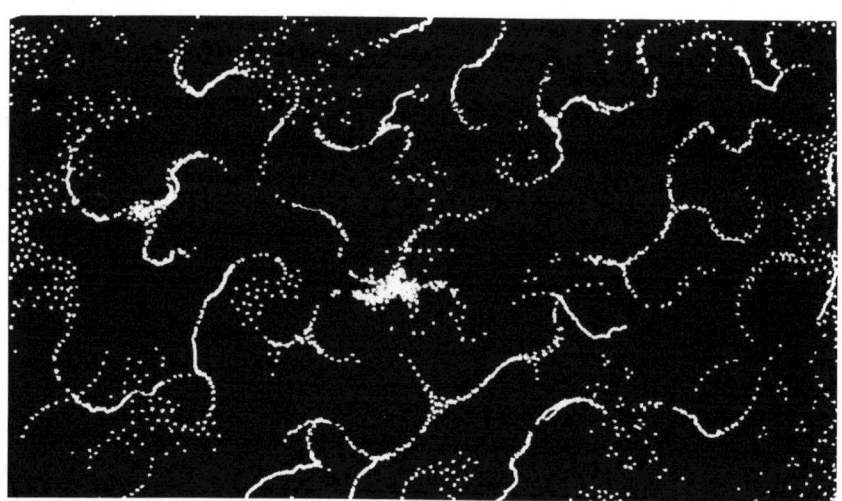

AN ELDERLY UNIVERSE - ABOUT 300 BILLION YEARS OLD
THE UNIVERSE IS 20 TIMES LARGER; THE EXPANSION HAS SLOWED AS STARS EXHAUST THEIR FUEL. THE HEAVENS ARE GOING DARK.

The tide has turned; the radiation flowing through space courses through clouds of dust and gas to form new particles. Each spark of new matter contracts space and exerts gravity on its surroundings; the particles will soon combine as atoms and add to the gathering clouds, which will catch still more light.

The shrinking universe will reach a rapid pace. New fires will kindle as new stars feed on fresh supplies of hydrogen gas. They start to release matter as light, but can do little to slow the implosion now occurring across a hundred-billion-year expanse.

Only after the murky unformed clouds of proto-galaxies begin to take shape as beautiful spirals; only after they are once again neighbors, near enough to occasionally collide, as they group into clusters and superclusters; only once they are fully ablaze and the heavens are filled with light, will the universe stop shrinking and pause.

Galaxies are now mature, dense, and hot. Millions of new stars are being born every day; and the universe starts to expand, slowly at first, then faster. We have come full circle. It will continue to expand, and then contract, in a cycle that lasts nearly a trillion years, according to Mills. And so for all time, forever, like the rise and fall of the tides in an eternal ocean of time.

We find ourselves on a small rocky planet orbiting a yellow Sun about thirteen billion years after the start of the expansion. We look up in wonder at the heavens, and our universe expands. But other beings, at other times, may look out and instead of seeing light from ancient galaxies shifted to the red, it may be shifted to the blue, as their universe contracts. Like us, they wonder at the source. Most confused, perhaps, will be those who live at the inflection point; the pause at the beginning of the cycle. They will look out and see a static universe, balanced on the head of a pin.

We expect our theories to explain known facts, but also predict new phenomena.

Mills had come up with a plausible rationale for the expansion of the universe. Whereas Einstein's general relativity predicted that the universe should either be *collapsing* or *decelerating* in its expansion, Mills's quantum gravity produced an equation of the universe that was a sinusoid.

Very early in the expansion phase, about where we are now, the universe is neither collapsing, nor decelerating. In fact it is expanding, and Mills predicted it is *accelerating* in its expansion. Mills published his equation for the oscillation of the universe quietly in the 1995 version of his book, and got back to his real job (Mills 1995).[91]

---

[91] The 1995 edition is LOC catalog number 94-077780, ISBN 0-9635171-1-2.

THE OSCILLATING UNIVERSE

MILLS PUBLISHED THESE EQUATIONS IN 1995, PREDICTING AN ACCELERATING, EXPANDING COSMOLOGY BEFORE IT WAS DISCOVERED. ACCORDING TO MILLS, SPACETIME EXPANDS AS MASS IS RADIATED AS ENERGY. STARS ARE THE ENGINES OF THE EXPANSION.

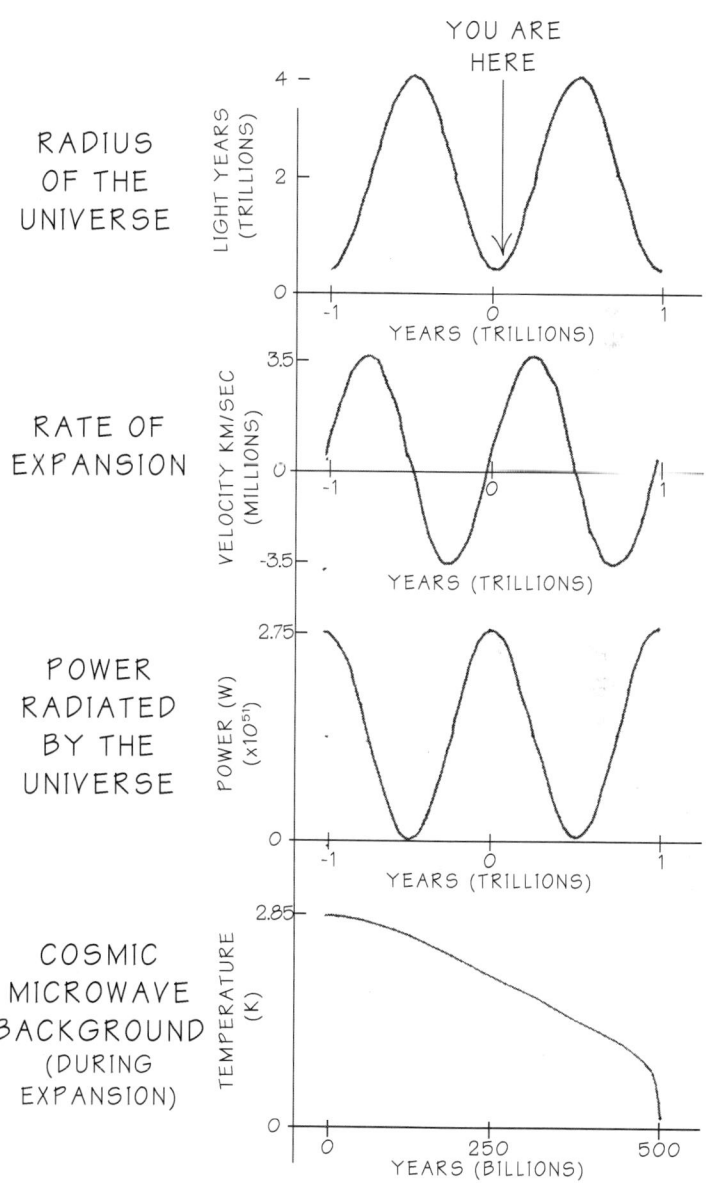

Somewhere, a star explodes.

Perhaps it is a white dwarf, with the mass of the Sun packed into the size of the Earth, cooling slowly in retirement after an active life of fusing hydrogen and helium. Now it has a dense core of carbon and oxygen, indigestible to a star of its mass.

Enter a companion star, which orbits closely.

The white dwarf begins to hungrily feed on the outer layer of the star. As new material adds to its weight, crushing its inner core, it may reach a density sufficient to ignite carbon fusion. When the critical mass is reached, much of the carbon will fuse suddenly, and the resulting explosion will blast the star apart in a blinding light that outshines its neighbors, even its whole galaxy. Hell hath no fury like a supernova.

The light spreads, over a billion years, in a widening sphere. A few photons from this event bounce off a mirror and are captured in the Hubble Space Telescope.

By the fall of 1997, two teams, the Supernova Cosmology Project (SCP) and the High-Z Team were searching for Type-1a supernova events and using their emission spectra as standard candles; the redshifts would tell them how much the universe is expanding, now and billions of years in the past.

Supernova are rare; only a few times each century in a galaxy with a hundred billion stars. So to find them the SCP and High-Z teams needed to monitor a lot of galaxies, and the administrators of the Hubble gave both teams time on the machine.

Their goal was to find out at what rate the universe was decelerating from its primordial explosion. The rate of deceleration tells us how much mass there is relative to the outward momentum of the galaxies (a value denoted Ω); too little mass (too high a deceleration) and the universe would expand forever (an "open" universe, in which $\Omega < 1$). Enough mass and the universe would eventually stop, and collapse back on itself, perhaps leading to another big bang (in which $\Omega > 1$). If $\Omega = 1$, then we have just the right amount of matter to collapse, and most theoreticians wanted this to be the case. A Goldilocks universe.

What the Hubble data gave us stunned both teams. The universe was not decelerating. It was *accelerating in its expansion* (Riess 1998). Ω was *negative*.

Mills apparently did not even issue a press release.

MIlls was not an academic, not aligned with a respectable institution, and his cosmological work was based on a modified form of General Relativity, based in turn on his entirely new theory of atomic and particle physics. Mills was busy searching for hydrino energy. No one was paying attention to Mills or his equations, and if his theories did cross the desk of a respectable astronomer, it was quickly tossed in the crackpot drawer. Adam Reiss's drawer was overflowing.

Although Mills's prediction was (and still is) utterly unknown in the scientific community, the volume in the Library of Congress is a historical artifact. If in the future, the scientific community finds that Mills's theories are an accurate description of nature, the book will be there to confirm that he anticipated the biggest surprise in modern astronomy.

In the wake of the discovery of the accelerating universe, theoreticians picked up Einstein's equations, and on the line where Einstein had erased his cosmological constant, scribbled it back in again. It was still unexplained; no theory supported it, but this didn't stop physicists from calling Einstein a genius once again, prescient even in his errors.

As to the phenomenon causing the expansion of the universe? Astronomers called it *dark energy*. Dark because, well, it was mysterious. And whatever it was, there was a lot of it; perhaps more than half of normal energy.

Energized by new realities, theoreticians began to theorize. But after twenty years, no account of the accelerating expansion has had any traction in the scientific community. Dark energy and dark matter have resulted in a dark age in modern physics.

Both Mills's theory and big bang theory agree that the universe should be expanding, that we should see a higher percentage of younger galaxies as we look back in time. But only Mills's theory predicts that even the most distant regions of space observable to us, those that go back 12 billion years or more, should nevertheless contain objects that are themselves very old. Recently, a quasar[92] was found that is 13 billion light years away, yet powered by a black hole about 2 billion times the mass of the Sun (Mortlock 2011). Such an object is ancient even as it appears to us today through a window in which we see 13 billion years back in time; it is the result of accumulation of matter over billions of years. Yet here it is, only hundreds of millions of years after the moment the universe began.

---

[92] The quasar ULAS J1120+064124.3.

When scientists encounter such anomalies, their first instinct is to find a way to include them in the present theory. This is the normal process of science, but it means that a theory often survives long past its expiration date. It becomes a hodgepodge of corrections.

In this case, physicists immediately hypothesized that that the universe seeded these structures very early on, which is in conflict with the experimental smoothness of the CMB, which implies that the big bang produced a largely uniform distribution of matter.

Another surprise was the recent discovery of a star, smaller than our Sun, which has almost no trace of elements heavier than hydrogen or helium.[93] In fact the ratio of helium was lower than that theoretically generated in the big bang. This star has earned the title, "The Star That Should Not Exist" (Caffau 2011).

Today big bang theory survives; neither of these discoveries is of the kind that can break a theory, but both only erode its plausibility. And neither is the kind that can make a theory, though it can lend it plausibility.

Mills's universe did not start with a bang. It may have structures that predate the beginning of the expansion by many billions of years. And it may have hydrogen-filled stars that postdate the expansion by billions of years. New stars can form from new hydrogen, produced by particle-production events, whereas, in Mills's universe, helium can come only from stellar nucleosynthesis.

At *every* point in the life of the universe, there is both the creation of matter, and the destruction of matter, occurring simultaneously. It is only the balance that shifts, like a spring, never arriving at equilibrium.

But what about the CMB radiation, the "echo" of the big bang?

It is well known that the CMB is a blackbody[94] spectrum, a spectrum that peaks at a certain value, indicating that it is a thermal emission at a specific temperature. The CMB is at a blackbody temperature of about

---

[93] The star SDSS J102915+172927.

[94] A "blackbody" is a theoretically ideal object that gives off light perfectly according to its temperature. To do this well, a blackbody must absorb all light that shines on it, reflecting none: you can place a light source inside an opaque object to produce something that acts like a blackbody. The CMB is, in fact, the most *perfect* blackbody spectrum that we have found in nature, and this makes sense considering that all light emitted by the universe must, eventually, be reabsorbed by it.

2.7 degrees Kelvin. This light arrives from all directions in space, as if the universe had an ambient temperature that is the same everywhere we look.

We ought to ask: absent a big bang, should the universe have an ambient temperature?

Mills says yes: the ambient temperature is related to the power output of the universe, and evolves over time with the expansion. He calculated the current temperature of the universe (early in the expansion phase) to be at about 2.7 Kelvin. It should be the same temperature throughout the universe. As the universe shrinks, the temperature goes up, and as it expands, the temperature goes down.

Lending support to Mills's theory is that the universe does appear to be of the same temperature (isothermal) in any direction we look, over vast distances that have been out of contact since the big bang. In an oscillating universe, the incredible age of the universe allows light to cross it many times over the course of the expansion cycle. The universe has, and will be, in thermal contact forever.

By the 1970s, big bang theory was growing stale; unanswered questions piled up. Why a bang? How did it produce the mass of our universe? How do we describe the moment before the bang, when the mass of the universe was, presumably, denser than that in a black hole?

Once gravity overcomes the strong nuclear force, general relativity describes matter as shrinking to a point, a *singularity*, where a finite quantity of matter is packed into an infinitesimal space, with an infinite mass density. When our equations produce infinities, we know something is wrong with the theory, and big bangs and black holes cannot be fully understood in general relativity prior to Mills.[95]

Big bang theory evolved. Quantum theorists imagined the creation of the universe from void as a spontaneous quantum event; the ultimate free lunch. They theorized that during the Bang, this quantum event would have created a negative gravitational pressure that pushed the universe out, determining its total mass. These ideas were plausible, but they did not predict an accelerating expansion.

Today, as we grow accustomed to this state of alarm at unexpected new data, we ought to recall the ease with which Newton's theory solved all

---

[95] As we discussed before, however, Mills's gravity does not reach a singularity. When the mass density is sufficiently high, matter annihilates and black holes erupt into gamma-ray bursts.

known physics of his day. Mysteries fell to his theory, naturally, effortlessly, like a house of cards. We long for those days.

In 1933, Lemaître's said, "From a cosmological point of view, the zero of space must thus must be treated as a beginning, in the sense that every astronomical structure with an earlier existence would have been completely destroyed there" (Lemaître 1933).

There are many, I think, who do not believe that the big bang represented a beginning, a moment of "creation." After all, no agent, whether a sentient maker or a law of nature, can bring the universe into existence, for that agent must exist before the act. Nothing outside of time can bring time about, for there would be no change, no medium in which, or means by which, an agent may act.

And our most sacred law of physics, the conservation of energy, tells us that energy cannot be created or destroyed. The total energy of the universe must have always been the same as it is now. How could it have *come* into being?

Yet an eternal universe has always posed logistical problems. Fred Hoyle argued that in an infinitely old universe, hydrogen should no longer exist, because it would have long ago been exhausted by stars converting it into helium (Hoyle 1950). Others have argued that in an eternal universe, the order that is inherent in complex structures and non-equilibrium systems would have been eroded due to entropy until we arrive at a lukewarm "heat death" from which complex structure can never arise.

We might say that Mills's universe enters a state of *negative* entropy during the contraction phase. This is because the creation of matter from energy is not typically captured by our laws of thermodynamics.

Yet, the universe does produce order in this phase, resetting the entropic balance sheet and refueling the universe for hundreds of billions of years. And we live on this order daily. Our metabolic activity can only maintain itself on highly ordered biochemical compounds, proteins, and amino acids. We use what we can to produce our own biological structure, and the rest we dispel as heat to our environment, heat that ends up as light, slowly exhausting the matter and structure of the universe.

Mills has suggested that complex biochemistry cannot exist in the contraction phase, but I see no reason why active suns are not possible in this phase. Where there is sunlight, and warmth, there is the means for life. It may be rare, a refuge in a vast, empty, and lonely universe, but life will go on, perhaps forever, throughout the cycle. A constant custodian, a constant presence.

There is something repellent about infinities. For one, infinity is not a number, it is a mathematical abstraction. I remember struggling with this question when I was very young, perhaps six years old. I asked my priest how it could be that God was infinitely old. Surprised, he thought for a moment, then he took his gold wedding band from his finger and traced a line around it; the circle has no beginning, no end.

Perhaps a more rigorous answer is to be found in a notion I would like to borrow from one of my professors. When we speak of what exists, we speak of what exists *now*, implicitly (Hinchliff 1996). Things that existed in the past are no longer in the category of things that exist, unless they exist still. This is called *presentism*. So we might speak about an infinitely old universe without admitting that anything in the universe exists in infinite quantity. A subtle distinction perhaps.

But it doesn't work for matter. The total amount of matter in the universe is, in fact, a finite physical constant, though we may never know it for sure, and certainly will never directly observe it. The history of astronomy is filled with discussions of infinite space and time; H.W.M. Olbers argued that if universe is eternal, and if it is infinitely large with infinite stars, then the light from the stars would be so intense that it would illuminate the surface of the Earth until it reached the brightness of the Sun! (Olbers 1826). This, of course, assumed that the universe is static, that stars do not exhaust their fuel, and a plethora of infinities.

Edmund Halley argued that if the number of stars in the universe was not infinite, then the universe would have a center of mass around which everything would collapse (Gregory 1715). He didn't anticipate a universe with curved space-time, where matter and energy circulate like the currents in the ocean that circumnavigate the globe: an idea I force myself to accept, resigned to the fact that I will never be able to visualize it in my mind's eye.

Mills's equation for the oscillation of the universe requires an estimate of the total mass, which he assumes equals: 400,000,000,000,000,000,000,000,000,000,000,000,000,000,000,000,000,000 kg. That's 4 with 54 zeros, the mass of 400 billion galaxies each with an approximate 400 billion stars. Just as the electron is imperfectly flat, so too is the universe imperfectly large. But we get an eternal, finite universe (Mills 2015, Ch. 32).

IN CONTEMPLATION OF ETERNAL TIME

There was once an old man who was an avid and expert gardener. He tended an orchard of trees aged to bear beautiful fruit. One day he brought his grandchild into the orchard. There she pointed to a large, wise-looking tree and asked: "How old is that one, grandpa?"

"Oh yes", he replied, "that one is special. That one has been there forever."

"So it was here before you tended the trees?" she asked.

"Certainly not. For I planted all these trees from seed. I remember it well."

The granddaughter was bright, and she didn't let anything get past her. "Well then," she insisted, "the tree can't be *forever* old, because you planted it!"

"Certainly it can," the man smiled, "for I have been here tending it, forever."

If we disregard the big bang as scientific fiction, do we dismiss, finally, arguments for a Creator? Perhaps religious beliefs will evolve as they have been forced to do before; instead of a creation: a continuum of change; instead of a creator: a custodian of time.

When we look to the heavens for the prime mover, we find only light and matter responsible for the rhythm of the universe, the ebb and flow that gives and takes life. Perhaps, what makes our place in the universe meaningful is simply that we are here to perceive it. We derive meaning from the beauty and experience of our lives, our activity, our advances in knowledge and art, our relationships, our happiness in a moment as we lay on the grass and watch the clouds through a shifting canopy of leaves, while a child crawls over our feet.

Eternal time may seem like an unsettling idea; like the notion that there is no ground beneath our feet; that the present moment hangs in an infinite void like the Earth does in space. How many civilizations have come and gone in an eternal past? The great drama of the universe has unfolded forever, into and beyond conceivable time, and we are here now, able to partake in its majesty for a brief moment. How many civilizations will come and go *after* we are gone? Will any of them know that we were here? Or will the end of the expansion, the death throes of dark stars, four hundred billion years from now, finally extinguish all our works?

I find eternal time a comfort. Whatever the fate of the human race, the universe will go on, and after coldness and darkness refold on itself, stars will emerge with planets kindling new life, new intelligences, who will look out on the world with curiosity and the desire to live.

CHAPTER 16

THE ARBITER OF TRUTH

In which hydrino experiments become "heat and serve" but the scientific community doesn't bite.

In May of 2008, BlackLight Power announced a "prototype power system" that could generate 50 kW of heat on demand, or about enough to heat a few homes. Not many details were initially given about the device, although supporting quotes were provided by BLP directors. There was no disclosure of the prototype itself, or how it worked.

Mills told the press "if you make cheap heat, you can make cheap electricity," but heat is a far more efficient use of any power source, since the conversion to electricity takes a serious toll on the output. Most power sources in small applications were around 30% efficient. Nevertheless, the anticipated date for delivery of this device was sometime in 2009 (BLP 2008a).

BLP had not been too active in the press in the preceding few years, and I was less in touch with Mills, again watching from the outside. The press release was broadcast throughout the web and picked up by blogs and the online version of news sites, followed by the inevitable long debates in the reader comments as to whether the company was legitimate.

To many, it appeared far more likely that BLP was a fraud, but the few who took the time to read the technical material on BLP's website were more optimistic. And occasionally one of BLP's cult followers would make a strong but lonely argument in their favor.

But there was, overall, little information to work from aside from BLP's word on the matter, until the next announcement five months later on October 20, announcing that Rowan University had independently replicated and validated BLP's 1 kW and 50 kW reactors (BLP 2008b). There was mention of the reactor being based on some kind of solid fuel.

In an effort to garner publicity, BLP offered commercial licenses for producing hydrino power: something that was certainly premature without a commercial product. These licenses were agreements to purchase power at specified rates, if and when such power was made available.

On December 11th of 2008, BLP announced that it had signed with Estacado Energy, a small, no-name electric cooperative in New Mexico

(BLP 2008b). Next was Farmers Electric Cooperative, serving rural customers in Texas. With more licenses that were apparently nondisclosed, BLP signed its sixth license with Akridge Energy. Akridge was not an energy company at all; John Akridge III was something of a green energy devotee and a property manager in the DC area who had apparently set up a subsidiary on paper for the sole purpose of delivering hydrino power to his commercial properties, when and if it became available.

There was some traction from these licensees: the story ran on CNN's Energy Fix, which took an optimistic look at BLP, though the host commented that it sounded almost too good to be true.

Although it was exciting to see BLP work toward an engineering concept, I began to feel that Mills was only sabotaging his own public reputation by announcing these licenses. They were non-exclusive, non-binding licenses with small utilities who had few resources to vet new major energy proposals, and zero ability to change minds about the legitimacy of BLP. Some licensees were asking for non-disclosure agreements – something I felt was a warning sign. BLP was making it difficult to distinguish itself, to outside observers, from a fraudulent scheme that might prey on small utilities. Most ignored the announcements, but a few blogs and news sites reposted the material, tossing the story like raw meat into a tank of piranhas, with a long train of fiercely negative reader comments following the article.

On August 12th, 10 months after the announcement that it had replicated BLP's reactors, Rowan finally released four technical reports: not journal articles, but nevertheless giving details about the new reactors (BLP 2009).

Peter Jansson led the nine-month study and told the press:

> The ability to generate such tremendous power in this controlled process demonstrates... repeatable heat experiments based on their technology can be replicated by independent scientists. (Jansson 2009)

BLP also filmed a short video of Jansson overseeing the reaction in BLP's laboratory and posted it online (Jansson 2009b). In the video, the BLP cell was loaded with hydrogen and some undisclosed material, and then the cell was turned on and a dramatic spike of heat was recorded on the data-acquisition system. Details were scarce, and it was obvious that the cell was not, in fact, a commercial prototype, but another bench-top laboratory experiment. Still, there was excitement in the air.

BLP was finally moving beyond basic science, willing to again be in the public eye.

PETER JANSSON

The basis for BLP's reactor—what Mills called "Generation Two" chemistry—was a cocktail of chemical compounds that, when heated in a cell, released both hydrogen and the catalyst and reacted to form hydrino. The reaction included a source of hydrogen and catalyst (KH or NaH), a reducing agent such as magnesium metal (Mg), a metal halide salt (such as $BaCl_2$, $SrBr_2$, or LiCl) and a high surface area conductive support material such as TiC.

The Rowan University Department of Engineering carried out experiments at their South Jersey Park calorimetry laboratory in the summer of 2009 (Mugweru 2009b; Jansson 2009). They ran a cell using KH, Mg, TiC, and MnI_2 or a variety of similar compounds ($FeBr_2$, SnI_2, InCl, CoI_2, $EuBr_2$, AgCl, and SF_6). They found that with these various cocktails, they produced from 2 to 6.5 times more heat than could be explained with conventional chemistry in the cell, depending on the recipe. Some of the most likely conventional reactions were, in fact, *endothermic*, they would actually cool the cell instead of heat it.

In the products from the reaction, they were also able to find a liquid NMR peak at -3.85, corresponding to BLP's reported peak for the hydrino ion $H^-(1/4)$.

Unlike electrolytic or plasma cells, this was an unsophisticated reaction, capable of being performed with off-the-shelf materials and equipment. Dump everything into a cell and throw it in the oven, and you were good to go. BLP and the Rowan team seemed to envision this experiment as the first step in a broad participation by the scientific community. They remarked that any moderately well-equipped team with a calorimeter that had an accuracy of at least 3% could reproduce the experiments with little difficulty.

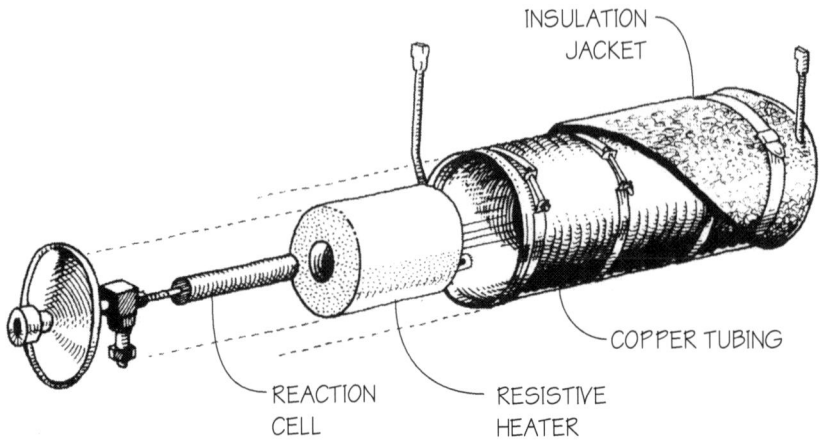

HEAT-FLUX CALORIMETER ASSEMBLY

The scientific investigations completed at Rowan University make it quite clear that there is a source of heat being generated in these numerous chemical reactions that cannot be explained in the confines of conventional modern chemistry. It is the sincere hope of the research team at Rowan University that other research laboratories across the world will find confidence from our results to begin reproducing these experiments for themselves. (Jansson 2009)

The Rowan team also issued a report demonstrating the accuracy of the calorimeter with reactants not expected to produce any hydrino chemistry (Jansson 2009b). Jansson also analyzed the purity of the chemical samples used in the reaction to conclude that there was no water, crystalline or elemental impurities in the cell. Leaving the door open to other explanations, Jansson did not claim to conclusively validate the hydrino theory, but encouraged the community to suggest possible alternatives.

After presenting at a conference in Marrakesh showing a power gain many times what was allowed by conventional chemistry, one attendee stood up and told Jansson that his results were rubbish, because they simply couldn't be true. Jansson said he replied by saying "that's why we're up here presenting these results" and asked for suggestions as to where the experiment could be flawed. But the experiment was so simple that there were few ways to criticize.

Reflecting on his difficulty introducing Mills's work to his peers, Jansson now believes that the scientific culture in physics is no longer letting data be the arbiter of truth. We are letting our minds be influenced by theory, by the mathematics, by the strong paradigms in the field.

Mills believed that he had found a way to commercialize hydrino power if he could simply engineer the cell to cycle continuously. The compounds in the solid fuel cocktail could be reinfused with hydrogen at high temperature, which would be easy to achieve if the reaction with hydrogen produced sufficient heat, which it did (Mills 2010, 2011c).

So it would have been a batch process in which individual cells were turned on to produce power, then turned off to consume some of the heat from other cells to rehydrogenate the ingredients, then turned back on. With enough cells, the net result would be a continuous heat source, with hydrogen as the fuel.

In one design, BLP proposed a stack of large cylindrical tubes, each tube 550 °C on the bottom and 400 °C at the top. During the reaction, the catalyst mixture would condense on the top of the cell, at which point hydrogen would be injected into the cell, and the entire tube rotated to heat back up and rehydrate the catalyst (Mills 2011).

In another design, BLP imagined bundles of thin, two-meter-long tubes. Each tube would go through a reaction phase, then a small chamber at the end would be cooled, cryopumping the catalyst out of the tube. The chamber would then be sealed off, the hydrino gas would be evacuated, new hydrogen would be pumped into the cell. Then the chamber would be rewarmed and opened back up to the remainder of the tube, initiating the reaction once again (Mills 2011b). By bundling the tubes, each would be warmed by the adjacent tubes, up to the 700 °C temperatures required to rehydrate the catalyst mixture.

Despite these proposals and announcements, Mills had not yet completely solved the problems of regenerating the catalyst mixture. These concepts also required significant investment in a large, central power plant, because it would require a steam cycle to generate power.

The greater value was the simplicity with which these experiments could be reproduced, completely independently of BLP. Yet after the announcement, there was no great rush to repeat Rowan's experiments. And because Jansson had history with BLP going back to when he performed due diligence for Atlantic, online observers were wary of considering Jansson or Rowan as independent sources, even if some of the Rowan papers did not have Jansson as an author.

In addition, BLP funded Rowan's research efforts to the tune of nearly

$650,000 between 2007 and 2010. Those who would argue that *any* financial tie corrupted the purity of science could doubt Rowan's results.

On November 29, 2010 David Agular, the media relations secretary at the Harvard Smithsonian Center for Astrophysics (CfA), started getting phone calls. One caller asked him if the CfA had just validated hydrino science. No one had told him anything, and when reporters asked if it was true, all he could say was that it was probably a hoax.

The work had been conducted by Alexander Bykanov, who with a PhD in Physics and Mathematics from the Moscow Institute of Physics and Technology, had spent most of his career studying plasma physics on contract to various industry groups such as SBIR, and GEN3 Partners, a network of scientists and engineers on contract to test new emerging technologies.[96]

PINCHED-DISCHARGE PLASMA

A HIGH-VOLTAGE PULSED DISCHARGE PLASMA APPARATUS FOR RECORDING EUV EMISSIONS FROM PURE HYDROGEN. AFTER (MILLS 2010, 2015).

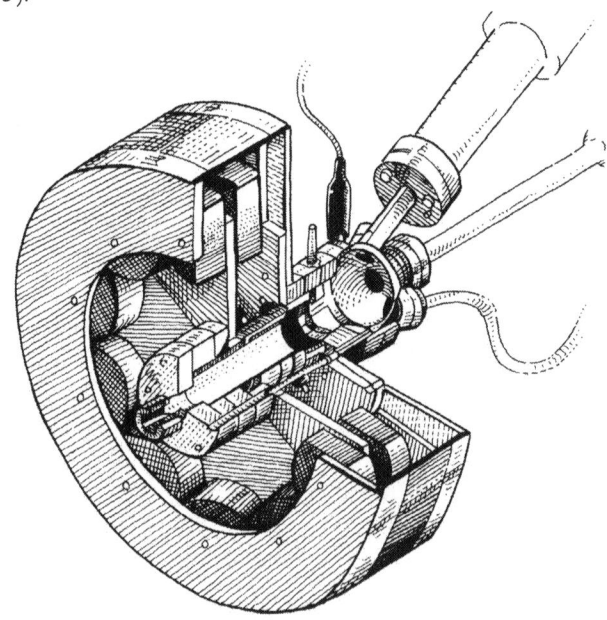

---

[96] GEN3 also performed validation work of water flow calorimetry. GEN3 2009)

BLP had recently performed an experiment using a pinch discharge plasma cell, an apparatus consisting of two large plate electrodes. When a high voltage was discharged between the plates, the resulting magnetic field compressed the gas (the "pinch") and briefly produced a plasma, essentially a lightning bolt between the electrodes.

Two small holes were bored through the center of the plates to allow the EUV spectrometer to see through. A high voltage was maintained between the plates, and an electron gun was pointed at the plates; when it fired at regular intervals, it would cause the plates to discharge through the plasma. BLP used pure hydrogen as well as mixed hydrogen gases, and used pure helium and argon as controls (Mills 2010).

They found a bell shape of continuum radiation in the EUV spectrum. Continuum radiation is the result of many closely spaced, overlapping emission lines that form a continuous curve. The shape of the band tells you something about the type of radiation being emitted.

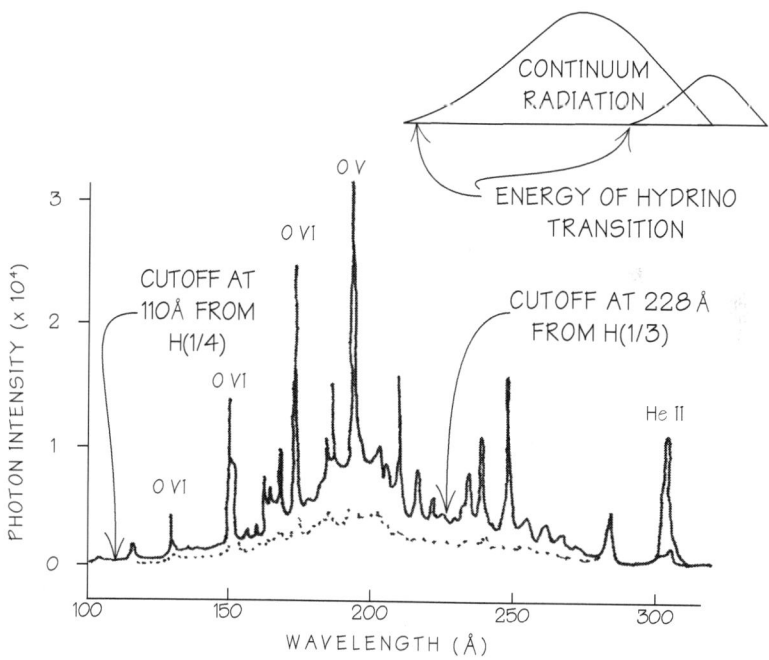

THE EMISSION SPECTRA OF A HIGH-VOLTAGE PULSED DISCHARGE FROM PURE HYDROGEN (330 mTORR) PRODUCING CONTINUUM RADIATION IN THE EUV. MILLS ASSIGNED TO HYDRINO TRANSITIONS WITH CUTOFFS AT 110Å AND 228Å. AFTER (BYKANOV 2010).

When a hydrino atom undergoes catalysis, it does so in two stages: First, energy is transferred to the catalyst, breaking bonds or ionizing electrons. Second, the electron of the hydrogen atom shrinks, releasing a number of photons in the process. There is a cutoff for how intense this radiation can be; it is the maximum energy of the electron's drop to its hydrino state. So in the spectrum, we should see a cutoff for each type of transition. The transition to an H(1/4) releases a total energy of 204 eV, but only releases 122.4 eV of that energy as light, corresponding to a cutoff at 101.3 Å. The transition to an H(1/3) hydrino releases a total energy of 108.8 eV, of which 54.4 eV is released as light, with a cutoff at 228 Å. The curve shows a cutoff at about 100 Å, and presumably the overlap with the radiation of the other transitions causes the bell shape.

The bell shape of continuum radiation at these frequencies and conditions was really unique, but most importantly, the lines could be made to appear in a *pure* hydrogen plasma. There was no conventional means by which to get EUV continuum radiation from hydrogen. Pinch plasmas had been studied for their ability to produce hot fusion with the release of X-rays and neutrons, but no one went looking for EUV lines, especially in the absence of fusion-enabling temperatures. Mills felt he had the smoking gun of hydrino catalysis.

Through their contacts at GEN3 Partners, BLP asked Bykanov to repeat the experiment. Bykanov wanted to be sure that the effect was real, and that it wasn't due to anything conventional. He considered Bremsstrahlung radiation, but dismissed it because it had a characteristic profile that tapered off to longer wavelengths, whereas this was a bell-shape. Perhaps it was an artifact of the spectrometer? He checked on how it performed with filters and controls. He dismissed the possibility of it being due to rovibrational lines from hydrogen because you simply couldn't get those lines to appear in a plasma of this temperature (Bykanov 2010).

It was merely incidental that he contracted space from the Harvard Smithsonian Center for Astrophysics. Because BLP's announcement overtly mentioned this fact, people immediately assumed that it represented, at long last, a prestigious university confirming the hydrino. This was another BLP press *faux pas*. It was also clear from reading the report that, although Bykanov was listed as the only author, he was referred to in the third person and much of the text was written by Mills.

When I caught up with Bykanov, he was not sold on the hydrino hypothesis. He had not seen the raw data files from the experiment until after the report had issued, and when he enlarged the helium control run, he found a similar bell shape buried there. Perhaps he had missed something; he hoped to do further experiments.

On the same day as the announcement of Bykanov's work, BLP also announced that Rowan had just performed additional validation work, this time for a fuel cell prototype.

A fuel cell is essentially an electrolytic cell with large electrodes; water is inserted into the cell, then splits into hydrogen and oxygen at the electrodes. BLP was busy designing what they called a Catalyst Induced Hydrino Transition (CIHT) cell. In the cell, water could act as a catalyst and source of hydrogen; it ionized the oxygen and broke its hydrogen bonds to make an H(1/4) hydrino. In nature, a water molecule is almost always found attached to other water molecules with very weak van der Waals forces transmitted from hydrogen to hydrogen. These interconnected molecules, which actually form lattice structures in a liquid, give water its viscosity. But BLP needed free, unbound water molecules to act as catalysts.

The first generation of CIHT cell reached maturity around 2010, but the second and far more promising cell was ready by 2012 for a swarm of independent verifiers to observe and validate.

The first generation used a nickel mat anode and a nickel oxide cathode. The electrolyte was lithium hydroxide and lithium bromide (LiOH-LiBr), which is a solid at room temperature and melts (becomes a molten eutectic salt) at high temperature. Water vapor was introduced in an argon gas. The cell was charged, during which it split water, then allowed to discharge as hydrino transitions occurred and produced an electric current. Hydrino gas and oxygen gas were released, and new water was introduced. BLP found that once started, the cell continued with very little or no further electrical input. The cells were small scale prototypes, and although only 2-3 mW of power issued from the cells, it was much greater than that required to electrolyze hydrogen and oxygen from water.

In 2011, a study by Rowan, headed by K.V. Ramanujachary, calibrated his experiment to 0.01% error, and found a gain that varied from 1.5 to 7.35. At the time of writing, only the summary of this paper had been disclosed. Another report from December of 2011, conducted by an anonymous investigator, reported that using molybdenum anodes, the cell's gain, averaged over 24 days, was up to 242, at which point the cell was turned off (Ramanujachary 2011).

Both of these reports were at the fault line between business and science. In the Ramanujachary paper, not all the details could be released because BLP was developing a commercial product. Mills wanted to give out enough information to interest investors and legitimize his progress, but not give out so much that he could aid a competitor or which would constitute a public disclosure that would invalidate his own patents.

And what of the anonymous validators? Individuals and companies, willing to work with BLP only if they were not exposed to the public ridicule BLP faced, were, ethically speaking, protecting themselves at Mills's expense.

I felt that these ('take my word for it') reports were unconvincing to those who were true skeptics of BLP, who did not personally know and had learned to trust Mills and his team. But the reports simultaneously gave out too many details of the prototypes to make secrecy useful.[97]

In May of 2012, BLP announced that six scientists (one anonymous[98]) had validated the next generation of BLP's CIHT cell. These were not fully independent verifications, but individuals with distinctive pedigrees who attested to satisfying for themselves that the experiments had been set up legitimately and conducted honestly, even if they left the experiments in BLP's hands.

Among them was Terry Copeland, a chemical engineer who had, among other positions, been the Director of Engineering for North America at Duracell. Copeland visited in November and December of 2011 and observed the preparation, fabrication, and testing of cells. The cells were made up of a pre-oxidized porous nickel cathode and a pressed porous nickel anode. A molybdenum anode could be used in place of the nickel, which generally had a much greater output. The electrolyte was made of $LiOH$-$LiBR$-MgO, which liquefied as the cell approached its maintained temperature of 450 °C. Argon and water vapor gas flowed through the cell.

Between visits to BLP, Copeland let the cells run and BLP forwarded the data to him. He reported accumulated power gains of 2, 5.5, and even 55, "well beyond any possible experimental error" to put it lightly. He

---

[97] BLP did publicly state that it was willing to provide the full reports to business partners operating under non-disclosure agreements, but as I was no longer with BLP or subject to such agreements, I could not obtain a copy for this book.

[98] See Anonymous 2012.

called BLP's efforts a "historic success" and suggested that they scale-up the device to 10 W (Copeland 2012).

Another validator included Nick Glumac, a Professor of Mechanical and Science Engineering at the University of Illinois. He was asked, through a fellow faculty member at the University, if he wanted to help out in some BLP work, and agreed; working occasionally on contract for BLP, and occasionally doing some research on his own dime.

He visited BLP in December of 2011 and observed a procedure similar to the other validators. He made careful notes of the assembly and execution of the cell and found gains of up to 20. He then stayed in communication as he received data from BLP. He was impressed by the thoroughness of the control experiments, done with different electrolytes or different electrodes, all of which produced a short burst of power as they absorbed water, then dropped by the end of the first day. In his report he stated that "I find no plausible alternative explanation for the observed energy release" (Glumac 2012). During his time on site, he saw no reason to doubt the accuracy of the results or the sincerity of the scientists at BLP.

Although electrochemistry was not Glumac's area of expertise, he was an expert at making accurate measurements of power and heat. He spent a lot of time looking at the data acquisition, voltage measurements, and calibrations. The CIHT cells were small scale, and the energy required to keep the cell warm dwarfed the electrical power generated. So the experiment, as a whole, used more energy than it consumed. But since there was no way for a warm cell to convert heat directly into electrical energy, the power output was real. Glumac felt it would be important to scale up the cell in order to get better measurements.

When I caught up with Glumac a few years later, he felt that it was a good attitude to be skeptical of everything, not only BLP's work but also that of mainstream theory. He thought that the evidence BLP had presented for its technology was compelling, and far beyond the standards most new technologies were required to meet. He looked forward to seeing more replications by third parties. As expected, Glumac quickly realized that he had no traction to get others interested. He was also forced to accept that human nature was infused in the scientific process at every level, that the scientific community was unable accept evidence that modified what had become, as he called it, "gospel" truth.

James Pugh and Dr. Ethirajulu Dayalan, both at ENSER Corporation (an engineering and fabrication services company), visited BLP in

February of 2012. They reviewed the data, observed experiments as they were constructed and operated, and received data from BLP thereafter. They found excess energy up to 100 times that required for electrolysis, produced over 60 days. The power gain varied from 3 to an incredible 144 in the case of a molybdenum anode, which ran for a total of 39 days. They also ran a variety of analytical tests (Pugh 2012).

Among their results, they found that the energy produced from cells with nickel anodes trailed off over time, but those with molybdenum anodes saw a consistently high output. From the peak that the cell reached at day 3, to when the cell was turned off 39 days later, they found only a 30% drop in power output. Like the early electrochemical cells from the 1990s, experimenters were finding that hydrino catalysis occurs slowly over time and the cell might *never* return to the baseline.

Another validator, W. Henry Weinberg, a retired professor with a long career in chemical engineering, visited BLP in January of 2012. From his study, Weinberg concluded: "Having participated in experimental design and execution, and having reviewed vast amounts of other data they have produced, I have found nothing that warrants rejection of their extraordinary claims." (Weinberg 2012).

Despite the extraordinary power output from the cell, Weinberg realized that if the source of power was the reaction to make H(1/4) hydrinos, the reaction rate was actually astonishingly *low*. Catalytic reaction rates in gas and liquid phases often were order of magnitude higher. In his mind, he felt that BLP could do better. Perhaps if they thinned the electrodes and increased their surface area, they could create even higher power densities.

When Harlan Bretz hiked across the scablands, he found braided streams etched across the landscape. Perhaps all of science is scouting the braided streams; the paths meander here and there.

BLP followed a path that began in electrochemistry, passed through a decade of plasma physics, then new catalysts, then back to electrochemistry, in a constant interplay of theory and experiment, each informing the other.

However, it was clear that in the wider scientific community, observation was no longer the arbiter of truth. Hydrino research would be ignored so long as it only manifested as low-grade heat, or light emitting plasma, or unusual materials, or high gains from tiny cells.

Mills needed *power* that could not be denied, a reaction rate that went beyond anything he had achieved to date. When the streams converged and Mills realized what was limiting hydrino catalysis all these years, the result was explosive.

CHAPTER 17

THE COSMIC CONSPIRACY

In which quasars are not doing as they are told, and we chew on Einstein's beef with Newton.

A QUASAR

We now believe that black holes lurk at the center of most galaxies. These are not your local dark stars, but supermassive, thousand-star behemoths. Around them orbits the luminous core of the galaxy, slowly but surely falling in.

In some galaxies, the black hole is pre-digesting its meal, tearing nearby stars into a flattened disk of plasma, the *accretion disk*. And just as the electron in the Bohr atom must give off energy as it spirals into the nucleus, so too the ionized plasma in the accretion disk emits light as it spirals to its death. The light is incredibly bright, and lasts millions of years: you might think it a star, but it isn't, it is a quasi-stellar object, or *quasar*.

Quasars are among the most awesome objects in space. They emit more light than that of an entire galaxy, and do so continuously. Beings who live dozens of light years from the quasar may perceive it as brightly in their sky as we perceive our Sun, which is only 7 light *minutes* from Earth. We see quasars across millions or billions of light years of space, and they obscure their own galaxies in the glare.

Unlike the spectrum of a star that peaks at a specific wavelength related to the star's temperature, quasars produce radiation across a broad range of wavelengths more or less equally. The radiation is emitted primarily along an axis centered on the accretion disk, and it must be pointing at us like a flashlight for us to see it well. If the quasar wobbles, even slightly, we notice the beam skirt across our position in space, changing slightly in luminosity. Most quasars wobble with a unique periodic frequency that might last hours to months.

Every quasar keeps time, like a clock, though each with its own tempo. Altogether they constitute the real world equivalent of what Einstein imagined in a thought experiment: a grid of clocks throughout space, all keeping time. And they may form an experimental test of a historical debate between Newton and Einstein on the nature of space.

Suppose we could reach out and prick the fabric of the world with a pin. We know the Earth rotates as it orbits the Sun, the Sun orbits about the center of the galaxy, and the galaxy orbits about a cluster of galaxies known as the Local Group. If that pin prick held its position in space, irrelevant to anything occurring around it, it would appear to us to fly off, at hundreds of kilometers per second, along the resulting vector of all our motions.

Even if it is not possible to do this in practice, there is something intuitively appealing about the idea that there is a fabric to the world there to be pricked. We say the Earth moves through space, as does the Sun and the galaxy. Isn't there an absolute space there to be moved through?

Newton believed there was; in the *Principia*, he suggested that in addition to relative motions between bodies, absolute motion was the movement from one "absolute place" to another. For Newton, absolute space was a real thing, made up of absolute places, as if there were an invisible grid laid over all the universe upon which we draw the line of our existence.

Newton also believed that time flowed uniformly throughout space; as if at each intersection of his absolute grid there sat a clock synchronized to every other, ticking along at the exact same rate.

He clearly realized that it may be impossible to measure absolute space or time; to measure space, for instance, we would need a stationary, immovable object that remains fixed for all of time to serve as a reference point. Since time is measured through periodic motion, we would need a perfectly regular motion (a perfectly ticking clock) to measure absolute time, as well as a way to synchronize clocks across vast distances.

Ernst Mach challenged Newton's notion of absolute space and time. For Mach, a definition must be operational (able to be measured) to be meaningful. The concepts of space and time have no meaning outside of the means by which we measure them, and if we *can't* make a measurement, we can't speak about it. As a result, Mach only accepted Newton's idea of relative motions, not absolute motions (Mach 1960, p. 272).[99]

Mach also criticized Newton's definition of mass as "the quantity of matter," since matter, itself, could not be directly observed or measured.

---

[99] "When we say a thing *A* changes with the time, we mean simply that the conditions that determine a thing *A* depend on the conditions that determine another thing *B*" (Mach 1960, p. 272).

We can see how an object behaves relative to other objects, but does this tell us anything about the world, really?

Mach refused to believe in real properties of the world independent from the relations we see between mutually dependent phenomena. Such real properties would be what Kant had called the "thing-in-itself," the thing that is really there, but forever beyond the reach of our perception.

Mach's criticisms were prescient, and found fertile ground in the young Einstein. In his famous 1905 paper on relativity theory, Einstein adopts Mach's language and philosophical outlook to introduce the theory of relativity.

Throughout the nineteenth century, it was believed that light propagated through space much like a surface ripple propagated on water. Physicists postulated the existence of a luminiferous ether filling all of space, serving as the medium through which light propagated. Physicists expected that as the Earth moved through this ether, a beam of light would move faster or slower, depending on which direction it was pointed.

In a famous experiment, it was found that whichever direction you pointed a beam of light, it propagated at the *same* speed. Light, perhaps the perfect motion Newton sought to measure absolute space and absolute time, was constant but independent of the motion of the source or observer. If the Earth moved, light would not tell.

Einstein felt that this result was tremendously important. Perhaps Mach was right. No ether, no absolute space; no absolute frame of reference in the universe. Perhaps all objects moved only relatively to one another. It became the conceptual basis for his theory of relativity, in which he drew out the full implications of equations that had been developed by Lorentz to account for objects moving at near light speeds.

The Lorentz transformations are perhaps best explained the way they have been for a century, in every textbook and popular reference. I will quickly discuss them here for any readers new to the subject.

Suppose you stand on the ground while a train goes by at very high speed, say 50% of light speed. Onboard, there is a passenger with a flashlight pointed at a mirror on the ceiling. As the train goes by you, the passenger flashes the light, which bounces off the ceiling and returns to the floor. From the point of view of the passenger, the light crosses the distance from the floor to ceiling and back, a total distance of 2L, where L is the height of the ceiling above the floor. The passenger measures the time for this round trip with a highly accurate timer. By dividing the distance by the time, the passenger calculates that light travels with speed *c*.

You, however, are on the ground. The train is moving by you as the passenger flashes his light, and as you watch through the train car window, the light ray travels a *diagonal* trajectory, moving L sideways as it traverses from the floor to the ceiling in the train car.

As a result, the path you observe the light following in its round trip from the ceiling to the floor is, in fact, two diagonals of a triangle with a height L and a base 1/2 L, resulting in a distance of about 18% longer than the path observed by the passenger. You track the time with your timer, and when you divide the distance by the time, you too calculate that light travels with speed *c*.

Both you, and the passenger, are watching and timing the same event, and yet, the round trip travel time observed by the passenger is *less* than the time observed by you, because the distance the light ray travelled was shorter!

You might conclude from this that time on-board the train must be progressing 18% slower than time on the ground. After all, that is the only way to explain why the passenger perceived less time passing than you did.

Let us reverse the roles. Suppose you have the flashlight and mirror on the ground, and the passenger on-board the train is watching you from their window. You flash the light to a mirror positioned a distance L over the ground, and you time the round trip. The passenger does likewise. Except this time, the passenger sees a diagonal light path, and observes a longer time than *you*. The passenger might conclude that time is advancing 18% slower for *you* than for himself.

For whom is time *actually* moving slower? Intuitively, we expect an answer to this question. But the question is not well-formed. Both scenarios are true at the *same* time.

When you are observing an object moving at relativistic speeds, that is, a significant fraction of light speed relative to you, you must use Lorentz's equations to describe the event. The length of the object contracts; the rate of passage of time slows; and the mass increases. These do not just *appear* to change; they are not simply an error of perception. They *actually* change, but they actually change only from your point of view. From the point of view of the passenger on-board the train, lengths, time, and mass actually change for objects on the ground, but only from his point of view. And thus the great lesson of relativity: length, time, and mass are quantities that vary depending on one's reference frame, one's inertial motion through space.

If your mind is boggled, prepare for another boggling. A further consequence of relativity theory is that the order of two events that are spatially distant can change depending on your point of view. Suppose we have two supernova explosions from star A and star B. The stars are 5 light years apart in space, but the two explosions both occur before light from one star's explosion reaches the other. These two explosions may be simultaneous, or in the order AB, or in the order BA, depending on the direction and velocity of your spacecraft.[100]

Such realities are another nail in the coffin for Newton's absolute space and time. Surely, the order of events must be clear in such a clockwork universe. It is also another way to vindicate Mach; an "operational" definition here is the only one allowed by the physics. You may determine the order of events based on your calculation of the time of flight of light rays reaching you from each event, and there is no third person omniscient narrator to tell you otherwise.

I should point out that this is not considered a speculative area of physics. The decay lifetimes of muons entering the Earth's atmosphere from space show a notable lengthening due to their speed. The International Space Station must adjust its clock speed to account for its motion relative to the Earth. The global positioning system uses relativistic corrections to determine your location. It is how the universe works. There has never been a case in which the principles of relativity were not found to be true of the world.

At least, until now.

Quasars are a unique opportunity to test relativity on a broad scale. They are a grid of clocks spread out over the universe and bright enough for us to see clearly across billions of years of space.

In a previous chapter, I described how the universe is expanding. Because it is expanding uniformly—that is, everywhere at once—galaxies farther away are moving away from us more quickly than galaxies nearby. As a result, the wobble of a quasar from the most distant reaches of space

---

[100] Note that this is true even if, on board your spaceship, you see star A before star B, or visa-versa. This is assuming you calculate the time it has taken the light to reach you from each star, making it not just an apparent order of events, but an actual order of events.

ought, on average, to exhibit a greater relativistic time dilation than one nearby. The clock should tick less often.

Mike Hawkins at the Royal Observatory, Edinburgh studied quasars his entire career. In 2001, he combined data from 400 quasars, observed over 24 years. He mathematically grouped them into bins containing a range of wobble rates, then looked at how the number of quasars in each bin were a function of the distance away, based on the quasar's redshift. He was startled to find that there was *no effect* with distance (Hawkins 2001).

Quasars, it seemed, were not exhibiting time dilation, despite moving away from us at great speed. What was going on here? Was Einstein wrong?

Hawkins desperately searched for any possibility that would account for this. Perhaps dark, massive objects in our galactic halo were lensing the light from these distant quasars and imparting to them their characteristic wobble. Perhaps the black holes in older, more distant galaxies exhibited a trend in frequency that perfectly cancels out the expected time dilation, for some unknown reason. Hawkins dismissed this as a "cosmic conspiracy" that would require a lot of fine tuning to pull off.

But his options quickly ran out. Are quasars not really that far away? No, we had taken good measurements by other means. Is time dilation not, after all, a feature of our universe? Hawkins threw up his arms. There was no satisfactory explanation.

If we have learned anything from the history of twentieth century physics, it is that subtle philosophical assumptions may have a strong influence on scientific reasoning. Ideas frame the problem and place constraints on how it may be solved.

The problem of time-dilation in quasars is a great example of this. On its face, there is no answer. What are we missing?

In his writings, Mach made the following point: We hold a pencil up in the air; it looks straight and we accept that it is straight. Then we place the pencil in a glass of water; it appears crooked, but we intuitively believe it is straight anyway despite the illusion. Mach wanted to change this notion. His goal was not to tell us that the pencil is really crooked, but rather that it *never was* straight.

What justifies us in declaring one fact rather than another to be the reality, and degrading the other to the level of appearance? In both cases we have to do with facts which present us with different combinations of the elements [senses], combinations which in the two cases are differently conditioned. (Mach 1914, p. 29)

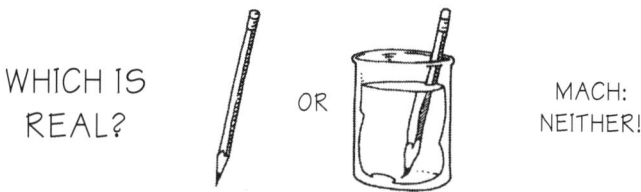

For Mach, sense experience was all there is. It was only an act of mental invention to say that the pencil *is* anything, whether straight or crooked, beyond what it appeared to be in a moment. Mach held that science ought not to make such distinctions, since there was no real pencil underlying appearances.

In Einstein's presentation of relativity theory, he treated all observers in all frames of reference equally, just as Mach treated all observers of straight or crooked pencils equally. This was actually Einstein's only innovation on Lorentz' understanding of the issue, but it was a conceptually significant one. It has boggled all our minds.

Yet, Einstein had a scientific realist core in him; he held that physical laws are *universal* regardless of one's point of view; relativity was merely a way of viewing the same phenomena from different angles. The pencil is there, regardless of how it is perceived.

Even after realizing that he was fundamentally opposed to Mach's philosophy, Einstein wrote a touching eulogy to Mach in 1916, only to discover in Mach's final, posthumously published manuscript, that Mach had repudiated his belief in Einstein's theories. In the end, Einstein's theories were too much about the real world for Mach.

Einstein continued to struggle with the idea that there was no absolute reference frame. In his 1915 paper on General Relativity, he imagined two bodies (say, moons) in the dead of space, spinning relative to one another. If you were on moon A, looking up at moon B, you would see B spinning. If you were on moon B, looking up at moon A, you would see A spinning. The rate of spin would be the same for each case. If there is no absolute frame of reference, how do you know which moon is actually spinning?

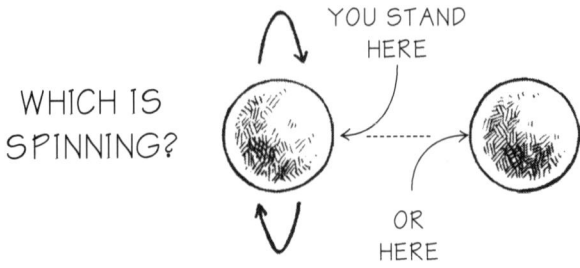

At this point, Einstein was still partially committed to Mach's instruction that definitions need to be operational to be meaningful:

> What is the reason for this difference in the two bodies? No answer can be admitted as epistemologically satisfactory, unless the reason given is an *observable fact of experience.* The law of causality has not the significance of a statement as to the world of experience, except when *observable facts* ultimately appear as causes and effects. (Einstein 1916)

We know which is spinning because if you are on the spinning moon, you will feel a force. The moon's spin may cause it to develop a noticeable oblate spheroidal bulge. And if you look out to the stars, they will also tell you whether your moon is spinning. This was a problem for Einstein. If his justification for relativity was correct, if all motion was only relative to other bodies, then the scenario in which moon A rotates and B does not, should be equivalent to the scenario in which moon B rotates and A does not. Let us call this the centripetal force paradox.

Einstein proposed that the answer to this enigma must have something to do with the stars and their gravitational fields. Perhaps the stars constructed something akin to an absolute frame of reference that instructed a spinning object to feel an outward force if it was moving relative to the stars. This idea is also known as "Mach's Principle," though different than the one discussed earlier.

I find this proposition extremely unsatisfactory. We throw out the idea of an absolute frame of reference, only to bring it back as an undiscovered physical mechanism by which the physics at my fingertips is influenced by the positions of stars light-years away?

In Einstein's time, the universe looked static. But things have changed; we now know that every star is moving relative to every other; every galaxy of stars relative to every other; the entire universe is expanding, and at an accelerating rate. Which of the thousands of neighboring stars establish our absolute frame?

THE "COSMIC CONSPIRACY"

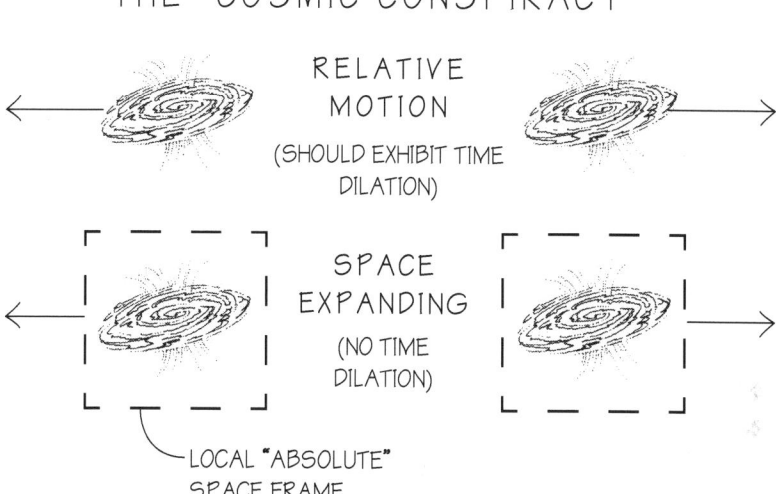

We face other quandaries as well. Einstein's Machian basis for relativity theory is unable to explain why the International Space Station (ISS) experiences absolute time loss associated with its relativistic motion, but the Earth does not. From the point of view of the ISS in orbit, the Earth is spinning underneath and those on the ground should be experiencing the absolute time loss. Yet it is the ISS that has to speed up its clocks to keep pace with Earth time.

These problems only stand unresolved if you make the same assumption that Einstein did at the outset, what he committed to prior to the analysis of the problem, and passionately defended throughout his career: *for absolute space to exist, it must be directly measurable.*

When Mills learned about the problem of the cosmic conspiracy, he offered the following, and I paraphrase: what if we suggest, without qualification, that absolute space exists? We perceive it whenever we are accelerated relative to it, because we feel a force, and we experience absolute time loss.

Light, however, passes through without regard to the absolute frame.[101]

Mills also argued that if all motion were relative, we could add any desired amount of mass-energy to the total mass inventory of the universe simply by choosing a reference frame. Remember that number with 54 zeroes? That is a fundamental constant, yet it gets bigger or smaller depending on our reference frame. Instead, we must choose an absolute reference frame for this purpose.

And Mills's position brings us back to quasars.

Recall that Mills predicted the accelerating expansion of the universe when he found that the release of matter as energy *pushes out* space. Every fusion event in every star in every galaxy is fueling the expansion.

In Mills's universe, galaxies are not *moving* through absolute space; rather, absolute space is *carrying* them outward as the universe expands. Those distant quasars still tick in a reference frame very similar to our own, despite the fact that the light from those galaxies is red-shifted as if they were racing away (Mills 2015, Ch. 34).

If spacetime expansion does not exhibit the effects of relativistic time dilation, then there must be something that defines an absolute place, and allows absolute places to be pushed around.

Perhaps everything is not relative; some things may exist though they may not be directly observed. Einstein was insightful, but he struggled with the bias of inherited ideas.

Within the sciences there has always been, and probably always will be, ideas transplanted from other domains of thought. When we reach a logical dead end, it means that somewhere along the way, in the labyrinth of the understanding, there was a wrong turn.

---

[101] Mills also argued that each particle, when it is created during pair production, acquires a unique absolute reference frame that may differ from that of other particles.

CHAPTER 18

THE QUANTUM QUAGMIRE

In which we find that those who attempt to prove it cannot be done, are usually wrong.

When I made a sincere attempt to learn quantum theory, I nearly fell under its spell. After my first full term of quantum mechanics, I came away with the sense that there must be a way to understand Mills's model in quantum terms; perhaps there were solutions to Schrödinger's equation for the hydrogen atom that allow fractional orbits?

I no longer think this way, but I understand the motivation to preserve what we know and what has been laboriously developed by others. We want to extend our understanding by merging it with new ideas. How would the scientific community reacted if instead of a revolutionary theory, Mills had offered (as one reporter put it) an "evolutionary" theory?

Perhaps what most intrigued me about quantum theory was how Nick Wheeler described it, as a mathematical extension of the classical tradition, in which we learn how to build particles out of waves. By 1927, experiments on free particles of both light and matter had been shown to exhibit wave behavior. Schrödinger was inspired by waves; his model of the hydrogen atom said something important about the wave-like nature of matter.

However, it didn't say everything we needed it to say, for a century later we are still baffled.

In 1965, Feynman introduced a topic in this way:

> [It is] a phenomenon which is impossible, absolutely impossible, to explain in any classical way, and which has in it the heart of quantum mechanics. In reality, it contains the only mystery. We cannot make the mystery go away by "explaining" how it works. We will just tell you how it works. (Feynman 1965)

He went on to describe a simple thought experiment. Fire a series of electrons at a barrier into which two thin slits have been cut. Place a screen on the far side that shows where the electrons land after passing through the slits. If electrons behave purely like classical particles, we would expect them to pile up in two narrow bands on the screen. If, however, they behave like waves, we should see something else entirely.

When a wave encounters a barrier with a small hole, it can pass through by forming a wavelet at the hole, which spreads out again as a new wave.[102] When a wave meets another wave, it interferes. The crests and troughs add constructively, but when a crest meets a trough, they cancel to nothing. If you have waves passing through two slits, the wavelets that emerge on the other side can interfere, like ripples from stones thrown in a pond. If electrons behave like this, we ought to see a series of narrow bands on the screen, a diffraction pattern.

In 2013, Roger Bach and his team at the University of Nebraska performed Feynman's thought experiment for the first time. But we knew what to expect. The experiment had been conducted in various configurations, first with light, then with matter, for 200 years.

The first experiment was conducted by Thomas Young in 1803, who showed that a fine wire could split a beam of light and produce color fringes resulting from interference (Young 1804). Maxwell's theory of light as electromagnetic waves led credence to the light-as-wave hypothesis. But the quantum revolution of 1900 forced physicists to think about light as particles.

The photoelectric effect, explained by Einstein in 1905, demonstrates this. If you shine a light on a metal surface in a vacuum, electrons will jump off the surface. If you increase the frequency (and therefore energy) of light, the same number of electrons will jump off, but at greater velocity. Only if you shine *more* light, more of what Einstein called *photons*, on the surface, do more electrons jump off. To make the jump, each electron needs to swallow a photon whole, so to speak.

If light is made of particles, how do they *wave*? I still remember my mathematics professor pacing around the room, chalk falling from his fingers, asking the class, or perhaps the universe out the window, "*What, actually, is waving?*"

Using the wave analogy, we might imagine that the stream of photons flowing on the left side of the wire is interfering with that from the right side. But what if we perform this experiment *one photon at a time* so there are no photons at the other side (or other slit) to interfere with? In 1909, G.I. Taylor did so (Taylor 1909). It must have been a shock to see, after many individual trials, a pattern emerge from the sum of the events that matched an *interference* pattern. Mind blown.

---

[102] According to Huygens' Principle.

THE CENTRAL MYSTERY OF QUANTUM THEORY: THE DOUBLE SLIT EXPERIMENT

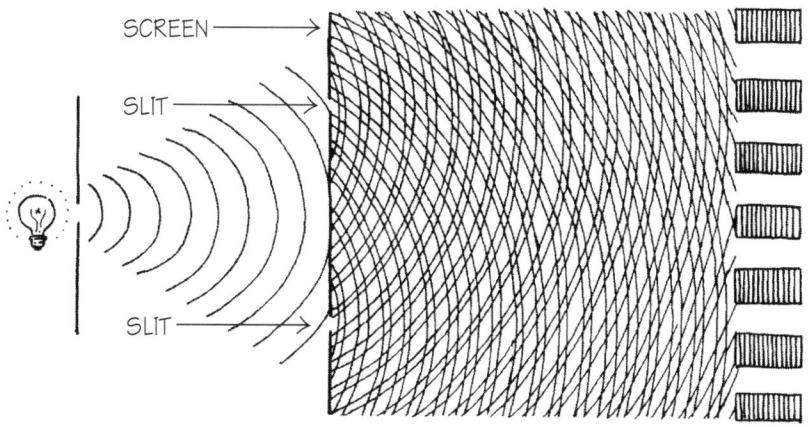

QUANTUM INTERPRETATION

A PHOTON PASSES THROUGH BOTH SLITS. THE EMERGING WAVELETS INTERFERE WITH ONE ANOTHER EN ROUTE TO THE SCREEN, AND THE WAVEFUNCTION COLLAPSES WHEN IT STRIKES THE SCREEN.

MILLS INTERPRETATION

A PHOTON PASSES THROUGH ONE SLIT. IT IS MOMENTARILY ABSORBED AND EMITTED BY THE SCREEN, WHICH IMPRINTS A CLASSICAL RADIATION PATTERN ON THE TRAJECTORY. IT PROCEEDS ALONG A STRAIGHT LINE TO THE SCREEN.

KOCSIS EXPERIMENT

THE RECONSTRUCTED AVERAGE TRAJECTORIES OF SINGLE PHOTONS IN THE DOUBLE-SLIT EXPERIMENT. A TEAM USED WEAK MEASUREMENTS THAT WERE ONLY ABLE TO YIELD APPROXIMATE INFORMATION ON THE MOMENTUM OF EACH PHOTON AS IT IMPACTED THE SCREEN. AFTER THAT IN (KOCSIS 2011).

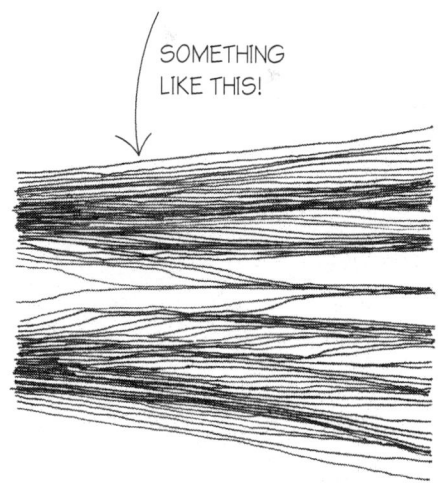

SOMETHING LIKE THIS!

This is not just limited to light.

In 1924, a young French physicist, Louis de Broglie, deduced that material particles might have a wavelength associated with their mass-energy. As it turns out, experimentalists were already scratching their heads over results that seemed to show electrons being diffracted in a crystal lattice. They had not published their results, of course, because they didn't know how to explain it: revealing again that we are often only confident in new observations when in the soothing embrace of new theory.

This began a century of double-slit-like experiments for particles of matter. A modified version of Young's experiment was called an electron biprism, where a very thin conducting wire was placed in the middle of the electron beam, causing the electron beam to split into two parts and interfere with each other on the far side. The first true double slit experiment was conducted in 1961;[103] and in 1989, Akira Tonomura was able to diffract one electron at a time, which still showed an interference pattern, just like the results with light (Tonomura 1989).

Roger Bach's experiment was the first *true* double-slit experiment with individual electrons, realizing the actual form of Feynman's thought experiment. Bach's team fired 600 eV electrons through slits milled in silicon-nitride windows coated with gold. Each slit could be opened or closed at will with a movable mask. Electrons were fired one at a time, and built up a series of bands. But when one slit or the other was closed, electrons showed no interference (Bach 2013).

We are left with many questions:

Does the particle pass through only one slit, or both at once? If the later, does it somehow interfere with itself? If it is spread out like a wave, how does it decide exactly where to land, and how quickly does it collapse from a wave to a point?

We have two conceptual pictures to explain this phenomena (waves or particles) but neither makes sense.

Beyond electrons, anything can in principle be diffracted; we have done it with neutrons, atoms, and molecules, and even carbon fullerenes (Arndt 1999; Nairz 2001). There are practical limits on our ability to do this because the more mass-energy the body possesses, the smaller its wavelength, and the finer the slits (or equivalent matrix) needed to diffract them. But theoretically, just as Archimedes once claimed "Give me a lever

---

[103] See Jonsson 1961, 1973.

long enough and a fulcrum on which to place it, and I shall move the world" so we might say: "give me a matrix fine enough and I will diffract the world!"

The explanation that quantum mechanics gives us (or, according to Feynman, fails to give us) for this wave-particle duality is deeply tied up in how we interpret the theory.

Recall that quantum theory models a particle as a wave group that forms a short pulse. Heisenberg was the first to realize that the model had some bizarre features.

Imagine, for a moment, three trains going by.

- ¤ The first is long; you hear each boxcar as it passes, and one passes each second for a full minute. If you know the length of a typical boxcar, you may easily calculate the velocity of the train.
- ¤ The second train is shorter, just a few boxcars long, and although you can still determine the velocity, it is less precise.
- ¤ Now the final train goes by, but it has only an engine and a caboose. There is no coherent beat as each boxcar passes, just a rise and fall in clamor as it goes by.

So there is a natural relationship here between the length of the train and your ability to discover the train's velocity.

Like the trains in the analogy, a quantum particle may be described by a wave-train which must be drawn out over space to have a regular beat, and the beat gives us the momentum of the particle. If we speak according to Born's interpretation, a quantum particle is a point, but the likelihood of measuring the particle's position at any given place is given by a spread-out probability distribution (given by the wavefunction). As we constrain the position to a narrower region of space—as we shorten the train—we widen the range of the particle's possible velocities.

Position and momentum are conjugate properties of a particle, according to quantum mechanics. The degree of accuracy with which you can know both properties are limited. Also limited is your ability to measure, because (in a confusing mix of empirical and theoretical postulates) as you measure the position of a particle, you disturb it by imparting a momentum burst that produces a random change to the particle's velocity. Both the theoretical postulate, and the experimental postulate, form what has come to be called the Heisenberg Uncertainty Principle.

When I was taught quantum mechanics, my professor felt that quantum theory tells us *what we can know* about a quantum system. We do not know if a particle passes through one or the other slit; in fact, we do not know where the particle is until it is observed. The goal of the theory is to give us a statistical estimate of where the particle will be found, when (and if) it is observed. Quantum mechanics is merely a statement about our knowledge, not about nature.

But Born's interpretation of the double-slit experiment suggested that perhaps, a particle exists in all of its possible states simultaneously, and the particle's probability distribution is a real object that passes through both slits, interferes with itself, and imparts to the particle a final location when measured. This would suggest that if we observe it at any point along its trajectory, we break the spell and collapse it into one place. And indeed, whenever we try to trick our particle into telling us which slit it went through, we lose the diffraction pattern. It disappears like a frightened ghost, and we are left with a classical pile-up of particles on the screen.

Perhaps the nature of the world must be observed to take on a singular value. Perhaps the world does not exist independent of our knowing it. Or perhaps we simply have a bad theory. Perhaps, perhaps, perhaps.

I am something of an endangered species of philosopher: a *scientific realist*. By this I mean that I believe that the goal of science is to give us a literally true story of what the world is like, and to accept a scientific theory is to believe that the theory is true.[104]

This is a very optimistic position. It implies that our minds are capable of understanding the universe and our senses are effective tools for perceiving it. We have limits, of course, but we come to know them and work around them. We use data acquisition systems connected to probes to help us observe; we compile data in databases and analyze them with statistics to refine our judgments.

More deeply, I believe that there is a universe outside my own head, beyond the sum of my experience of it; a vast, incredible universe that will delight me until my last breath. We might call this the objective world premise. Einstein, who in the latter part of his life was an outspoken defender of the scientific realist position, wrote the following in 1948:

---

[104] For further reading on scientific realism see Psillos 1999.

> If one asks what is a characteristic of the realm of physical ideas independently of the quantum theory, then above all the following attracts our attention: the concepts of physics refer to a real external world, i.e. ideas are posited of things that claim a real existence independent of the perceiving subject (bodies, fields, etc.), and these ideas are, on the other hand, brought into as secure a relationship as possible with sense impressions. (Einstein 1948)

Scientific realists, like Einstein, have struggled with quantum theory. Unable to refute physicists, philosophers are often led to reject one or more of realism's tenants. Some are willing to interpret the statistical interpretation literally; allowing mathematical entities (probability distributions) to exist in reality. We might call this *mathematical realism* (McMullin 1984; Chew 1973). Heisenberg is counted among them.

> 'All things are numbers' is a sentence attributed to Pythagoras. ...In modern quantum theory there can be no doubt that the elementary particles will finally also be mathematical forms, but of a much more complicated nature. (Heisenberg 1958, p. 72)

Heisenberg felt that elementary particles would turn out to be solutions of some eternal law of motion for matter. The particles are real, but they are mathematical rather than physical. Nancy Cartwright, once a strong realist, later argued "quantum realists should take the quantum state seriously as a genuine feature of reality" (Cartwright 1999, p. 232).

Hilary Putnam went a different route; he relaxed his scientific realist position to something called *internal realism* in which propositions are only true relative to some favored descriptive framework or conceptual scheme (Norris 2000, p. 165; Putnam 1973). Here Putnam gave up the notion that words are literal and have genuine meaning; he cut off our connection to the world at our tongue.

Scientific realists must resort to arguing that quantum theory is not true of nature, or if it is partially true, then incomplete in some important way; or if its mathematics is effective, it must admit of a more reasonable explanation. Someday, perhaps, we will have a better theory.

Many physicists struggled to find alternative interpretations. Erwin Madelung supposed that the wavefunction is a kind of hydrodynamic fluid of electricity. In 1927 de Broglie offered what he called a "double-solution" in which a particle is a singularity in a wave field: here the particle remains classical but is guided by a pilot wave that gives it the illusion of wave behavior (Jammer 1974, p. 4).

David Bohm suggested that there must be hidden variables that work in conjunction with Schrödinger's equation, and guide the system with new laws (Bohm 1952). Although Bohm believed that his interpretation would offer some testable discrepancies with quantum mechanics on a very small scale, neither his nor any other interpretation of quantum theory have given us any new, useful physics.

Perhaps the problem is not with the physics, but that our minds are not well-equipped to deal with the realm of the atom.

Bohr thought so, and proposed a new style of thinking in which we use different conceptual lenses to look at the same problem, even if those lenses are inconsistent. He called these lenses "complementary" and he called the inconsistencies, "reciprocal" properties of a thing.

We can only look at a quantum particle with a particle-analogy or a wave-analogy, but not both. Bohr imagined that perhaps all of our concepts would be improved by this kind of thinking, and gave another example: the experience of free will versus the physical machinery of our brain. Perhaps these are complementary in the same way.

Bohr spoke about the quantum world as if it were real, but when pressed against a wall, he sounded a lot like Mach:

> There is no quantum world. There is only an abstract physical description. It is wrong to think that the task of physics is to find out how nature is. Physics concerns what we can say about nature. Quoted in (Peterson 1963)

Among the many interpretations of quantum theory, Bohr's view (also known as the Copenhagen Interpretation) was common, and often discussed in conjunction with the Born and Heisenberg statistical view.

But Einstein, Schrödinger, Planck, and even de Broglie expressed reservations with this way of thinking, and kept the faith that there must be something going on that we don't understand.

I love the words that Grover Maxwell used in 1962 to voice his position; even though he was well aware that electrons were theoretically impossible to observe according to quantum mechanics, he said he would "put his head on a block" to argue that electrons would in the future become observable (Maxwell 1962, p. 40). J.J.C. Smart was another advocate of this point of view (Smart 1963, p. 44).

Almost every day we see news about some new experiment that confirms quantum mechanics, whether the discovery of a new particle, or the teleportation of a particle, or a step forward in quantum computing. Quantum mechanics is hailed as "spectacularly successful: in terms of power and precision, head and shoulders above any theory we have ever had" (Ismael 2004). Nobel prizes are regularly awarded. Philosophers are buckling under the pressure.

There are a few left standing, including Stathis Psillos and Christopher Norris. The latter argued:

> From the realist viewpoint... there is something irrational in the very idea that a branch of science so fraught with unresolved puzzles and paradoxes should be thought to require a wholesale change in our basic conceptions of truth, knowledge, and physical reality. After all, it could well be argued that ever since its inception quantum theory has been in a state of more-or-less permanent crisis, a protracted version of what Kuhn describes as 'pre-revolutionary' science but without—as yet—any sign of a breakthrough to the new (post-revolutionary) paradigm. (Norris 2000, p. 196)

Mills has a long list of criticisms that substantiate Norris's complaint: Schrödinger's equation was never compatible with special relativity; it failed to predict that the electron spins (Messiah 1969, p. 419); it failed to predict observed properties of the atom such as the Lamb Shift, the Fine Structure, and the Hyperfine Structure. The equation only accurately solved hydrogen, and failed with heavier elements. Any system with more than one electron became a computational nightmare.

Dirac's reformulation of quantum theory allowed for electron spin, and (arguably) predicted the positron, but it allowed the electron to have properties that are not physical, such as negative rest mass and negative kinetic energy. Dirac's attempt to rationalize these away required proposing a feature of reality never observed: a sea of electrons over all space filling the disallowed electronic energy levels.

This reminds me of something Imre Lakatos remarked: "In a progressive research programme, theory leads to the discovery of hitherto unknown novel facts. In degenerating programmes, however, theories are fabricated only in order to accommodate known facts (Lakatos 1978).

Feynman and others developed quantum electrodynamics as a way to describe the interactions of charged particles mediated by photons. But Feynman himself was critical of the mathematical methods needed to make it work. The theoretician must divide infinites by infinities to remove them from equations, or arbitrarily truncate power series that diverge (Dyson 1952).

And what did quantum theory get us? Most of the useful technologies in the twentieth century are a result of Maxwellian physics. I cannot attest to whether semiconductor physics was improved by quantum theory, but high temperature superconductors were certainly a surprise, and the founders of quantum theory felt that the laser was impossible (Mead 2001).

Perhaps quantum theory was merely an accompanist to an incredible surge in applied research, desperately trying to keep up and rationalize new discoveries within its paradigm. To substantiate this view would be a topic for another book.

While quantum theoreticians had forgotten about the problem of radiation in the atom, and obsessed over the double-slit experiment, Mills only turned his attention to it fifteen years after solving the problem of radiation. It happened to be the year I was in the office.

Mills realized photons should not interfere, they should superimpose. Noise-canceling headphones can use sound to negate sound, but you can't use light to negate light because it would violate the conservation of energy. Instead, the interference pattern must be an *emission* pattern from the slits.

If there cannot be interference, then exiting a slit is the last opportunity for the photon to experience a causal influence. Yet we know that if we close off one of the slits, they do not produce the interference pattern. This means that the photon passing through the slit has to be aware of the existence of other slit at the moment it passes through. This is strange, but might make sense. As the photon passes through the slit it may be momentarily absorbed and emitted with a new trajectory that takes it along a straight line to the screen (Mills 2015, Ch. 8).

This is consistent with the results of a modern double-slit experiment, performed in 2011. A team used weak measurements that were only able to yield approximate information on the momentum of each photon as it impacted the screen. By taking many measurements over multiple trials, the study revealed an average trajectory for all photons at each point in space (Kocsis 2011).

We must be careful how we interpret this, since the data does not give us the path of any individual particle, but the average of many trajectories. If we do allow ourselves to assume that the average data is representative of individual paths, then the photons appear to have straight-line trajectories from the slit to the screen. No interference.

Mills found that a diffraction pattern seen on the screen matches a *classical* radiation pattern if we treat the slits as something like radio antenna, yet one that preserves the momentum of the photon as it passes through.

Before 1900, physicists thought that radiation was a continuous spread of electromagnetic energy. Now we know that large fields are made up of many individual photons. If you feel an electromagnetic field, it is because your measuring device (your radio receiver) is capturing some of these photons, which are statistically distributed across the classical energy spread.

This distribution is deterministic; it is due to subtle realities that give a statistical result over many trials. The same is taking place in the double-slit experiment.

The case with electrons is a little different.

When you perform a double-slit experiment with electrons, you must first allow the mask to be conductive (the Bach study used gold). Otherwise, electric charge just piles up at the slits. If you run a current through the mask, you also preclude the interference pattern. This is because when a charged particle approaches the slits, image charges emerge on the slit and photons are exchanged between the electron and the slits. These photons scatter with electrons and *imprint* the classical radiation pattern on those that pass through the slits. Like the previous case with photons, once the electrons are done interacting with the slits they follow straight line trajectories until they hit the screen.

Compton scattering is the sudden and abrupt change in the electron's trajectory when it interacts with a photon. Mills conjectured that how much the trajectory changed was due to the time it took for the photon to be emitted after being absorbed. A small time of interaction will result in a very small scattering; a long absorption time will cause a wide scattering angle, and the Heisenberg uncertainty principle becomes a statistical relationship in how electrons scatter from photons.

The uncertainty is due to very small differences in how the two particles come together and fly apart. This does limit our observations because if we are trying to extract information from a particle, scattering a photon from it is the finest scalpel we have. But this uncertainty is not intrinsic to the nature of reality. It is consistent with a scientific realist world view, even if it is mildly disappointing that there will always be limitations.

I am not afraid of limitations. It was the ancient Greeks who felt that one is defined by one's limitations; "Know Thyself" was written above the Oracle at Delphi. It is through a knowledge of our own limits that we better ourselves.

When Mills handed me his solution for the first time, it soon dawned on us that we may be able to test whether his explanation was right. Each electron is polarized when it passes through the slit into either a parallel or antiparallel state. If we could see the contribution of only one slit to each interference band, we would see that each band represents a spin-flip on the part of the electron (Mills 2015, Ch. 8).

Perhaps if we polarized the incoming electron beam, selecting for, say, only the parallel orientation, then we analyzed the spin orientations of electrons, say, with an electric field that shifts spin-up electrons one way and spin-down electrons another way, we should see a pattern of alternating spins, up-down-up-down, marching across the screen.

I was excited by this possibility and I began talks with the electron microscopy faculty at Princeton. Performing the experiment would be expensive and time consuming; they wanted us to substantially fund the laboratory for a year, which was not possible. If I saw it through, it would probably amount to a doctorate thesis. If the experiment matched Mills's predictions, it would be a landmark study; I wouldn't be surprised if it earned the experimenter, or Mills, a Nobel Prize.

I took a moment to imagine that life. I had set myself on a path that could give me incredible opportunities in physics and engineering; to be at the edge of change. I was in the right place at the right time. But I was also beginning to sense my own limits.

I didn't know where I would end up; we conduct our lives like a quantum particle, with every choice we visualize the range of futures we are making available for ourselves, but we never know how we will act when faced with that future.

The experiment has not yet been performed as of this writing, and I look forward to learning if it will turn out as Mills predicted. It is another confirmable prediction that may force us, kicking and screaming, from one paradigm to the next.

Einstein didn't have a better theory, but he desperately sought to communicate to other physicists his qualms with quantum. In 1935, he, Podolsky and Rosen (EPR) wrote a paper that was the classic argument against quantum theory from a scientific realist viewpoint, but by a turn of fate became part of quantum's strongest defense (Einstein 1935).

EPR argued that for a theory to be successful, it ought to be both *correct*, and *complete*, by which there should be an element in the theory that corresponded to every element in the world, and by which we should be able to predict the outcome of any experiment.

The Heisenberg Uncertainty Principle says we can know the position of a particle, or its momentum, but not both, which means either a particle does not, in reality, possess both position and momentum at once, or a particle does, but our theories are unable to describe both at once. If the latter is true, we have an *incomplete* theory.

EPR then suggested a thought experiment. Suppose we allow two quantum particles to interact, and then allow them to move apart in opposite directions. By interacting, the wavefunctions describing the two particles have become *entangled*, each particle's state depends, to some extent, on the state of the other, at least until a measurement is made. We allow them to move apart an arbitrarily large distance. It could be a few meters, or a few light years, or across the universe.

Now take one of the particles and measure its position. If we know its position, we now know something about the other particle's position, because the two wavefunctions are entangled. However, if instead of measuring position we had measured momentum, then we would have known something about the other particle's momentum.

We could perform *either* experiment, and the other particle can't know which we are performing, because it could be much too far away to be told what is going on, even if it were able to communicate with its entangled mate at light speed.

Einstein had made it his life's work to show that the speed of light was instrumental for any kind of causal propagation through space; the idea of two quantum particles interacting faster than light, *nonlocally*, offended every fiber of his being: "No reasonable definition of reality could be expected to permit this." EPR concluded that quantum theory was incomplete; a particle must possess both a definite position and a definite momentum when it parts ways with the other particle.[105]

EPR concluded with the following:

> While we have thus shown that the wave function does not provide a complete description of the physical reality, we left open the question of whether or not such a description exists. We believe, however, that such a theory is possible. (Einstein 1935)

Bohr begged to differ, and responded to EPR's paper with an arguments from complementarity (Bohr 1935). Bohr felt that it was an extension of Einstein's own Machian approach to physics that motivated relativity theory, but Einstein had renounced most of his Machian ties by that point, asking his colleague in frustration "Do you really think the moon exists only when you look at it?"

This debate was largely a philosophical one for many years, until 1965, when John Bell took a modified version of EPR's thought experiment and asked what would happen if quantum theory really was incomplete. Would we expect an experiment to yield a different result?

Suppose we take two electrons emitted with opposite spins, or two photons emitted with opposite polarizations from an excited atom. We allow them to move apart, and simultaneously measure their spins or polarizations.

Suppose there is an unknown variable that predetermines the results of our measurements on the two particles, and the variable is *local*, unable to communicate superluminously with the entangled mate. Bell found that that we ought to see a correlation in spins which is different than that predicted by quantum theory.

Bell argued that *any* local, realistic theory must differ from the results of quantum mechanics; this is called Bell's theorem.

---

[105] It is worthy to note here that if the particles were allowed to move a light year apart, and we measured one of the particles, for the signal to reach the other particle in time for a simultaneous measurement a light-year away, the signal would need to travel *backwards in time* in order to reach the other particle.

In 1982 Alain Aspect performed a definitive experiment to test Bell's theorem using pairs of photons emitted by a beam of excited calcium atoms. Aspect used rotating polarizers to measure the photon's polarization, and the results confirmed the predictions of quantum theory to high accuracy (Aspect 1982).

The conclusion drawn by physicists was that quantum theory *had* to be a complete theory; for no local theory containing "hidden variables" could possibly give the results that were found in experiment.

This brought about something of a mass extinction event among scientific realists. Most physicists found it disturbing, but were unable to think of a way around Bell's results. It seemed that there was no way out of the flood dam brought about by the double-slit experiment and the Aspect experiments; we had to accept a world in which particles inhabit statistical ensembles of possible states until measured, and pairs of particles can share in their statistical limbo across time and space until measured by a knowing being; a phenomena that Einstein had aptly called "spooky actions at a distance."

In a general sense, the goal of Bell's theorem was an interesting one: it was an explicit attempt to test our theory against all possible theories that differed in a paradigmatic way. We might think of it as a ladder to get from one paradigm to the next. To do this well, however, one must be sure to assume *nothing* of the current paradigm, and this was where Mills believed Bell's theorem was flawed.

Quantum theory made the implicit assumption that the unknown variables affecting the outcome of the spin measurements are somehow stored, metaphorically speaking, in a kind of disk drive on-board the quantum particle, which is still described, geometrically as a *point*.

Suppose instead of measuring the spin of a single quantum particle in Aspect's experiment, we sent through two, or four, or ninety-six particles to each detector at the same time. Suppose also there were some way to establish a complex, aggregate pattern of motion among the group of particles, such that the angular momentum of the group is stored in three-dimensional space.

They need not all be orbiting in the same direction, as angular momentum may be distributed across the collective motion of the ensemble. Let the groups of particles we send to each detector have opposite aggregate "spins.". Suppose our detector could measure the spin of each *group*, instead of the spin of an individual particle.

In our thought experiment, we may now match the predictions of quantum theory without assuming superluminous interaction.

According to Mills's theory, a particle is not a point, but an extension, and its spin is distributed across a three-dimensional spherical shell. Measurements of spin or polarization are therefore influenced by a complex geometrical function that describes all moving charge (or fields) throughout the particle's surface, and our calculation must take this into account (Mills 2015, Ch. 42).

Mills theory is thus not a member of the set of possible theories described by Bell's theorem; it is not a "hidden variables" interpretation of quantum mechanics. Mills's theory allows us to match experiment, but with a *local* and *realistic* theory.

If quantum mechanics is an incomplete theory—or moreover, if the theory is outright wrong—it is amazing that its predictions for the double-slit and Aspect experiments were right at all. Obviously, there are features of the world that quantum theory captured with some regularity.

The murky meaning of the theory is a problem; physics is not just about math, it is about the physical world. And while our minds should be open to new possibilities, we cannot lose sight of our most fundamental philosophical assumptions about the nature of the universe: causality, determinism, realism, and locality. These assumptions work. Our understanding of them allowed us to climb out of the cave.

But it is worthy to ask, why is quantum mechanics still around?

I believe that quantum theory has survived because it evolves easily. It can approximate and adjust parameters to feign success.

Recall that Mach believed that the purpose of a scientific theory was to create an economical "systematization of experience" in which the conceptual part of the theory, inasmuch as it is useful, only serves to facilitate the creation of "direct descriptions" of observable phenomena, i.e. descriptions not dependent on natural laws or unobservable entities.

We sometimes call this an *instrumentalist* theory.

From the beginning, quantum theory was a theory of this kind, one that removed meaningful theoretical notions and replaced them with instructions for calculating and for observing. Perhaps it is a general feature of all such theories that as the set of axioms and sophistication of its instructions increases, it becomes capable of accounting for any phenomena. Just as an argument with contradicting premises can prove any result, a murky theory can accommodate any result. It feeds on new data but it loses the ability to predict.

It is ironic that although quantum mechanics opposed the unobservables of the electron orbiting the atom, it did end up positing a variety of unobservable features of reality such as virtual particles, hyperdimensions, effective nuclear charge, zero-order vibration, polarization of the vacuum, parallel universes, and so on; features that were offered to rationalize mathematics, rather than flowing from our intuitions.

Before the Copernican revolution, we had the Ptolemaic celestial system, in which each planet moved on an epicycle revolving on its deferent, offset by an equant that was different for each planet. The resulting system was able to map very well onto the observed celestial motions, but the epicycles were postulated unobservables that only served the math.

In retrospect, the system, in all its complexity, could map onto *any* potential celestial motion as observed from the Earth, because mathematically it is equivalent to a Fourier series expansion. You can refine it forever.

Perhaps quantum theory has inadvertently become something similar.

Can we give it up after a century of thought? After thousands of articles in journals of physics and philosophy? After all the coffee shop conversations and popular mystic movements?

We will, no doubt, go unwillingly, the scientists desperately attempting to salvage what they can, the mystics clinging to the washed-up science like the astrologer's zodiac and the alchemist's potions.

Eventually, we will accept it and move on.

CHAPTER 19

THE POWER OF THE SUN

In which we seek the ultimate source of energy.

CORONAL LOOPS ON THE SURFACE OF THE SUN, WHICH EMIT IN THE EUV AND X-RAY BANDS.

Energy is the ultimate enabler of human life and prosperity, a prosperity in which a billion people still do not fully share. And whatever our motivation for doing science, the ultimate end is, as Francis Bacon asserted, "that human life be endowed with new discoveries and powers" (Bacon 1620).

These powers are, for many, a matter of life and death, of subsistence or freedom, of ignorance or a thoughtful life. A family without access to an efficient energy source is in a kind of abject poverty that requires an effort to survive almost every waking moment: gathering firewood, carrying water, or grazing livestock, much of which is a disproportionate burden on women and children. A child whose effort goes to meet survival needs cannot attend school; a woman who cannot participate in a larger economy is married young. A branching fan of opportunities in life are cut off at the source.

Historically, our advancement as a species may be directly charted by our energy use. A hunter-gatherer able to build a fire consumed, on average, 6 kWh per person per day; a farmer employing oxen and horses consumed 14 kWh; an early industrial worker using coal-fired steam engines consumed 89 kWh, and a modern person in a first world nation consumes 257 kWh (Cook 1971; Jansson 1997).

That's a one-hundred-fold multiplier over the 2,000 calorie diet (2.3 kWh) we need daily to stay alive.

Energy access correlates with every measure of standard of living. Where there is an energy problem, there are also water access and sanitation problems. Where there is a water problem, there is a crop irrigation problem. Where families burn wood and coal daily, people are subjected to pollutants as airborne particulates, oxides of sulfur and nitrogen, or the threat of carbon monoxide poisoning, all of which may cause millions of deaths per year.

Developing countries with some access to modern energy sources quickly become dependent on them, either as imports or as exports, resulting in a fragile situation. Rising or falling energy prices may put enormous strain on these countries. They may fall into debt while fighting to maintain political stability.

The resources are rarely equitably distributed. It has been estimated that with modern innovations in energy efficiency, only a kilowatt per capita is enough to vastly lift the standard of living for the citizens of many in developing countries, providing not only clean drinking water and safe heating sources, but refrigeration and lighting as well. But the infrastructure is not there to serve everyone (Goldemberg 1985).

We are chasing this global poverty problem, but we are barely running in place. Eight hundred million people in China were added to the grid in the 1980s, but the world population increased over that time such that the number of people still without access was the same. Billions more will need to be added to the grid in the twenty-first century, challenging our energy sources and our infrastructure.

Meanwhile, those with access now realize that the ecological impact of our existing energy sources is unacceptable. About 80% of our energy comes from fossil fuel sources, which stress our ecosystems with chemicals like lead, oil, cadmium, sulfur, and mercury; require extraction and transportation of billions of tons of coal and oil; and contribute massive quantities of carbon dioxide into the atmosphere. Much of this CO_2 is absorbed by the Earth's oceans, acidifying them rapidly, with severe impact on ocean life.[106]

If we continue altering global surface land and water temperatures, not only do we stress existing ecosystems, but we risk melting the Greenland ice sheet and raising the sea level by 7 meters over the next 150 years. Projections show that we could still escape this fate, but it would require a substantial reduction in CO_2 emissions *now*, or a total abandonment of them within a century.

While the complete exhaustion of fossil fuel sources is unlikely in the coming centuries, it is likely that costs will rise as we struggle to exploit smaller deposits with more difficult extraction methods, which may occur in sensitive ecosystems, and be combated by ever more fierce environmental policy.

---

[106] Although our contribution to CO_2 levels is only about 5% of natural flows, our contribution is expected to double the atmospheric concentration of CO_2 since pre-industrial times by 2070. For more information see GEA 2012; WEA 2000; and WEI 2011.

Few alternatives to fossil fuels are attractive. Hydroelectric dams (which contribute about 18% to world energy use) are often viewed as among the most sustainable sources as they do not result in CO_2 emissions. However, they impede the flow of nearly every major river on the planet, concentrating the impact to river ecosystems while altering the landscape on a massive scale.

Nuclear power, although once hailed as the power source of the future, has turned out to be more expensive than we expected, unable to fulfill the promised length of operation. It produces radioactive waste with long-term storage requirements, and the power plants are vulnerable to catastrophic failure. Further, nuclear power plants are a source for weapons-grade plutonium, inciting battles over who gets to use it.

Renewable energy sources such as solar and wind have seen rapid expansion and incredible decreases in cost. Solar panels alone have fallen to a tenth of what they cost in 2000, and a *hundredth* of what they cost in the 1970s. While 90% of power generated in a central plant is lost in transmission before it reaches the end year, wind and solar are easily decentralized, placed closer to or within cities, leading to a *microdistributed* power infrastructure. This allows renewable sources to compete with central generation, though they are often dependent on the elements.

So far, renewables have only made an impact equivalent to the amount of nuclear power taken off-line over the same period, and have had a negligible impact on fossil-fuel consumption. We may, however, be at a turning point. As of the writing of this book, costs from solar electricity have recently dropped below the average cost of electricity for most users in the United States.

A wide-scale replacement of fossil fuels would involve a tapestry of green technologies deployed on many levels, deploying renewables while lowering consumption with ultra-low energy buildings, smart-grid technology, electric vehicles, denser communities with more mass-transit, organic or permaculture farming, recycling, reuse, or cradle-to-cradle life cycling of materials, and so on.

In developing countries, renewables have occasionally been implemented, such as the SolaWin project, a hybrid solar and wind power system that pumps groundwater to be used for drinking or irrigation, producing a local answer to the coupled challenges of food, water, and energy (WEI 2011). These have been deployed as demonstration projects, not economically fertile systems for wide implementation.

Yet, even with inexpensive solar power, implementation would be expensive, slow, require broad and intense will on the part of individuals and politicians, and we would need to remain tolerant of rising energy costs. The transition would be fighting ongoing increases in energy demand, especially from developing and undeveloped countries, for many years.

Energy scarcity spills over into every facet of materials and manufacturing. If the steel mill can't turn on their arc furnace, there will be a steel shortage.

While the tapestry is certainly feasible in concept, it would be among the most difficult tasks the human race has ever attempted, not the least because it would require all us to curb our own excesses while we continue to boom in numbers and affluence.

We seek the *ultimate* source of energy.

This is a source that does not rely on geopolitically scarce natural resources; that does not require resource extraction that degrades habitat; that does not produce radioactive or chemical waste; that is an unlimited source, renewable like wind and sun, but ideally able to run day and night, anywhere; that may be implemented in large scale power plants or smaller, microdistributed plants; that is not vulnerable to catastrophic failure; and finally—and most importantly—the ultimate source of energy is cheap, to encourage the transition and absorb the implicit costs.

For 50 years, humanity has placed its hopes and dreams in the fire of the Sun: hot fusion. In fusion, hydrogen nuclei crash together at millions of degrees, forming helium, releasing a substantial amount of energy in the process. We have funded research at about $300 million per year, for a total bill of about 20 billion.[107]

Perhaps, if we doubled, or tripled, or quintupled that amount, we would achieve fusion energy. Yet dollars do not always equate to discoveries.

The legacy of the fusion research program has been the failure of the technology to prove that it was a viable solution in the near-term. There remain many scientific problems to be solved before a feasible fusion reactor could be engineered, and progress had been plagued by administrative problems common to public works projects.

Even if we were successful at harnessing fusion, it may not be the ultimate energy source. A fusion plant is likely to be a central power source,

---

[107] The annual fusion budget was equivalent to three times Mills's total 25-year research budget.

large and complex, perhaps modeled on a Tokamak reactor, in which a hydrogen plasma is held within a large, toroidal magnetic trap while it is superheated to millions of degrees. It is not cheap power, it is not easily deployable in the third world, and comes with significant risk. Large superconducting magnets need to be kept at liquid helium temperatures; if they warm up beyond their critical superconducting temperature, they may be destroyed.

Further, fusion would likely come with significant amounts of low-grade radioactive waste. The neutrons that are emitted from nuclear reactions are uncharged and effortlessly escape magnetic confinement to impinge on reactor materials.[108]

Fusion may not be the *ideal* source of energy, but we have pursued it anyway; we seek an energy source that steps lightly on Earth.

Hot fusion is a cruel temptress. We look into the sky and we see the power of the Sun radiating down to Earth; its energy filtering through the whole biosphere. We bathe in its radiance, but we would like to reach out, capture the power of the Sun, and bring it down to Earth. This has eluded us. Perhaps it is because we don't yet understand the Sun; while we have proven that the Sun *is* powered by fusion, there are deeply disturbing mysteries surrounding its source of power.

What we know about the Sun comes from what we can see; yet this is only the outer layer of the Sun's surface; the *photosphere*, together with the atmosphere of the Sun, the *corona*, which we can see especially well from Earth during a total solar eclipse.

The surface of the Sun is a tumultuous place, with incredibly strong magnetic fields laced among explosive events, dark spots, coronal loops, coronal mass ejections, and flares that emit everything from radio waves to gamma rays while sending shock waves across the entire solar disk.

Physicists calculate that the majority of the Sun's mass, and nearly all of its fusion activity, is contained within only a quarter of its radius, deep in its interior.

Nature has given us a way to see deep into this interior, with a kind of light that effortlessly passes through the outer layers of the Sun: the

---

[108] The design would likely use a water bath around the reactor to trap many of the neutrons, thereby also helping to produce the deuterium and tritium used in reactor.

neutrino. Neutrinos are emitted from nuclear reactions and carry away some of the energy, but they react only very rarely with matter.

Proton-proton fusion releases neutrinos, but in order to see a neutrino you need to be able to capture it. The isotope Chlorine-37 seems particularly good at absorbing neutrinos. When it does, it ejects an electron, converting a neutron to a proton, thereby transmuting to Argon-37, which as it happens, is well equipped to absorb any left-over energy it receives from the neutrino in its many nuclear excitations.

Neutrinos produced by proton-proton fusion are of too low an energy to be absorbed by Chlorine-37. However, one of the reaction pathways for fusion involves the creation of a Beryllium-7 nucleus by fusion of Helium-3 and Helium-4. Beryllium-7 can capture a proton to make Boron-8, which releases a neutrino.

In 1958, we discovered that even though only two out of every thousand fusion events lead to Beryllium-7, the production of Beryllium-7 was a thousand times more likely to occur than we expected. This was a breakthrough, because the neutrino energy was high enough to be captured by Chlorine-37. Physicists found hope that they could see neutrinos from deep inside the Sun.

The first attempt to detect solar neutrinos was a 3,800-gallon tank of tetrachloromethane, buried about 19 feet down at Brookhaven.

It was mocked for inaccuracy: "one would not write a scientific paper describing an experiment in which an experimenter stood on a mountain and reached for the moon, and concluded that the moon was more than eight feet from the top of the mountain" (Bahcall 1982), though we were not trying to reach the moon, we were trying to reach the Sun.

Raymond Davis pioneered the project to build a 100,000 gallon tank of tetrachloroethene (C_2CL_4) (Davis 1964, 1968). It needed to be deep within the Earth, because cosmic rays entering the Earth's atmosphere produce particles such as muons at relativistic velocities that would interfere with the detection of neutrino capture events. So they found a mine at Homestake and built the tank 1,200 meters below the surface. By flowing helium and Argon-36 through the massive tank, they were able to collect the Argon-37 and analyze it in a detector. Each Argon-37 atom detected meant a neutrino had been captured.

How poetic: we must go deep underground, in order to see clearly into the interior of the Sun.

We can calculate how many neutrinos we should see from the rate of fusion in the Sun, which on the first level of approximation should be directly related to the Sun's luminosity, i.e. a neutrino for every 25 MeV or so. This calculation is, of course, different for the Boron-8 neutrino. Physicists arrived at a number: 7.9.

But the Homestake experiment found only 2.1.

That's only *60%* of the neutrinos we expected to find.

Like dark matter, the solar neutrino problem was neglected by physics for decades. It took a full 35 years to convince many physicists that solar neutrino research was telling us something important (Bahcall 2003).

Prior to Homestake, many thought that an underground neutrino detector could not be made sensitive enough to detect neutrinos, and the experiment would be too expensive. There were arguments between the particle physicists and the astrophysicists as to whose budget would fund the project. Bahcall even sold the experiment to particle physicists by suggesting that the best possible result would be a discrepancy with theory, because it would prove to the particle physicists that astrophysicists couldn't do experimental science.

Even as the chlorine experiment was finding a clear discrepancy, Homestake was the only neutrino detector on Earth for 20 years, from 1968-1988. Bahcall gave talks everywhere and tried to interest others in the problem. But it was a complex problem at the intersection of multiple areas of research.

Why so few neutrinos? Fewer neutrinos means fewer fusion events. The fusion of hydrogen to form helium releases the most energy with the fewest reactions, so we needed to make this kind of fusion dominate in the Sun. To do that, we need to bring down the core temperature of the Sun to the point at which this kind of fusion is favorable deep in the interior. However, bringing down the temperature is a big problem, because the temperature produces a pressure which is directly related to the Sun's size. A lower temperature means a smaller Sun.

Perhaps, since heavy elements catalyze fusion events, we might hypothesize that there are fewer heavy atoms in the Sun than we see on the surface. The abundance we see on the surface could be due to the Sun collecting space dust (the "dirty Sun" theory).

Perhaps the core is rotating very rapidly, or the Sun's magnetic fields are very strong and boosting the pressure.

Or perhaps the Sun is simply more opaque to neutrinos than we thought.

Another possibility is that the neutrinos are a true indicator of fusion in the core of the Sun: that the core output had severely diminished but we wouldn't know it from the surface luminosity for thousands of years.

Hollywood thought the dying Sun theory was a fun idea: in the movie *Sunshine* we send a mission to reboot the Sun, but we have to fight a monster in the process.

Others suggested there was something wrong with the physics of the neutrino. Physicists suggested that neutrinos can change (oscillate) from the state they are created, such as an electron neutrino, into more difficult to detect states such as muon and tau neutrinos. If neutrinos have mass, a resonance in matter could efficiently convert them.[109]

Although physicists were not wild about the idea at first, they later became excited by this and began to support more experimental work. Perhaps the astrophysicists could do something useful.

When our experiments don't give us what we expect to see, the next step is usually to do another experiment. Another suitable neutrino-sensitive element was identified: Gallium-71, which can absorb a neutrino to become Germanium-71. The experiment required about three times the world's annual output of Gallium, but Russia did it, using liquid Gallium in the SAGE experiment, and $GaCL_3$/HCl in the GALLEX experiment. Both were sensitive to neutrinos above 233 keV.

Another type of experiment used by the Kamiokande and Super-Kamiokande experiments in Japan uses water, and waits for a neutrino to scatter from an electron. When this happens, the electron absorbs so much energy from the neutrino that it is excited to faster than the speed of light in water, which causes it to emit Cerenkov radiation,[110] allowing photomultiplier tubes on the walls of the tank to detect the neutrino *and* its direction. Similarly, the Sudbury Neutrino Observatory (SNO) uses heavy water, which also has neutrino interactions with deuterium.

Each detector has a characteristic range of neutrinos it can observe, but in all cases, there is a serious discrepancy between our models and

---

[109] This was first suggested by Vladimir Gribov and Bruno Potecorvo in 1968, and further described by Stanislav Mikeyev, Alexei Smirnov, and Loncoln Wolfenstein.

[110] The radiation is emitted in a characteristic shape, see the illustration in chapter 4.

A NEUTRINO OBSERVATORY

reality. The neutrino deficit has remained on the order of 60%, with slight fluctuations for each range of energies.

Yet we carefully calibrate the experiment with a radioactive source, and our theoretical calculations have not yielded in half a century.

Our theory seems right, our experiment seems right, but they contradict.

Bahcall reflects on this work, "if you can measure something new with reasonable accuracy, then you have a chance to discover something important. The history of astronomy shows that, very likely, what you will discover is not what you were looking for..." (Bahcall 1999).

The neutrino mass was a hot topic in 2005 when I was trying to get my professors interested in Mills's work. Mills, in typical fashion, has his own theory: a neutrino is a photon with an elliptical (instead of circular) polarization. It has no mass, and is incapable of oscillating between types (Mills 2015, Ch. 4).

Soon after going online in 1987, the Super-Kamiokande observed a burst of neutrino captures that correlated well with an astronomical observation of a supernova event. It was the type of supernova that occurs when the heavy core of a sun exhausts its supply of fusible fuel, and collapses under its own gravitational weight. Protons and electrons merge to form neutrons, releasing an intense burst of neutrinos. The detection was the first time neutrinos were detected from a distant source. Apparently, they can travel at least *very close* to light speed through long distances of space (Hirata 1988). At CERN, they were actually clocked at *faster* than light speed—which made a press sensation—but was soon retracted as a mistake.

Finding muon and tau neutrinos in our Cerenkov detectors was the best evidence for neutrino oscillations, and it persuaded scientists. But this was theoretically entangled evidence; our detection of muon and tau neutrinos was just that: observation of neutrinos, not neutrino *oscillation*. That is, unless physicists could independently verify our model of the interior of the Sun, or we could independently verify that neutrinos had mass.

And the solar neutrino problem is only one of many mysteries surrounding the Sun.

Galileo was the first to observe Sun spots, yet we are only beginning to understand them, let alone solar flares, mass ejections, and the often associated coronal waves. These are powerful explosive events, which can sometimes emit more light than the entire surface of the Sun. The shock waves (visible in X-rays or Extreme Ultraviolet) will travel at supersonic velocity in expanding arcs, but sometimes the arcs will linger inexplicably.

It is clear that there are powerful magnetic fields involved; while the fields are, at least in principle, strong enough to store the needed amount of energy for these explosions, we don't know yet whether they are concentrated releases of magnetic energy or merely interacting with some explosive chemical or nuclear process. We do see fusion, and we even see electron-positron annihilation events (with the signature 511 MeV light emission). Standard textbooks on solar physics are full of unanswered questions: "How is the energy stored in the magnetic field? By which instability is it released? How are the particles accelerated? How is the ejected mass set in motion?" (Phillips 1995).

And there is a final mystery: *the corona appears hotter than the photosphere.*

The temperature clearly rises with elevation; whereas the surface is only about 5,000 °C, the highly-ionized neon, magnesium, and silicon species we see in the corona appear to be at five *million* degrees.

This makes no sense; the atmosphere should cool as it radiates energy into the vacuum of space. But simultaneously we see species in the corona such as (unionized) hydrogen that could not exist if it were so hot. We see strong hydrogen lines corresponding to the Lyman alpha series. So the corona must be less than 10,000 K, but must have thermally excited species at millions of degrees.

Astrophysicists are baffled.

In this book we have seen evidence of a broken paradigm, in which there are unanswered questions in nearly every field of physics. We have also seen how one discovery can spread like a shock wave through an entire body of scientific knowledge, deciphering widely differing phenomena with a single explanation.

This is how it should be; we seek simplicity in our theories; we seek to bind the loose threads of a thousand observations to solve old problems and predict new realities. Perhaps the solar astronomers did discover something they were not looking for, but it is the same as that found by electrochemists and plasma physicists and those hunting for the missing matter in the universe; and in a literal interpretation of Francis Bacon's famous conjecture, *knowledge is power*,[111] perhaps the answer to our mysteries will give us the power of the Sun.

On January 14th, 2014, BlackLight Power announced a breakthrough.

With a new kind of experiment, they had achieved a power density far higher than anything they had done in twenty-four years of research. With the success of the new generation of electrolytic cells, Mills's attention had returned to water.

Typically, a water molecule is bound by weak van der Waals attractions to other water molecules, but if you can produce them without these intermolecular bonds, the chemical splitting of water into its constituent atoms is 81.6 eV, or 3 times 27.2 eV, the energy release needed to create an H(1/4) hydrino. The hydrogen atom dissociates from the water molecule, releasing the energy needed to break the bonds, then falls to the H(1/4) orbit with the release of one or more photons totaling another 122.4 eV (101 Å). The total release from the reaction is 204 eV.

In this scenario, you don't even need to rely on collisions for catalysis, because all the ingredients start off together in one package.

However, water does not typically exist as isolated molecules. And

---

[111] "ipsa scientia potestas est" or "knowledge itself is power" found in Bacon 1957.

water molecules do not spontaneously hydrino-catalyze, thankfully for life on this planet. BLP's microwave plasmas successfully used water vapor, but Mills always ran into a road block when trying to scale up or increase the power density of his cells. In even his best cells, only a tiny fraction of the hydrogen was catalyzed to hydrino.

Hydrinos must be catalyzed by an atom or molecule, which usually ionizes one or more electrons; these electrons build up in the plasma, attaching to whatever they find, producing a net *charge* which causes all the species to repel one another. It limits the catalysis reaction.

Mills wondered if he put a sufficiently intense current through a conductive medium containing liquid water, perhaps he could use brute force to pull the excess charge off the water molecules and enable more reactions.

Water, by itself, is a poor conductor, but when there are free ions present in the water, such as that due to a fine metal powder, it becomes highly conductive.

BLP took water with some titanium or copper metal powder, wrapped it in aluminum foil, and placed it carefully between two electrodes of a spot welder. The sample only weights about a tenth of a gram. When they zapped the sample with ~12,000 amps of current (at very low voltage), it produces a bright flash of white light, a loud crack, and a shock wave.

Yeah, that's an *explosion*.

It brought me back to a moment, ten years before, when I was asked by Mills to do some research for a collaborating defense contractor. It would be only a few hours of work, but it forced me into a mental pause.

I reminded Mills that I had come to work for him to create technologies for the benefit of mankind, not to make us better at blowing people up.

But explosive power is good sign. If you can produce a controlled explosion, you have an energy source with a power density sufficient to generate electricity or power a vehicle. You can replace the internal combustion engine. You can replace fossil fuels.

BLP quickly came up with a conceptual design for a reactor that used magnetohydrodynamic conversion to capture energy from a 1,000 cycle per second explosion occurring between rolling electrodes. They announced to the press that they had achieved "millions of watts" (BLP 2014a), though, again, the power had not yet been harnessed as electrical energy. They announced a demonstration to be in two weeks' time, on January 28th.

When the day came, BLP filled its general purpose room with investors and professionals. With the room full of observers and the cameras rolling, the upper electrode of the spot welder falls onto the capsule, and with a sharp crack the capsule is gone: vaporized instantaneously.

Mills also demonstrated the bomb calorimeter used for measuring the total energy output, as well as the spectroscopy of the light produced. In his discussion, Mills felt he had finally demonstrated that quantum theory was invalid, as there was no quantum chemistry in the pellet that could produce an explosion of *any* kind.

"You can't prove a theory," Mills admitted, "but you can *disprove* a theory by experiment."

And he had done just that.

EXPLOSIVE POWER

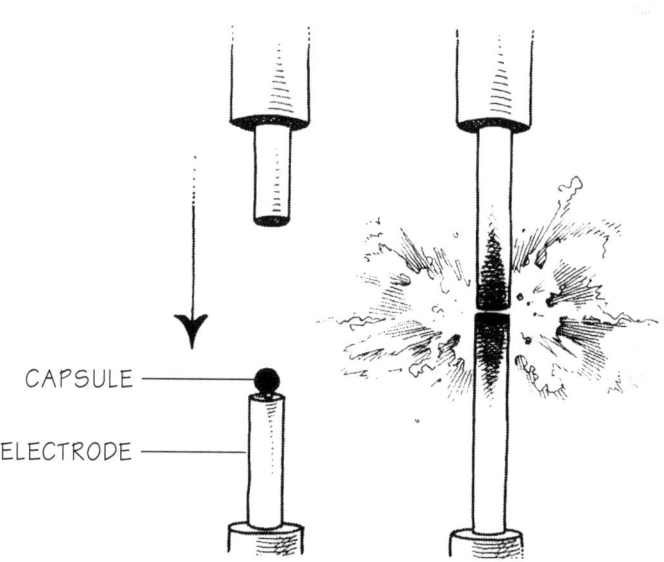

APPARATUS USED TO GENERATE MICRO-EXPLOSIONS. HIGH CURRENT IS PASSED THROUGH 100mg CAPSULES CONTAINING WATER AND METAL POWDER. THE BLAST INSTANTLY VAPORIZES THE CAPSULE.

BLP's hydrated powders included titanium (Ti), copper (Cu), aluminum (Al), or gold (Au) often in combination with their oxides (TiO, CuO, AlO). Ti and Au was used in combination with magnesium chloride and zinc chloride.

In the best reported reaction, 70 mg of titanium powder with 30 mg of water produced a net excess energy of 866 Joules, a power gain of 7. That's 8,660 J/g from the sample, or twice the energy output of TNT after totally subtracting for the input power. Not all of the input power needs to go into the sample, but to be conservative we subtract it all. Also, since the titanium is recoverable, the consumed weight in the reaction is only the water (30%) although we will ignore this too in our calculation. Since the reaction takes place in less than a millisecond, the power output from the reaction is astonishing: at least 8.6 MW/g (Mills 2014).

It appeared that Mills had found a way to overcome the rate-limiting processes and take hydrino catalysis to completion; all of the hydrogen in the sample was being catalyzed *at once*.

They made sure they were making $H_2(1/4)$ two ways: they found a Raman peak that corresponded to the rotational energy of $H_2(1/4)$, and they found an XPS peak that corresponded to the double ionization energy of $H_2(1/4)$, a peak that has no previously known assignment.[112]

Most of the energy released from the process is in the form of light. To the naked eye, the light is difficult to see, because most of it is emitted in the EUV, and absorbed very quickly by surrounding gases.

In one experiment, BLP allowed the gases from the explosion to expand into a larger vacuum chamber. As the gas expanded, it became optically "thin," allowing it to be analyzed. Although the burst of current occurred only over one microsecond, the gases continued to emit light over 19 microseconds, as they expanded from the source at supersonic velocity.

Amazingly, the emission spectrum revealed that the gases were at a temperature of over 5,000 ° C, closely matching the temperature of the surface of the Sun (Mills 2015). It was also good match for a broad 587 Å peak seen in the diffuse EUV background from the interstellar medium, suggesting once again a link to dark matter (Jelinsky 1995).

BLP also found evidence of "fast" hydrogen atoms produced by the rapid dissociation of each water molecule. Just like in the plasma studies from the previous decade, BLP found a broadening of the emission lines from hydrogen excited states as they were Doppler shifted in all directions. The line was broadened almost beyond belief, from 1.2 Å to a whopping 24 Å.

---

[112] Metal foils subjected to 50 explosions studied with Raman produced an absorption peak at 1982 cm[-1] (0.2414 eV) with a width of 40 cm[-1]. XPS produced a 498.5 eV XPS peak. (Mills 2014)

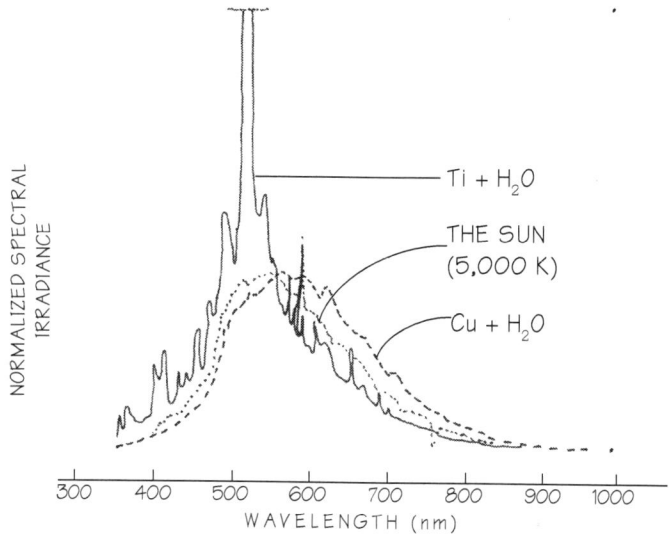

THE SPECTRUM OF THE SUN COMPARED TO THE SPECTRUM EMITTED BY THE EXPLOSION OF FOIL CAPSULES OF WATER AND METAL POWDER IN 11,000 AMPS OF APPLIED CURRENT. AFTER (MILLS 2015).

Six months later, BLP held another demonstration to show off a semicontinuous system in which pellets of the fuel were rolled between rotating electrodes, producing something that looked like a string of firecrackers. They also released several technical reports and letters from outside validators who came in to study the reaction.[113]

Although the first concept for a reactor involved directly capturing the energy of a high-velocity ionized plasma with magnetohydrodynamic conversion, they soon realized that more of the energy was being released as *light*.

There was a moment of illumination. Why not use *solar cells*?

It was a breakthrough that would massively simplify the engineering. "It is a gift from Nature" Mills excitedly told an audience at a demonstration. But it was also a gift from man; we had been developing solar cells for decades, investing billions of dollars in the effort to manufacture them inexpensively. Of course, they were typically used at the moderately low energy density of natural sunlight, but concentrator cells had also been developed that could take thousands of times more light and convert it to electricity at a much higher efficiency. It was as if the world had been preparing for the hydrino for thirty years.

[113] See Crouse 2014; Glumac 2014; Ramanujachary 2014; Weinberg 2014.

A sun in a box.

I laughed with surprise when I heard this. In the demonstration, BLP equipped their semicontinuous system with a box of solar panels and a 70 W LED bulb. As the explosions rolled off the wheels, the lights went on.

BLP released a new conceptual design showing a 50 MW generator with internal solar panels capturing light from a continuous reaction. It was obviously conceptual, and problems remained to be solved; they hoped that a water-powder mixture could simply be dropped through the rotating electrodes, and it was unclear how they would recover and reuse the metal that was vaporized in the blast.

Another problem was that the reaction primarily released light in the EUV and soft X-ray, which would require some kind of conversion to emit in the visible spectrum, which is the range of wavelengths our solar cells have been designed to capture. Details remained to be worked out, but it was an exciting concept to investors, and it seemed that all that was left was engineering. They raised another 11 million dollars to continue development.

Mills called it the *SunCell*.

Perhaps Phillip Anderson was on to something when he suggested that Mills's discovery would "fuck around with the energy process in the Sun" (Baard 1999). In 2002, Mills proposed that hydrinos were forming in the Sun (Mills 2002e).

The idea is compelling: it would add a power source that relies only on hydrogen, does not produce neutrinos, and could conceivably make up the remaining 40% of the Sun's power.

Hydrino catalysis may also help explain solar activity on the surface. High-current filaments discharging through water vapor in the photosphere and corona could produce explosive outbursts, emitting EUV and soft X-ray light and ionizing surrounding gas, explaining the coronal loops that arc beautifully high above the Sun and glow in these wavelengths.

Further, the high-energy light from hydrino catalysis in the photosphere may be captured by species in the corona, causing them to be photoionized to high states of ionization. We assumed these were being thermally ionized, but perhaps not. So the corona need not be millions of degrees warmer than the surface.

If dark matter in the universe is hydrino, we might expect it to behave much like normal matter. It will be gravitationally bound, fall into nebulae, and condense to forms new stars. It may have been in our star from the beginning; and perhaps even in the planets. The gas giants consist almost entirely of hydrogen. We know that Jupiter emits far more energy than it receives from the Sun, and has its own extremely intense magnetic field. We also know it emits in the EUV. Yet, it is not massive enough for hot fusion to occur.[114]

If we are host to a fusion-hydrino hybrid star, we ought to find lines in the photosphere and corona that correspond to disproportionation reactions, those due to self-catalysis by hydrogen and hydrino. In 1969, an EUV grazing-incidence spectrometer was flown in an Aerobee rocket launched from White Sands. It was flown during a period of some solar activity, recording the spectrum of the entire solar disk (Malinovsky 1973).

Mills carefully walked through this data and found many line energies corresponding to hydrino disproportionation reactions. Few of them jump out as large peaks, but many of them did not have previous assignments in the literature, making a hydrino assignment the only available explanation. Some of them were assigned to highly ionized elements, but may have been better assigned to hydrino. A few were assigned to well-known peaks that may be at least partially due to hydrino (Mills 2002e).

We should also find these lines in other stars. White dwarfs are very strong EUV emitters, and consist largely of heavier elements which it cannot fuse, though they still have helium and hydrogen on the surface. The smooth continuum band of a white dwarf has clear cut-offs at 912 Å (H to H(1/2) transition), 228 Å (H to H(1/3) helium-catalyzed transition), and 101 Å (H to H(1/4) transition). A white dwarf may have exhausted its fusion energy, but it continues to give off light as it cools. Perhaps, it is a hydrino star.

---

[114] On this interpretation, our Solar System is a binary star system with one hydrino-fusion hybrid star, and one hydrino-powered brown dwarf!

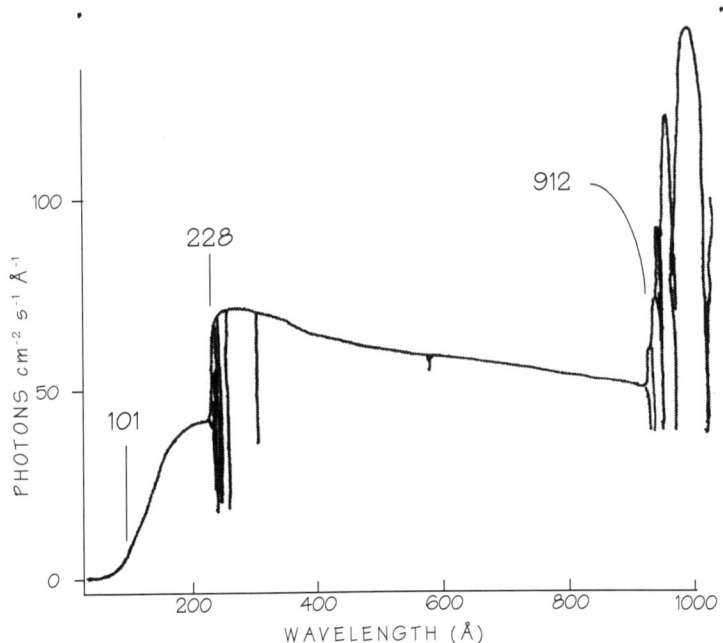

THE WHITE DWARF: A HYDRINO STAR?

THE SPECTRUM OF A WHITE DWARF. CLEAR CUT-OFFS AT 912, 228, AND 101 Å CORRESPOND TO THE FORMATION OF HYDRINO STATES H(1/2), H(1/3) AND H(1/4). AFTER (BARSTOW 2003).

Solid fuel, though spectacular, is not an ideal substance for a continuous power source. We prefer liquids or gases. But the SunCell taught Mills that water was a great catalyst. Water had always been there, in every "cold fusion" cell, in every BLP electrochemical cell. If you could produce water as an isolated molecule, unbonded to its brethren, it was good at making hydrino.

In 2014, Mills announced a new generation of high-power electrochemical cells (Mills 2014b). It used anodes with molybdenum and Mo alloys with nickel or copper, and cathode of nickel oxide in an electrolyte of molten LiOH-LiBr maintained at 420 °C.

The cell was supplied with water vapor in argon, and electrolysis occurred at the electrodes; at the cathode, oxygen and water combined to form hydroxyl radical (OH-) and hydrogen and at the anode, hydroxyl radical and hydrogen combined hydrogen and water. Except that H(1/4) was formed in the process. The cell was intermittently powered, and left open to air.

The power density of these cells was huge. The Mo, MoCu and MoNi anodes allowed power gains of 2 to 5 with a density over 10 mW/cm². An ideal electrode would have a high surface area, and be stable to corrosion. Their best results came from anodes made of CoCu, made by ball milling, sintering, and tape casting Co and Cu powders on a nickel permeable membrane. These were found to be highly stable, with almost no weight loss during electrolysis, and able to sustain a power density of 7.3 mW/cm², or 36 times the previous generation of electrochemical cells, which ran at only 0.2 mW/cm².

BLP ran cells for two and half days with a nearly constant power output and a gain of 1.76. After about 72 hours the cell began to fizzle out. Although there was a little weight loss from the anodes, when they took an image with a scanning electron microscope (SEM) it appeared that the loss was due to sintered particles breaking loose from the electrodes, rather than corrosion.

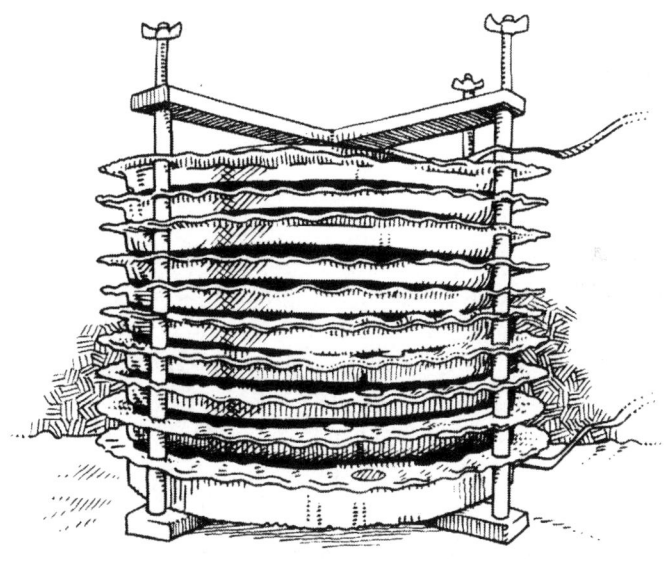

CIHT: A NEW GENERATION OF ELECTROLYTIC CELL WITH A MOLTEN ELECTROLYTE AT 420 °C.

BLP also explored water as a catalyst in solid fuel reactors, the kind that you heat and serve with off-the shelf compounds in an enclosed cell

(Mills 2014b). The reaction simply needs to produce hydrogen and water. You can do this a variety of ways, with a hydroxide and an oxide, or both in one, or a hydroxide and an oxyhydroxide, or with a hydroxide-halide exchange reaction, or even an acid-base reaction. BLP found energy outputs of up to 60 times what was allowed by conventional chemistry, with a notable thermal burst as the cell was heated.

Our energy sources define us. The more we produce, the more we can mechanize, and the more our minds are free to learn, invent, and create. Fossil fuels gave us the industrial revolution; they gave us science, medicine, democracy, flight, the music of Rachmaninoff, the microprocessor, and the unified theory. But they also contributed to the Sixth Great Extinction, global warming, acidified oceans, and melting icecaps.

What will the hydrino age bring?

In the Pacific Northwest, an area between the mountains and the sea, much of the water that falls west of the Rockies ends up in the Columbia River, which flows through the gorge on the Washington-Oregon border to the ocean. The walls of the gorge are gouged from Bretz's cataclysmic floods fifteen thousand years ago. When Louis and Clark crossed the continent, they came through the gorge and found a center for trade and plenty with a native population density unmatched in their journey, at Celilo Falls.

At Celilo, millions of salmon once desperately fought their way up the falls, in an effort to reach the exact place where they were spawned far upstream. The people there built large platforms from which they stood with nets over the water to catch them; one man could catch in a day enough to feed his family for a year. Celilo was the epicenter of trade routes that went up and down the coast and inland; artifacts are found there that were traded from thousands of miles away. Beautiful petroglyphs ornamented the rock walls.

Now, Celilo Falls is submerged year-round. The hundreds of dams on the Columbia combined with our intense fishing and pollution of the river ecosystems have severely declined salmon runs, and on some rivers in the Northwest, driven some local species to extinction. A food source, an ecological blood vessel, a historical and cultural center, and a spiritual center for native tribes has been lost, transformed into a source of energy. That energy is traded North and South to serve half the continent, but the

CELILO FALLS

ecology of the place was once just as powerful, reaching out over the ocean to sustain pods of whales with members that counted in the hundreds.

When we have a clean, sustainable source of energy, I hope to see the dams torn down and salmon runs restored; I hope to see the falls return to Celilo and recapture the soul of the Pacific Northwest.

But this is only one example of the impact such power will have on communities across the globe; from those living in smog-filled cities to those living in the Amazon rainforest who depend on cutting endangered trees for cooking fuel.

I believe that humanity has a deep emotional connection with the natural world; we do not exploit nature for its own sake, but have accepted it as a consequence of our survival.

Hydrino power may resolve many environmental issues of our day, but our race will always be faced with new questions regarding the ethical stewardship of the Earth. Hydrino compounds are super-inert, ten times more inert than traditional inert compounds. While this means they will likely not have biological or environmental reactivity, it also means that materials made from hydrino compounds may be so inert that they may be nearly indestructible. We may face a disposal problem worse than for carbon based plastics. It is a new frontier of chemistry and we must be smart.

Further, hydrino catalysis is, literally, the permanent removal of hydrogen from the Earth's biosphere. If water is the fuel, the oxygen is released, but the hydrogen is permanently altered. Yet hydrogen is the most abundant atom in the universe and on Earth, present in not just water but the Earth's crust. Dust and ice containing hydrogen regularly fall on the Earth from space. It may be a truly inexhaustible resource.

We might expect there to be a radical increase in energy production once hydrino power is available, but we also might expect our technology to improve, allowing us to reach deeper hydrino states and thereby increase by orders of magnitude the energy yield of each hydrogen atom consumed.

Perhaps, even, take hydrino catalysis to the point at which it catalyzes fusion events, in a hybrid hydrino-fusion reactor.

With unlimited power comes unlimited means. The world's deserts are almost empty of life. Are they ours for the taking? We could desalinate water from the ocean and, using some of the hydrogen to fuel the process, irrigate some of the 50 million square kilometers of the Earth's land area that is now covered in desert. This would magnify the carrying capacity of the Earth, not only for us, but for all life, in an act of geoengineering that would actually *increase* our impact on the Earth's oceans and atmosphere. We may open doors to new problems, such as the safe disposal of the salt from desalination, or our unpredictable impact on weather patterns around the world.

The new "green" will react to new realities. If energy generation is safe, we may turn to systems that rely on *high* energy use, but *low* resource consumption, such as the manufacturing of synthetic products instead of harvesting natural products on a scale that alters natural ecosystems. Ultimately, our goal is to reduce our impact, while continuing to unleash our potential in a technologically limitless future.

For decades, BLP had a problem of insufficient power density; now they had a problem of too great a power density. They needed a controlled and tunable explosion. They needed to dilute their fuel, but also sustain the explosion at a rate such that it would produce continuous light for the solar panels—at least a thousand flashes per second.

Building on their rotating electrode concept, they tried to pneumatically inject their solid fuel powder through the rolling electrodes, but they couldn't get that to sustain a continuous, bright reaction light even while continuously injecting high-current.

Instead of a continuous 10,000 A supply, they hired an engineering firm to design a pulsed ignition source at high current and high frequency, so that it was injecting current only 2-3 times per second. But the micro-explosions were destroying the electrodes.

There were other logistics: if they were going to explode pellets at a thousand times a second, they needed to manufacture pellets at a thousand times a second, and they developed a way to do so by dropping molten silver into water. Silver doesn't react with water or oxygen, and the water mixes itself into the silver in just the right proportion.

In light of the complications of the solid fuel system, they tried pouring a slurry of titanium through the electrodes. This generated a continuous bright light, but titanium reacts with water and oxygen, making it difficult to reuse. They tried running it in an argon atmosphere instead of oxygen. They tried substituting TiO, which is, oddly, just as conductive as titanium, but won't react chemically. Unfortunately it didn't work.

In January of 2016, two years from the first demonstration of the explosive reaction, BLP again hosted a public demonstration to show off its latest prototype. They had found a solution to a sustained reaction. Mills also announced a new name change: *Brilliant* Light Power.

"We've been very busy..." Mills explained, "and we did a lot of work, had trials and travails. Some led to innovations, some led to other ideas, some were a total waste of time. That's the way it is in science and engineering" (Mills 2016).

In a breakthrough experiment on November 14th, 2015, they had injected water vapor into molten silver and poured it between tungsten electrodes, hitting it with rapid bursts of current. The intensity of hydrino catalysis *vaporized* the silver as it passed through. They found they could create, and sustain, a brilliant glow.

In the prototype reactor now on the bench as of the completion of this book, the alloy is heated to melting point, and pushed up with an electromagnetic pump into a basin between the electrodes. When the silver reaches the electrodes, it triggers the current flow, injecting a rapid succession of high-current sparks from a bank of supercapacitors.

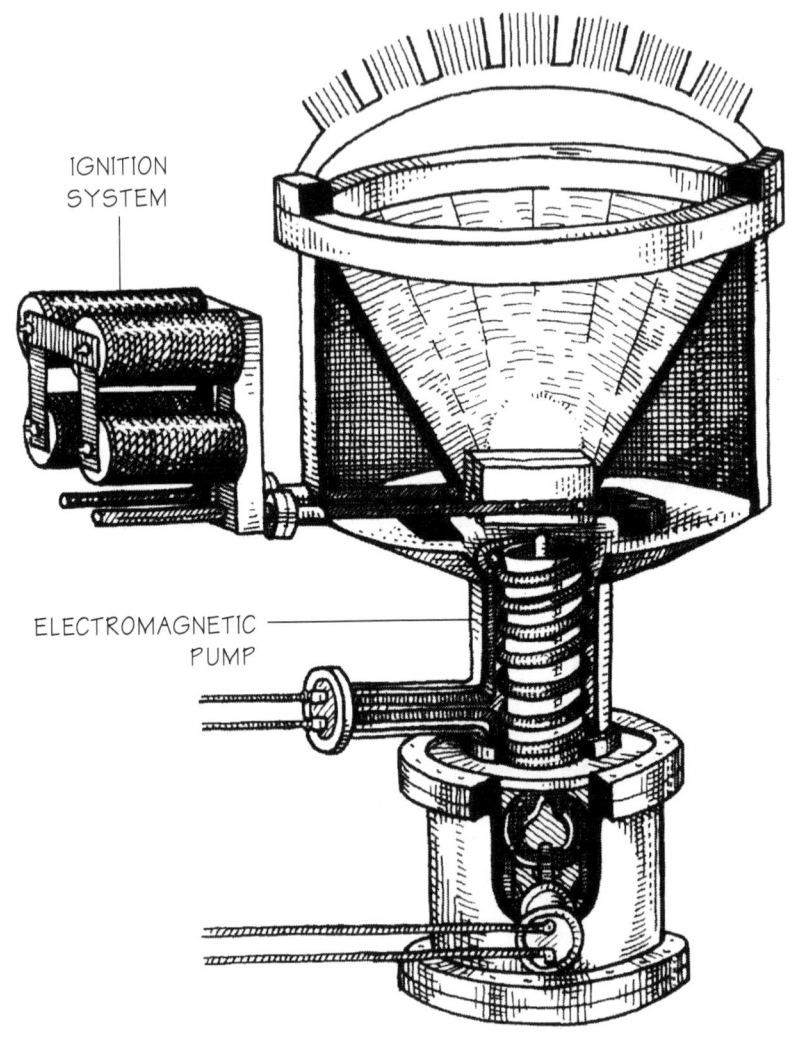

FIRST SUNCELL PROTOTYPE

WATER VAPOR IS INJECTED INTO A MOLTEN SILVER-COPPER ALLOY THAT IS PUMPED BETWEEN TUNGSTEN ELECTRODES AND INJECTED WITH RAPID BURSTS OF CURRENT, PRODUCES A SUSTAINED BRILLIANT EMISSION OF LIGHT, PRIMARILY IN EUV AND X-RAY BANDS. THIS LIGHT MAY THEN BE CONVERTED INTO THE VISIBLE SPECTRUM AND CAPTURED WITH SOLAR CELLS (NOT PART OF PROTOTYPE).

At first, the green sparks emit primarily in the EUV and soft X-ray wavelengths. There is not much for the human eye to see. Then you see beautiful golden light emerge, flickering, with molten metal spitting out like a volcano boiling over. It is fragile, struggling, and almost masked by the smoke of vaporized metal that plumes from beneath.

Beyond the smoky plume is a light that grows, steady but surely, penetrating through, until it enraptures you in its golden light, like watching a glowing campfire in the middle of the night. And though you don't expect it, it grows still, washing over you in waves, and when you feel it could not be more beautiful, the gold, now solid and unwavering, grows to white, and the white begins to beam. It overwhelms everything in your peripheral vision, and you find yourself staring into an impossible brilliance. The night no longer exists, for the campfire has become the Sun. [115]

It is a sun that we can make at will; it is capable of growing food through an Arctic winter and carrying water to a parched land; a sun that may be used to power every facet of our civilization in ways we have not yet imagined.

In time we will be swept into a new era, with its own struggles. But the waters will spill over Celilo falls and we will look out over the expanding landscape with a benevolent view of our own future and our lasting place on this Earth.

---

[115] In BLP's conceptual design, a tungsten shield absorbs all the heat energy and converts it to a thermal spectrum of light suitable to be captured by a parabolic shield of solar cells. It is a light-emitting plasma, similar to BlackLight's earlier plasma cells, but at atmospheric pressure, producing a tremendous amount of light.

CHAPTER 20

TRUTH AND DELIGHT

In which we take a post-quantum view on the nature of scientific theories and belief.

Occasionally theories have come along and uprooted our philosophical, religious, or cultural notions. The Copernican theory taught us that we were not at the center of the universe; Darwin's theory taught us that we were not special in the tree of life. Quantum theory counts among these; it presumed that the universe was not even made in such a way that it was accessible to our understanding. The debate it rose among scientists and philosophers was intense, and in a century of thought, resulted in a widespread cultural habituation of its position on the nature of knowledge and reality.

Mills's theory does not delete quantum theory from our shared history. It will not revert us to the philosophical stance of eighteenth-century physics, but rather push us into a *post*-quantum paradigm. And now is the moment to decide what that paradigm will be.

For the latter half of the twentieth century, a new vision of the nature of scientific theories and belief has been slowly described, one largely unencumbered by the quantum world view, and one whose time has come.

In the early decades of the twentieth century, there formed a group of mathematicians and philosophers organized under Moritz Schlick of Vienna University. They came to be known as the Vienna Circle, though they called themselves the Ernst Mach Society.

The influential group adopted Mach's general attitude towards science, but with important modifications.

Henri Poincaré made one such change. Whereas Mach believed that theoretical terms (terms that describe theoretical entities, laws, or processes) were useful only inasmuch as they led to *direct descriptions* of sensory experience, Poincaré believed that theoretical terms were inherently meaningful, but only inasmuch as they were abbreviations of what could be said in an *observation language*, one referring only to sensory experiences (Henri 1905; Suppe 1977).[116]

In retrospect this view is rather cunning. Suppose a scientific realist, like myself, walks up to Poincaré and makes the following argument:

> Dear Sir, if you believe that electrons don't exist, you are simply ignoring the evidence! How do you explain how a beam of electricity can be curved in a magnetic field if there is no underlying stream of particles with the required ratio between mass and charge?

To which Poincaré might reply:

> I do not doubt that as a scientist you are exposed to a great deal of experimental evidence for what you call an "electron," but you do not even understand the words you use. For the word "electron" does not refer to a thing that exists in nature, but rather it is merely something you use to refer to your *perception* of the experimental evidence. Without such evidence the word would be meaningless! And whenever you use the word, I can remove it and replace it with a detailed list of your evidence. So you see, you *can't* tell me that electrons exist, because the word refers only to your experiences.

Mach would have been jealous of the reasoning used by Poincaré. Even the most stalwart realist was foiled by the very meanings of the words he used. This idea requires, however, that theoretical terms are completely defined in terms of observable terms, a condition that is difficult to accept.

The Vienna circle, being largely composed of mathematicians, also took a strong interest in the work of Frege, Cantor, and Russell, and the recent interest in expressing mathematics as an axiomatized deductive system. They synthesized these influences into the view that scientific theories ought to be expressed as axiomatized systems in mathematical logic, with scientific language divided into three vocabularies: logical and mathematical terms; terms referring to observables; and theoretical terms defined in terms of observables.

---

[116] Poincaré also believed that Mach didn't sufficiently embrace the role that mathematics plays in science (Henri 1905). Poincaré embraced mathematics on the basis that it could, like theoretical terms, be used merely as a simplified way for talking about observations.

The idea here was that we could create a bulleted list of definitions for our theoretical terms that were written entirely in terms of observables; and the logical and mathematical terms served as the means by which we did so. Each theoretical term was defined in terms of observables by way of a *correspondence rule*.

Rudolf Carnap analyzed what form such a rule would take in mathematical logic. Trying several different forms, he ultimately found that a theoretical term could never be *completely* defined using observable terms.[117] It is a criticism that applied similarly to the view of P.W. Bridgeman, called operationalism (Bridgman 1945). Here each theoretical term was given an "operational" definition such that a theoretical term applied to a particular case if a certain action we performed yielded a certain result in that case (Hempel 1965, p. 124).

But any change in the experimental procedure used to measure a physical quantity, such as temperature, would need its own operational definition. There could be millions of ways of measuring temperature, and there is no way to contain all the possibilities within an operational definition.[118]

Even if the logistics of generating correspondence rules could be solved, we might wonder what the advantage would be.

In 1951, William Craig formulated a proof in mathematical logic that showed that if you had a theory which consisted of a vocabulary of theoretical terms, and a vocabulary of observational terms, and given that the theory was axiomatized in first-order logic, you could construct a new theory whose observational vocabulary and predictions were identical to the first theory, but which retained none of the original theoretical vocabulary. Hempel realized this was the proof that Carnap was looking for in a classic essay entitled *The Theoretician's Dilemma* (Hempel 1965, p. 173; Boolos 2002, p. 260).

One prerequisite for doing science this way is that you must also have a rigorous and fool-proof distinction between theoretical and observable terms. To observe something in the best sense is to *directly* experience

---

[117] For further reading from the scientific realist viewpoint, see Psillos 1999, p. 4. Also see Carnap 1936, 1966.

[118] Operationalism formed the basis for B.F. Skinner's behaviorism in psychology which continues to have influence today (Skinner 1953). This was the idea that cognitive states may be completely described in terms of a person's behavior, without reference to the complex internal life of the human mind.

it with your senses, but devices such as microscopes and telescopes expand the range of our eyes, allowing us to see microscopic (hitherto "unobservable" objects and properties) in the same way as we experience everyday objects.[119]

This is a luxury not afforded to those who observe the signature of an atomic nucleus with a NMR spectrometer. They must interpret the information with a complex theory. But we've learned to trust such devices because we understand how they work, and they yield highly consistent results. Using an NMR is an accepted act of observation. It is by the same logic that we trust the working of our sensory organs, despite the fact that we understand very little about how perceptual information is processed in the brain and delivered to our consciousness.

At the end of the day, "observable" and "theoretical" must be relative terms determined by context. We may observe an atom, but our observation is more indirect and reliant on theoretical interpretation than our watching a bacterium under a microscope. There may be no way to clearly break all examples into exclusive categories. And just as operationalism requires a list of all the possible ways of measuring a physical quantity, this approach to theories requires you to list all possible ways of observing a theoretical object or property.

Perhaps the most important criticism Hempel had to offer was that using this system made it difficult to combine theories, integrate them, and generate novel predictions. After all, history shows us that when two different theories of nature merge, there are consequences that go beyond the sum of the parts of the independent theories.

Mach's goal for science was to create a *deductive* systematization of experience, but a theory reduced to a set of syntactic rules loses its value for generating new connections between phenomena, that which allows us to extrapolate from our limited experiences into a wide range of new possibilities, what Francis Bacon called *induction* (Hempel 1965, p. 222).

For the first half of the twentieth century, the syntactic view was the only option on the table. Throughout the latter half of the century a new view took form in the writings of philosophers such as Evert Beth, Patrick Suppes, and Bas van Fraassen, and developed further by Frederick Suppe and Ronald Giere, among others.[120] These thinkers believed that, at some level, theoretical terms were indispensable. This became the *semantic* view.

---

[119] For more discussion of this see Churchland 1985.
[120] See Beth 1960; Suppes 1967; Fraassen 1980; Suppe 1989; Giere 2004.

These thinkers were motivated by the fact that theoretical terms allow us to extrapolate existing knowledge to new situations, allowing us to make predictions. They allow us to account for new phenomena with a known theory, and allow theories to be cross-fertilized with others to generate new knowledge. They are broadly functional, multifaceted mental representations of things in the world, and the ideas they denote allow our mind to contain, in a small amount of matter, a complex understanding of the world that enables us to survive a changing environment.

Philosophers of the semantic view have developed the idea of a *model*. According to Giere this consists of a set of principles that express important relationships between objects (or properties of objects) that are part of the model (Giere 2004; Teller 2001).

What is important here is the meaning of the relationships (the *semantics*), not the specific linguistic form (the *syntax*) of the principles that constitute the model. We should never forget that a model is an idea stored in the brain, a cognitive object. Words refer to this object, they don't make it up. So principles may be expressed in many different ways without altering the substance of the theory.

The most enduring principles seem to be artful and efficient propositions that communicate the important relationships of the theory. They can be statements of fundamental laws of nature, but very rarely. They may be true without perfectly describing any real scenario in nature.

From a cognitive point of view, it doesn't matter if the principle is a shallow generalization, a useful idealization, or an absolute truth. Only from a historical point of view, seen over time, do fundamental relationships endure without being usurped by later discoveries, and prove useful in their formulation. Though Einstein modified Newton's Laws, I have no doubt they will always be taught to school children.

When we combine a series of principles as a deduction or derivation, we can create a narrative that helps guide the logic of our thought. This amounts to a group of propositions that correctly articulate the various relationships present in the model. Sometimes these relationships require elaboration; Newton found it important to discuss in depth the meanings of the words he used when formulating his laws because he was introducing the meaning of these concepts in their modern form. But even if we add to our list of principles enough exposition to satisfy a new student, there are innumerable concepts that borrow from adjacent areas of thought. Throw in related textbooks and an encyclopedia, but still the branches spread outward, exponentially multiplying in an ever-widening sphere. Let us add all written knowledge to the body of the theory, would that be enough?

I believe that a limited set of principles can never *fully* describe all features of a model; it can never fully capture its meaning.[121] An idea in our brain is always tied up in an interconnected web of existing knowledge. Principles implicitly leave something out, something we must tacitly assume in our presentation.

This is why we cannot confuse language with the model described *by* language. Language can never fully describe a model, and therefore language can never serve as a placeholder for real cognitive understanding.

Models describe classes of things. The Bohr model applies to many different structures including each atom in the periodic table, and all possible isotopes, ions and anions of each atom, as well as molecular structures. Every model contains a range of free parameters, and if we lock some of these down we narrow the range of physical situations the model can describe. Lock down the number of protons and electrons and we have a specific element; lock down the number of neutrons and we have a specific isotope. Lock down the physical position of an isotope we have isolated in a penning trap, and we have a physical concrete: only one object in the world can satisfy it.[122]

In short, our theories establish relationships and leave many parameters free to vary in a kind of cognitive algebra. Some of these parameters are essential to the theory (such as the number of protons in an atom), but some are inessential (whether the atom is in Princeton or Copenhagen).

---

[121] This is my refinement of the semantic view. Giere believed that a model obeys "all and only those characteristics specified in the principles" (Giere 2004, p. 745). Suppe speaks of "full formulations" of a theory, but doesn't ask if this is really possible (Suppe 1989, p. 88).

[122] Van Fraassen argues that we would call a model that gives a class of things a "model-type" but I believe that *all* models are model-types (Fraassen 1980, p. 44). Frederick Suppe also hints at this feature when he describes a theory as a "domain of logically possible states" (Suppe 1989, p. 84). Giere then describes a model as something that is only born when married to a set of specific conditions, yielding a "more specific, but still abstract object" that can be used to represent reality (Giere 2004, p. 745). In my view, a model is irreverent to how many free parameters are locked down; we may have a model that is capable of describing a class of physical systems in the abstract, as well as a highly specific model capable of describing only one real-world object.

Realist philosophers have reacted to quantum mechanics by trying to fuse mathematics more deeply into the semantic view than is needed. For instance, van Fraassen argued for an idea of a model as a "state-space" or mathematical model of the world, complete with a list of measurable quantities, statements about those quantities, and statements comparing those quantities to the real world (van Fraassen 1970, p. 328).

I think it is important to point out that not all theories are quantitative (even if in principle they could be made so) so there is no reason to force a mathematical view onto all of them.

In the semantic view, mathematics does not play a central role. Many of the relationships that make up a model *may* be mathematical, but such a relationship is like any other, capable of being expressed as a proposition. Where mathematical expressions differ is that they use a unit of measure to relate properties of objects: a meter stick can be used to express the diameter of an atom or that of a galaxy. So a unit is a currency for comparing common characteristics. So there is nothing special, ethereal, or mystical about mathematics.

Again and again, philosophers use quantum theory to test their beliefs on the nature of theories. Can quantum theory now be taken completely out of the equation?

If we have a highly predictive, classical model for matter, and if we can understand experiments without recourse to statistical explanations (or "hidden-variables" versions thereof), we have turned the page on the quantum century.

We are all *post*-quantum now.

Without bending our philosophy to serve quantum mechanics, we ought to accept the semantic notion that a model is a truly cognitive object with the abstract power to represent classes of objects in the world to any degree of generality or specificity.

If the reader finds it important to distinguish a "theory," from a "model," we might agree with Bob Park's thesis instructor that a theory is something that is done with a pencil; an idea written and transmitted. But in most cases the two words can be interchangeable. I am not fickle.

Perhaps this view on the nature of scientific theories is not unique only to science, but a good way to describe all knowledge. After all, theories begin as ordinary knowledge; and become scientific through refinement, rigor, precision, and abstract power, but they are merely an extension of the underlying structure. Science in the twentieth century underwent explosive growth, but it also carried with it an infatuation with ideas that are counter-intuitive to everyday life, from the paradoxes of relativity to the contradictions of quantum mechanics.

Perhaps, in this century, we will return to a view that the world is made up of ordinary objects that behave in sensible ways; that the theories we use to describe them need only be good common sense taken to a higher level of refinement.

Perhaps we will find profundity, in simplicity.

If our theories are merely ordinary knowledge taken to a higher level of refinement, how then are we to accept scientific theories as *true*?

There are those who say we can never know anything, though I feel if we were to accept this in practice, we should be paralyzed by fear to take a step lest the ground drop from beneath our feet. There is no *perfect* knowledge, yet the Sun rises. From the moment we rise in the morning we accept that our day will be guided only by practical knowledge, obtained from experience, and we place our faith in it with every step we take.

Those who advocate the semantic view of theories often take one of two positions on the nature of belief.

The *scientific realists* believe:

1. Good scientific theories are largely true.

By contrast, the *empiricists* believe:

2. Good scientific theories *may* be largely true.

For a realist, our scientific theories tell of the behavior of things in the real world and if we use a theory we commit ourselves, in some important way, to its truth. By contrast, empiricists don't commit themselves so wholeheartedly. Bas van Fraassen, a philosopher with his own unique dialect of the empiricist tradition, claimed: "Science aims to give us theories which are empirically adequate, and acceptance of a theory involves as belief only that it is empirically adequate."[123]

The empiricist position is rather safe. After all, if a theory demonstrably works, then we are justified in saying so, and perhaps not justified in saying much more. Would van Fraassen's position allow us to avoid the pitfall of psychological attachment to a prior, outmoded theory? The empiricist remains uncommitted and detached, the epistemological bachelor.

We might wonder if acting on acceptance of a theory as 'empirically adequate' is any different than acting on acceptance of 'truth.' Someone

---

[123] See Fraassen 1980, p. 12, 1985.

watching through binoculars might not be able to tell the difference. And philosophical puzzles have little or no value outside how they influence our behavior in the world (though this aphorism is often forgotten by philosophers). But I find this distinction important, because it has a strong impact on how we theorize.

Truth does have a way of gripping the mind in a way that 'empirical adequacy' does not. Science is the story of great minds struggling to comprehend the universe; and those that fail do not find solace in the fact that their model is at least useful, though it be untrue.

But van Fraassen's position was actually more subtle. He believed that we could believe in theories concerning easily observable, macroscopic entities, but that we could not believe in those concerning microscopic entities or those more difficult to observe.[124] So van Fraassen was something of a hybrid between realist and empiricist, a position which he called *constructive empiricism*, and an advocate of the position implicitly taken by quantum theorists.

There is some arrogance to the notion that philosophers can create a criterion for belief that applies as a blanket statement over all scientific knowledge. The logistics alone would be a nightmare: should we categorize all entities difficult to observe that are, say, smaller than a microbe, as things we cannot believe in?[125]

Scientific knowledge is highly contextual and highly differentiated. Often, it is only the experts in a field, those who have studied it their entire lives and absorbed it into their bones, who are able to give accurate statements about the plausibility of theories, and even then it may be difficult.

Van Fraassen argued for his empiricist position by posing two questions (Fraassen 1980, p. 20-21). He asked:

1. How we are able to judge the truth of a theory beyond its empirical adequacy?
2. Is there any value in doing so? How much farther does it get us to know that a theory is *true* beyond being empirically adequate?

These questions get at the heart of this book. I believe that good

---

[124] I don't mean to distinguish here between entities, processes, or properties, all of which can be observable or unobservable.

[125] Philosophers—including yours truly—have argued endlessly over whether it is possible to have a crystal clear distinction about what counts as an "observable" or "theoretical" entity. See Holverstott 2007 and references contained therein.

theories come from seeking truth, from engaging in the meaning of our physical concepts, of taking literally the words we use, and of ensuring that the mathematics is describing something plausible, something that may be visualized in the mind's eye. A theory without a clear meaning can become an addiction, its concepts shadowy, and its predictive ability unproductive. We seek to explain our experiments and observations, but more deeply we seek theories that tell us about nature, that allow us to predict the next experiment we have not yet conducted.

Seeking truth forces us to imagine nature watching over our shoulder. Are we creating coherent, internally consistent theories? If we accept a theory because it works, without having to insist that it is true, why shouldn't the theory allow the kinds of dualities we find in quantum theory?[126]

Scientists so loved quantum theory that new theories of knowledge and reality were proposed to explain why it didn't make sense. Bohr's complementarity, Heisenberg's mathematical realism, and others that I have not discussed, such as the many-worlds hypothesis. There will never be perfect clarity in science, but we should try to avoid institutionalizing our contradictions to such a degree that they are passed down for generations with no progress, while precluding other avenues of research.

The universe is deterministic, simple, and singular. It is composed of ordinary objects, ultimately knowable by man, and our failures are no excuse to impose on it a jumbled metaphysics.

With a commitment to truth we seek the whole truth, to integrate adjacent areas of knowledge, to understand interrelated phenomena. The universe is not like our textbooks; phenomena are not neatly categorized into disciplines. This is why we seek a unified understanding of physics, as opposed to a stack of theories, one for each need.

True theories give us sweeping predictive power. We seek them for good reason, and though the progress of future scientists may render them redundant, there is a sense in which each successful theory is taking a hearty bite of the pie. It may be proven wrong, or it may be contextualized; just as Mills believes that Newton's law of gravitation *is* exactly true on a local scale during particle production.

But if most theories are ultimately surpassed, what theories from the past can we say, are in fact true? And how do we know that theories that prove themselves empirically adequate are today are, in fact, true?

---

[126] They may be rejected because they are *epistemologically* unsatisfactory, but they ought to also be rejected as *metaphysically* unsatisfactory.

The empiricist points at the scientific realist and laughs, but then the scientific realist calmly asks the empiricist "how do we know that theories that we have today are, in fact, empirically adequate?"

Some theories are successful at explanation and prediction, such that their effectiveness appears effortless. For this the scientific realists have a classic argument: the "No Miracles" argument.

It goes as follows: if some theories were not true, it would be a miracle for them to be as empirically adequate as they are.

Consider the theory of atoms and molecules; the theory of evolution; the theory of pathogen transference of disease; these all are highly successful because they are true. If they weren't, it would simply be impossible for them to predict the wide range of phenomena under their umbrella. We continue to refine these theories, but we have not usurped them.

Mills's ability to match the ionization energies of atoms and ions to high accuracy with simple equations is inexplicable if the theory were not true. As is the ability to match the state lifetimes and line intensities of the hydrogen excited states. Or the energies of the helium excited states. Or the functional groups of chemistry. And so on.

It is even more amazing when a theory makes predictions that we did *not* expect, such as the hydrino, and another that we will discuss in the next chapter.

From a psychological point of view, it is dangerous to be too committed to our theories, to believe too deeply. Perhaps this is the motivation for the empiricist's program. They don't feel the need to commit. But theories that are designed to be empirically adequate are more likely to allow scientists to ignore new evidence that is inconsistent with the theory because any new evidence can, with trouble, be absorbed into an algorithm of sufficient complexity, and made sense if the conceptual framework of the theory is sufficiently vague.

Van Fraassen also argued that it could be expected, over time, for scientific theories to achieve a high level of empirical adequacy because they were subject to a kind of scientific Darwinism. By this, I assume he imagined bad theories evolving through permutations in some kind of genetic algorithm. In fact, theories evolve in unexpected ways, sometimes in a nonlinear series of twists and turns and leaps of creative insight; sometimes linearly, deductively, from a compelling idea; sometimes starting with advances in technology that produce new instrumentation that in turn produces new data for theoreticians; sometimes developed by groups focusing on different areas of research in various stages of competition or collaboration; however it happens, ultimately a good idea is born. It succeeds in explaining nature, predicting nature, because there is some truth in it.

Quantum theory is one of the last strongholds in science that has an institutionalized a constructive empiricist view of the world. The old guard are fond of this view, but they will find that the young physicists will not put up with it. The future belongs to those who seek a mechanistic model of nature; the future belongs to the truth-seekers and model-builders.

Truth inspires the imagination, it forces us to be careful about how we construct theories, and it forces us to use models that make sense. Just as Soviet-era social planners used outside capitalist markets to set prices, empiricists must look to the truth-seekers to know how to theorize.

Is there any *value* in seeking the truth of theories?

It is here that the story of this book comes to a point. We have seen quantum theory drift into the twenty-first century on inertia alone, despite being built on weak assumptions and internal inconsistencies, supported by a philosophical artifice. We have seen this theory stagnate, become sterile and unproductive, despite the thousands of minds dedicated to its development. We have seen it concoct new ways of recycling empirical data to produce calculations; concoct new physical concepts to explain its math; or proceed by brute force progress: spending billions of dollars on successive generations of supercolliders to hunt for new physics.

We have followed the career of a brilliant man whose ideas are not yet accepted by the scientific community, despite his theoretical advances on paper and his advances in the laboratory. We have seen those who jumped into the fray, because they believed there was a chance Mills was right. They were driven by a need to know, a love of knowing, a delight of discovery, and an understanding of the wider impact of their work. They overcame the pressure of their peers and the stigma of the community to make a contribution.

I count myself among them; and the glowing, overwhelming drive that pushed me into action was among the most powerful emotions I have ever experienced.

The world is built by the truth-seekers, and it is torn down and rebuilt, by the truth-seekers.

The next generation will go forward with the view that science is a profound interaction with the natural world, in which all things are laid open to our understanding; that our imagination is a useful tool, not an impediment, enabling us to form a conceptually rich picture of how the world works—as Mills likes to say—from the scale of the quarks to that of the cosmos. They will delight in the many predictions that flow from our theories, they will turn them into useful technologies, and look to the future with a burgeoning sense of possibility.

CHAPTER 21

THE PATH TO THE STARS

In which a new theory of gravity produces some useful physics, and 2152 may be a very good year.

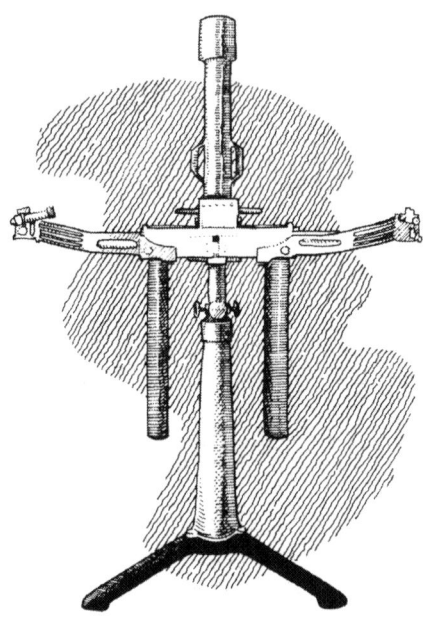

A TORSION BALANCE USED TO TEST THE EQUIVALENCE OF GRAVITATIONAL AND INERTIAL MASS.

In 1890, some stone piers were laid into the ground during construction of the new physics building at the University at Budapest. The one-meter-square piers were isolated from the foundation, so they would provide a stable, vibration-free surface to allow Loránd Eötvös, chair of the department, to carry out a highly sensitive experiment.

On the piers Eötvös placed an instrument of his invention: a torsion balance. As with any balance, if the mass of the two samples was exactly the same, the bar would remain perfectly horizontal. But the balance may also rotate. The piers on which the balance sit are attached to the surface of the Earth, and therefore rotate with the Earth at a thousand miles per hour. If the *inertial* mass of one side varied from the other in the slightest, the outward centripetal forces of the samples, as they describe curved paths through space, would cause the balance to rotate, ever so slightly. A beam of light reflected by a mirror on the balance amplifies even the slightest movements.

Eötvös placed a number of chemical samples on the torsion balance. He was answering a question that had intrigued physicists since Newton: is *gravitational* mass the same thing as *inertial* mass?

Newton's laws gave us the foundation of modern physics. An object in motion will remain in motion along a straight line, unless a force acts upon it. The greater the object's mass, the greater the force needed to produce the same acceleration. This is inertia.

But Newton also gave us the Law of Universal Gravitation: bodies attract one another due to their mass. But these laws give us two *different* definitions of mass, two different ways to measure it. Are they the same thing?[127]

Eötvös wanted to know, at a higher precision than had ever been possible, whether there was any variation with different substances. And so he set his stone piers in the Earth.

---

[127] Mass can both *act on*, and be *acted upon* by other mass; we may call this "active" and "passive" gravitational mass, though we have never seen any discrepancy in experiment.

Eötvös' believed his experiment was able to confirm the equivalence of gravitational and inertial mass to within about one part in twenty million. With an improved setup, his students were able to refine the precision to one part in two hundred million. And still others improved where he left off.

Is the issue closed? Over the last century, we have discovered that there are many different kinds of matter: bound, free, leptons, baryons, quarks, antiparticles and antimatter. There is, apparently, much remaining to test with Eötvös' experiment, ensuring job security for the next generation of experimental physicists.

In 1957, Phillip Morrison and Thomas Gold suggested that matter and antimatter might repel, assigning a "gravitational charge" much like electric charge (Morrison 1958a).

Let us suppose this were true; we have a capsule containing an equal amount of matter and antimatter in magnetic confinement. The capsule has no weight, so we raise it high above the surface of the Earth. We then allow the matter and antimatter to meet, resulting in an annihilation event, producing high-energy photons. We let the photons rain back down to Earth; as they do, they increase in energy, shifting to the blue spectrum. When they reach the surface, we capture the light, and use it to recreate our matter and antimatter in a particle production event.

Suppose we could do this efficiently. What is left over? A little bit of extra energy, captured by the photon as it fell in Earth's gravitational field. We now have a perpetual motion machine (Morrison 1958b).

It started a dialogue. In 1957, at a conference at the University of North Carolina, Brice DeWitt took a piece of chalk, threw it in the air, and caught it.

"We know almost nothing about gravitation," he told the audience, "There is only one experiment which we do over and over again, and that is what I have just done. In fact we don't even know whether that experiment works for antimatter. It is perfectly possible, and even plausible, that antimatter falls upward!" (Everitt 1990).

In the audience was the Bill Fairbank, a professor of physics, known for his infectious enthusiasm, who could be found discussing ideas late into the night. When Fairbank accepted a professorship at Stanford in 1959, he showed up with plans for a number of low-temperature physics experiments involving superfluids and superconductors.

Any experiment, he would often say, could be done better at liquid helium temperature. His many original ideas would fill a pioneering career.[128]

Fred Witteborn was a graduate student attending a solid state physics course taught by Fairbank, who was an entertaining lecturer but would often digress to discuss experiments his research group were doing. One day he described to the class an experiment he would like to perform on the free fall of positrons. The trick was to shield them from electromagnetic forces with a metal tube held at superconducting temperature. Witteborn was intrigued. For the last couple of years he had been working at Stanford's linear accelerator, so he was comfortable working with ions. He dropped by Fairbank's office and expressed an interest: he had taken the bait.

Although the large-scale structure of the universe is dominated by gravity, it is a very weak force, 40 orders of magnitude weaker than electromagnetism. Other forces will always win over gravity on a small scale; the pull of a single proton on an electron a few meters away is enough to overcome the gravitational pull of the entire Earth. Eötvös had studied gravity on neutral, bulk matter, not charged particles, and of course not antiparticles.

Electromagnetism is also a complex force. A charged particle can be attracted or repelled by electric fields, polarized by electric field gradients; attracted or repelled by magnetic fields; it may precess in magnetic field due to its magnetic moment and interact with magnetic gradients through its diamagnetic polarizability. All of these effects must be controlled within very tight bounds to allow the influence of gravity to be revealed. Working with charged particles would be difficult enough, let alone working with positrons, so they quickly decided to perform the experiment with electrons first.

Witteborn was starting to design the experiment when the Varian Physics Laboratory was being built, and like Eötvös, they needed to plan ahead. They didn't know yet how tall the free-fall drift tube would need to be, so they asked the engineer to leave a small unreinforced square in each slab of the building that could easily be broken open (the first ceiling of the lab was almost opened right away). They also asked to allow a pit beneath the floor in the basement, to allow enough room for a small particle accelerator that could be a positron source. (The pit, which is still

---

[128] For a survey of Fairbank's work see Meyer 2011.

visibly covered with sheet metal, has become the source of mythology among the students there.)

Witteborn was tasked with constructing a meter long copper tube, machined as perfect as could be manufactured by man, to be used for shielding electrons during the experiment. He sought to avoid any variations in the thickness or crystalline structure of the metal, called patches, that are only a few hundredths of a millimeter across, but able to produce "excessively large" variations in the surface potential, and thus ruin the experiment.

The solution was to manufacture a polished aluminum cylinder, on which was electroplated a uniform layer of copper. The aluminum would then be melted away with acid, leaving the copper with an atomically smooth surface; any left-over variations would, hopefully, not have an impact at superconducting temperature, and be uniformly distributed around the tube.

Any variation in temperature could also throw off the results. The tube was held in a deep vacuum, in contact with liquid helium at its base to keep the copper at a superconducting temperature. The tube could not, in fact, be completely immersed in the helium because the variation in the pressure of the helium over a depth of only one meter in Earth's gravity would change its boiling point ever so slightly and, incredibly, cause an unacceptable temperature gradient in the tube!

An electron emitted into this tube induces mirror charges on the walls of the tube, and it will want to interact with them, like Peter Pan with his shadow. So Witteborn wrapped a solenoid around the tube to produce a magnetic field. An electron entering the field will follow a helical path with an axis aligned with the tube. When the electron is orbiting in the direction opposite to its intrinsic spin, the magnetic moments cancel (this is called the electron ground state) and the electron has very little interaction with gradients in the magnetic field. So Witteborn was able to use the fields to pick out electrons in the ground state.

In the experiment, Witteborn released a burst of electrons from a cold cathode source at the top of the tube. The majority of electrons were moving too quickly, as only those with about 10^{-10} eV of energy were suitable for the experiment. They fell through the tube, reached a sensor at the bottom, and the time of flight was measured. Witteborn conducted a pilot experiment as part of his doctorate, and in the years after, refined the experiment (Witteborn 1967, 1977).

He could not get electrons to fall more than 9% of the acceleration due to Earth's gravity.

But this result was not easily interpreted. Because gravity is acting also on the shielding tube, there may be an electric field induced in the tube that, by a rude coincidence, is almost exactly what is needed to counteract the gravitational field on a single charged electron. Witteborn performed his own calculation, but he and Fairbank asked the Stanford physics department chair to perform a refined analysis; he and a graduate student obtained a similar answer (Schiff 1966).

The calculation was messy; quantum theory could only approximate the metal surface, which was in reality covered with small patches and surface contaminants such as oxide layers. There was a debate among theoreticians. Humphrey Marris (who we met in an earlier chapter) argued that the electric fields produced by the thermal vibrations of atoms in the tube ought to have completely swamped Fairbank and Witteborn's result. Others thought that the acceleration due to gravity should, in fact, be *amplified* by about 100,000 times!

On the bleeding edge of science, we often find that there is much more to be done. Most needed is a way to control for the effects of these gravitationally-induced charges in the shielding tube. We might imagine placing the entire apparatus in a centrifuge to simulate gravitational fields with centripetal forces. This was tried, but not with the same apparatus, and not at cryogenic temperature, and certainly not while the experiment was taking place. A larger tube radius and length would increase the sensitivity; we could punch out the remaining floors of the Varian building.

We could try a muon in place of an electron, or, of course, a positron. To perform the experiment with positrons, more problems would need to be solved, and Witteborn and Fairbank had assumed that a string of later graduate students would solve the parts and pieces of how to make positrons and ensure they were moving slowly enough. But the theoretical debate was precluding more work. It was pointless to continue without a better understanding of the results, or a better way of doing the experiment.

There was a lot of interest in the work. At one point Oppenheimer walked in the lab, sat down in Witteborn's desk chair, and suggested that back in the day, they wouldn't have thought twice about a 1 Curie source. That would do the trick for supplying the necessary positrons. But that's about a gram of Radium-226 and extremely dangerous. A 3 MeV accelerator, occupying about 6-feet square, could also generate positrons, hence the pit.

Such things add complexity to an already complex experiment. But we live in an era of supercolliders. Surely, mankind can make an electron fall.

We ought to expect a good theory of quantum gravity to give us something new. Mills's new theory was only a slight modification to the equations of general relativity (specifically the Schwartzchild metric) but it allowed him to calculate the classes of fundamental particles and the relationships in their masses. It also allowed him to predict the accelerating, expanding universe before its discovery.

Mills's dedication to hydrino research required him to ignore his other innovations: Luminide drug delivery compounds, Mossbauer cancer therapy, magnetic susceptibility imaging, Millsian molecular modeling, and so on. However, there was another idea that Mills had discovered by the first publication of his theory in 1990, but about which he spoke little for twenty years. He had no time to think about it or run experiments, and whenever he mentioned it to the press, it resulted only in ridicule.

It was a new connection between *electromagnetism* and *gravity*.

Recall that according to Mills, gravitation is a result of electromagnetism, or rather, relativity. It is a field of contracted spacetime that is produced by circulating currents when a particle is born. Mills reasoned that if those currents define a three-dimensional surface of constant curvature, such as a sphere, a particle responded normally to gravity. After all, everything we see around us is made from particles that have this structure.

If, however, a particle's currents did not have this curvature, the particle should have *no* gravitational mass. Recall that when unbound to the atom, the free electron (as well as the muon and tau) is a disk of charge with no curvature. So Mills conjectured that free electrons shouldn't fall. And it is plausible that Mills is right: perhaps this was why Witteborn had so much trouble.

Of course, we won't know *for sure* until we perform a better experiment. But there's more.

Suppose we were to create a particle with a surface of constant negative curvature. Would it react negatively to gravitational fields? There are two types of surfaces that meet this requirement: tractricoids and saddles. Both are problematic as particles because they extend out forever (a tractricoid approaches an asymptote, but goes to infinity).

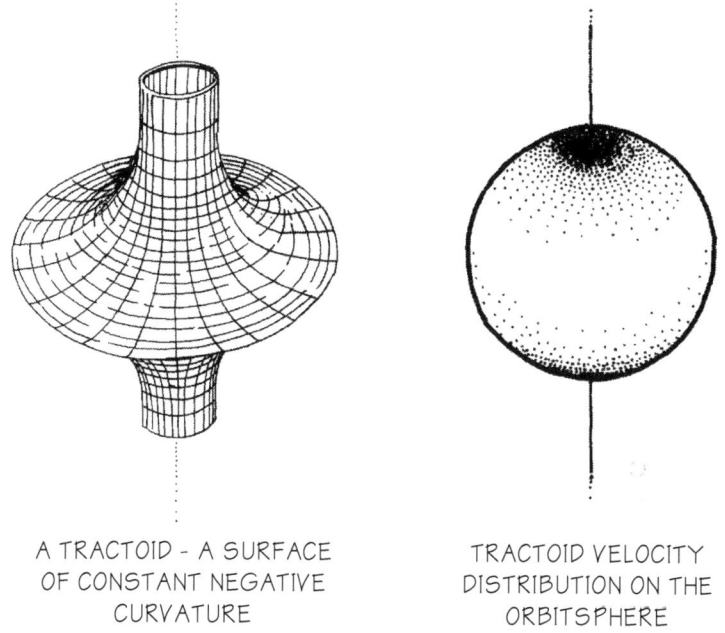

A TRACTOID - A SURFACE OF CONSTANT NEGATIVE CURVATURE

TRACTOID VELOCITY DISTRIBUTION ON THE ORBITSPHERE

But Mills imagined a tractricoid-like distribution of angular velocity of electron current superimposed on a spinning spherical shell. Currents at the equator move very slowly, but the currents at the top and bottom would almost reach the speed of light.

Mills conjectured that if the electron could be put in such a state (what he calls a pseudo-electron), it would *repel* gravitational fields. It would do so with an intensity much more powerful than the force of gravity itself.

Mills designed a simple experiment in which a beam of electrons intersects a noble gas beam, such as helium. The helium beam, colliding with the free electrons, might impart the right amount of energy to the free electron to flip it into a pseudo-state. In the process of colliding with an atom, the electron may absorb a photon (like excited atomic states) and the electron may assume states with l and m quantum numbers. If these electrons can be made, and trapped, and if they are at least momentarily stable, they could form the basis of a new form of lift.

Sometimes our ideas stretch so far into the realm of science fiction that we simply can't believe they are feasible. Mills had discovered a new energy source, and that kept him busy enough. He set aside the possibility of anti-gravity for twenty years before he designed an experiment to test his prediction.

Although I will report on it here, I should remind the reader that—*unlike everything hitherto discussed in this book*—this study has not been published in an academic journal, it has not been repeated by any party, nor has it been publicly demonstrated. It is also worthy of note that *not once* in my experience at BLP and in my research of twenty-five years of BLP's scientific output have I seen any evidence of fraud. But one experiment is *never* enough.

It is my hope, of course, that with a wider dissemination of Mills's theories, others may decide to repeat the study, to confirm or disconfirm it.

Mills predicted that pseudoelectrons may form when scattered at specific energies determined by the mass of the electron and strength of Earth's gravitational field. The resulting pseudoelectron orbitspheres have distinct radii, which are in some cases quite large, on the order of one centimeter.

BLP scientists designed a stainless steel chamber, held under vacuum, with two metal cylinders to shield outside electromagnetic fields. An electron gun was targeted to intersect a flow of gas from a nozzle. An electrode above and below the collision point recorded electron current. As the electron beam energy and gas pressure was varied over a range of values, the ratio of the top detector current over the bottom detector was measured. The distance between the detectors was also varied. Further, the gas flow could be turned off as a control.

Mills and Ying Lu, operating the experiment, found that as the electron beam and gas pressure were varied, there were clear spikes in the top collector current at *precisely* the energies predicted by Mills's theory. When the electron gun was turned off, the charge lingered; the electrons appeared to have a half-life of more than a minute.

When Mills calculated the strength of his new phenomena, what he came to call the *fifth force*, he found it was stronger than Earth's gravity by about one trillion times (Mills 2015).

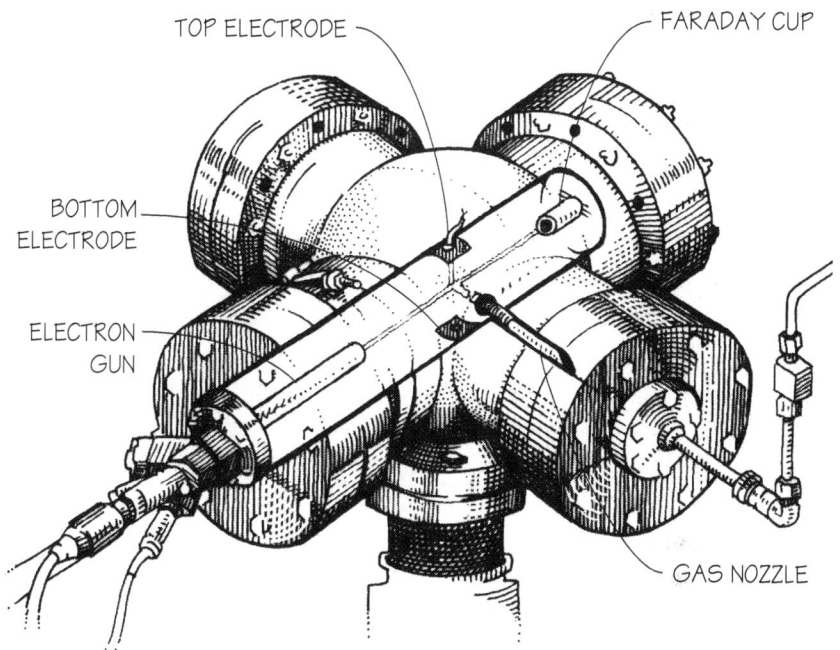

"FIFTH FORCE" TEST CHAMBER

AN ELECTRON BEAM WAS CROSSED WITH A NOBLE GAS BEAM. THE ENERGY WAS VARIED, AND CLEAR SPIKES WERE FOUND IN THE RATIO OF TOP TO BOTTOM COLLECTOR CURRENT. THESE MATCHED MILLS'S PREDICTIONS FOR THE CREATION OF PSEUDOELECTRONS - WHICH MAY REPEL GRAVITATIONAL FIELDS WITH A STRENGTH OF ONE TRILLION TIMES THE FORCE OF GRAVITY.

Let us suppose, for a moment, that Mills has discovered a new form of lift. It will open up a new frontier of flight. We will be able to more easily and cheaply transport people and goods around the planet. And, we can hope, flying cars.

But what about space flight? At present, we use the gravity and momentum of planets to fling our space-borne crafts around the solar system. If we approach a planet from behind, following a free fall trajectory, that planet will pull our craft into its orbit, accelerating it. Since our craft is now moving more quickly, it can sling shot around and escape from the planet's gravitational field more easily with a total net gain of momentum on the part of the craft.

But with anti-gravitational lift, this maneuver is now two-phase. First, we let the gravity of a planet pull the craft along a free fall trajectory. Then, at the moment where the acceleration wanes, we turn on a "space drive," and use it to repel away from a planet at an acceleration limited only by the g-forces that can be sustained by the craft or the people on board, and our energy source. Better to accelerate as much as possible, as close as possible to the planet, for maximum gain. As the craft accelerates away, the space drive will get diminishing returns, and eventually the craft will return to a free fall through space toward its next destination, unless we marry this system with some other form of chemical propulsion.

When NASA first began to seriously contemplate space flight, we thought a mission to the outer planets of the solar system would be expensive and, pardon the pun, a long way off. But we were amazed to discover that a unique arrangement of the planets would occur around 1976 that would allow a single probe to sling shot around *all* of the outer gas giants—Jupiter, Saturn, Uranus, and Neptune—in a single mission.

It caught us by surprise, but it was an opportunity not to be missed: it occurs only once every 176 years. Using the Voyager I and II missions, we took advantage of it. In fact, both probes are still out there, now beyond the orbit of Pluto, entering interstellar space. It is a rather amazing feat for a civilization that had just recently become space-faring.

This magical moment next occurs around 2152. Imagine what a Mills space drive would allow us to achieve: a pull and push from each of the outer gas giants; four opportunities in rapid succession. Perhaps 2152 will be the year that mankind sends the first manned mission to a neighboring star. Perhaps we will go to an exoplanet that is a good candidate for life. Perhaps we will use this interstellar superhighway to send out a host of probes to targets in deep space. The crafts will approach neighboring stars after decades—or centuries—of travel, and the space drive ought to allow them to decelerate directly against the gravitational field of the approaching star to slow down again.

I look forward to seeing the fifth force independently confirmed or disconfirmed. After all, it is a rather simple experiment, and one that may set us on a path to the stars.

One afternoon while we were chatting in Mills's office, we imagined how one might go sideways in a craft equipped with an engine that only produces lift. Perhaps the craft could spin like a top, and use angular momentum to precess through space along curved trajectories.

Mills brought up another option: go *straight up*.

When you stand on the surface of the Earth, you rotate with the Earth, but when you climb in altitude, you lose angular velocity. If you plan to go West, you need only go straight up, let the Earth spin beneath you, and gently come back down to your destination.

I remember the suggestion, because we laughed.

New ideas sometimes come with an elegance that makes the struggles of the past seem amusing. We are all a product of our time; there was a time when quantum mechanics was a beautiful innovation; now it is washed away by a vision of dynamic membranes of flowing charge, building spheres and ellipsoids, and fullerenes and nucleic acids, and the infinite array of forms we see around us. There was a time when crude oil, pumped from the ground and refined, and fed into powerful jet engines, was a symbol of technological prowess; now we face a future of flight in which we can rise from the ground on a whisper and soar.

I often laugh simply out of joy.

It is an infectious joy that Mills carries around with him, that endears him to friends and colleagues, and reveals that he has been driven for twenty-five years by his *love* of the work, at once discovery, experiment, and invention, guided by the belief that the purpose of new ideas is to allow new works. He has spent half a lifetime trying to bring his work to fruition.

I hope he succeeds, for the satisfaction of his soul, for the benefit of mankind, and because it will be fun to watch.

Bibliography

Mills's Books *(cited editions)*

Mills, R., & Farrell, J. (1990). *The Grand Unified Theory*. Ephrata, PA: Science Press.

Mills, R. (1995). *The Grand Unified Theory of Classical Quantum Mechanics*. Malvern, PA: HydroCatalysis Power Corp. Library of Congress Catalog Number 94-077780.

Mills, R. L. (2015). *The grand unified theory of classical physics*. Blacklight Power.

Journal articles and conference proceedings authored by Mills / BLP

This is a comprehensive list of publications, organized by year. Those cited in this work are indicated with a (*).

Experimental Publications

*Mills, R., Lotoski, J., Good, W., & He, J. (2014a). Solid Fuels that Form HOH Catalyst. *Int. J. Hydrogen Energy* **39**: 11930-11944. doi:10.1016/j.ijhydene.2014.05.170

*Mills, R., Lotoski, J., Kong, J., Chu, G., He, J., & Trevey, J. (2014). High-power-density catalyst induced hydrino transition (CIHT) electrochemical cell. *International Journal of Hydrogen Energy*, *39*(27), 14512-14530.

Mills, R., Booker, R., & Lu, Y. (2013). Soft X-ray continuum radiation from low-energy pinch discharges of hydrogen. *Journal of Plasma Physics*, *79*(05), 489-507. doi:10.1017/S0022377812001109.

Mills, R. L., Nansteel, M., Good, W., & Zhao, G. (2012). Design for a BlackLight Power multi-cell thermally coupled reactor based on hydrogen catalyst systems. *International Journal of Energy Research*, *36*(6), 778-788. doi:10.1002/er.1834.

Mills, R. L., & Lu, Y. (2011). Time-resolved hydrino continuum transitions with cutoffs at 22.8 nm and 10.1 nm. *The European Physical Journal D*, *64*(1), 65-72. doi:10.1140/epjd/e2011-20246-5.

Mills, R. L., Zhao, G., Akhtar, K., Chang, Z., He, J., Hu, X., ... & Chu, G. (2011). Thermally reversible hydrino catalyst systems as a new power source. *International journal of green energy*, *8*(4), 429-473. doi:10.1080/15435075.2011.576287.

*Mills, R. L., Lotoski, J., Zhao, G., Akhtar, K., Chang, Z., He, J., ... & Lu, Y. (2011). Identification of new hydrogen states. *Physics Essays*, *24*(1), 95. doi:10.4006/1.3544207.

Mills, R. L., Zhao, G., & Good, W. (2011). Continuous hydrino thermal power system. *Applied Energy*, *88*(3), 789-798. doi:10.1016/j.apenergy.2010.08.024

*Mills, R. L., Zhao, G., Akhtar, K., Chang, Z., He, J., Hu, X., ... & Chu, G. (2011). Thermally reversible hydrino catalyst systems as a new power source. *International journal of green energy*, *8*(4), 429-473.

*Mills, R. L., & Lu, Y. (2010). Hydrino continuum transitions with cutoffs at 22.8 nm and 10.1 nm. *international journal of hydrogen energy*, *35*(16), 8446-8456. doi:10.1016/j.ijhydene.2010.05.098

Mills, R. L., & Akhtar, K. (2010). Fast H in hydrogen mixed gas microwave plasmas when an atomic hydrogen supporting surface was present. *international journal of hydrogen energy*, *35*(6), 2546-2555. doi:10.1016/j.ijhydene.2009.12.148.

Mills, R. L., Akhtar, K., Zhao, G., Chang, Z., He, J., Hu, X., & Chu, G. (2010). Commercializable power source using heterogeneous hydrino catalysts. *international journal of hydrogen energy*, *35*(2), 395-419. doi:10.1016/j.ijhydene.2009.10.038

Mills, R. L., Lu, Y., & Akhtar, K. (2010). Spectroscopic observation of helium-ion-and hydrogen-catalyzed hydrino transitions. *Central European Journal of Physics*, *8*(3), 318-339. . doi:10.2478/s11534-009-0106-9

Mills, R., Good, W., Jansson, P., & He, J. (2010). Stationary inverted Lyman populations and free-free and bound-free emission of lower-energy state hydride ion formed by an exothermic catalytic reaction of atomic hydrogen and certain group I catalysts. *Open Physics*, *8*(1), 7-16. doi:10.2478/s11534-009-0052-6

Akhtar, K., Scharer, J. E., & Mills, R. L. (2009). Substantial Doppler broadening of atomic-hydrogen lines in DC and capacitively coupled RF plasmas. Journal of Physics D: Applied Physics, 42(13), 135207. doi:10.1088/0022-3727/42/13/135207

Mills, R. L., Good, W., & He, J. (2009). Excess power and the product molecular hydrino H 2 (1/4) generated in a K 2 CO 3 electrolysis cell. *Electrochimica Acta*, *54*(17), 4229-4236. doi:10.1016/j.electacta.2009.02.079

Mills, R. L., & Akhtar, K. (2009). Tests of features of field-acceleration models for the extraordinary selective H Balmer α broadening in certain hydrogen-mixed plasmas. *international journal of hydrogen energy*, *34*(15), 6465-6477. doi:10.1016/j.ijhydene.2009.05.148

Mills, R. L., Zhao, G., Akhtar, K., Chang, Z., He, J., Lu, Y., ... & Dhandapani, B. (2009). Commercializable power source from forming new states of hydrogen. *international journal of hydrogen energy*, *34*(2), 573-614. doi:10.1016/j.ijhydene.2008.10.018

Mills, R., Good, W., Jansson, P., & He, J. (2010). Stationary inverted Lyman populations and free-free and bound-free emission of lower-energy state hydride ion formed by an exothermic catalytic reaction of atomic hydrogen and certain group I catalysts. *Open Physics*, *8*(1), 7-16.

Mills, R. L., Dhandapani, B., & Akhtar, K. (2008). Excessive Balmer α line broadening in capacitively coupled rf water-vapor plasmas. *International Journal of Hydrogen Energy*, *33*(2), 802-815. doi:10.1016/j.ijhydene.2007.10.016

Mills, R. L., He, J., Nansteel, M., & Dhandapani, B. (2007). Catalysis of atomic hydrogen to new hydrides as a new power source. *International Journal of Global Energy Issues*, *28*(2-3), 304-324. doi:10.1504/IJGEI.2007.015882

Mills, R. L., Zea, H., He, J., & Dhandapani, B. (2007). Water bath calorimetry on a catalytic reaction of atomic hydrogen. *International*

Journal of Hydrogen Energy, *32*(17), 4258-4266. doi:10.1016/j.ijhydene.2007.06.017

Mills, R. L., He, J., Lu, Y., Nansteel, M., Chang, Z., & Dhandapani, B. (2007). Comprehensive identification and potential applications of new states of hydrogen. *International Journal of Hydrogen Energy*, *32*(14), 2988-3009. doi:10.1016/j.ijhydene.2007.03.035

*Mills, R., He, J., Chang, Z., Good, W., Lu, Y., & Dhandapani, B. (2007). Catalysis of atomic hydrogen to novel hydrogen species H-(1/4) and H2 (1/4) as a new power source. *International Journal of Hydrogen Energy*, *32*(13), 2573-2584. doi:10.1016/j.ijhydene.2007.02.023

Mills, R., Ray, P., & Dhandapani, B. (2006). Evidence of an energy transfer reaction between atomic hydrogen and argon II or helium II as the source of excessively hot H atoms in radio-frequency plasmas. *Journal of Plasma Physics*, *72*(04), 469-484. doi:10.1017/S0022377805004034

*Mills, R. L., Ray, P. C., Mayo, R. M., Nansteel, M., Dhandapani, B., & Phillips, J. (2005). Spectroscopic study of unique line broadening and inversion in low-pressure microwave generated water plasmas. *Journal of plasma physics*, *71*(06), 877-888. doi:10.1017/S0022377805003703

Mills, R., He, J., & Dhandapani, B. (2005). Highly stable amorphous silicon hydride from a helium plasma reaction. *Materials Chemistry and Physics*, *94*(2), 298-307. doi:10.1016/j.matchemphys.2005.05.002

Mills, R., He, J., Chang, Z., Zea, H., Akhtar, K., Lu, Y., ... & Dhandapani, B. (2005, August). Catalysis of atomic hydrogen to novel hydrides as a new power source. In *230th ACS National Meeting*.

*Mills, R., Sankar, J., Voigt, A., He, J., Ray, P., & Dhandapani, B. (2005). Role of atomic hydrogen density and energy in low power chemical vapor deposition synthesis of diamond films. *Thin Solid Films*, *478*(1), 77-90.

*Mills, R., & Ray, P. (2004). Stationary inverted Lyman population and a very stable novel hydride formed by a catalytic reaction of atomic hydrogen and certain catalysts. *Optical Materials*, *27*(2), 181-186. doi:10.1016/j.optmat.2004.02.026

Mills, R., Ray, P., Dhandapani, B., Good, W., Jansson, P., Nansteel, M., ... & Voigt, A. (2004). Spectroscopic and NMR identification of novel hydride ions in fractional quantum energy states formed by an exothermic reaction of atomic hydrogen with certain catalysts. *The European Physical Journal Applied Physics*, *28*(1), 83-104. doi:10.1051/epjap:2004168

Mills, R. L., Lu, Y., Nansteel, M., He, J., Voigt, A., & Dhandapani, B. (2004). Energetic Catalyst-Hydrogen Plasma Reaction as a Potential New Energy Source. *Prepr. Pap.-Am. Chem. Soc., Div. Fuel Chem*, *49*(1), 392.

*Mills, R. L., Sankar, J., Ray, P., Voigt, A., He, J., & Dhandapani, B. (2004). Synthesis of HDLC films from solid carbon. *Journal of materials science*,*39*(10), 3309-3318. doi:10.1023/B:JMSC.0000026931.98685.59

Mills, R. L., Lu, Y., Nansteel, M., He, J., Voigt, A., & Dhandapani, B. (2004). Energetic Catalyst-Hydrogen Plasma Reaction as a Potential New Energy Source. *Prepr. Pap.-Am. Chem. Soc., Div. Fuel Chem*, *49*(1), 392.

Mills, R. L., Lu, Y., Nansteel, M., He, J., Voigt, A., & Dhandapani, B. (2004). Energetic Catalyst-Hydrogen Plasma Reaction as a Potential New Energy Source. *Prepr. Pap.-Am. Chem. Soc., Div. Fuel Chem*, *49*(1), 392.

*Mills, R., Sankar, J., Ray, P., Dhandapani, B., & He, J. (2003). Spectroscopic characterization of the atomic hydrogen energies and densities and carbon species during helium-hydrogen-methane plasma CVD synthesis of diamond films. *Chemistry of materials*, *15*(6), 1313-1321. doi:10.1021/cm020817m

*Mills, R., & Ray, P. (2003). Extreme ultraviolet spectroscopy of helium–hydrogen plasma. *Journal of Physics D: Applied Physics*, *36*(13), 1535. doi:10.1088/0022-3727/36/13/316

Mills, R. L., Chen, X., Ray, P., He, J., & Dhandapani, B. (2003). Plasma power source based on a catalytic reaction of atomic hydrogen measured by water bath calorimetry. *Thermochimica Acta*, *406*(1), 35-53. doi:10.1016/S0040-6031(03)00228-4

Mills, R. L., Dhandapani, B., & He, J. (2003). Highly stable amorphous silicon hydride. *Solar energy materials and solar cells*, *80*(1), 1-20. doi:10.1016/S0927-0248(03)00107-7

*Mills, R. L., Ray, P. C., & Mayo, R. M. (2003). Potential for a hydrogen water-plasma laser. *Applied Physics Letters*, *82*(11), 1679-1681.

doi:10.1063/1.1558213

*Mills, R. L., Ray, P. C., & Mayo, R. M. (2003). Stationary inverted Lyman population formed from incandescently heated hydrogen gas with certain catalysts. *Journal of Physics D: Applied Physics*, *36*(13), 1504. doi:10.1088/0022-3727/36/13/312

Mills, R. L., Ray, P. C., Nansteel, M., Chen, X., Mayo, R. M., He, J., & Dhandapani, B. (2003). Comparison of excessive Balmer α line broadening of inductively and capacitively coupled RF, microwave, and glow-discharge hydrogen plasmas with certain catalysts. *IEEE Transactions on Plasma Science*, 31(3), 338-355. doi:10.1109/TPS.2003.812340

* Mills, R. L., Ray, P. C., & Mayo, R. M. (2003). CW HI laser based on a stationary inverted Lyman population formed from incandescently heated hydrogen gas with certain group I catalysts. *IEEE Transactions on Plasma Science*, 31(2), 236-247. doi:10.1109/TPS.2003.810174

*Mills, R. L., Ray, P., Dong, J., Nansteel, M., Dhandapani, B., & He, J. (2003). Spectral emission of fractional-principal-quantum-energy-level atomic and molecular hydrogen. *Vibrational Spectroscopy*, 31(2), 195-213. doi:10.1016/S0924-2031(03)00013-4

Mills, R., He, X., Ray, P., Dhandapani, B., & Chen, X. (2003). Synthesis and characterization of a highly stable amorphous silicon hydride as the product of a catalytic helium–hydrogen plasma reaction. *International journal of hydrogen energy*, 28(12), 1401-1424. doi:10.1016/S0360-3199(02)00293-8

Mills, R.L., Ray, P. "A Comprehensive Study of Spectra of the Bound-Free Hyperfine Levels of Novel Hydride Ion H-(1/2), Hydrogen, Nitrogen, and Air". *Int. J. Hydrogen Energy* **28** (8): 825–871. doi:10.1016/S0360-3199(02)00167-2

*Mills, R.L., Nansteel, M., Ray, P. (2003b). "Excessively Bright Hydrogen-Strontium Plasma Light Source Due to Energy Resonance of Strontium with Hydrogen". *J. Plasma Physics* **69**: 131–158. doi:10.1017/S0022377803002113

Mills, R.L. (2003). "Highly Stable Novel Inorganic Hydrides". *J. New Materials for Electrochemical Systems* **6**: 45–54.

Mills, R.L., Ray, P. (2002). "Substantial Changes in the Characteristics of a Microwave Plasma Due to Combining Argon and Hydrogen". *New Journal of Physics* **4**: 22.1–22.17. doi:10.1088/1367-2630/4/1/322

*Mayo, R.M.; Mills, R.L.; Nansteel, M. (2002). "Direct Plasmadynamic Conversion of Plasma Thermal Power to Electricity". *IEEE Transactions on Plasma Science* **30** (5): 2066–2073. doi:10.1109/TPS.2002.807496

*Mills, R.L.; Nansteel, M.; Ray, P. (2002b). "Bright Hydrogen-Light Source due to a Resonant Energy Transfer with Strontium and Argon Ions". *New Journal of Physics* **4**: 70.1–70.28. doi:10.1088/1367-2630/4/1/370

Mayo, R.M.; Mills, R.L.; Nansteel, M. (2002). "On the Potential of Direct and MHD Conversion of Power from a Novel Plasma Source to Electricity for Microdistributed Power Applications". *IEEE Transactions on Plasma Science* **30** (4): 1568–1578. doi:10.1109/TPS.2002.804170

Mills, R.L. (2002). "Highly Stable Novel Inorganic Hydrides from Aqueous Electrolysis and Plasma Electrolysis". *Electrochimica Acta* **47** (24): 3909–3926. doi:10.1016/S0013-4686(02)00361-4

*Mills, R.L.; Dayalan, E.; Ray, P.; Dhandapani, B.; He, J. (2002). "Comparison of Excessive Balmer alpha Line Broadening of Glow Discharge and Microwave Hydrogen Plasmas with Certain Catalysts". , *J. of Applied Physics* **92** (12): 7008–7022. doi:10.1109/TPS.2003.812340

Mills, R.L.; Ray, P.; Dhandapani, B.; Mayo, R.M.; He, J. (2002). "Comparison of Excessive Balmer alpha Line Broadening of Glow Discharge and Microwave Hydrogen Plasmas with Certain Catalysts". *J. of Applied Physics* **92** (12): 7008–7022. doi:10.1109/TPS.2003.812340

Mills, R.L.; Ray, P.; Dhandapani, B.; Nansteel, M.; Chen, X.; He, J. (2002). "New Power Source from Fractional Quantum Energy Levels of Atomic Hydrogen that Surpasses Internal Combustion". *J. Mol. Struct.* **643** (1-3): 43–54. doi:10.1016/S0022-2860(02)00355-1

Mills, R.L.; Dong, J.; Good, W.; Ray, P.; He, J.; Dhandapani, B. (2002). "Measurement of Energy Balances of Noble Gas-Hydrogen Discharge Plasmas Using Calvet Calorimetry". *Int. J. Hydrogen Energy* **27** (9): 967–978. doi:10.1016/S0360-3199(02)00004-6

Mills, R.L.; Ray, P.; (2002). "Spectroscopic Identification of a Novel Catalytic Reaction of Rubidium Ion with Atomic Hydrogen and the Hydride Ion Product". *Int. J. Hydrogen Energy* **27** (9): 927–935. doi:10.1016/S0360-3199(02)00002-2

Mills, R.L.; Voigt, A.; Ray, P.; Nansteel, M.; Dhandapani, B.; (2002). "Measurement of Hydrogen Balmer Line Broadening and Thermal Power Balances of Noble Gas-Hydrogen Discharge Plasmas". *Int. J. Hydrogen Energy* **27** (6): 671–685. doi:10.1016/S0360-3199(01)00172-0

Mills, R.L.; Greenig, N.; Hicks, S. (2002). "Optically Measured Power Balances of Glow Discharges of Mixtures of Argon, Hydrogen, and Potassium, Rubidium, Cesium, or Strontium Vapor". *Int. J. Hydrogen Energy* **27** (6): 651–670

Mills, R.L.; Ray, P. (2002). "Vibrational Spectral Emission of Fractional-Principal-Quantum-Energy-Level Hydrogen Molecular Ion". *Int. J. Hydrogen Energy* **27** (5): 533–564. doi:10.1016/S0360-3199(01)00145-8

*Mills, R.L.; Nansteel, M.; Ray, P.; (2002c). "Argon-Hydrogen-Strontium Discharge Light Source". *IEEE Transactions on Plasma Science* **30** (2): 639–652. doi:10.1109/TPS.2002.1024263

Mills, R.L.; (2002). "Spectral Emission of Fractional Quantum Energy Levels of Atomic Hydrogen from a Helium-Hydrogen Plasma and the Implications for Dark Matter". *Int. J. Hydrogen Energy* **27** (3): 301–322. doi:10.1016/S0360-3199(01)00116-1

Mills, R.L.; Ray, P. (2002). "Spectroscopic Identification of a Novel Catalytic Reaction of Potassium and Atomic Hydrogen and the Hydride Ion Product". *Int. J. Hydrogen Energy* **27** (2): 183–192. doi:10.1016/S0360-3199(01)00093-3

Mills, R.L.; Dayalan, E. (2002). "Novel Alkali and Alkaline Earth Hydrides for High Voltage and High Energy Density Batteries". *Proceedings of the 17th Annual Battery Conference on Applications and Advances*: 1–6. doi:10.1109/BCAA.2002.986359

Mills, R.L.; Good, W.; Voigt, A.; Dong, J. (2001). "Minimum Heat of Formation of Potassium Iodo Hydride". *Int. J. Hydrogen Energy* **26** (11):

1199–1208. doi:10.1016/S0360-3199(01)00051-9

Mills, R.L. (2001). "Spectroscopic Identification of a Novel Catalytic Reaction of Atomic Hydrogen and the Hydride Ion Product". *Int. J. Hydrogen Energy* **26** (10): 1041–1058. doi:10.1016/S0360-3199(01)00041-6

Mills, R.L.; Dhandapani, B.; Nansteel, M.; He, J.; Voigt, A.; (2001). "Identification of Compounds Containing Novel Hydride Ions by Nuclear Magnetic Resonance Spectroscopy". *Int. J. Hydrogen Energy* **26** (9): 965–979. doi:10.1016/S0360-3199(01)00027-1

Mills, R.L.; Onuma,T.; Lu, Y.; (2001). "Formation of a Hydrogen Plasma from an Incandescently Heated Hydrogen-Catalyst Gas Mixture with an Anomalous Afterglow Duration". *Int. J. Hydrogen Energy* **26** (7): 749–762. doi:10.1016/S0360-3199(01)00004-0

*Mills, R.L.; (2001a). "Observation of Extreme Ultraviolet Emission from Hydrogen-KI Plasmas Produced by a Hollow Cathode Discharge". *Int. J. Hydrogen Energy* **26** (6): 579–592. doi:10.1016/S0360-3199(00)00122-1

*Mills, R.L.; Dhandapani, B.; Nansteel, M.; He, J.; Shannon, T.; Echezuria, A.; (2001). "Synthesis and Characterization of Novel Hydride Compounds". *Int. J. of Hydrogen Energy* **26** (4): 339–367. doi:10.1016/S0360-3199(00)00113-0

Mills, R.L. (2001b). "Temporal Behavior of Light-Emission in the Visible Spectral Range from a Ti-K2CO3-H-Cell". *Int. J. Hydrogen Energy* **26** (4): 327–332. doi:10.1016/S0360-3199(00)00099-9

Mills, R.L.; (2001). "Observation of Extreme Ultraviolet Hydrogen Emission from Incandescently Heated Hydrogen Gas with Strontium that Produced an Anomalous Optically Measured Power Balance". *Int. J. Hydrogen Energy* **26** (4): 309–326. doi:10.1016/S0360-3199(00)00098-7

*Mills, R.L.; (2000b). "Synthesis and Characterization of Potassium Iodo Hydride". *Int. J. of Hydrogen Energy* **25** (12): 1185–1203. doi:10.1016/S0360-3199(00)00037-9

*Mills,R.L.;Dong,J.;Lu,Y.; (2000c)."Observation of Extreme Ultraviolet Hydrogen Emission from Incandescently Heated Hydrogen Gas with

Certain Catalysts". *Int. J. Hydrogen Energy* **25**: 919–943. doi:10.1016/S0360-3199(00)00018-5

Mills, R.L.; (2000). "Novel Inorganic Hydride". *Int. J. of Hydrogen Energy* **25**: 669–683. doi:10.1016/S0360-3199(99)00076-2

*(2000) BlackLight Power Technology: A New Clean Energy Source with Potential for Direct Conversion to Electricity. *Global Foundation Inc*, Nov 26-28, 2000. Presented at International Conference on Global Warming and Energy Policy, Ft. Lauderdale, FL.

*Mills, R.L.; (2000). "Novel Hydrogen Compounds from a Potassium Carbonate Electrolytic Cell". *Fusion Technology* **37** (2): 157–182.

*Mills, R.L.; Good, W.; (1995). "Fractional Quantum Energy Levels of Hydrogen". *Fusion Technology* **28** (4): 1697–1719.

*Mills, R.L.; Good, W.; Shaubach, R. (1994). "Dihydrino Molecule Identification". *Fusion Technology* **25** (103).

*Mills, R.L.; Kneizys, S. (1991). "Excess heat production by the electrolysis of an aqueous potassium carbonate electrolyte and the implications for cold fusion". *Fusion Technology* **20** (65).

Theoretical Publications

Mills, R.L.; Good, W.; Makawana, A.; Holverstott, B.; Hogle, N. (2011). "Millsian 2.0: A Molecular Modeling Software for Structures, Charge Distributions and Energetics of Biomolecules". *Physics Essays* **24**: 200–212. doi:10.4006/1.3567145

Mills, R.L.; Holverstott, B; Good, W.; Makwana A. (2010). "Total Bond Energies of Exact Classical Solutions of Molecules Generated by Millsian 1.0 Compared to Those Computed Using Modern 3-21G and 6-31G Basis Sets". *Phys. Essays* **23**: 153–199. doi:10.4006/1.3310832

*Mills, R.L. (2007). "Physical Solutions of the Nature of the Atom, Photon, and Their Interactions to Form Excited and Predicted Hydrino States". *Physics Essays* **20**: 403–460. doi:10.4006/1.3153414

*Mills, R.L. (2008). "Exact Classical Quantum Mechanical Solution for Atomic Helium which Predicts Conjugate Parameters from a

Unique Solution for the First Time". *Physics Essays.* 21(2): 103–141. doi:10.4006/1.3009282.

*Mills, R.L.; (2006). "Maxwell's Equations and QED: Which is Fact and Which is Fiction". *Physics Essays* **19**: 225–262. doi:10.4006/1.3025792

Mills, R.L. (2005). "Exact Classical Quantum Mechanical Solutions for One- through Twenty-Electron Atoms". *Physics Essays* **18**: 321–361. doi:10.4006/1.3025747

Mills, R.L. (2005). "The Fallacy of Feynman's Argument on the Stability of the Hydrogen Atom According to Quantum Mechanics". *Ann. Fund. Louis de Broglie* **30** (2): 129–151.

Mills, R.L. (2004). "The Nature of the Chemical Bond Revisited and an Alternative Maxwellian Approach". *Physics Essays* **17**: 342–389. doi:10.4006/1.3025699.

*Mills, R.L.; (2003). "Classical Quantum Mechanics". *Physics Essays* **16**: 433–498. doi:10.4006/1.3025609

Mills, R.L.; (2002). "The Grand Unified Theory of Classical Quantum Mechanics". *Int. J. Hydrogen Energy* **27** (5): 565–590. doi:10.1016/S0360-3199(01)00144-6

Mills, R.L.; (2001). "The Nature of Free Electrons in Superfluid Helium—a Test of Quantum Mechanics and a Basis to Review its Foundations and Make a Comparison to Classical Theory". *Int. J. Hydrogen Energy* **26** (10): 1059–1096. doi:10.1016/S0360-3199(01)00023-4

Mills, R.L.; (2000). "The Hydrogen Atom Revisited". *Int. J. of Hydrogen Energy* **25** (12): 1171–1183. doi:10.1016/S0360-3199(00)00035-5

Xie, W., R.L. Mills, W. Good, A. Makwana, & B. Holverstott. (2011) "Millsian 2.0: A molecular modeling software for structures, charge distributions, and energetics of biomolecules." *Physics Essays* 24. 200-212

Journal articles from non-BLP primary authors concerning hydrino research

Bas, Erdal, & Funda Metin. (2015) "Spectral Analysis for Fractional Hydrogen Atom Equation." *Advances in Pure Mathematics* 5: 767–663.

Becker, Kurt, Nigel Mason, & Claude Fabre. (2011) "Editorial by the Editors-in-Chief regarding the highlighted paper "Time-resolved hydrino continuum transitions with cutoffs at 22.8 and 10.1 nm" by R.L. Mills and Y. Lu." *European Physics Journal D* 64: 63.

Bush, Robert. (1992) "A light water excess heat reaction suggests that 'cold fusion' may be 'alkali-hydrogen' fusion." *Fusion Technology* 22: 301–322.

Bush, Robert, & R. Eagleton. (1994) "Calorimetric Studies for Several Light Water Electrolytic Cells with ALkali Salts of Potassium, Rubidium, and Cesium." *Proceedings: Fourth International Conference on Cold Fusion (Electric Power Research Institute)* 2: 13–5.

Conrads, H, R Mills, & Th Wrubel. (2003) "Emission in the deep vacuum ultraviolet from a plasma formed by incandescently heating hydrogen gas with trace amounts of potassium carbonate." *Plasma Sources Sci Technol* 12: 389–395.

Driessen, N. M., E. M. van Veldhuizen, P. Van Noorden, R. J. L. J. De Regt, & G. M. W. Kroesen. (2005) "Balmer-alpha line broadening analysis of incandescently heated hydrogen plasmas with potassium catalyst." In XXVIIth ICPIG, Eindoven, the Netherlands. 18-22 July.

Jansson, Peter Mark. (2007) *Hydrocatalysis: A New Energy Paradigm*. Master's thesis, Rowan University, 1997.

Mayer, Fred. (1991) "Comments." *Fusion Technology* 20: 511.

Naudts, Jan. (2005) "On the hydrino state of the relativistic hydrogen atom." *ArXiv Preprint* .

Noninski, V. C. (1992) "Excess heat during the electrolysis of a light water solution of K2CO3 with a nickel cathode." *Fusion Technology* 21: 163–167.

Notoya, Reiko. (1993) "Cold Fusion by Electrolysis in a Light Water-Potassium Carbonate Solution with a Nickel Electrode." *Fusion Tech* 24, 2: 202–204.

Phelps, A. V. "Comment on "Water bath calorimetric study of excess heat generation in resonant transfer plasmas"." *J. App. Phys.* 98.

Phillips, Jonathan, Chun Ku Chen, & Randell Mills. (2008) "Evidence of energetic reactions between hydrogen and oxygen species in RF generated H2O plasmas." *Int. J. of Hydrogen Energy* 33, 10: 2419–2432.

Phillips, Jonathan, C.K. Chen, Kamran Akhtar, Bala Dhandapani, & Randell Mills. (2007) "Evidence of catalytic production of hot hydrogen in RF generated hydrogen/argon plasmas." *Int. J. of Hydrogen Energy* 32, 14: 3010–3025.

Phillips, J.; Chen, C. K.; Akhtar, K.; Dhandapani, B.; Mills, R.L.; (2007). "Evidence of Catalytic Production of Hot Hydrogen in RF-Generated Hydrogen/Argon Plasmas". *Int. J. Hydrogen Energy.* 32(14): 3010–3025. doi:10.1016/j.ijhydene.2007.01.022

Phillips, Jonathan, Randell MIlls, & Xuemin Chen. (2004) "Water bath calorimetric study of excess heat generation in 'resonant transfer' plasmas." *J. App. Phys.* 96, 6: 3095–3102.

Rathke, Andreas. (2005) "A critical analysis of the hydrino model." The New Journal of Physics 7: 127.

Sisovic, N.M., G. Majstorovic, & N. Konjevic. (2005) "Excessive hydrogen and deuterium Balmer lines broadening in a hollow cathode discharges." Eur. Phys. J. D. 32: 347–354.

Serendipitous experimental studies related to hydrino research

Lu, C, J Hu, JH Kwak, Z Yang, R Ren, & T Markmaitree. (2007) "Study the Effects of Mechanical Activation on Li-N-H systems with 1H and 6Li solid-state NMR." *Journal of Power Sources* 170: 419–424.

Ulrich Andreas, Jochen Wieser, Daniel Murnick (1998) Excimer formation using low energy electron beam excitation. *SPIE*, Vol. 3403

Wishnow, Edward. *The far-infrared absorption spectrum of low temperature hydrogen gas.* Ph.D. thesis, University of British Columbia, 1993.

Unpublished technical reports regarding hydrino research

Anonymous, (2012) "Independent Technology Evaluation Study. Phase 1 – Test Plan Development for BlackLight Power CIHT Technology" Technical report. January 23.

Bykanov, Alexander. (2010) "Validation of the observation of soft x-ray continuum radiation from low-energy pinch discharges in the presence of molecular hydrogen." Technical report, GEN3 Partners.

Copeland, Terry. (2012) "Catalyst Induced Hydrino Transition (CIHT) Electrochemical Cell Validation." Technical report, January 5.

Craw-Ivanco, M.T., Tremblay, R.P., Boniface, H. A., Hilborn, J. (1994) "Calorimetry for a Ni/K2CO3 Cell" Chemical Engineering Branch, Chalk River Laboratories. June.

Crouse, Gilbert. (2014) "Differential Scanning Calorimeter Analysis of Hydrino-Producing Solid Fuel" Auburn University Department of Aerospace Engineering.

GEN3 Partners, (2009) "GEN3 Validation Report" Water Flow Calorimetry, Experimental Runs and Validation Testing for BlackLight Power, Inc." Technical Report. August.

Gernet, Nelson, & Robert Shaubach. (1994) "Nascent Hydrogen: An Energy Source." Technical report, Thermacore, Inc., Prepared for Aero Propulsion and Power Directorate, Wright Laboratory, Air Force Material Command (ASC), Wright-Patterson Air Force Base, Ohio 45433-7659. SBIR Contract No. F33615-93-C-2326, Report No. 11-1124.

Glumac, N. (2012) "Final Consultant Report" Technical report. January 21.

Glumac, N. (2014a). "Report from Visit to BlackLight Power on Friday, January 17, 2014" Technical report.

Glumac, N. (2014b). "Scientific Test Report" Mechanical Science & Engineering Department, University of Illinois. Technical report. April.

Haldeman, C.W., Savoye, E.D., Iseler, G.W., & Clarke, H.R. (1995) "Excess Energy Cell Final Report ACC Project 174." Technical report.

Jacox, M. G., Watts, K. D., (1993) "The Search for Excess Heat in the Mills Electrolytic Cell" Idaho National Engineering Laboratory, January 7.

Jansson, Peter, Amos Mugweru, KV Ramanujachary, & Heather Peterson. (2009) "Anomalous Heat Gains From Multiple Chemical Mixtures: Analytical Studies of "Generation 2" Chemistries of Black-Light Power Corporation." Technical report, Rowan University, November.

Jansson, Peter, Amos Mugweru, KV Ramanujachary, & John Schmaizel. (2010) "Anomalous Heat Gains from Regenerative Chemical Mixtures: Characterization of BLP Chemistries Used for Energy Generation and Regeneration Reactions." Technical report, Rowan University, November.

Jansson, Peter, Ulrich Schwabe, Matthew Abdallah, Nathaniel Downes, & Patrick Hoffman. (2009) "Water Flow Calorimetry, Experimental Runs and Validation Testing for BlackLight Power, Inc." Technical report, Rowan University, May.

Marchese, Anthony, Peter Jansson, & John Schmalzel. (2002) "The Black-Light Rocket Engine: Phase I Final Report." Technical report, College of Engineering, Rowan University. Phase I Study funded by the NIAC CP 01-02 Advanced Aeronautical/Space Concept Studies Program.

Mugweru, Amos, KV Ramanujachary, Heather Peterson, & John Kong. (2009a) "Report on Synthesis and Studies of "Generation 2" Lower Energy Hydrogen Chemicals." Technical report, Rowan University.

Mugweru, Amos, K.V. Ramanujachary, Heather Peterson, John Kong, & Anthony Cirri. (2009b) "Synthesis and Characterization of Alkali Metal Salts Containing Trapped Hydrino." Technical report, Rowan University.

Neterov, Sergei & Kryukov, Alexei. (1993) "In re Application of Mills Appl. No. 07/825, 845" MPEI Cryogenics Center. 26 February.

Niedra, Janis. (1996) "Replication of the Apparent Excess Heat Effect in a Light Water Potassium Carbonate-Nickel Electrolytic Cell. Technical Memorandum No. 107167." Technical report, NASA.

Payne, Philip. (2010) "OH Radical." Technical report. April 16.

Peterson, S.H., (1994) "Evaluation of Heat Production from Light Water Electrolysis Cells of Hydrocatalysis Power Corporation" Technology Department, Westinghouse STC. February 25.

Phillips, Jonathan, Julian Smith, & Kurtz, Stewart. (1996) "Report on Calorimetric Investigations of Gas-Phase Catalyzed Hydrino Formation." Technical report, Department of Chemical Engineering, Penn State University.

Phillips, Jonathan. (1996) "Consulting Report: Additional calorimetric examples of anomalous heat from physical mixture of K/carbon and Pd/carbon." Technical report, Department of Chemical Engineering, Penn State University.

Pugh, James, & Dayalan, Ethirajulu. (2012) "Evaluation of Electrical Power Generation by BlackLight Power's Catalyst Induced Hydrino Transition (CIHT) Cells" The ENSER Corporation. Technical report. April 4.

Ramanujachary, K. V., (2011) "Validation of Electrical Power Generation by Second-Generation CIHT Technology" Technical report. Department of Chemistry and Biochemistry, Rowan University. November.

. "Validation of SF-CIHT Technology" (2014) Technical report. Department of Chemistry and Biochemistry, Rowan University. February.

Shaubach, Robert, & Nelson Gernet. (1993) "Anomalous Heat from Atomic Hydrogen in Contact with Potassium Carbonate." Technical report, Thermacore.

Spittznagel, John. (1994) "Review of ESCA Evidence for Fractional Quantum Energy Levels of Hydrogen" Science and Technology Center, Westinghouse. Letter. January 18.

Weinberg, Henry. (2012) "CIHT Validation Report" Technical report. January.

. (2014) "Report of Visit to BlackLight Power on January 14 and 15, 2014" Letter. January 29.

Journal articles from Mills unrelated to hydrino research

Mills, Randell, & Guo Zhang-Wu. (2004) "Synthesis and Evaluation of Novel Prodrugs of Foscarnet and Dideoxycytidine with a Universal Carrier Compound Comprising a Chemiluminescent and Photochromic

Conjugate." *Journal of Pharmaceutical Sciences* 93, 5: 1320– 1336.

Mills, R. (2006c) "Novel method and system for pattern recognition and processing using data encoded as fourier series in fourier space." *Engineering Applications of Artificial Intelligence* 19: 219–234.

Mills, Randell. (1988) "A novel cancer therapy using a Mossbauer-isotope compound." *Nature* 336: 787–89.

Also see Mossbauer Cancer Therapy

Mills, R. L. & Y. Lu. (2011) *Fifth Force.* Unpublished.

BlackLight power press releases (2008-2014)

May 28, 2008 "BlackLight Power Inc. Announces Commercial-Ready Alternative Energy Solution"

Oct. 20, 2008 "BlackLight Power Inc. Announces Independent Replication of New Energy Source."

Dec. 11, 2008 "BlackLight Power Inc. Announces First Commercial License with Estacado Energy Services."

Jan. 6, 2009 "BlackLight Power Inc. Announces Second Commercial License with Farmers' Electric Cooperative, Inc. of New Mexico."

July 30, 2009 "BlackLight Power Inc. Announces Sixth Commercial License Agreement."

Aug 12, 2009 "BlackLight Power, Inc. Announces Independent Validation of Breakthrough New Energy Source Based on a New Form of Hydrogen and Chemistry Capable of Continuous Regeneration"

March 23, 2010 "BlackLight Power Inc. Announces First Commercial License in Europe with GEOENEGIE SpA, Energy Subsidiary of Geogreeen."

Nov 29, 2010 "BlackLight Power Inc. Announces Production of Electricity from a New Form of Hydrogen."

May 22, 2012 "Electricity generated from water: BlackLight Power announces validation of its scientific breakthrough in energy production."

Jan 14, 2014 "BlackLight Power, Inc. Announces Game Changing Achievement of the Generation of Millions of Watts of Power from the Conversion of Water Fuel to a New Form of Hydrogen."

Apr 3, 2014 "BlackLight Power, Inc. Announces Sustained Production of Electricity Using Photovoltaic Conversion of the Millions of Watts of Brilliant Plasma Formed by the Reaction of Water to a More Stable Form of Hydrogen."

Documents related to patent disputes

BlackLight Power, Inc. v Dickinson 109 F. Supp.2d 44, 55, USPQ.2d 1812, DD, 15 August 2000 (No CIV. A. 00-422 (EGS)).

BlackLight Power, Inc. v Rogan 295 F.3d, 1269-1274, 63 USPQ.2d, C.A. Fed. (Dist. Col.) 28 June 2002 (No. 00-1530).

BlackLight Power v The Comptroller-General of Patents [2008] EWHC 2763 (Pat.)

Allen, John. (2003) "Letter from John Allen, of John Allen & Associates Int'l, Ltd. to the Honorable Donald Evans, Secretary of the US Department of Commerce" dated May 12. Patent File Wrapper 10575345, 2003.

. . (2003b) "Letter from John Allen, of John Allen & Associates Int'l, Ltd. to the Honorable Johnie Frazier, US Dept of Commerce dated June 7." Patent File Wrapper 10575345, 2007.

Brewer, Shelby. (2001) "Letter from Shelby T. Brewer to the Honorable James e. Rogan, Director, US Patent and Trademark Office" dated December 21. Patent File Wrapper 10575345, 2011.

Hicks, Frances. (2000) "Letter from Frances Hicks, Petitions Examiner, to Farkas & Manelli, PLLC" dated February 17. Patent File Wrapper 10575345, 2000.

Kepplinger, Esther. (2000) "Declaration of Esther Kepplinger, as part of the civil action No. 00 0422 EGS." Dated April 14. Patent File Wrapper 10575345.

Marchant, P. (2008) UK Intellectual Patent Office Decision BL O/076/08, March 14.

. (2008b) UK Intellectual Patent Office Decision BL O/114/08, April 17.

. (2009) UK Intellectual Patent Office Decision BL O/170/09, June 19.

Melcher, Jeffery. (2001) "Letter from Jeffery Melcher, Farkas & Manelli PLLC to Ms. Esther Kepplinger, Director of Group 1700, US Patent and Trademark Office, dated Jan 19." Patent File Wrapper 10575345.

Rimmer, Matthew. (2011) "Patenting free energy." *Journal of Intellectual Property and Law* 6, 6.

Also see references contained therein

Siehndel, Kathryn. (2014) "Re: Freedom of Information Act (FOIA) Request No. F-15-00004" and included attachments (43 pp). Dated October 9.

Simenauer, Jeffrey, & Jeff Melcher. (2000) "Letter from Jeffrey Simenauer and Jeffrey Melcher to Thomas Heinemann, Attorney Advisor, United States Department of State, dated July 10. Signed April 14." Patent File Wrapper 10575345.

USPTO (1999) "Media Contact Policy. Memorandum from the Acting Assistant Secretary of Commerce and Acting Commissioner of Patents and Trademarks." June 22.

Wyden, Ron. (2000) "Letter from Ron Wyden, United States Senator, to the Honorable Q. Todd Dickinson, Commissioner of Patents and Trademarks. dated April 5 2000." Patent File Wrapper 10575345.

Patents Granted in the United States by Mills / BLP and collaborators

Genert, Nelson J., Robert M. Shaubach, Donald Ernst. (1993) Electrolytic Heater. US 5273635 A

Mills, R., (1989) Mossbauer cancer therapy US 4815447 A

Mills, R., (1990) Paramagnetic dynamo electromotive force detector and imaging system incorporating same. US 4969469 A

Mills, R., (1995) Prodrugs for selective drug delivery. US 5428163 A

Mills, R., (1996) System and method for providing localized Mössbauer absorption in an organic medium. EP 0316440 B1

Mills, R., (1998) Prodrugs for selective drug delivery. US 5773592 A

Mills, R., (1999) Chemical Compounds and pharmaceutical compositions capable of releasing a drug. EP 0414730 B1

Mills, R., (2000) Lower-energy hydrogen methods and structures. US 6024935 A

Mills, R., (2001) Pharmaceuticals providing diagnosis and selective tissue necrosis using Mossbauer absorber atom. US 6224848 B1

Mills, R., (2002) Resonant magnetic susceptibility imaging (ReMSI) US 6477398 B1

Mills, R., (2006) Pro drugs for selective drug delivery. US 7015352 B2

Mills, R., (2010) Molecular Hydrogen Laser US7773656 B1

Mills, R., (2010) Method and system of computing and rendering the nature of the excited electronic states of atoms and atomic ions. US 7689367 B2

General publications

"Hydrogen is Potential New Energy Source." *Reuters* .

"'Cold Fusion': Still Going." Focus, *Newsweek* .

"Fusion Facts Names Bush, Eagleton, and Mills as Fusion Scientists of the Year 1991.", *Fusion Facts,* University of Utah Research Park, 1992.

"Climbers Rescued." (1964) The Round Up: University Park New Mexico LVI, 10.

Baard, Erik. "Quantum Leap." *The Village Voice.*

. "Research Claims Power Tech That Defies Quantum Theory." *Dow Jones NewsWires.*

. "Dr. Molecool: Quantum Iconoclast Randell Mills' Grand Visions of Microscopic Medicine." *The Villiage Voice*.

. "The Empire Strikes Back: Alternative Energy Scientist Fights to Save Patent." *The Village Voice*.

. "Eureka? Hydrino Theorist Gets Nod from NASA-Funded Investigation." *The Village Voice*.

BBC Horizon (1994) *Too Close to the Sun* (Video)

Bishop, Jerry. (1992) "More Labs Report 'Cold Fusion' Results." *Wall Street Journal* B5.

Brewer, Shelby. "Review of Randell Mills The Grand Unified Theory of Classical Quantum Mechanics." Online via BlackLightPower.com.

Broad, William. (1991) "Two Teams Put New Life in 'Cold Fusion' Theory." *New York Times*. April 26.

CNN (2008), *Energy Fix*. Airdate: December 11.

Dume, Belle. (2005) "Hydrogen result causes controversy." *PhysicsWorld*,

van Eijk, Ernst. (2005) "Waterstof-plasma produceert onverklaarde straling en energie." *Het Zwarte Licht* July/August Issue. English translation by Bob Kelly.

Engelmann, Reinhart. (1996) "Review of Randell Mills The Grand Unified Theory of Classical Quantum Mechanics." Online via BlackLightPower.com.

Jakab, Spencer. (2006) "Energy Play Draws Money and Ire." *Wall Street Journal*

Jansson, P. (2009) "BlackLight Power's Independent Validation: BLP's independent validation of 50KW system by Rowan University" Online video clip. Youtube. Sept 24.

Jha, Alok. (2005) "Fuel's paradise? Power source that turns physics on its head." *The Guardian* November 4.

Mallove, Eugene. (2000a) "Breaking Through: Welcome to ICCF-8-Liberate Science!" *Infinite Energy Magazine* 31: 4–5.

———. (2000b) "New Energy and the News Media." *Infinite Energy Magazine* 34: 4.

Matthews, Robert. (2003) "Take Water and Potash, Add Electricity and Get – A Mystery." *Daily Telegraph*. May 18.

———. (2005) "Hydrino Power: Hype or Hope?" *BBC Focus Magazine* 157.

Newmyer, Jacqueline. (2000) "Academics question the science behind Black-Light Power, Inc." *The Harvard Crimson*. May 17.

Park, Robert. (2000) *Voodoo Science: The Path from Foolishness to Fraud.* Oxford University Press.

———. (2002) *"What's New? Online Column."* September 6.

———. (2008) *"What's New? Online Column."* June 6.

Port, Otis, John Carey, Neil Gross, & Gary McWilliams. (1992) "Power In A Jar: The Debate Heats Up." *BusinessWeek*. October 25.

Reichhardt, Tony. (2000) "New form of hydrogen power provokes scepticism." Nature 404. March 16.

———. (2002) "Out of this world (news feature)." Nature 420: 10–11.

Setzer, Luther. (1999) "The John Galt of Quantum Mechanics." *The Daily Objectivist*. December 1.

Srinivasan, Mahadeva. (1997) *Cold Fusion Times* 5, 1: 3.

Stolper, Thomas. (2006) *Genius Inventor: The controversy about the work of Randell Mills, America's Newton, in historical and contemporary context.* CreateSpace. 348 pp.

Suplee, Curt. (1991) "Two New Theories on Cold Fusion Swiftly Produce Heat Among Scientists." *Washington Post* A11. April 26.

Wales, J. Quoted in: "Wikipedia Core Content Policies." Wikipedia: The Free Encyclopedia. Wikimedia Foundation, Inc.

Zimmerman, Peter. (2000) "Touching the Third Rail: Encounters with Pseudoscience and Pseudoscientists." Speech summary dated March 16, 2000 for a talk to be given April 30th at the FBS-Session Business Meeting.

Philosophy, psychology, & sociology of science

Bacon, Francis. (1620) *Novum Organum Scientiarum*.

Beth, Evert. (1960) "Semantics of Physical Theories." *Synthese* 12: 172–175.

Boolos, G., J. P. Burgess, & R. C. Jeffrey. (2002) *Computability and Logic*. Cambridge University Press.

Carnap, Rudolf. (1936) "Testability and Meaning." *Philosophy of Science* 3, 4: 420–468; 1–40.

. (1966) *Philosophical Foundations of Physics*. New York: Basic Books.

Cartwright, Nancy. (1983) *How the laws of physics lie*. Oxford: Clarendon Press.

. (1999) *The Dappled World*. Cambridge University Press.

Chew, Geoffrey. "Impasse for the Elementary-Particle Concept." *Great Ideas Today* 367–389.

Churchland, Paul M. (1985) "The Ontological Status of Observables: In Praise of the Superempirical Values." In *Images of Science*, edited by Paul M. Churchland, and Clifford A. Hooker, Chicago and London: University of Chicago Press, 35–47.

van Fraassen, Bas. (1970) "On the Extension of Beth's Semantics of Physical Theories." *Philosophy of Science* 37, 3: 325.

. (1980) *The Scientific Image*. Clarendon Library of Logic and Philosophy. Oxford: Clarendon Press.

———. (1980) "Empiricisim in the Philosophy of Science." In *Images of Science*, edited by Paul M. Churchland, and Clifford A. Hooker, Chicago and London: University of Chicago Press, 245–305.

Giere, Ronald. (2004) "How Models are Used." *Philosophy of Science* 71: 742–752.

Gilovich, Thomas. (1991) How we know what isn't so: the fallibility of human reason in everyday life. *Free Press*.

Hempel, Carl G. (1965) "Aspects of Scientific Explanation and Other Essays" in *The Philosophy of Science*. New York, NY: *The Free Press*.

Hicks, Stephen R. C. (2004) *Explaining Postmodernism: Skepticism and Socialism from Rousseau to Foucault*. Scholargy Publishing.

Hinchliff, Mark. (1996) "The Puzzle of Change." In *Philosophical Perspectives 10: Metaphysics*, edited by James Tomberlin, Oxford: Blackwell, 119–136.

Hollingsworth, Rogers. (2004) "Institutionalizing Excellence in Biomedical Research: The Case of Rockefeller University." In Creating a tradition of biomedical research, edited by Darwin Stapleton, *The Rockefeller University Press*.

Holton, Gerald. (1968) "Mach, Einstein, and the Search for Reality." *Daedalus* 97 No. 2: 636–673.

Holverstott, Brett. (2007) *Scientific Realism, Empiricism, and Quantum Theory*. Bachelors thesis, Reed College.

Jammer, Max. (1974) *The Philosophy of Quantum Mechanics*. John Wiley & Sons, Inc.

Kant, Immanuel. (1951) *Prolegomena to a Future Metaphysics*. The Liberal Arts Press.

Kuhn, Thomas. (1970) *The Structure of Scientific Revolutions*. University of Chicago.

Lakatos, Imre. (1978) *The Methodology of Scientific Research Programmes*. Cambridge University Press.

Lord, Charles, Lee Ross, & Mark Lepper. (1979) "Biased Assimilation and Attitude Polarization: The Effects of Prior Theories on Subsequently Considered Evidence." *Journal of Personality and Social Psychology* 37: 2098–209.

Mach, Ernst. (1914) *The Analysis of Sensations*. The Open Court Publishing Company.

———. (1960) *The Science of Mechanics*. The Open Court Publishing Company.

Maxwell, Grover. (1962) "The Ontological Status of Theoretical Entities." In *Scientific Explanation, Space, and Time*, edited by Herbert Feigl, and Grover Maxwell, Minneapolis: University of Minnesota Press, volume III of Minnesota Studies in the Philosophy of Science, 3–27.

McMullin, Ernan. (1984) "A Case for Scientific Realism." In *Scientific Realism*, edited by Jarrett Leplin, Berkeley: University of California Press.

Mueller, Jennifer. (2012) "The bias against creativity: why people desire but reject creative ideas." *Psychological Science* 23(I): 13–17.

Norris, Christopher. (2000) *Quantum Theory and the Flight from Realism*. Routledge.

Petersen, A. (1963). The philosophy of Niels Bohr. Bulletin of the Atomic Scientists, 19(7), 8-14.

Poincaré, Henri. (1902) *Science and Hypothesis*. New York: The Science Press, 1905. Originally published as La Science et l'hypothes´e.

Popper, K. (1959) *The Logic of Scientific Discovery*. New York: Basic Books.

Psillos, Stathis. (1999) *Scientific Realism: how science tracks truth*. Routledge.

Putnam, Hilary. (1973) "What Theories are Not." In *Theories and Observation in Science*, edited by Richard Grandy, Ridgeview Publishing Company.

Skinner, B. F. (1953) *Science and Human Behavior*. New York: Macmillan.

Smart, J. J. C. (1963) *Philosophy and Scientific Realism*. International Library of Philosophy and Scientific Method. London: Routledge & Kegan Paul.

Suppe, Frederick. (1977) *The Structure of Scientific Theories*. University of Illinois Press, 2 edition.

———. (1989) *The Semantic Conception of Theories and Scientific Realism*. Board of Trustees of the University of Illinois.

Suppes, Patrick. (1967) "What is a Scientific Theory." In *Philosophy of Science Today*, edited by Sidney Morgenbesser, New York: Basic Books, Inc., 55–67.

Teller, Paul. (2001) "Twilight of the Perfect Model Model." *Erkenntris* 55: 393–415.

Tweney, Ryan D., Michael E. Doherty, & Clifford R. Mynatt. (1981) *On Scientific Thinking*. New York: Columbia University Press.

also see: Heisenberg in Quantum and General Physics

Scientific publications by topic

Classical electron theory and radiation physics

Abbott, Tyler, & David Griffiths. (1985) "Acceleration without radiation." *American Journal of Physics* 53, 12: 1203.

Dirac, P. A. M. (1938) "Classical theory of radiating electrons." *Proceedings of the Royal Society of London. Series A. Mathematical and Physical Sciences* 167, 929: 148–169.

Friedman, F.L., & L. Sartori. (1965) *The Classical Atom*, Volume I. Addison-Wesley.

Goedecke, G. H. (1964) "Classically Radiationless Motions and Possible Implications for Quantum Theory." *Physical Review* 135, 1 B: B281.

Haus, H. A. (1986) "On the radiation from point charges." *American Journal of Physics* 54, 12: 1126.

Jackson, John David. (1999) *Classical Electrodynamics.* John Wiley & Sons, Inc, 3rd Edition.

Jimenez, J. L., & I. Campos. (1999) "Models of the Classical Electron after a Century." *Foundations of Physics Letters* 12, 2: 127–145.

Joannopoulos, J., Karalis, A. & Solijacic, M. (2010) *Wireless Nonradiative Energy Transfer.* Patent number 7,741,734 B2.

Kragh, Helge. (2010) "Before Bohr: Theories of atomic structure 1850-1913." *RePoSS: Research Publications on Science Studies* 10.

Levine, H., E. J. Moniz, & D. H. Sharp. (1977) "Motion of extended charges in classical electrodynamics." *American Journal of Physics* 45, 75.

Nagaoka, H. (1904) "On a dynamical system illustrating the spectrum lines and the phenomena of radio-activity." *Nature* 69: 392–393.

Pearle, Phillip. (1982) "Classical Electron Models." *In Electromagnetism: Paths to Research*, edited by Teplitz, New York: Plenum.

Schott, G. A. (1933) "On the Electromagnetic Field of a moving Electrified Sphere and its Orbits." *Philosophical Magazine* 15: 752–61.

Thomson, J.J. (1904a) *Philosophical Magazine* 7: 237.

. (1904b) *Electricity and Matter.* Constable and Co.

. (1907) *Corpuscular Theory of Matter.* Constable and Co.

Weisskopf, V. F. (1949) "Recent Developments in the Theory of the Electron." *Reviews of Modern Physics* 21, 2: 94.

Quantum & general physics

Aspect, Alain. (1982) "Experimental Realization of Einstein-Podolsky-Rosen-Bohm Gedankenexperiment: A New Violation of Bell's Inequalities." *Physical Review Letters* 49, 2: 91–94.

Bohm, David. (1952) "A Suggested Interpretation of the Quantum Theory in Terms of Hidden Variables." *Physical Review* 84-85: 166–179, 180–193.

Born, Max. (1927) *Mechanics of the Atom*. London: Bell.

———. (1964) "The statistical interpretation of quantum mechanics." In *Nobel Lectures: Physics 1942-1962*, edited by Nobel Foundation, Amsterdam -New York: Elsevier Publishing Company, 1964, 256–267. Original lecture delivered on 11 December.

———. (1968) "Quantum Mechanics of Collision Processes." In *Wave Mechanics*, edited by Gunther Ludvwig, Pergamon. English translation of original 1926 papers in Zeitshrift fur Physik.

Bohr, Niels. (1935) "Can Quantum-Mechanical Description of Physical Reality be Considered Complete?" *Physical Review* 48: 696–702.

Campagnari, Claudio, & Melissa Franklin. (1997) "The discovery of the top quark." *Reviews of Modern Physics* 69: 137–211.

Davisson, C., & L. H. Germer. (1927) "Diffraction of Electrons by a Crystal of Nickel." *Phys. Rev.* 30: 705740.

Dirac, Paul. (1930) *The principles of quantum mechanics*. Oxford: The Clarendon Press.

———. (1978) *Directions in Physics*. New York: Wiley.

Dyson, F. J. (1952) "Divergence of perturbation theory in quantum electrodynamics." *Physical Review* 85, 4: 631.

Einstein, Albert. (1905) "On the Electrodynamics of Moving Bodies." *Annalen der Physik* 17: 891.

———. (1916) "The Foundation of the General Theory of Relativity." *Annalen der Physik*

———. (1948) "Quanten-Mechanik und Wirklichkeit." *Dialectica* 2: 320–24.

Feynman, et al, Richard. (1965) *The Feynman Lectures on Physics*, Volume 2. California Institute of Technology.

Feynman, Richard. (1985) QED: The Strange Theory of Light and Matter. Princeton University Press.

Galilei, Galileo. (1632) *Dialogue on the Two Chief World Systems.*

Griffths, David J. (1995) *Introduction to quantum mechanics.* Upper Saddle River, NJ: Prentice Hall.

Heisenberg, Werner. (1927) "ber den anschaulichen Inhalt der quantentheoretischen Kinematik und Mechanik." *Zeitschrift fr Physik* 43: 172–198.

. (1958) *Physics and Philosophy: The Revolution in Modern Science,* Volume 19 of World Perspectives. New York: Harper & Brothers Publishing.

. (1971) *Physics and Beyond.* Harper and Row.

Ismael, Jenann. (2004) "Quantum Mechanics." In *The Stanford Encyclopedia of Philosophy*, edited by Edward N. Zalta.

Kramers, Hendrik. (1924) "The quantum theory of dispersion." *Nature* 113: 310.

Lumb, MD. (1978) Luminescence Spectroscopy. *Academic Press.*

McQuarrie, Donald A. (1983) *Quantum Chemistry.* University Science Books.

Mead, Carver. (2001) "The Spectator Interview." *American Spectator* 34, Issue 7: 68.

Mehra, Jagdish, & Helmut Rechenberg. (1982) *The Historical Development of Quantum Theory*, volume 2. Springer-Verlag New York Inc..

Messiah, Albert. (1969) *Quantum mechanics.* Amsterdam: North-Holland.

Newton, Issac. (1687) *Mathematical Principles of Natural Philosophy.*

von Neumann, John. (1932) *Mathematische Grundlagen der Quantenmechanik.* Berlin: Springer.

Sommerfeld, Arnold. (1925) "Zur Theorie dees periodischen Systems." *Phys. Zs.* 26: 70–74.

Young, Thomas. (1804) "The Bakerian Lecture: Experiments and Calculations Relative to Physical Optics." *Philosophical Transactions of the Royal Society of London* 94.

Tests of Wave-Particle Duality

Arndt, Markus, Olaf Nairz, Julian Vos-Andreae, Claudia Keller, Gerbrand van der Zouw, & Anton Zeilinger. (1999) "Wave-particle duality of C60 molecules." *Nature* 401: 680–682.

Durr, S., Rempe G., Nonn, T. (1998) "Origin of quantum-mechanical complementarity probed by a which way experiment." *Nature* 395: 33–37.

Jonsson, Claus. (1961) "Interferenz von Elektronen am Doppelspalt." *Zeitschrift fur Physik* 161: 454.

——. "Electron Diffraction at Multiple Slits." *American Journal of Physics* 48. English translation by Dietrich Brandt and Stanley Hirschi.

Kocsis, Sacha, Boris Braverman, Sylvain Ravets, Martin Stevens, Richard Mirin, L. Shalm, & Aephraim Steinberg. (2011) "Observing the Average Trajectories of Single Photons in a Two Slit Interferometer." *Science* 332: 1170–1173.

Nairz, Olaf, Bjorn Brezger, Markus Arndt, & Anton Zeilinger. (2001) "Diffraction of Complex Molecules by Structures Made of Light." *Physical Review Letters* 87: 160,401.

Rozema, Lee, Ardavan Darabi, Dylan Mahler, Alex Hayat, Yasaman Soudagar, & Aephraim Steinberg. (2012) "Violation of Heisenberg's Measurement-Disturbance Relationship by Weak Measurements." *Physical Review Letters* 109: 100,404.

Taylor, G. I. (1909) *Proceedings of the Cambridge Philosophical Society* 15: 114.

Tonomura, Akira. (1989) "Demonstration of single-electron buildup of an interference pattern." *American Journal of Physics* 57: 117–120.

Group Additivity Theory

Benson, S. & Buss, J. (1958) "Additivity Rules for the Estimation of Molecular Properties. Thermodynamic Properties." *The Journal of Chemical Physics* 29: 546

Cohen, N., & S. W. Benson. (1993) "Estimation of Heats of Formation of Organic Compounds by Additivity Methods." *Chemical Review* 93: 2419–2438.

Mossbauer Cancer Therapy

Barbieri, A., B.F. Matzanke, S. Giesselmann, W. Jelkmann, V. Schunemann, & A.X. Trautwein. (1998) "In the Quest of the Mirage Effect: The Interaction of Fe(III) with DNA and the Role of Ferritin." *Hyperfine* 112: 129–132.

Brenner, D.J., C. R. Geard, & E.J. Hall. (1989) "Mossbauer cancer therapy doubts." *Nature* 339(6221): 185–186.

Ortalli, I., G. Pedrazzi, V. Fano, W.Y. Ma, S.Z. Cai, N. Giuliani, & M. Passeri. (1996) "Effects of hematin and Mossbauer gamma-radiation on human osteosarcoma cell lines." Il Nuovo Cimento D 18: 359–363.

Ortalli, I., G. Pedrazzi, K. Jiang., X. Zhang, C. Carlo-Stella, L. Mangoni, & V. Rizzoli. (1992a) "Effects of Mossbauer radiation on bone marrow cultures." Hyperfine Interactions 71: 1267–1270.

Ortalli, I., G. Pedrazzi, K. Jiang., X. Zhang, C. carlo Stella, & V. Rizzoli. (1992b) "Gamma-rays from Mossbauer sources: a low-dose approach to cancer therapy." Il Nuovo Cimento D 14: 351–358.

Reiff, W. M., Randell Mills, & John Farrell. (1990) "On the Potentialities of Nuclear Gamma Resonance (Mossbauer Effect) Spectroscopy as a New Low-Dose Approach to Cancer Radiation Therapy." Hyperfine Interactions 58: 2525–2534.

Cold Fusion

Chien, C. C., D. Hodoko, Z. Minevski, & J. Bockris. (1992) "On an electrode producing massive quantities of tritium and helium." Journal of

Electroanalytical Chemistry 338: 189.

Fleischmann, M., & S. Pons. (1990) "Calorimetry of the palladium deuterium-heavy water system." Journal of Electroanalytical Chemistry 287: 293.

Jones, Jonathan. (1999) "Faradaic Efficiencies Less Than 100 in Water Can Account For Reports of Excess Heat in "Cold Fusion" Cells." Journal of Physical Chemistry 99: 6973–6979.

Miles, M. H., B. F. Bush, G.S. Ostrom, & J.J. Lagowski. (1991a) "Heat and Helium Production in Cold Fusion Experiments." In Proc. Conf. The Science of Cold Fusion, edited by T. Bressani, E. Del Giudice, and G. Preparata.

. (1991b) "Helium Production During the Electrolysis of D2O in Cold Fusion Experiments." Journal of Electroanalytical Chemistry 304: 27.

Miles, M. H., R. A. Hollins, B. F. Bush, J.J. Lagowski, & R. E. Miles. (1993) "Correlation of Excess Power and Helium Production during D2O and H2O electrolysis using palladium cathodes." Journal of Electroanalytical Chemistry 346: 99.

Shkedi, Zvi. (1995a) "Calorimetry, Excess Heat, and Faraday Efficiency in Ni-H2O Electrolytic Cells." Fusion Technology 28, 4: 1720–1731.

. (1995b) "Letter." Fusion Facts 7, 6: 20–21.

Taubes, Gary. (1993) *Bad Science: The Short Life and Weird Times of Cold Fusion*, Random House.

Yamaguchi, E., & T. Nishioka. (1993) "Direct Evidence for Nuclear Fusion Reactions in Deuterated Palladium." Proceedings of the 3rd International Conference on Cold Fusion Nagoya, Japan.

Solar & neutrino physics

Bahcall, John, Sarbani Basu, & M. H. Pinsonneault. (2008) "How Uncertain Are Solar Neutrino Predictions?" Elsevier Preprint.

Bahcall, John, & Raymond Davis Jr. (1999) "The evolution of neutrino astronomy." *Millennium Essay for the PASP.*

Bahcall, John, & Raymond Davis Jr. (1982) "An Account of the Development of the Solar Neutrino Problem." In Essays in Nuclear Astrophysics, Cambridge University Press.

Davis Jr., Raymond. (1964) "Solar Neutrinos. II Experimental." *Physical Review Letters*: 12, 11: 303-305

Davis Jr., Raymond, D. Harmer & K. Hoffman. (1968) "Search for Neutrinos from the Sun" *Physical Review Letters*. 20, 21: 1205-1209

Hirata, K. S., *et al.* (1988) "Observation in the Kamiokande-II detector of the neutrino burst from supernova SN1987A." Physical Review D 38.

Malinovsky, Monique, & L. Heroux. (1973) "An analysis of the solar extreme-ultraviolet spectrum between 50 and 300 A." *The Astrophysical Journal* 181: 1009–1030.

Phillips, Kenneth. (1995) *Guide to the Sun.* Cambridge University Press.

Dark matter & related EUV & X-ray astronomy

Barstow, Martin, & Jay Holberg. (2003) *Extreme Ultraviolet Astronomy.* Cambridge University Press.

Bournaud, Frederic, Pierre Alain Duc, & Elias Brinks. (2007) "Missing Mass in Collisional Debris from Galaxies." Science 316: 1166–1169.

Bowyer, Stuart. (1994) "Extreme Ultraviolet Astronomy." *Scientific American* August. 32–39.

Bulbul, Esra, Maxim Markevitch, Adam Foster, Randall Smith, Michael Loewenstein, & Scott Randall. (2014) "Detection of an unidentified emission line in the stacked x-ray spectrum of galaxy clusters." *The Astrophysical Journal* 789.

Elmegreen, Bruce. (2007a) "Dark Matter in Galactic Collisional Debris." *Science* 316: 1132.

Kahn, F. D., & L. Woltjer. (1959) "Intergalactic Matter and the Galaxy." *Astrophysical Journal* 130, 3.

Labov, Simon, & Stuart Bowyer. (1991) "Spectral Observations of the Extreme Ultraviolet Background." *Astrophysical Journal* 371: 810–819.

Oort, J. H. (1940) "Some Problems Concerning the Structure and Dynamics of the Galactic System and the Ellliptical Nebulae NGC 3115 and 4494." *Astrophysical Journal* 91, 3.

Ostriker, J. P., & P. J. E. Peebles. (1974) "The Size and Mass of Galaxies, and the Mass of the Universe." *The Astrophysical Journal* 193: L1–L4.

Rubin, Vera, & W. Kent Ford. (1970) "Rotation of the Andromeda Nebula from a Spectroscopic Survey of Emission Regions." *Astrophysical Journal* 159: 379.

Sanders, Robert. (1996) "EUV Explorer satellite discovers huge, unexplained new gas component in clusters of galaxies." *UC Berkeley Public Affairs* News Release. Nov 18.

Sciama, D. W. "Dark Matter Decay and the Ionization of H I Regions in the Galaxy." *Astrophysical Journal* 364: (1990) 549–554.

Smith, Sinclair. (1936) "The Mass of the Virgo Cluster." *Astrophysical Journal* 83: 23.

Vallerga, John, & Jonathan Slavin. (1998) "The diffuse extreme ultraviolet background." *The Local Bubble and Beyond Lyman-Spitzer-Colloquium Lecture Notes in Physics* 506: 79–82.

Zwicky, F. (1933) "Die Rotverschiebung von extragalaktischen Nebeln (The Redshift of Extragalactic Nebulae)." Helvetica Physica Acta 6: 110–127. Republished in English translation in *Gen. Relativ Gravit* (2009) 41: 207-224.

also see (Panek 2011) in Cosmology

Cosmology

Caffau, Elisabetta, *et al* (2011) "An extremely primitive star in the Galactic halo." *Nature* 477: 7362.

Costa., E. *et al*, (1997) "Discovery of an X-Ray Afterglow Associated with the Gamma-Ray Burst of 28 February 1997." *Nature* 387: 783–785.

Gregory, D. (1715) *The Elements of Astronomy ...to which is annexed Dr. Halley's synopsis of the astronomy of comets*, vol. 2, London.

Hubble, Edwin. (1929) "A Relation Between Distance and Radial Velocity Among Extra-Galactic Nebulae." *Proc. N. A. S.* 15: 168– 173.

Lemaitre, Abbe Georges. (1933) "L'Univers en expansion." Annales de la Societe Scientifique de Bruxelles A53: 51. See English translation reprint in *General Relativity and Gravitation*, Vol. 29, No. 5 1997.

Mortlock, Daniel, *et al.* (2011) "A luminous quasar at a redshift of $z = 7.085$." *Nature* 474: 616–619.

Olbers, H. W. M. (1826) "Ueber die Durchsichtigkeit des Welt-raums," *Astromisches Jahrbuch*, vol. 51, ed. Johan Elert Bode, Berlin

Panek, Richard. (2011) *The 4 Percent Universe: Dark Matter, Dark Energy, and the Race to Discover the Rest of Reality*. Houghton Miflin Harcourt.

Penzias, A. & Wilson, R., (1965) A measurement of the Excess Antenna Temperature at 4080 mc/s. *The Astrophysical Journal*, 142: 419-421.

Riess, Adam, Alexiei Filippenko, & Peter Challis. (1998) "Observational Evidence from Supernovae for An Accelerating Universe and a Cosmological Constant." *The Astronomical Journal* 116: 1009– 1038.

Rocket propulsion & planetary exploration

Drake, Bret. (2009) "Human Exploration of Mars Design Reference Architecture 5.0." Technical report, NASA. NASA-SP-2009-566.

NIAC (2003) "5th Annual Report." Technical report, NASA Institute for Advanced Concepts.

Petropoulos, Anastassios, James Longuski, & Eugene Bonfiglio. (2000) "Trajectories to Jupiter via Gravity Assists from Venus, Earth, and Mars." Journal of Spacecraft and Rockets 37: 776–783.

Zubrin, Robert, & Richard Wagner. (1997) *The Case for Mars: The Plan to Settle the Red Planet and Why We Must*. Free Press.

Also see Jansson, 2005

Exotic ions in liquid helium

Doake, C. S. M., & P. W. F. Gribbon. (1969) "Fast ions in liquid helium." *Physics Letters* A 252.

Ihas, G. G. Ph.D. thesis, University of Michigan, 1971.

Ihas, G. G., & Jr. T. M. Sanders. (1971) "Exotic negative carriers in liquid helium." *Physical Review Letters* 27: 383.

Maris, Humphrey J. "Electrons in Liquid Helium." *Journal of the Physical Society of Japan* 77: (2008) 1110,008.

Wei, W., Z. L. Xie, G. M. Seidel, & H. J. Maris. "Experimental Investigation of Exotic Negative Ions in Superfluid Helium." *Journal of Low Temperature Physics* 171: (2013) 178–186.

Also see Mills, 2001

On electron free fall

Everitt, C. W. F., & M. Demianski, editors. (1990) Summary of the Meeting of the First William Fairbank Meeting on Gravitational Experiments in Space. *ICRA*.

Meyer, Horst, Blas Cabrera, & Peter Michelson. (2011) "William Martin Fairbank Sr. (1917-1989) A Biographical Memoir." National Academy of Sciences.

Morrison, Philip. (1958) "Approximate nature of physical symmetries." *Am. J. Phys* 26: 358–368.

Morrison, Philip, & Thomas Gold. (1958) "On the gravitational interaction of matter and antimatter." In Essays on Gravity, Nine Winning Essays of the Annual Award (1949-1958), *Gravity Research Foundation*, 45–50.

Schiff, L. I., & M. V. Barnhill. (1966a) "Gravitation-Induced Electric Field near a Metal." Physical Review 131, 4: 1067–1071.

Witteborn, F. C., & W. M. Fairbank. (1967) "Experimental Comparison of the Gravitational Force on Freely Falling Electrons and Metallic Electrons." Physical Review Letters 19, 18: 1049.

. (1977) "Apparatus for measuring the force of gravity on freely falling electrons." Rev. Sci. Instrum. 48, 1: 1–11.

Also see Mills, 2015

Energy & society

Cook, Earl. (1971) "The Flow of Energy in an Industrial Society." *Scientific American* September.

Goldemberg, Jose, Thomas Johansson, Amulya Reddy, & Robert Williams. (1985) "Basic Needs and Much More with One Kilowatt per Capita." *Ambio* 14: 190–200.

Kim, Younghoon David. "Making the Green Revolution Work." In *World Energy Insight* 201, World Energy Council, 2011.

Global Energy Assessment, (2012) International Institute for Applied Systems Analysis, Cambridge University Press

World Energy Assessment: Energy and the challenge of sustainability, (2000) United Nations Development Programme

World Energy Insight 2011, World Energy Council, 2011

Paradigm-shifting discoveries

Soennichsen, J., (2010) *Bretz's Flood: The Remarkable Story of a Rebel Geologist and the World's Greatest Flood*. Sasquatch Books.

Grand, H. E. Le. (1988) *Drifting Continents and Shifting Theories*. Cambridge University Press.

Nuland, Sherwin. (2004) *The Doctors' Plague: Germs, Childbed Fever, and the Strange Story of Ignac Semmelweis*. Great Discoveries. W. W. Norton & Company.

Brett Holverstott holds a BA in Philosophy from Reed College, obtained after three years of coursework in physics and chemistry. He worked at Brilliant Light Power over several years while attending college, and coauthored two scientific papers. He also holds a Masters in Architecture from the University of Oregon.

Made in the USA
San Bernardino, CA
14 December 2016